The Rise of Illiberalism

The Rise of Illiberalism

Thomas J. Main

BROOKINGS INSTITUTION PRESS
Washington, D.C.

The Brookings Institution is a private nonprofit organization devoted to research, education, and publication on important issues of domestic and foreign policy. Its principal purpose is to bring the highest quality independent research and analysis to bear on current and emerging policy problems. Interpretations or conclusions in Brookings publications should be understood to be solely those of the authors.

Library of Congress Control Number: 2021942751

ISBN 9780815738497 (pbk)
ISBN 9780815738503 (ebook)

9 8 7 6 5 4 3 2 1

Typeset in Janson

Composition by Elliott Beard

To my wife, Carla Main

Contents

Acknowledgments

I wish to thank the following people and institutions for assistance that made this book possible. The Marxe School of Public and International Affairs at Baruch College, City University of New York, my professional home for almost thirty years, has been very supportive. David Birdsell, Dean of the Marxe School, has been especially helpful. Marxe School faculty who have given me assistance on this project include Neil G. Bennett, Hillary Botein, and Daniel W. Williams. Academics at other institutions who have helped me include William G. Howell, Roman Hoyos, Terry M. Moe, Robert F. Williams, and Naomi Zack. I have received useful comments as a result of presentations of my work I have made to the Faculty Research Seminar of the Marxe School; the Society for the Study of Africana Philosophy, organized by Alfred Prettyman; and Oasis New York, an academic discussion group organized by Lawrence M. Mead of New York University. Jessica Miller has been my indispensable research assistant and is co-author of chapter 3. Pascal Cohen has been my contact person at SimilarWeb, the internet research firm that provided the data on which the web traffic analysis of chapter 3 is based. His troubleshooting was essential to the success of this project. A Dean's Research Award I received from the Marxe School made the data purchase possible. My wife, Carla T. Main, helped with her expertise in journalism and law, as well as with her emotional support. My sons, Henry S. Main and Joshua

E. Main, my brother, William Main, and my cousin, Margaret Gallacher, took an interest in my work and helped me to clarify my thinking. My parents, George Main and Catherine Main, and my grandmother, Catherine Gallacher, provided for me and raised me to respect education and good storytelling. All quotes from outside sources are provided verbatim unless otherwise noted. All remaining errors and omissions are my own.

The Rise of Illiberalism

1

Illiberalism in American Political Culture Today

After Charlottesville

A wave of revulsion and anti-racist organizing followed the violent "Unite the Right" rally in Charlottesville, Virginia, in August 2017, during which a counterdemonstrator was murdered by an Alt-Rightist participant. So potent was the response to the rally that many observers concluded the Alt-Right and other white supremacist movements were all but dead. *Newsweek* asked, "Is the Alt-Right Dying?" *The Guardian* concluded, "The Alt-Right is in decline." Antifascist organizers were particularly pleased by and took credit for the shrinkage of the movement's web presence. The leftist news organization Truthout declared, "In the wake of Charlottesville, they [Alt-Right sites] were forced off social media, web hosting, podcast platforms and just about every outreach tool available, leaving them only to the back alleys of the internet." The Daily Stormer, the most extreme and offensive Alt-Right outlet, was denied access by responsible service providers and as a result "is now isolated and marginalized" opined the *Anti-Racist News*.

1

But unfortunately, reports of the death of the Alt-Right are greatly exaggerated. In terms of the crucial measure of web audience size, the movement, if defined narrowly, has indeed shrunk somewhat since its supposed Waterloo at Charlottesville. But the Alt-Right has a significant and steady audience. And adding other racist, anti-Semitic, anti-democratic, and otherwise illiberal movements to the picture reveals an audience of many millions.

Using data from the digital analytics firm SimilarWeb for the period of January to November 2019, I calculated traffic to ten prominent Alt-Right sites that I identified in an earlier study. I also had data on traffic to those sites for the period October 2015 to February 2018. With these data, I was able to analyze the impact that the events in Charlottesville in August 2017 had on the audience of the Alt-Right.

Looking at only the ten Alt-Right sites I identified in my earlier research, from October 2015 to July 2017 the average number of visits per month to all ten sites combined rose steadily from about 1.6 million to 4.5 million visits. For the month of August 2019—that is, two years after the Charlottesville tragedy—these Alt-Right sites received about 3.2 million visits. Thus, visits to these sites were down by about 29 percent.

Consider the Alt-Right site with the most visitors, the ferociously radical Daily Stormer. In the month before Charlottesville, the site received about 1.9 million visits. Immediately after that debacle, a deplatforming campaign hit the Daily Stormer hard, depriving it of access to major web services. The site received only about 13,000 visits in November 2017, in effect a nearly 100 percent decline. But in August 2019 the Daily Stormer was back to about 1.4 million visits per month on average, which is a decline of about 25 percent.

Thus, visits to the original ten Alt-Right sites are down since the period immediately before Charlottesville but have been holding steady at about 3 million visits on monthly average for the period January to November 2019. So by this measure, the movement is down somewhat from its heyday but seems to have found a significant and stable audience. The Alt-Right, even by this narrow standard, is not dead.

Why should the continued presence of the Alt-Right be a matter of concern? The reason has nothing to do with the movement's support of Donald Trump, protectionism, nationalism, immigration restriction, or any other issue debatable within the wide spectrum of traditional American politics. The Alt-Right is objectionable because it is an illiberal, anti-democratic movement. The essential elements of its ideology are racialism and white supremacy; secession, disunion, and anti-Americanism; a rejection of liberal democratic principles; and a reliance on vituperative, intolerant rhetoric. All expressions of such radical illiberalism are worrisome insofar as they undermine the nation's broad consensus that favors a free and open society. Therefore the real questions are, how large is the Alt-Right and how expansive is the total presence of all illiberal ideologies on the web?

Using data from SimilarWeb along with ideological classifications of political outlets by the nonprofit watchdog group Media Bias/Fact Check and other sources, I calculated visits to the websites of 215 rightist illiberal political outlets. The methods by which I identified these sites are described in detail in chapter 3. I included the ten original Alt-Right sites and others that I identified later, for a total of thirty-two Alt-Right sites. The analysis also included the websites of traditional hate movements; sites that disseminate conspiracy theories and fake news; Alt-Lite sites that are superficially less radical than the Alt-Right; and a range of reactionary movements such as the Manosphere, the Dark Enlightenment, the Alt-South, and hyperorthodox religious groups. To measure the web footprint of these right-wing illiberal sites compared to other, more mainstream tendencies, I also collected data on sites of all political orientations, from the extremist or Illiberal Left through to the traditional Right. I ended up with data on a total of 1,952 sites for the period January 2019 to November 2019. Unless otherwise noted, all figures used below refer to this time period.

All of the 215 sites that are the most radically right wing—identified here as Hard-Core Right Illiberal—had a monthly average of about 186 million visits. This is nearly one-third the size of the monthly average traffic to sites of the mainstream Right, which received about 604 million visits. This is an impressively sized audience, especially given the extreme radicalism of these Hard-Core Right Illiberal sites.

Moreover, not only is explicit, radical illiberalism a concern, but so too are its less overtly anti-democratic characteristics such as nasty, alienating rhetoric; hyperpartisanship; race baiting; highly biased reporting; treatment of adversaries as enemies; and acidic scorn of democratic institutions. Has this illiberal style of discussion penetrated into mainstream political culture?

Documenting the audience for a style of political discussion is difficult, but there is relevant evidence. Breitbart News, once described by its former editor Steve Bannon as "the platform of the alt-right,"[1] has one of the largest audiences of any political web magazine, with about 51 million visits and 5.5 million unique visitors on monthly average. (If one person visits a site five times in a month, that represents five visits and one unique visitor.) Ann Coulter, Michelle Malkin, and Pat Buchanan are long-time practitioners of the illiberal style. All of them have their syndicated columns appearing in the Alt-Right outlet VDARE and Malkin and Buchanan also appear in American Renaissance. The traffic to their websites is not large, but they reach many millions of people through their columns, best-selling books, and television appearances. Tucker Carlson's website also receives relatively few visits, but he reaches an audience of millions through his Fox News program. Carlson's style is clearly illiberal. Andrew Anglin, editor of the Daily Stormer, described Carlson's Fox News show as "basically Daily Stormer: The Show," referred to Carlson as "literally our greatest ally," and has featured Carlson in 265 stories on the site.[2] And the greatest exponent of illiberal style, Donald Trump, became president and continues to be a major influence in American politics.

In short, the Alt-Right and related illiberal ideologies remain, in both substance and style, a major presence in American political culture. Charlottesville and the deplatforming efforts that immediately followed did not have the impact that was expected. The long march of extremism through American political culture and on to an authoritarian future continues.

After Trump

The above analysis and the data they are based on were conducted and collected before the presidential election of 2020. At that point there was optimism that Donald Trump would be overwhelmingly defeated, that Democrats would achieve unified government with control of the White House and both chambers of Congress, and that a political realignment away from the illiberalism lite of Trump would begin.

Democrats did achieve a unified government, but with only the absolutely slimmest of margins in the Senate, a reduced majority in the House, and a sound but not landslide win for Joe Biden. We have a unified government but not political realignment. In fact, by some criteria the grip of illiberalism on American political culture looks stronger than ever. The stunning spectacle of angry mobs of Trump supporters, deluded by widespread fake news of a rigged election storming the U.S. Capitol and shutting down the final counting of the electoral vote, was perhaps the most dramatic manifestation of widespread illiberal sentiment in modern American history. For electoral democracy is a central component of liberal democracy and a corrosive cynicism about the legitimacy of elections in the face of overwhelming evidence of their fairness is an expression of illiberalism. Yet, according to a poll conducted for Reuters, 52 percent of Republicans think that Trump "rightfully won" the 2020 election, and 68 percent were concerned that the election was "rigged." Further, the poll showed that "more Americans appear to be more suspicious about the U.S. election process than they were four years ago. . . . The 28% who said they thought the election was 'the result of illegal voting or election rigging' is up 12 points from four years ago."[3] A substantial percentage of the population believes in still more florid conspiracy theories. An NPR/Ipsos poll asked respondents whether they believe "a group of Satan-worshipping elites who run a child sex ring are trying to control our politics and media."[4] This bizarre recycling of themes from the *Protocols of the Elders of Zion* is the central message of the online conspiracy mongering movement QAnon. Seventeen percent of respondents believed the claim while 37 percent said they did not know, which makes for 54 percent of the American public who give some credence to a movement that has been accurately described by a scholar of genocide studies as "a Nazi cult, rebranded."[5]

This susceptibility to lies, disinformation, and conspiracy theories is a clear threat to democracy. Thomas Jefferson was correct when he wrote "If a nation expects to be ignorant and free, in a state of civilization, it expects what never was and never will be."[6] But America's current situation is graver than that envisioned by Jefferson. The people who stormed the Capitol are not merely ignorant but are among the "active misinformed," who are convinced that their false beliefs are true and who are willing to take action—even illegal, violent, and anti-democratic action—based on those false beliefs. Moreover, the chief misinformation fomenter, Donald Trump, earned more than 74 million votes, retains his grip on the Republican Party, and is the most popular man in America.[7] And perhaps most concerning of all, a PBS NewsHour/Marist Poll conducted on January 6, 2021, found that 8 percent of adults and 18 percent of Republicans expressed support for the disruption of the electoral vote process at the Capitol.[8] The corruption of public opinion and the disorder it provokes are signs of the enduring presence of illiberalism in America.

Outline of the Book

This book is, in part, about the development and growth of a right-wing extremist ideology and rhetorical style that have penetrated deeply into American political culture. Call it the rise of illiberalism. The current size and influence of illiberal ideology, its intellectual origins, the social and political developments that facilitated its spread, and what to do about it are the main issues that this book addresses.

The book explores the full range of illiberal ideologies. By "illiberal" I mean any political ideology that explicitly rejects liberal democracy or some central principle of liberal democracy, such as political egalitarianism, human rights, electoral democracy, the rule of law, an enlightened ethics of controversy, and tolerance. Illiberal ideologies include all of the right-wing extremisms mentioned above, as well as leftist illiberal movements such as various schools of communism, anarchism, and some varieties of antifascist or antifa movements. But to recognize ideologies that reject liberal democracy, liberal democracy itself must first be defined, and chapter 2 accomplishes that necessary methodological step.

The analysis of illiberalism begins in chapter 3, which includes a quantitative analysis of illiberal outlets of political opinion on the web. One purpose of this chapter is to address the objection that, even when all its many expressions are wrapped up together, illiberalism is still an insignificantly small phenomenon and so focusing on it is alarmist. To tackle this issue, chapter 3 presents an analysis of data on hundreds of websites that identify themselves as illiberal or are identified as such by expert observers of this material. I compare the audiences for these sites with the audiences of opinion outlets that fall within the traditional liberal democratic political spectrum, running from the Left through the political center to the traditional Right. Altogether 1,952 websites are included in the analysis, which shows that, by many measures, the audience for illiberalism is nearly as large as the audience for outlets of mainstream political ideologies. Other important findings are that left-wing illiberal movements such as Antifa—a favorite bugaboo of conservative media—are vanishingly small in terms of their digital audience; audiences for rightist illiberal sites are much more engaged with and visit their favorite websites more often than is the case with websites of other orientations; and in between the Hard-Core Illiberal Right sites and sites of the conventional Right are a set of In-Between Right sites that facilitate transmission of Hard-Core ideology into mainstream political culture.

Chapter 3 also documents and critiques the content of Hard-Core Illiberal Right ideology. To facilitate that process, the analysis sorts the pertinent websites into subcategories such as Hate, Alt-Right, Alt-Lite, Manosphere, Dark Enlightenment, and others, then reviews the content of the sites identified within each subcategory as having the largest audiences. One of the main findings is that, although there is some variation among these sites, for the most part the ideology of the Hard-Core Illiberal Right is extremely radical. In fact, this material is so radical that it had to be laid out at length and in depth; otherwise the extremism of the Hard-Core Illiberal Right would be hard to believe. Suffice it to say that the ideology of these sites is not simply a slightly more populist, rightist, or hyperbolic version of the mainstream conservativism that dominated American politics during the 1980s. Today's Hard-Core rightist illiberalism is an explicit, root-and-branch break with liberal democracy and embraces a mash-up of fascist, reactionary, racialist, inegalitarian, anti-Semitic, and anti-democratic principles. Another feature of this ideology is a rhetorical style based on open scorn of tolerance, including an insistence that politics is war, an embrace of the friend-versus-enemy conception of politics, an unconstitutional definition of treason that is applied to all political opponents, and a vituperative style of criticism. Further, respect for the idea that political discourse should be based on reasoned debate, established facts, and a search for common ground is rejected by the Illiberal Right. Instead, words are used as weapons, seeking consensus is repudiated, facts are countered with factoids and fake news, and conspiracy theories are disseminated. Here again, the illiberal rhetorical style is so extreme that ample documentation is necessary to overcome the generally helpful disinclination to think too ill of political opponents.

But documenting the rise of illiberal ideology is only part of what this book seeks to accomplish. The real question is why this political vision has crystalized, found a significant audience, and exerts influence throughout American political culture, even all the way to the White House. There is no one answer to any of these questions, so they require a comprehensive overview of American politics. Chapters 4 to 7 seek to provide such an overview, with each chapter looking at one aspect of political life that in combination provide a 360-degree picture of American politics today.

Chapter 4 concerns identity. Political deliberation has to start from somewhere in particular, from a set of cognitions that are taken for granted, at least provisionally. This starting point may be thought of as the identity of a given polity, and in this sense, identity is a necessary aspect of political life. Moreover, identity is relevant because Right Illiberals have made a racialistic theory of identity into the lance tip of their attack on liberal democracy. So chapter 4 rebuts the Right Illiberal conception of identity and develops a conception of identity compatible with liberal democracy. Much of chapter 4 is devoted to an intellectual history of the development of the illiberal, or identitarian, conception of political identity. Very briefly put, illiberals have learned there are rhetorical advantages to be gained by painting themselves—rather than African Americans, women, or gays—as the true outsiders to liberal democratic society and thus the only group possessed of critical distance from society and capable of instigating fundamental change. The discussion of how illiberals made use of what has been called the "inversion thesis" is the main theoretical contribution of this book. Understanding how this maneuver turned out to be more effective than might be thought requires going back to mid-twentieth-century efforts to protect scientific communities from the pitfalls of groupthink. Rebutting identitarianism also involves a review of the empirical sociology that shows Americans widely share a sense of political identity that is compatible with liberal democracy.

Chapter 5 takes up another key aspect of political life, ideas—the units that make up the arguments advanced in the course of political discourse. The chapter explains how a certain type of ideas, public ideas, played a positive role in American politics that was undermined by developments in the twenty-first century. The argument is that from about the early 1970s to the turn of the millennium, the United States had a system for producing and disseminating public ideas that were simple enough to be grasped by mass audiences but also had roots in more complex ideas produced by experts. This system was shattered by the traumatic political and social developments of the early twenty-first century, and also by the rise of digital communications technologies that called the whole notion of expertise into question and undermined the cultural gatekeeping functions of public intellectuals. This digital revolution is irreversible, and the gatekeeping power of public intellectuals cannot be fully restored. What intellectuals can do, however, is abandon some of the dogmas that weakened their position even before the transformational changes of the twenty-first century. Intellectuals can also facilitate the development of a progressive New American Majority based on the oncoming minority-majority population by interpreting these developments as consistent with the existing American political identity.

Chapter 6 describes the role of ideas in American political culture now that the process of developing public ideas that are linked to expert knowledge has been undermined. The result, on the internet at least, is a world of weaponized irony and total ambivalence, where the meaning of words and the intent of their writers are often almost impossible to determine for sure. Public ideas that trace back to expert understanding have been replaced by digital memes that trace back to other memes ad infinitum and, in the end, to nothing at all. The rhetoric of weaponized irony that now dominates the web needs to be balanced by a rhetoric of assent that helps build a social consensus around ideas that have passed the inspection of qualified gatekeepers and that merit provisional acceptance. To achieve this, internet service providers must be pressured to more strongly moderate the content they carry than they do now.

Chapter 7 is devoted to interests, the final major aspect of political life covered here. Interests are a major motivation behind political action. Even if the United States sorts out the issues related to identity politics and revives its capacity to develop useful public ideas, the power of interest groups will remain strong and the well-known problems of pluralistic politics will remain, creating problems that illiberalism will seek to exploit. These problems are exacerbated by the notoriously fragmented American Constitution, which encourages the development of interest groups and, as a result, makes collective action unnecessarily difficult. Chapter 7 therefore proposes constitutional amendments to reduce fragmentation and improve rationality in policymaking. The key to making constitutional change realistic is to advance only proposals that have been road tested at the state level. In general, state constitutions are much easier to change than the federal Constitution, and some of these mechanisms for change should be adopted at the federal level. Chapter 7 also explores a constitutional amendment designed to improve coherence in policymaking by strengthening the hand of the president in forming a legislative agenda. Chapter 8 offers some elaborations on and qualifications of the book's major themes.

2

What Is Illiberalism?
What Is Liberal Democracy?

Establishing criteria that define illiberalism not only is an essential methodological step, but also gets to a central issue of this book. What is it about illiberalism that makes it so great a concern? Illiberalism is a political ideology—that is, a fixed and fairly consistent set of ideas about politics. But so, too, are all the varieties of conservativism, progressivism, socialism, and many other systems of political thought that are not problematic in the same sense as illiberalism. Indeed, any political ideology that is consistent with the political philosophy of liberal democracy is unproblematic in terms of this investigation. It is ideologies that break with or reject flatly the principles of liberal democracy that are of concern here. So to define illiberalism, one must first identify those liberal democratic principles.

Doing so could involve a review of a vast literature. But wading through and taking a position on the many arguments and issues in that huge body of work would require a book in itself and would not serve present purposes. Instead, this analysis requires a ready-at-hand tool that does not introduce controversies of its own. The solution is not a new, up-to-the-minute contribution to the literature, but rather a consensus definition—

one that lays out the widely recognized features of liberal democracy, and enjoys something like universal recognition and respect.

Fortunately the second paragraph of the Declaration of Independence provides just such a definition of liberal democracy.

> We hold these truths to be self-evident, that all men are created equal, that they are endowed by their Creator with certain unalienable Rights, that among these are Life, Liberty and the pursuit of Happiness.—That to secure these rights, Governments are instituted among Men, deriving their just powers from the consent of the governed,—That whenever any Form of Government becomes destructive of these ends, it is the Right of the People to alter or to abolish it, and to institute new Government, laying its foundation on such principles and organizing its powers in such form, as to them shall seem most likely to effect their Safety and Happiness. Prudence, indeed, will dictate that Governments long established should not be changed for light and transient causes; and accordingly all experience hath shewn, that mankind are more disposed to suffer, while evils are sufferable, than to right themselves by abolishing the forms to which they are accustomed. But when a long train of abuses and usurpations, pursuing invariably the same Object evinces a design to reduce them under absolute Despotism, it is their right, it is their duty, to throw off such Government, and to provide new Guards for their future security.[1]

The main points of Thomas Jefferson's iconic statement can be operationalized for this study's purposes as follows:

Political Egalitarianism: All human beings are politically equal to one another however much they may differ or be unequal in other respects. No one has a political status that is any better or worse than anyone else's.

Human Rights: All people hold a set of political privileges that are not to be infringed by anyone or anything. Exactly what these privileges should be is subject to discussion. In Canada they are the rights to peace, order, and good government, while in the United States the privileges are the rights to life, liberty, and the pursuit of happiness. In any case, the same rights are enjoyed by all, and while these rights can be violated, they cannot be alienated in the sense of being voided or nullified.

Limited Government: Liberal democracy insists government in some form is necessary to protect the rights of everyone. All forms of anarchism and other ideologies that reject the need for government are antithetical to liberal democracy. And a central function of government is the protection of human rights.

Democracy: Liberal democratic government derives its just powers from "the consent of the governed."

Change and Revolution: Liberal democracy holds there must be a government but does not specify any particular form of government as long as liberal democratic principles are not violated. People have the right to change or abolish their form of government as they see fit. Even revolutionary change is consistent with liberal democracy but only in the extreme case when, in light of long experience, the alternative is "absolute Despotism."

These are the principles of liberal democracy that are explicit in the Declaration, but others are implicit. In its first paragraph the document states that, given the gravity of the issues at hand, "a decent respect to the opinions of mankind requires that they [the colonists] should declare the causes which impel them" to their decision, which in this case is to become independent. So, out of respect for others, those seeking political change must lay out their reasons. In exercising their right to form and change government, people should act on principles they think "seem most likely to effect their Safety and Happiness." Thus, political action is grounded in principles and aimed at safety and happiness, although perhaps other principles may apply in certain situations. In acting, people should show "prudence" and not be moved by "light and transient causes." Jefferson goes on to offer proof of his case with "facts . . . submitted to a candid world." The penultimate paragraph of the Declaration, in which Jefferson recounts the colonies' relations with the British people, suggests how political adversaries should engage: The British were "warned," "reminded," and "appealed to," and were still considered "friends" until war broke out.

In all this, an ethics of controversy is implied. Treat other people's opinions decently, with respect, and give reasons for political decisions. Base political action on principles and fundamental issues, not minor considerations, and take action prudently. Prove points with facts intelligible to anyone who is candid enough to appreciate them. Pay attention to those who disagree, and address them respectfully and not as enemies, short of war.

Another principle in the ethics of controversy is implicit in the Declaration. Scholars often note that the second paragraph of the document is a recognizable paraphrase of key passages from John Locke's *Second Treatise*. Indeed, by modern standards Jefferson simply plagiarized Locke. The similarity is so close that it is fair to say Jefferson deliberately invoked Locke, who was the most influential political philosopher in the eighteenth-century Anglo-American world. In other words, Jefferson engaged his British adversaries by clearly seeking out shared ground with them.

Thus the main features of the ethics of controversy implicit in the Declaration are respect, reasoning, deliberation, prudence, argument, facts, candor, the search for common ground, and avoidance of demonizing political adversaries. In summary, then, a liberal democratic principle implicit in the Declaration is a political culture based on tolerance.

But as seminal and widely respected as Jefferson's account of liberal democracy is, consider that after more than 200 years some clarifications and additions may be appropriate, even given the present limited circumstances. For example, although the Declaration says that governments derive their just powers from consent of the governed, the document does not specify how to obtain that consent. For a long time now, that consent has been almost always determined by elections. Joseph Schumpeter recognized this reality when he provided his now widely accepted operational definition of democracy as "that institutional arrangement for arriving at political decisions in which individuals acquire the power to decide by means of a competitive struggle for the people's vote."[2] Today, after the civil rights movement and other extensions of political equality, the "people" are understood to include all adults. Thus, Jefferson's concept of the consent of the governed means electoral democracy in the form of periodic contested elections before a universal adult franchise, which is an essential principle of liberal democracy.

There is another key principle of liberal democracy that the Declaration does not mention explicitly: the rule of law. The document says government must "secure these rights" but says little about how to do it. However, today the consensus is that (as Locke said)[3] government, in all it does, must act through laws that are binding on all.

In recent decades, scholars have advanced other institutions as essential to liberal democracy. The idea that capitalism is a necessary, but not sufficient, condition for democracy has been argued at length by Friedrich Hayek in *The Road to Serfdom* and elsewhere by many others. This concept was widely accepted in the 1990s, when the collapse of communism seemed to prove that socialism—at least the centrally planned, Soviet variety—was incompatible with democracy. More recently, however, globalization and "creative destruction" (another famous formulation by Schumpeter) have reminded people of the limitations of capitalism. Additionally, there is the difficulty of defining capitalism widely enough to embrace all countries that are democratic. For instance, from the 1940s through the 1960s, Scandinavian nations were obviously democratic and yet considered their economies socialist. For present purposes, then, this analysis does not consider capitalism to be an essential feature of liberal democracy.

What about the welfare state? Arguably, all stable democracies today have a welfare state, but whether it is a necessary condition of democracy is not clear. Until very recently, conservatives were often harshly critical of the welfare state and some argued it is inimical to democracy. Hayek waded into this debate too and argued against the welfare state in *The Constitution of Liberty*, although elsewhere he was less critical or even positive.[4] Today even libertarians are making peace with the welfare state. Thus the Niskanen Center, a free-market-oriented think tank, publishes material such as "Why Libertarians and Conservatives Should Stop Opposing the Welfare State."[5] The question of whether the welfare state is essential to liberal democracy falls into the same definitional issues as the debate about capitalism and is not likely to reach a consensus soon.[6] Thus the welfare state does not figure in the definition of liberal democracy used here.

Therefore, the main principles of liberal democracy are political egalitarianism, human rights, limited government, electoral democracy, the legitimacy of change and revolution, the rule of law, and tolerance, broadly defined to include an ethics of controversy based on reasoned discussion. It is important to understand that in identifying the main principles of liberal democracy, I do not claim to have identified all principles of liberal democracy, nor an exclusive list of all the desiderata of political action. My goal is to come up with criteria with which to clearly identify an outlet of political opinion as illiberal. The definition of liberal democracy used here is by design a minimal one. To break with liberal democracy thus defined is a radical step and therefore illiberalism, as it is understood here, is a radically anti-democratic ideology.

With a definition of liberal democracy, illiberalism, which is the rejection of liberal democracy in whole or in part, can be defined. For purposes of illustration some of the findings of the rest of this book, which are based on traffic to political websites in the first eleven months of 2019, are anticipated below.

All forms of political inegalitarianism are illiberal. These include but are not limited to all types of discrimination based on race, creed, color, ethnicity, sex, or gender. Anti-Semitism, sexism, and all forms of racism are obvious examples. White supremacy also is obviously illiberal. Some commentators claim not to know what white supremacy is or that it has no meaning. After Joe Biden in his inaugural address referred to "political extremism, white supremacy, domestic terrorism that we must confront and we will defeat," Fox News pundit Tucker Carlson asked "What does it mean to wage war on white supremacists? Can somebody tell us in very clear language what a white supremacist is?"[7] Carlson suggested that white supremacy refers to people who celebrate the Fourth of July, support federal border security, or use the term "American exceptionalism," even though Biden referred to none of this in his address. (Neither did he speak of waging war on anyone.) Similarly, Heather MacDonald, writing of Biden's address in the Manhattan Institute's *City Journal*, objected to Biden's repudiation of white supremacy, which she claimed was one of the "au courant, shallow terms of the moment, lacking depth or weight."[8] But "white supremacist" has a well-known meaning, one with at least as much depth and weight as any other term frequently used in journalistic and academic literature. It is defined by the *Oxford English Dictionary* as "an advocate or supporter of the doctrine that white people are superior to other peoples, and should therefore have greater power, authority, or status."[9] Chapter 3 documents a set of websites that, even in the narrowest terms, are accurately defined as white supremacist. Outright hate sites, which are only a portion of all Hard-Core Illiberal Right sites, received on average about 1.2 million visits per month.

Another form of illiberal inegalitarianism is rejection of the proposition that all people are created equal. It is, of course, well understood that the equality referenced by Jefferson's words is not equality of any trait, such as strength, intelligence, or virtue, but political equality. There are plenty of thinkers and websites that explicitly deny Jeffersonian equality. Among them is American Renaissance, a key Alt-Right site, which declares: "[W]e ought to laugh out of town every goofball who claims the Declaration proves everyone is equal to everyone else. It's a form of insanity."[10] And there are hyper-fundamentalist outlets that claim "Jefferson's statement in the Declaration of Independence is unfortunate, and taken at face value it is manifestly untrue . . ." and ". . . our people have been inundated with the propaganda that all men are created equal . . ."[11] Chapter 3 shows that these and other websites that explicitly deny political egalitarianism receive many millions of visits each month.

Any ideology that rejects electoral democracy is illiberal. An expression of anti-democratic illiberalism is "What Democracy?" an article from the platform *Zero Hedge*, an extreme libertarian blog that declares "Democracy's pitting of individuals against each other leads to moral degeneration and impairs capital accumulation."[12] In a similar vein, Paul Craig Roberts, a former supply-side economist now turned illiberal idealogue, asserts "The American Republic was a *democracy of male property owners*. . . . Whereas a democracy of property owners is stable, a one person one vote democracy is not."[13] These and other arguments against electoral democracy as it is now practiced are common coin in the illiberal websites analyzed in this book.

Illiberalism also takes the form of an attack on human rights. Chapter 4 discusses Alain de Benoist, the European New Right (ENR) thinker and author of *Beyond Human Rights* who has been highly influential on American Alt-Rightists and other illiberal sites. Benoist writes: ". . . today the discussion of human rights . . . is above all an instrument of domination, and should be regarded as such."[14] Chapter 4 also discusses Guillaume Faye, another more radical but still influential ENR writer who repudiates "Human Rights, Human Rightism: The cornerstone of the modern ideology of progress and individualistic egalitarianism—and the basis upon which the thought police have been set up to destroy the people's rights to exist as a people."[15] Illiberal sites such as Counter-Currents Publishing and Occidental Observer have frequently published and commented on Benoist and Faye.[16] Through their influence and that of others, opposition to human rights became a staple of illiberalism.

Illiberalism can take the form of a principled rejection of the ethics of controversy based on tolerance that, as described earlier, is implicit in the Declaration of Independence. It is important to understand that not every intemperate op-ed or poorly argued essay is illiberal in this sense. It is not the failure of a writer or publication to always live up to enlightened standards of debate that makes for illiberalism. Rather, illiberalism is the explicit rejection of those standards, the celebration of irrationalism, the sedulous dissemination of obvious lies, and regular indulgence in vituperation. Nothing better encapsulates the illiberal ethics of controversy than the stylebook for the infamous Daily Stormer, which receives about 1.3 million visits on average per month. The stylebook explains the following to its contributors:

> The goal is to repeat the same points over and over and over and over again. . . . [T]o the extent possible everything should be painted in completely black and white terms. . . . The basic idea is that everyone on our side is 100% good and everyone who isn't on our side is 100% evil. . . . There should be a conscious agenda to dehumanize the enemy to the point where people are ready to laugh at their deaths. . . . and the more hyperbole, the better.[17]

Chapters 3 and 4 document other proponents of the illiberal style, including Vox Day, editor of a web outlet that receives about 694,000 visits on average per month, and the popular right-wing pundit Ann Coulter. The embrace of hyperbole, dehumanization, name-calling, and extremism, as well as the rejection of meaningful communication, are hallmarks of the illiberal rhetorical style.

Inherent in this imperative to exaggerate and oversimplify is an indifference to truth. Thus, consistently trafficking in falsehoods, unverified rumors, conspiracy theories, and the like when the subject is political affairs is another expression of illiberalism. What is meant here is not tabloid gossip about Hollywood stars or tall tales about UFOs and bigfoot but the deliberate dissemination of lies and highly biased stories to advance a political agenda. This form of illiberalism is exemplified by Alex Jones's InfoWars, which receives a monthly average of about 6.9 million visitors and is most famous for circulating the fiction that the Sandy Hook Elementary School shooting was a false flag operation designed to discredit the Second Amendment. Another example is QAnon, the conspiracy theory spread by various social media networks that portrays Donald Trump as leading a secret war against satanic, pedophile Democrats. The Drudge Report and Breitbart News are outlets that have hawked less surreal falsehoods. Drudge has featured phony Clinton family scandals and Obama birtherism, while Breitbart has gone with climate change denial, bogus election fraud claims, and decrying "mask fascists." The Drudge Report and Breitbart News had, respectively, 84.9 and 50.9 million visits on average per month. This mix of inaccurate reporting, hyperpartisanship and bias, and regularly circulating falsehoods all undermine the democratic ethics of controversy and are characteristic of illiberal outlets.[18]

The liberal ethics of controversy require that adversaries be treated with respect, not as enemies short of war, and that common ground with them be sought. All of this means that the friend-versus-enemy conception of politics, most famously developed by the National Socialist jurist Carl Schmitt, is illiberal. Counter-Currents Publishing, one of the most philosophically oriented illiberal sites, is again relevant as it has published scores of articles by and about Schmitt and often invokes the friend-versus-enemy idea.[19] One such article, "Why Are We Political Soldiers?," gets right to the illiberal implications of politics as friend versus enemy: "Our soldierly faith and duty is wedded to the national-revolutionary ideal that seeks a new political, aristocratic, hierarchical, anti-democratic, and anti-egalitarian order. . . . For us, as for Carl Schmitt, politics is that privileged arena in which the enemy and the friend is clearly designated."[20]

Variations on this illiberal theme are the notions that politics is war and that political opponents are traitors. Of course, normal democratic politics can be heated and adversaries often speak harshly of each other. But loose talk about war or treason is not the issue. Illiberalism is seriously advancing the principle that politics is war and opposition is treason. These concepts are central at FrontPage Magazine, which receives about 684,000 visits per month, and other sites managed by David Horowitz. One of his outlets asserts: "The David Horowitz Freedom Center . . . sees its role as that of a battle tank, geared to fight a war . . . [and] is best seen as a School of Political Warfare."[21] And in a campaign manual circulated to Republican strategists, Horowitz advised: "Politics is War. Don't forget it."[22] FrontPage Magazine also frequently equates ordinary opposition with treason, as in a typical article "Borderline Treason: How Democrats Continue to Betray Their Country."[23] The ideas that politics is war and adversaries are traitors are commonplace in illiberal discourse, as chapters 3 and 4 show.

Probably most readers will need little convincing that liberal democracy is a very positive, perhaps the best, form of government and that opposition to it is negative. But it might be asked what makes liberal democracy so desirable. Answering that question in the detail it deserves would go far beyond the scope of this book. Reviewing all the forms of government that humankind has known, or even those on offer today, toting up their pros and cons, and coming to a final judgment is the work of many lifetimes. But a few observations can be made here. One is that the most recent attempts at synoptic evaluations of the world history of government are in favor of liberal democracy. These include S. E. Finer's three volumes on *The History of Government from Earliest Times* and Francis Fukuyama's *The Origins of Political Order* and *Political Order and Political Decay*. Finer insisted that his magisterial history was not teleological and that later forms of government are not necessarily better than earlier forms. But he did note that ". . . the European modern state—the territorial nation-state that proclaims democratic and secular values—has become the model for the entire contemporary world."[24] And in a "prolegomenon" to his history, he suggested a conclusion that could be drawn from it:

> Would there be what the Victorians would have called a "moral" to this long tale? . . . Could this lead, at the end of the story, to comparing the different polities in respect to their care for the well-being of their populations? . . . The more interesting question would indeed be whether, for the western world, any period in the entire history of government has afforded so high a proportion of the population such material prosperity, such domestic security, such changes for upward mobility and such freedom of expression, person and domicile than the period which set in after 1945.[25]

Thus, a plausible moral to be drawn from Finer's history is that the modern democratic and secular state—what is here called liberal democracy—has likely done a better job of caring for the well-being and freedom of its population than any other governmental form.

Fukuyama's volumes are similar to Finer's in that they cover an enormous amount of material and conclude that something like liberal democracy is what most nations do and should want to achieve. He writes: "I believe that a political system resting on a balance among state, law, and accountability is both a practical and a moral necessity for all societies. . . . [T]here is no alternative to a modern, impersonal state as guarantor of order and security, and as a source of necessary public goods."[26] The system Fukuyama is describing here is a liberal democracy, with the rule of law and democratic accountability and a limited state to implement both. In short, the upshot of Finer's and Fukuyama's extensive historical research is that liberal democracy is a particularly desirable form of government, which is why the rise of illiberalism today is a serious problem.

Knowing clearly what illiberalism is clarifies certain terminological issues. In the literature on illiberal movements the terms "extremist," "radical," and "far"—as in "far right" or "far left"—come up often. But they are usually unhelpful as the baseline from which a given ideology or movement is held to be far, or extreme, or radical is not specified. For the purposes of this book, liberal democracy is taken as the baseline; that is, the default political philosophy that is given a rebuttable benefit of a doubt as a desirable basis for social organization. Only ideologies or movements that make a clean break with liberal democracy count as radical or extreme for present purposes.

All of this means that there is a certain phenomenon that is sometimes called illiberalism but that is not the subject of this book. When some people speak of illiberalism they are talking about such things as the centrist editor Bari Weiss being criticized by progressive colleagues and quitting her job at the *New York Times*, someone getting flack for insisting there are two sexes, harsh critics of Israel, protesters who want to take down memorials to Washington and Jefferson, disorderly demonstrators, writers who belittle conservatives, and the like. Published concerns about such issues include Dinesh D'Sousa's *Illiberal Education: The Politics of Race and Sex on Campus* and Kim R. Holmes's *The Closing of the Liberal Mind: How Groupthink and Intolerance Define the Left*. In July 2020, *Harper's Mag-

azine published "A Letter on Justice and Open Debate," which was signed by many distinguished intellectuals and decried:

> [A] censoriousness . . . spreading more widely in our culture: an intolerance of opposing views, a vogue for public shaming and ostracism, and the tendency to dissolve complex policy issues in a blinding moral certainty. . . . Editors are fired for running controversial pieces; books are withdrawn for alleged inauthenticity; journalists are barred from writing on certain topics; professors are investigated for quoting works of literature in class; a researcher is fired for circulating a peer-reviewed academic study; and the heads of organizations are ousted for what are sometimes just clumsy mistakes.[27]

Whatever might be said of these developments, they are not what this book is about. The concern here is with political ideologies explicitly opposed to liberal democracy. The cultural trend referenced above is a strong form of political correctness that seldom flatly rejects liberal democracy in the way that the right and left illiberal ideologies of concern to this book do as a matter of course. One might argue that there is a leftist "censoriousness" analogous to the harsh rhetorical style of the Illiberal Right. But few readers will want to make that claim after they have looked over the material in chapter 3 from Hard-Core Right Illiberal outlets, which are vituperative, hateful, and hyperbolic to a degree not found elsewhere. This book will show that right illiberalism is much more radical, salient, and corrosive of liberal democratic values than is the political correctness of the academic and intellectual left.

With these clarifications made, and a definition of liberal democracy based on an updated version of Jefferson's world historical account in hand, the analysis can begin.

3
The Audience for Illiberalism Today

Thomas J. Main and Jessica Miller

This chapter is devoted to a quantitative analysis of illiberal outlets of political opinion on the web. One purpose is to counter the objection that, even when all its many expressions are wrapped up together, illiberalism is still an insignificantly small phenomenon and, therefore, focusing on it is alarmist. To address this issue, we present our analysis of data on hundreds of English-language websites that identify themselves, or have been identified by expert observers of this material, as illiberal. We compare the audiences for these sites with the audiences of opinion outlets that fall within the traditional liberal democratic political spectrum running from the conventional left through the political center and to the conventional right. All together the analysis includes 1,952 websites and covers the time period from January 2019 to November 2019, unless otherwise noted.[1] The numbers show that, by many measures, the audience for illiberalism is fairly large relative to the audience for outlets of mainstream political ideologies. This chapter also tests the broader hypothesis that illiberal ideologies are not expressed only through outlets that are isolated from the mainstream of American political culture, but rather these ideologies pass through a spectrum of sites and so become steadily normalized.

Methodology

A central goal of this analysis is to identify websites with an extremist-right political orientation, such as that of the Alt-Right, but not confined to that particular movement. To avoid the pitfall of picking sites based on personal judgment alone and thus biasing the results, the study relies on choices made by sites that self-identify as Alt- or extremist-right. These source sites of an extremist right orientation that provided blog rolls and links to other similarly oriented sites were Affirmative Right, Mapping the Dark Enlightenment, Occidental Dissent, Occidental Observer, VDARE, and Who Is White? SimilarWeb, a web-traffic analytics firm, was the source for data on visits and unique visitors to these sites from January 2019 to November 2019. (If one person visits a given site ten times in a month, that represents ten visits but only one unique visitor.) Unless otherwise noted, all statistics on audience size presented here are monthly averages for this period.

We eliminated sites that had no measurable traffic in one or more months. Since we were interested in sites that have a political orientation, we eliminated sites of government agencies, such as the Drug Enforcement Administration (DEA), Immigration and Customs Enforcement (ICE), and Department of Homeland Security (DHS); web pages of higher education institutions or their departments, such as the Harvard Kennedy School and Columbia University; entry portals to digital services such as Gab; home pages of nonpolitical, nonprofit institutions, such as Monticello and Mount Vernon; and other sites with no political orientation. Sites in languages other than English were eliminated, but English-language sites based in foreign countries were retained. The result was 360 sites that we refer to as Right Illiberal.

A key goal was to measure the size of the audience for illiberal sites. But in this context, size is a relative matter and so we had to identify websites of other political orientations for comparison. Again, site selection relied on classifications of sites made by an independent organization, the nonprofit Media Bias/Fact Check (MBFC), which organizes hundreds of sites into the following political categories: Left Bias, Center-Left Bias, Least Biased, Center-Right Bias, and Right Bias. After applying the criteria for elimination described above, there were 246 Left sites, 425 Center-Left sites, 355 Least Biased sites, 212 Center-Right sites, and 207 Right sites.

Another relevant comparison group is Left Illiberal sites. Since MBFC does not provide a list of such groups, selection relied mostly on the same technique used to identify Right Illiberal sites—that is, lists provided by sites that self-identify with an ideology that can fairly be identified as Left Illiberal. Therefore, Left Illiberal sites included those that self-identified with communism or anti-democratic Marxism, anarchism, or Antifa (a particular left-wing, antifascist movement). We identified eleven such Left-Illiberal sites that provided link lists or blog roles.[2] We also consulted Discover the Networks (DTN), a site that is described as "A Guide to the Political Left" and that is maintained by the David Horowitz Freedom Center, a right-wing advocacy organization. The vast majority of sites mentioned by DTN hardly qualify as radical or illiberal, but some relevant sites were included.[3] The result was a list of 131 Left-Illiberal sites.

Sorting websites in this manner raised several ambiguities. The sources we used sometimes placed the same site in different categories. For example, fourteen sites were categorized by MBFC as Right but also appeared in the lists of sites compiled by the Illiberal-Right sources. And two sites categorized as Center Right by MBFC also appeared in the lists compiled by Far-Right sources. We put these sixteen sites in their own category of Right-Ambiguous sites. Readers can judge for themselves how these outlets should be counted.

Similarly, four sites categorized by MBFC as Left also appeared in the lists of sites compiled by Left-Illiberal sources. There were also four sites that MBFC placed in the Left category that were not mentioned by the Far-Left sources and yet were very explicit about their Marxist or anarchist orientation. Indeed, all eight of the sites in question here were explicit about being Marxist, anarchist, or communist. We therefore counted all these sites in the Illiberal-Left category.

Finally, two sites devoted to Jewish and Israeli affairs appeared in both the lists of the Illiberal-Right sources and in the Left or Center-Left lists of MBFC. Neither of these sites had anything in common with the other Illiberal-Right sites. Perhaps they found their way into that category to provide anti-Semites with information they could repurpose to their own ends. We left these sites—The Forward and Haaretz—in the categories to which MBFC assigned them (Center Left and Left, respectively) and did not count them as Illiberal Right.

As illiberalism is the main focus of this book, we paid special attention to the sites that ended up in the Right-Illiberal or Left-Illiberal categories. In the Right-Illiberal category, it became clear that some of the sites listed by our extremist source sites had little relation to illiberalism or even to politics at all. For example, Overcoming Bias describes itself as "a group blog on the general theme of how to move our beliefs closer to reality, in the face of our natural biases such as overconfidence and wishful thinking. . . ."[4] NextBigFuture "provides science-focused news that covers disruptive technologies and trends globally. . . ."[5] Other sites dealt with political issues but were not obviously relevant to the issue of illiberalism. For example, Steve Keen's Debt Deflation page concerns "Australia's private debt bubble," and Overlawyered is devoted to "Chronicling the High Cost of Our Legal System."[6] But other sites clearly fit into the illiberal category. These included kkk.bz, "The Knights Party: The Premier Voice of America's White Resistance," and Alt-right.com, "an academic think-tank on the alternative right."[7] Thus, some distinctions needed to be made.

We decided it was necessary to sort out sites that, even though they had been mentioned in the blog rolls or link lists of illiberal source sites, had little to do with the political ideology of illiberalism. Not eliminating these irrelevant sites would artificially pump up the audience size of the illiberal sites and make the issue we are investigating seem more serious than it is. On the other hand, there was the disadvantage of imposing our own judgments on the data. We decided that distinguishing the truly illiberal sites from the rest would be less misleading than not doing so, but only if we could develop clear criteria for what constituted illiberalism, which led to the creation of a research strategy for identifying those criteria.

Our research strategy for sorting out Hard-Core Illiberal sites from the tentative list our source sites provided was as follows: We visited and became familiar with all of the 360 sites associated with right illiberalism by our sources. We then consulted research by organizations whose mission is to investigate and document what they often describe as "extremist" movements and outlets. These organizations were the Southern Poverty Law Center (SPLC), the Anti-Defamation League (ADL), and the Counter Extremism Project. Another useful source was RationalWiki ("a community working together to explore and provide information about a range of topics centered around science, skepticism, and critical thinking"), which provided much information on right-wing extremism.[8] We also looked at Metapedia[9] and InfoGalactic,[10] two sites that identified with the Far Right and compiled information on that movement. MBFC was also useful even though it devotes most of its attention to mainstream sites and did not have a separate category for Right Illiberal sites. It did have categories for "Conspiracy-Pseudoscience" and "Questionable" sites, and in its descriptions of particular sites sometimes provided relevant information.

For each of the 360 sites our sources associated with right illiberalism, we consulted all or most of the databases cited above. If one or more of the databases described a site as "Alt-Right," "extreme," "neo-Nazi," "racist," "anti-Semitic," a "hate group," or similar terms, we took that as a second, independent judgment that the site was illiberal. (The first judgment was the inclusion of the site in the blog rolls or link lists of the illiberal source sites that were preidentified.) However, we did not consider the judgments of the databases to be dispositive. If a site was identified in one of the databases as illiberal, we did not accept that as automatic proof the site was in fact illiberal. Similarly, if a database did not describe a site as illiberal, we did not necessarily accept that judgment. The SPLC and RationalWiki especially had interests that extended far beyond obvious illiberal groups and devoted attention to right-wing outlets they found objectionable on other grounds.[11]

Therefore, although we consulted all the sources mentioned above and were guided, to a considerable extent, by their material, in the end we sometimes had to exercise our own judgment in determining which sites were accurately described as illiberal. One of us (Main) was particularly qualified to do so.[12] Moreover, the reader should keep in mind that our judgment came into play only after we had gone through all the methodological steps and only in the process of eliminating sites. Our concern was that applying an entirely mechanical approach to identifying illiberal sites would overstate the true size of the movement's audience and be open to the charge of alarmism. Below we describe the content we found at the sites we visited and are transparent about the judgments we made. Readers can decide for themselves if we made accurate choices. We ended up putting the 360 Right-Illiberal sites into two categories: Soft-Core Right Illiberal (145 sites) and Hard-Core Right Illiberal (215 sites). When we refer to all of the 360 Right Illiberal sites collectively, we use the term "Combined Illiberal Right (HC+SC)."

One final methodological point: We did not attempt to distinguish between Hard-Core and Soft-Core Left Illiberal sites as we did with Right-Illiberal sites. One reason for not doing so is that there are fewer research resources available for that task. While there are several organizations with the mission of documenting and analyzing the extreme Right, there are few that follow the extreme Left. The only resource that approaches doing so is DTN, which does have write-ups on some radical Left sites. But as its name suggests, DTN is more concerned with documenting connections between a wide range of left-of-center actors and does not focus as narrowly on extremist groups as, for example, SPLC and ADL do. To the best of our knowledge, there are no other independent resources available for researching the contemporary Illiberal Left. Moreover, on reviewing the sites that our sources associated with the Illiberal Left, none looked to us to be obviously out of place. Therefore, we did not break down the Illiberal-Left sites into Hard Core and Soft Core or in any other way.

Findings: Visits and Unique Visitors

Table 3-1 shows website audiences in terms of visits, unique visitors, and engagement rates. All figures discussed below are based on monthly data for the period from January through November 2019.

The ideologies that had the largest audiences in average monthly visits were the Center Left, with about 2.3 billion visits; Least Biased, with about 1.6 billion visits; and the Left, with about 995 million visits. Together these three ideologies account for about 79.3 percent of the total average monthly visits over the time period. So in terms of visits, the audience for online outlets skews strongly toward the Center Left. It follows that the audience for the Right ideologies is much smaller in number of visits. Together the Right (about 604 million average monthly visits), the Right Ambiguous (about 13.4 million average monthly visits), and the Center Right (about 483 million average monthly visits) account for about 17.5 percent of the total average monthly visits over the time period.

Looking at audience size in terms of unique visitors raised methodological issues. Taking the average number of monthly visits for, say, each of the 425 Center-Left sites and adding them to get about 2.3 billion visits on monthly average raises no issue. But adding up the average number of

Table 3-1. Monthly Traffic to Websites, January 2019–November 2019

Ideology	Number of Sites	Mean Monthly Visits	Mean Unique Visitors	Median Unique Visitors	Mean Engagement Rates	Median Engagement Rates
Left Illiberal	131	2,464,707	10,928	1,338	1.76	1.77
Left	246	994,773,084	1,573,617	49,272	1.95	1.56
Center Left	425	2,348,888,608	2,565,003	231,943	1.84	1.60
Least Biased	355	1,631,514,089	1,366,673	103,617	1.95	1.63
Center Right	212	482,506,802	1,037,338	106,239	1.86	1.67
Right	207	603,611,620	823,845	49,506	2.43	1.82
Right Ambiguous	16	13,354,416	314,165	120,589	1.88	1.68
Right Illiberal, Soft Core	145	8,942,739	18,534	2,131	2.42	1.89
Right Illiberal, Hard Core	215	185,772,634	83,972	3,415	3.07	1.95
Sum	1,952	6,271,828,699				
Right Illiberal, All (SC + HC)	360	194,715,373	57,581	2,980	2.81	1.93

unique visitors to each site presents a problem. Imagine that one person visits Website A ten times in a given month and also visits Website B ten times in the same month. At first glance this eventuality might seem to show ten visits and one unique visitor to Website A, and ten visits and one unique visitor to Website B, for a total of 20 visits and two unique visitors. But there was, in fact, only a single unique visitor. In other words, the data on unique visitors involve double counting and, therefore, unique visitor figures for a series of websites in a given period cannot be summed up. But we can still get a fix on the size of the audience across a set of sites based on unique visitors, by looking at the mean and median number of unique visitors for a site within a category of sites.

Looking at the audience for the various ideological categories shows that the category with both the highest mean and highest median of unique visitors is the Center Left, with a mean of about 2.6 million and a median of about 232,000 unique visitors. Based on unique visitors, after the Center Left comes the Left, with a mean of about 1.6 million unique visitors per month. In terms of median unique visitors, the Ambiguous Right was second, with about 121,000 unique visitors. The Least Biased category had a mean of about 1.4 million and a median of about 104,000 unique visitors. Also behind the Center Left is the Center Right, with a mean of about 1 million and a median of about 106,000 unique visitors.

Off the mainstream liberal democratic spectrum are the categories of the Illiberal Left and the Illiberal Right. Both varieties of illiberalism combined are a small, but not insignificant, part of the audience for all websites, with average monthly visits representing 3.1 percent of the total audience. But the category of Combined Illiberal Right (HC+SC) is vastly larger in every measure of audience size than the Illiberal Left. The Combined Illiberal Right (HC+SC) sites received about 195 million visits on monthly average, with a mean of about 58,000 unique visitors and a median of about 3,000. The Illiberal Left was far behind, with about 2.5 million visits on monthly average, and a mean and median of about 11,000 and 1,300 unique visitors, respectively. Further, the Illiberal Right makes up the great majority of the audience for all Illiberal sites. If the Illiberal audience is defined as that of the Illiberal Left plus the Hard-Core Illiberal Right, the Illiberal Left audience is only about 1.3 percent of the total Illiberal audience.

The Combined Illiberal Right (HC+SC) category also represents a far larger percentage of the audience for all right-wing sites than the Illiberal Left does of all left-wing sites. In monthly visits, all of the Combined Illiberal Right (HC+SC) sites represent about 15 percent of the audience for all right-of-center sites (that is, the sites of the Combined Illiberal Right (HC+SC), the Ambiguous Right, the Right, and the Center Right). In contrast, monthly visits to Illiberal Left sites represent less than one-tenth of one percent of the audience for all left-of-center sites (that is, the Illiberal Left, the Left, and the Center Left). Further, the Hard-Core Illiberal Right has an audience of about 30.8 percent the size of the mainstream Right audience, while the Illiberal Left audience is just 0.2 percent of the mainstream Left audience. In short, the Hard-Core Illiberal Right is an important part of the audience for right-of-center outlets, while the Illiberal Left is a vanishingly small part of the audience for left-of-center outlets.

As discussed above, the Illiberal Right was split into two subcategories, the Hard-Core Illiberal Right and the Soft-Core Illiberal Right. In both visits and unique visitors, the Hard-Core Illiberal Right is much larger than its Soft-Core counterpart. The Hard-Core Illiberal Right received, during the time period, about 186 million visits and had a mean of about 84,000 and a median of about 3,400 unique visitors. In contrast, the Soft-Core Illiberal Right received only about 9 million visits and had a mean of about 19,000, and a median of about 2,100 unique visitors. We separated out the Soft-Core sites from the Hard-Core sites in order not to inflate the size of the Illiberal Right by counting sites that, although they were mentioned by our illiberal sources, seemed upon review to contain little distinctly illiberal content. But we need hardly have bothered. The Hard-Core Illiberal Right received about 95.4 percent of all monthly visits to Illiberal Right sites, while the Soft-Core sites received only about 4.6 percent of monthly visits.

We can also analyze website audience engagement—that is, on average, how many times a unique visitor visits a given website in a month. The more often a unique visitor visits a given website during that period, the more engaged he or she is. The engagement rate for a given site during a given month can be calculated by dividing visits by unique visitors. To get a sense of how engaged unique visitors are with the sites of a given ideological category, we can look at the mean and median engagement rates for the sites in that category.

The category with the highest engagement rate was the Hard-Core Il-liberal Right, with a mean engagement rate of 3.07 visits by every unique visitor and a median of 1.95. The category with the next-highest engage-ment rate was the Combined Illiberal Right (HC+SC), with a mean en-gagement rate of 2.81 visits by every unique visitor and a median of about 1.93. The category with the third-highest mean engagement rate was the Right, with an average of 2.43 visits per unique visitor, and the Soft-Core Illiberal Right had the third-highest median engagement rate at 1.89 visits per unique visitor.

The audience for the sites on the left were mostly less engaged than the sites on the right. The Illiberal Left had the lowest mean engagement at 1.76 visits per unique visitor and the mainstream Left had the lowest median engagement with 1.56 visits per unique visitor.

Moreover, if we look at the top fifty sites in terms of engagement from the entire sample of 1,952, we find that the Hard-Core Illiberal Right dominates (table 3-2A).

In terms of mean engagement rates, nineteen of the top fifty sites are Hard-Core Right Illiberal and another five are Soft-Core Right Illiberal (table 3-2B). Thus, almost half of the fifty sites with the highest mean engagement rates are Right Illiberal. Ten of the fifty sites with the highest mean engagement rates are from the Right category. Thus, 68 percent of the sites with the top fifty engagement rates are right wing. Left, Center Left, and Least Biased categories have, respectively, seven, five, and four sites with a top-fifty mean engagement rate.

The story is much the same in terms of median engagement rates. Nineteen of the fifty sites with the highest median engagement rates were Hard-Core Right Illiberal. Five of the sites with the highest median engagement rates were Soft-Core Right Illiberal. So, again, in terms of median engagement rates nearly half of the top fifty sites were Right Il-liberal. Another nine of the sites with the highest median engagement rates were Right. Therefore, 66 percent of the fifty sites with the highest median engagement rates were right wing. The Left, Center Left, and Least Biased categories have, respectively, eight, four, and five sites with a top-fifty median engagement rate.

The extraordinarily high engagement rates of the Right Illiberal sites are one of the most striking findings of this analysis. Without demo-graphic data on the sample's audiences, it is not possible to explain this

Table 3-2A. Top 50 Domains by Mean Engagement Rate

Rank	Domain	Category	Mean Engagement Rate
1	voxday.blogspot.com	Right Illiberal Hard Core	21.54
2	drudgereport.com	Right Illiberal Hard Core	20.49
3	ace.mu.nu	Right Illiberal Soft Core	19.06
4	therightstuff.biz	Right Illiberal Hard Core	18.53
5	weaselzippers.us	Right	18.31
6	memeorandum.com	Least Biased	16.3
7	jsmineset.com	Right Illiberal Soft Core	14.52
8	whatfinger.com	Right	13.47
9	oneindia.com	Center Left	13.33
10	palmerreport.com	Left	12.32
11	theconservativetreehouse.com	Right Illiberal Hard Core	11.44
12	dailystormer.name	Right Illiberal Hard Core	10.92
13	electoral-vote.com	Left	10.88
14	zerohedge.com	Right Illiberal Hard Core	10.69
15	forum.thepurityspiral.com	Right Illiberal Hard Core	10.31
16	freerepublic.com	Right	10.04
17	citizenfreepress.com	Right	9.69
18	westhunt.wordpress.com	Right Illiberal Hard Core	9.64
19	breitbart.com	Right Illiberal Hard Core	9.32
20	whitedate.net	Right Illiberal Hard Core	9.27
21	twitchy.com	Right	9.13
22	market-ticker.org	Right Illiberal Hard Core	9.08
23	democraticunderground.com	Left	8.92
24	moonofalabama.org	Left	8.83
25	patriotnewsalerts.com	Right	8.78

Rank	Domain	Category	Mean Engagement Rate
26	xyz.net.au	Right Illiberal Hard Core	8.77
27	politicalwire.com	Least Biased	8.69
28	wonkette.com	Left	8.53
29	thezman.com	Right Illiberal Hard Core	8.45
30	newsnow.co.uk	Least Biased	8.38
31	thepurityspiral.com	Right Illiberal Hard Core	8.03
32	wdtprs.com	Right Illiberal Soft Core	7.88
33	intoday.in	Least Biased	7.62
34	conservativeinstitute.org	Right	7.56
35	nakedcapitalism.com	Center Left	7.49
36	newsandgutsmedia.com	Center Left	7.38
37	powerlineblog.com	Right	7.07
38	crooksandliars.com	Left	6.8
39	hotair.com	Right	6.68
40	rawstory.com	Left	6.57
41	lionoftheblogosphere.wordpress.com	Right Illiberal Hard Core	6.47
42	lewrockwell.com	Right Illiberal Hard Core	6.43
43	forum.nobodyhasthe.biz	Right Illiberal Hard Core	6.4
44	presstv.com	Center Left	6.39
45	msn.com	Center Left	6.35
46	heartiste.wordpress.com	Right Illiberal Hard Core	6.28
47	vivalamanosphere.com	Right Illiberal Soft Core	6.2
48	marginalrevolution.com	Right Illiberal Soft Core	6.17
49	thinkinghousewife.com	Right Illiberal Hard Core	5.95
50	pjmedia.com	Right	5.88

Table 3-2B. Top 50 Domains by Median Engagement Rate

Rank	Domain	Category	Median Engagement Rate
1	voxday.blogspot.com	Right Illiberal Hard Core	21.19
2	drudgereport.com	Right Illiberal Hard Core	21.16
3	weaselzippers.us	Right Illiberal Hard Core	19.64
4	ace.mu.nu	Right Illiberal Soft Core	18.64
5	therightstuff.biz	Right Illiberal Hard Core	18.53
6	memeorandum.com	Least Biased	16.37
7	whatfinger.com	Right	15.14
8	jsmineset.com	Right Illiberal Soft Core	13.89
9	oneindia.com	Right Illiberal Hard Core	12.82
10	theconservativetreehouse.com	Right Illiberal Hard Core	12.06
11	palmerreport.com	Left	11.89
12	dailystormer.name	Right Illiberal Hard Core	11.64
13	citizenfreepress.com	Right	11.54
14	xyz.net.au	Right Illiberal Hard Core	11.03
15	electoral-vote.com	Left	10.79
16	zerohedge.com	Right Illiberal Hard Core	10.62
17	moonofalabama.org	Left	10.18
18	twitchy.com	Right	9.93
19	freerepublic.com	Right	9.67
20	politicalwire.com	Least Biased	9.46
21	breitbart.com	Right Illiberal Hard Core	9.4
22	democraticunderground.com	Left	9.16
23	thezman.com	Right Illiberal Hard Core	8.75
24	market-ticker.org	Right Illiberal Hard Core	8.66
25	patriotnewsalerts.com	Right	8.31

Rank	Domain	Category	Median Engagement Rate
26	whitedate.net	Right Illiberal Hard Core	8.17
27	wonkette.com	Left	8.13
28	newsnow.co.uk	Least Biased	8.11
29	intoday.in	Least Biased	7.9
30	wdtprs.com	Right Illiberal Soft Core	7.75
31	nakedcapitalism.com	Center Left	7.69
32	conservativeinstitute.org	Right	7.64
33	powerlineblog.com	Right	7.42
34	vosizneias.com	Least Biased	7.29
35	altleft.com	Right Illiberal Hard Core	6.97
36	newsandgutsmedia.com	Center Left	6.91
37	westhunt.wordpress.com	Right Illiberal Hard Core	6.89
38	crooksandliars.com	Left	6.78
39	rawstory.com	Left	6.76
40	hotair.com	Right	6.76
41	pjmedia.com	Right	6.56
42	lionoftheblogosphere.wordpress.com	Right Illiberal Hard Core	6.44
43	lewrockwell.com	Right Illiberal Hard Core	6.43
44	presstv.com	Center Left	6.42
45	msn.com	Center Left	6.34
46	bloodandsoil.org	Right Illiberal Hard Core	6.29
47	barnhardt.biz	Right Illiberal Hard Core	6.05
48	americanindependent.com	Left	5.96
49	hawaiianlibertarian.blogspot.com	Right Illiberal Soft Core	5.92
50	marginalrevolution.com	Right Illiberal Soft Core	5.9

finding. One possibility is that right illiberalism attracts zealots or "true believers" in search of a cause to dedicate themselves to. Another is that rightist illiberals have lost or failed to gain employment due to globalization, capitalist creative destruction, or some other cause and therefore have time on their hands to spend on the web. These two possibilities are also not mutually exclusive. But without further data, this issue cannot be resolved.

But whatever the causes of the high engagement of the Hard-Core Illiberal Right audience, the political implications are clearer. Political scientists have long known that dedicated minorities can often win out against indifferent majorities. It may be that, in regard to political effectiveness, the relatively small size of the Hard-Core Illiberal Right audience is counterbalanced by its very high engagement. The data show that it is a mistake to dismiss the Hard-Core Illiberal Right as too miniscule to be of importance. In fact, the size of the audience for this movement is considerable. Moreover, focusing exclusively on the size of that audience misses an important part of the story. What the Hard-Core Illiberal Right lacks in size, it makes up for in engagement.

The structure of the categories on the right and left wings of the ideological spectrum is also telling. The rightward-most category is the Hard-Core Illiberal Right, followed by the Soft-Core Illiberal Right, the Ambiguous Right, the Right, and the Center Right. Occupying a position on the political spectrum between the Hard-Core Illiberal Right and the mainstream Right are the Soft-Core Illiberal Right and the Ambiguous Right, which may be thought of as the In-Between Right. The sites in the categories of the Hard-Core and Soft-Core Illiberal Right were all included in the blog rolls and link lists of the illiberal sources noted above. This means even though we decided to separate out the Soft-Core sites as being less radical than the Hard-Core sites, nonetheless the illiberal sources we consulted saw something of interest to them in the Soft-Core sites. Put another way, our illiberal sources saw some kind of affinity with the Soft-Core sites even though those sites were less radical than other sites those sources noted.

A similar story can be told about the Ambiguous Right sites. These were sixteen sites that appeared in the lists compiled by our illiberal sources but were categorized by MBFC as mainstream Right or Center Right. In other words, to the nonpartisan analysts at MBFC, these sites

were within the spectrum of ordinary American politics, but the editors at the illiberal sources saw something of interest in them too. Some
of these Ambiguous Right sites—such as the Manhattan Institute, the
Hudson Institute, and the American Enterprise Institute (AEI)—seemed
to us quite removed from right illiberalism. This was so even though these
think tanks sometimes take up illiberal themes such as nationalistic foreign policy options and criticism of feminism, and even though AEI is the
home base of Charles Murray, whose forays into eugenics are of interest to
illiberals. However, other Ambiguous Right sites are nearer to the gravi-
tational pull of illiberalism. These include the paleoconservative outlet
Chronicles, whose interim Editor in Chief, Paul Gottfried, has been described as one of the co-founders of the Alt-Right.[13] The American Conservative and American Greatness are both Ambiguous Right sites that
often feature illiberal themes. The American Conservative has published
articles condemning liberal democracy. An example is "The End of Liberal Democracy?," which asserts ". . . liberal democracy is fundamentally
irreconcilable with what it means to live a Good life. . . ."[14] American
Greatness features articles endorsing the friend-versus-enemy conception
of politics formulated by the Nazi theorist Carl Schmitt. Thus, one of
its authors asserts: "What Schmitt gets right is the irreducible nature of
the friend-enemy distinction in politics.[15] In other words, the Ambiguous Right sites represent outlets that straddle the illiberal and traditional
conservative worlds.

The point is that on the right end of the political spectrum, there exists
a bridge between the Hard-Core Illiberal Right and the ordinary Right
sites—a space where both the Illiberal Right and the ordinary Right see
ideas and issues that are of interest to them being discussed and debated.
This bridge is the In-Between Right sites. These sites are of interest to
illiberals but are seen by nonpartisan observers as still within the bounds
of the ordinary Right. The 161 In-Between Right sites have a monthly audience of 22.3 million visits, about 1.7 percent of the total right-of-center
audience (Hard-Core Right Illiberal, Soft-Core Right Illiberal, Ambiguous Right, Right, and Center Right), which is small but not insignificant.

The relationship of the Illiberal Left to the mainstream Left is very
different. Only four sites were mentioned both by our Illiberal Left
sources and classified as ordinary Left by MBFC, thus potentially quali-
fying as an Ambiguous Left. These sites were revcom.us, the outlet of the

Maoist Revolutionary Communist Party, USA (RCP); worldcantwait.net, another site of the RCP; workers.org, the platform of the Workers World Party, self-described as "a revolutionary Marxist-Leninist party";[16] and its goingdown.org, which says it is "a digital community center for anarchist, anti-fascist, autonomous anti-capitalist and anti-colonial movements."[17] In their professed dedication to Leninism, Maoism, and anarchism, these sites were all clearly Illiberal Left as defined here. With their total audience of 146,000 visits on monthly average, these apparent Ambiguous Left sites have only about a hundredth of a percent of the audience of the mainstream Left.[18] Moreover, the radically illiberal nature of these sites was so obvious that, for the purposes of calculations, we included them all in the Illiberal Left category. In our judgment and based on their self-descriptions, these sites did not represent any kind of bridge between the Illiberal Left and mainstream Left categories.

The Illiberal Left audience is much smaller than that of the Hard-Core Illiberal Right, about 1.3 percent the size of its right-wing counterpart in terms of visits. Also, the Illiberal Left audience is much less engaged than that of the Hard-Core Illiberal Right. The latter, as we saw, has the highest engagement rates of any ideological category, while the Illiberal Left has the lowest mean engagement rate, at 1.76 visits by each unique visitor, and a median engagement rate of 1.77 visits per unique visitor. Moreover, further analysis of the relationship between the fringes of the political spectrum and their neighbors within the limits of liberal democratic politics reveals another weakness of the Illiberal Left and a strength of the Hard-Core Illiberal Right. The Illiberal Left is utterly isolated from the traditional Left. The distinctive concerns of the Illiberal Left include various forms of Marxism, communism, and anarchism; proletarian revolution; international working-class solidarity; the disappearance of the state; antifascist activism; and similar old Left and new Left themes. The Illiberal Left sources we consulted very seldom link to ordinary Left sites and thus, in effect, acknowledge there are very few sites of the ordinary Left that take up their concerns or are of any interest to them. The Illiberal Left is a tiny island—hardly even a sandbar—completely cut off from the continent of the liberal democratic Left.

Some might object that the revival of interest in socialism on the Left indicates some Illiberal Left themes are making their way into the discourse of the liberal democratic Left. Certainly, socialism is a theme associated with and often discussed by the Illiberal Left. One might think that the Illiberal Left sources we consulted would be interested in the animated discussion of socialism on the ordinary Left and would therefore link to sites of that orientation. But it is not hard to see why this does not happen. The sites of the mainstream Left that discuss socialism of course have in mind democratic socialism. For example, *Dissent* is a magazine site categorized as Left by MBFC and not mentioned by the Illiberal Left sources. Michael Walzer, the magazine's co-editor, published an article in 2010 entitled "Which Socialism?" where he noted that "the socialism of the West today is so modest that it can't be called either revolutionary or reformist; it has become conventional." He defended "today's socialism— social democracy is probably the more accurate name," and distinguished democratic socialism from its illiberal forms:

> Anarchists and communists talk, or used to talk, of doing away with power and wealth—literally: so that no one would ever exercise power over anyone else and no one would be able, after the abolition of market exchange, to "make" more money than anyone else. Socialists and social-democrats, by contrast, believe in the uses of power, so long as it is democratically delegated and limited; and they have come to believe in the market's capacity to coordinate economic activity, so long as it is subject to democratic control.[19]

The brand of socialism advocated by the Illiberal Left has little to do with such democratic socialism. PopularResistance.org is recognized by the Illiberal Left sources but not noted at all by MBFC. The site's account of socialism differs strikingly from the one offered by the liberal democratic *Dissent*. An article by the Marxist economist Richard D. Wolff on PopularResistance.org, entitled "Socialists Need to Fight for Economic Change—Not Just another Version of Capitalism," distinguished the Illiberal Left's understanding of socialism from that of the mainstream Left:

> Two major—and clashing—interpretations have prevailed over others. Both interpretations use the same word, "socialism," but they give it very different meanings.
>
> In one camp are those who believe socialism would involve a fundamental change in the structure of our economy, to completely undo our

current system's division of people into categories of employee and employer. Those who support this interpretation point to Marx's explanation of capitalism. . . .

Others think very differently. . . . Realism, these thinkers often insisted, placed limits on what could be done. These socialists called their position "social democracy," or "democratic socialism," to indicate a progressive, state-regulated private capitalism . . . a gentler, kinder form of capitalism. . . .

This interpretation of socialism—the social democracy of the Nordics—has come to dominate the public debate about socialism. But this misses the bigger picture. It is a limited interpretation of socialism, better characterized as state capitalism, that fails to redraw the oppressive employer/employee relationship.[20]

Wolff's proposal for more democracy within places of employment, whatever one makes of it, is not, on its own, necessarily illiberal. But his position becomes more problematic when it turns out to dovetail with a denigration of electoral democracy, as when he writes, "Such elections are the cheapest and least dangerous way to secure the distance that capitalism keeps between itself and real democracy."[21] Thus the socialism of PopularResistance.org and that of *Dissent* are two different things.

There is a more blatantly illiberal account of socialism on the website In Defense of Marxism, which was noted by the Illiberal Left sources but not by MBFC. On this site, Ben Gliniecki published "What Will Socialism Look Like?" According to his account, socialism, once it is fully developed, will look a great deal like anarchy:

Under socialism . . . wages could gradually disappear as the economy develops. . . . Over time wages could be replaced by coupons, which in turn could be replaced by nothing at all, as people would be able to take anything they need. . . . [M]oney as a whole will wither away as these functions of measuring the health of an economy will be superseded by *administrative*, instead of financial control. . . . Just as money will eventually wither away under socialism, so too will the state.[22]

By these lights, under full socialism there would be no profits, no wages, no money, and no state, yet somehow there would be a planned economy. Let us put aside the question of how there can be planning when there is no state to make and implement decisions and no money economy to generate information and incentives. The point here is that any definition of socialism along these lines qualifies as illiberal because it amounts to anarchy and thus violates the liberal democratic principle that government is necessary to secure the rights of the people.

In short, though both the Illiberal Left and the liberal democratic Left these days are much focused on socialism, there is no real overlap of interest between them. The ordinary Left is speaking of democratic socialism on the Scandinavian model, of universal health insurance, more subsidies for higher education, more redistributive fiscal policies, and similar extensions of the welfare state. This democratic socialism is a few steps further to the left than mainstream American politics ventured to go in the twentieth century, but it is well within the bounds of the liberal democratic spectrum. The socialism of the Illiberal Left is frankly Marxist and unsympathetic with the electoral democracy at the heart of modern liberal democracies.

It is, then, no wonder that the Illiberal Left sources we consulted seldom included traditional Left outlets in their blog rolls and link lists. *Dissent* is not mentioned there, nor is *The Nation*, nor even is *Jacobin*, which is often strongly critical of liberal democracy but finally acknowledges its importance. The point is that even apparent overlaps of concern between the Illiberal Left and the liberal democratic Left are, in fact, no such thing. The Illiberal Left is isolated from the mainstream of American political discourse while the Hard-Core Illiberal Right is a sort of peninsula, connected to the mainland by the bridge of the In-Between Right.

If the penetration of illiberalism into American political culture is a matter of concern, the problem is to be found exclusively on our right flank. The Illiberal Left is minute, entirely isolated, and unengaged. The Illiberal Right is sizeable, closely connected with mainstream political tendencies, and dramatically more engaged with political discourse than any other ideological tendency.

But is the penetration of illiberalism into the mainstream really a matter of concern? To answer this question, we must look at the content of the various sorts of Illiberal Right sites and see if they really do reject the principles of liberal democracy. If the Illiberal Right is merely a variation on conventional conservativism, it does not represent a challenge to the

American liberal democratic order. But if the Illiberal Right really does reject liberal democracy, it represents a radical challenge to American democracy that requires a response.

The Political Principles of the Illiberal Right

Sorting out Hard-Core Illiberal Right sites into more specific political orientations is difficult. There is a blizzard of terms that might be applied to such sites: Hate, Alt-Right, Alt-Lite, Manosphere, Dark Enlightenment, New Right, Anti-Immigrant, White Supremacist, Conspiracy/Pseudoscience, Questionable, and many more. The definitions of these terms vary and the sources mentioned above are sometimes at odds in their classification of a particular site. We attempted to do a cluster analysis on the Hard-Core Right Illiberal sites, but due to a lack of demographic data, the results were unilluminating.

In the end, we broke the Hard-Core Illiberal Right sites into subcategories using the same resources and methodology we used to break the Illiberal Right sites into Hard-Core and Soft-Core varieties (table 3-3). We worked with the vocabulary used by our sources and the websites themselves, and did not try to invent new categories or terminology. We also did not try to assign every Hard-Core site to mutually exclusive ideological categories. If a Hard-Core site's ideology was hard to further categorize, we did not attempt to do so and simply identified that site as unclassified.

It important to note that the main purpose in dividing the Hard-Core Illiberal Right sites into subcategories was to facilitate reviewing the sites' political content. When sites can be organized into groups, it is easier to describe their content than to describe each individual site as if it were *sui generis*. Undoubtedly other observers of these ideological tendencies will reasonably disagree with at least some of the choices made here. But this analysis attaches no great importance to whether a particular site belongs to one subcategory or another, so long as the reader gets a fair sense of the ideas espoused by the Hard-Core Illiberal Right.

It is also important to understand that although all the sites discussed below are classified as Hard-Core Illiberal Right, there is considerable variation among them in their degree of radicalism. The notorious Daily Stormer is about as radically illiberal, coarse, and hateful as a political outlet can be. But many of the sites in the Hard-Core category are not always so vicious. A few, like VDARE.com, are forum sites with some contributors who occasionally come almost within hailing distance of the mainstream Right. Breitbart specializes in inflammatory rhetoric, race baiting, crude ethnic humor, and similar provocations, but it is usually careful not to explicitly deny basic liberal democratic propositions such as "all people are created equal." Some outlets contain a great deal of conventional conservative boilerplate but also attack the idea of democracy or espouse illiberal principles such as the friend-versus-enemy vision of politics. And there are sites that primarily offend against liberal democracy with intolerant rhetoric and dissemination of false and misleading information that undermines the democratic ethics of controversy. In short, not every site and every author always violate every principle of liberal democracy at every turn and as flagrantly as possible. What follows is a nuanced review of the content of the sites classified here as Hard-Core Illiberal Right. Readers will have to judge for themselves if we are correct in our evaluation that on balance this material represents a serious break with and threat to the principles of liberal democracy.

Hate Sites

Identifying Hate sites is relatively easy, both because there is a large literature on them and because they typically are quite clear about what they are. The sites categorized as Hate are blatantly illiberal, to say the least. The very names of some of them shout out their orientation: kkk .com, third-reich-books.com, national-socialist-worldview.blogspot.com, radioaryan.com, and even nwordrmania.com (the actual URL uses the full racial expletive). Other sites are only slightly more subtle by incorporating Nazi code elements into their web addresses, including wau14.com, nsm88.org, and davidlane1488.com. The number 14 is a reference to the following fourteen words: "We must secure the existence of our people and a future for White Children." This phrase was coined by David Lane, founder of The Order, a white nationalist terror organization.[23] And according to the ADL, the number 88 "is a white supremacist numerical code for 'Heil Hitler.' H is the eighth letter of the alphabet, so 88 = HH = Heil Hitler."[24]

Obviously, sites that flaunt Nazi and Klan nomenclature have broken

Table 3-3. Monthly Traffic to Categories of Hard-Core Illiberal Right Websites, January 2019–November 2019

Ideology	Number of Sites	Mean Monthly Visits	Mean Unique Visitors	Median Unique Visitors	Mean Engagement Rates	Median Engagement Rates
Alt-Catholic/Religious	13	219,722	4,359	1,994	2.81	2.46
Alt-Lite	9	51,723,492	642,823	45,159	3.14	2.40
Alt-Right	32	4,052,939	19,173	5,158	4.18	2.32
Alt-South	6	104,028	7,824	4,851	2.37	1.94
Conspiracy/Questionable	20	125,767,765	504,762	107,643	4.92	3.56
Dark Enlightenment	17	116,651	3,318	1,740	2.15	1.78
Hate	66	1,186,576	7,140	1,667	2.45	1.87
Manosphere	7	972,130	61,138	40,578	2.62	1.63
Right Illiberal HC Uncategorized	45	1,579,331	11,123	3,325	2.93	1.92
Sum	215	185,772,634				

with liberal democracy. Sometimes these outlets try to soft-pedal their historical affinity for racism, anti-Semitism, and violence. For example, the "25 Point Plan" of the National Socialist Movement (www.nsm88.org) at points reads as if it is reaching out to New Age millennials, as when it says, "Healthcare is a human right, not a business opportunity," "All current student loan debt shall be forgiven," and "Mistreatment of animals, either by private or corporate forces, shall be banned."[25] But elsewhere the illiberal nature of the plan and its movement are clear:

> Only members of the National Community may be citizens of the State. Citizenship in the Homeland must therefore be limited to White persons who share our values, and White persons alone. . . .
>
> Key industries should be in the hands of the nation. . . . This process of nationalization will remove the Jewish, internationalist, and capitalist stranglehold on information and resources and put these to work for the benefit of the nation and people, not international stockholders or Jewish oligarchs. . . .
>
> The National Socialist Movement, as the banner carrier and embodiment of the State and our People's Revolution, shall be the sole political party of the nation. . . . The liberal modern "multi-party" state, where the people are split in half and pitted against itself in destructive electoral circuses, will be retired.[26]

The Hate sites with the largest audiences, both in average monthly visits and unique visitors, are stormfront.org (about 281,000 visits and 113,000 unique visitors on monthly average), renegadetribune.com (about 90,000 visits and 44,000 unique visitors on monthly average), and national vanguard.org (about 68,000 visits and 26,000 unique visitors on monthly average). These sites also show high engagement rates, with Stormfront having 2.48 visits per unique visitor on monthly average, and renegade tribune.com and nationalvanguard.org having 2.03 and 2.65 visits per unique visitor on monthly average, respectively.

Stormfront's illiberal credentials are unquestionable. The site was created in 1990 by Don Black, a former Alabama Klan boss, as an online bulletin board for David Duke's Senate campaign and went public in 1994.[27] An Italian journalist reports the following exchange with Black:

So I ask him if Stormfront is nothing but the new Ku Klux Klan, the Klan of the 21st century without hoods and Aryan symbols. "Yes, it is so," he replies instinctively. . . . "I would never tell an American journalist, but you know it's true." . . . "The Klan has great merits, it has restored order in the South after the Civil War, today we try to rewrite history but it was a truly positive force."[28]

A post entitled "Intro Material for People New to Stormfront" presents the essence of the site's ideology, which is one of inegalitarianism, racism, and anti-Semitism:

In a nutshell, the problem with humanity is not so much one of ideology—this or that religious, political, social, or economic doctrine—but rather one of blood. . . . If the genetics of a people are "bad" it's pretty much hopeless regardless of the political/economic system (e.g., Africa). . . . If Blacks or Mexicans become a majority, then they will not be able to maintain the White man's social, cultural and economic systems because they do not have to [sic] minds needed to do so. . . . We want a few areas on the Earth (and states in the US) that are reserved for Whites, and Whites only. . . . The origin of the problem with the Jews is, once again, in the blood. As a group, a *race*, they suffer from psychopathy—a mental disorder whose main symptom is the ability to lie like there is no tomorrow.[29]

Renegade Tribune is edited by Kyle Hunt, best known for prompting the sparsely attended "White Man March" scheduled for the weekend of Saint Patrick's Day in 2014. The site features an eleven-part series entitled "National Socialism—the Fundamentals," which describes itself as a "series of blog posts that break down the core fundamental teachings of National Socialism":

These "fundamentals" come, for the most part, directly from Hitler's book, "Mein Kampf," which was written in 1925, and other sources. . . . The ongoing & constant vilification & demonization of Adolf Hitler in the Jewish-controlled media is utilized to prevent & discourage the disclosure of Hitler's *(German)* Economic & Social miracle, which, during his reign, kicked out the parasitic influence of International Jewry. . . . No matter if mistakes were made . . . Long live National Socialism![30]

About nationalvanguard.org and the rest of the Hate outlets, little needs to be said. All are openly neo-Nazi, Klan-related, anti-Semitic, racist, or otherwise oriented toward traditional anti-democratic, right-wing extremism.

Overall the sixty-six sites in the Hate category received about 1.2 million visits on monthly average, with a mean of about 7,100 and a median of about 1,700 unique visitors, and had a high engagement rate, with a mean of 2.45 visits per unique visitor and a median of 1.87. This is an audience much smaller than some mainstream sites but larger than or on a par with others. Thus *National Review*, the flagship publication of traditional conservatism, has an audience far larger and nearly as engaged as that of the Hate sites, with nearly 8.9 million visits, 3.9 million unique visitors on monthly average, and a mean engagement rate of 2.30. On the other hand, the Hate audience by most measures easily beats out that of such established conservative sites as *Commentary* (315,000 visits, 224,000 unique visitors, 1.41 mean engagement rate) and *American Spectator* (828,000 visits, 281,000 unique visitors, 2.95 mean engagement rate). Hate sites also draw more of an audience than progressive standards, including *Dissent* (145,000 visits, 83,000 unique visitors, 1.75 mean engagement rate) and *American Prospect* (388,000 visits, 301,000 unique visitors, 1.29 mean engagement rate).

As for the ideology purveyed by Hate sites, the "Intro Material" on Stormfront expresses the orientation for all of them: What people think—ideas—is insignificant. What people are—in terms of race—is decisive. The races are unequal, not merely in certain traits, but in their inherent worth and value as citizens. Note the claim is not that Jews, on average, are merely different from other groups. The claim is that Jews are morally worse—liars, psychopaths, mentally disordered—than other groups. And this moral inferiority is congenital, "in the blood." Peoples with "bad" genetics make for a "hopeless . . . political/economic system" and must therefore be exiled from states "reserved for Whites, and Whites only."

Of course, all this qualifies as illiberal due to, among other things, its florid expression of political inegalitarianism. As we will see, this line of argument is embraced not only by Hate sites, but also by many illiberal sites of other varieties. While they often prudently eliminate the coarse racist and anti-Semitic rhetoric, these sites nonetheless accept the argument that starts with the denigration of ideas, posits race consciousness as the essence of politics, then slips in one form or another of racism, and ends up with political inegalitarianism and full-blown illiberalism.

Alt-Right

Alt-Right sites are another particularly radical sort of Hard-Core Illiberal Right outlets. Through interviews with declared Alt-Right editors and thought leaders, site self-identification, lists compiled by Alt-Right sites, and consultations with academic experts, Main identified the following ten Alt-Right sites: affirmativeright.blogspot.com, altright.com, amren.com, counter-currents.com, dailystormer.name, occidentaldissent .com, theoccidentalobserverl.net, radixjournal.com, VDARE.com, and therightstuff.biz.[31] Together these sites had, from January to November 2019, a monthly average of about 3 million visits; a mean and a median, respectively, of about 42,000 and 28,000 unique visitors; and, in monthly engagement rates, a mean of 5.3 visits per unique visitor and a median of 5.5, both of which are very high. This is down from the period analyzed earlier, from September 2016 to February 2018, when these Alt-Right sites had a monthly average of about 4.4 million visits.[32]

However, this decline is somewhat misleading. At least two of the Alt-Right sites identified earlier—Radix Journal and ALTRIGHT.com—which were founded and edited by Richard Spencer, were mostly inactive for much of 2019. New personalities have since started their own sites, such as nicholasjfuentes.com. Further, in his earlier studies of the Alt-Right, Main defined sites of that orientation narrowly and for the most part followed the judgments of proclaimed adherents of the movement.[33] Now that we have greater familiarity with the Alt-Right, and given that there is a more substantial literature on the subject, we are more confident about designating other sites as outlets of that ideology.

Based on the original ten Alt-Right outlets and the movement's history, the Alt-Right status of other sites was an easy inference. For example, following a presentation to the H.L. Mencken Club, Paul Gottfried and his editor, Richard Spencer, coined the term Alternative Right, so hl menckenclub.org can safely be put in that category. Kevin MacDonald's pseudo-Darwinian anti-Semitism and racialism is widely acknowledged as foundational to Alt-Right ideology. Thus, kevinmacdonald.net counts as Alt-Right, as do the online journals he edits, Occidental Observer (theoccidentalobserverl.net) and Occidental Quarterly (toqonline.com). Washington Summit Publishers, an outlet for Alt-Right books, was established by Spencer, once the most prominent Alt-Right spokesman, so washsummit.com can be added to the Alt-Right category. RationalWiki has a long entry on the Alt-Right and identifies many sites in that movement.[34] Using this and other databases, site self-identification, and other resources, we ended up with thirty-two sites in the Alt-Right category. During the relevant time period, these sites received about 4.1 million visits; had a mean of about 19,000 unique visitors per month and a median of about 5,200; and in terms of monthly engagement rate, had a high mean of 4.18 visits per unique visitor and a median of 2.32.

One of us, Main, has already discussed Alt-Right ideology in his book on that movement. There, Main demonstrated that the essence of Alt-Rightism is the insistence that all people are not created equal, meaning not merely that people are unequal in many different traits and abilities, but also that people are not equal politically, in the rights they hold and should hold, and before the law. And indeed, when we look at recent postings on the sites newly added to the Alt-Right category, we find the open political inegalitarianism characteristic of the movement.

Vox Day is the pseudonym of Theodore Beale, a science fiction writer and game designer who was involved in the Gamergate controversy, a formative episode of the Alt-Right that will be discussed in chapter 4. He now edits the site Vox Popoli, which RationalWiki categorizes as Alt-Right.[35] True to form, Day's site dispenses the political inegalitarianism characteristic of the Alt-Right. Here is an example:

> As I have repeatedly observed, there is no such thing as equality, the grand rhetorical flights of Thomas Jefferson notwithstanding. The artificial distinctions that conservatives attempt to make between equality of opportunity and equality of result, and between equality before the law and equality of condition *simply do not exist*. Literally every day we see material evidence to the contrary.[36]

Day then sites a news article that reports on a NYPD officer who was found guilty of sexual harassment but did not receive due punishment since his father was a high department official. Day therefore concludes the following:

This is not at all surprising, of course. Just as one does not expect off-duty police to receive speeding tickets or DUI citations, one does not expect the influential or their family members to be treated just like anyone else in the courts of law. But as petty as it is, this episode serves to effectively demonstrate that the conservative concept of equality is just as fantastic, just as utopian, just as nonexistent and just as ludicrous a basis for societal policy, as the leftist concept of equality.

God does not believe in equality. Nature does not believe in equality. Neither should Man believe in it, much less attempt to order his societies around it, *because it does not exist.*

The reason that Jefferson found it necessary to claim it was self-evident that all men are created equal is because he could not find a single observable example of that imaginary equality to cite, not in religion, philosophy, history, nature, or law. The assertation is not a self-evident truth, it is nothing more than a logical and empirical falsehood, and easily proven to be so by every possible standard.[37]

This explicit rejection of Jeffersonian egalitarianism is quintessential illiberalism, Alt-Right style, as is its shoddiness of thought. Jeffersonian egalitarianism is a moral and political demand that all people should be equal politically and before the law. That every day we see people are unequal in various traits in no way speaks against this claim. Nor are the examples Day cites of people being treated unequally and unfairly relevant. Day's counterexamples show that political equality is not always enforced, not that it is nonexistent.

In terms of visits, Vox Popoli is the second-largest Alt-Right site, with about 694,000 visits and about 32,000 unique visitors on monthly average, and a whopping average monthly engagement rate of 21.5 visits per unique visitor. The Alt-Right site with the largest audience is the Daily Stormer, with about 1.3 million visits and about 122,000 unique visitors on monthly average, and an extremely high monthly average engagement rate of 10.9 visits per unique visitor.

The Daily Stormer is the most notorious site of the Hard-Core Illiberal Right, and there is a large literature on this site.[38] No detailed analysis of dailystormer.name is necessary to establish its extremely radical illiberalism, for, as lawyers say, the thing speaks for itself. In 2017 the *Huffington Post* obtained the Daily Stormer's style guide.[39] Here are a few excerpts:

Morals and Dogma

It should be understood first and foremost that the Daily Stormer is not a "movement site." It is an outreach site, designed to spread the message of nationalism and anti-Semitism to the masses. . . . The basic propaganda doctrine of the site is based on Hitler's doctrine of war propaganda outlined in Mein Kampf, Volume I, Chapter VI.

Prime Directive: Always Blame the Jews for Everything

Dehumanization

There should be a conscious agenda to dehumanize the enemy, to the point where people are ready to laugh at their deaths. So it isn't clear that we are doing this—as that would be a turnoff to most normal people—we rely on lulz. . . . Dehumanization is extremely important, but it must be done within the confines of lulz.[40]

Interestingly, unlike many neo-Nazi and white supremacist sites that are suspicious of any and all politicians, dailystormer.name supports Donald Trump. The site's founder and editor, Andrew Anglin, has written, "Trump just keeps hitting all of our issues. Left and right. Is there anyone who could argue at this point he isn't a reader of the Daily Stormer?"[41] and "Heil Donald Trump—*The Ultimate Savior.*"[42]

Despite its gross anti-Semitism and racism, the Daily Stormer in some cases beats out, and in others nearly matches, well-established platforms within the mainstream American political spectrum. Anglin's unfortunate outlet easily surpasses The Forward, a Center Left Jewish media outlet with an audience, on monthly average, of about 954,000 visits, 692,000 unique visitors, and a mean engagement rate of 1.38 visits per unique visitor. Other mainstream outlets have audiences somewhat larger in size than the Daily Stormer but cannot touch it in terms of audience engagement. The flagship think tank of the conventional Right is the Heritage Foundation, whose website pulls in about 1.5 million visits and about 858,000 unique visitors on monthly average. On the Left is the iconic *New Republic*, with about 1.6 million visits and 1.1 million unique visitors on monthly average. Somewhat further to the left is Democracy Now!, with about 1.5 million visits and 678,000 unique visitors on monthly average. These mainstream outlets, with their respective engagement rates of 1.76,

1.48, and 2.26 visits per unique visitor on monthly average, are left in the dust by the Daily Stormer, with its engagement rate of 10.9 visits per unique visitor on monthly average.

Manosphere

Based on self-reporting and the literature, seven sites fall within what is called the Manosphere, that is, extremist anti-feminist sites. These seven sites of the Manosphere receive, on monthly average, about 972,000 visits. In terms of unique visitors, their mean is about 61,000 and the median is about 41,000. Their mean engagement rate is about 2.62 visits per unique visitor and their median is about 1.63.

If one accepts the popular formulation that "feminism is the radical idea that women are human beings," then feminism is a corollary of liberal democratic political egalitarianism. But if feminism is thought of as a collection of progressive political positions—such as pro-choice, comparable worth, the Equal Rights Amendment, and so on—then anti-feminism, whatever one thinks of it, is perhaps not necessarily illiberal. But the Manosphere sites jump right from their usually unconvincing critiques of feminist politics to a flat rejection of liberal democracy. Their argument is similar to that of the Alt-Right's racialism: as women have achieved political equality and moved into positions of power, American liberal democracy has been degraded and no longer merits the loyalty of the "masculine men" for whom Return of Kings—the second largest of the Manosphere sites—claims it is published. That site had a monthly average of about 271,000 visits and 200,000 unique visitors with an average monthly engagement rate of 1.36 visits per unique visitor. A site article entitled "6 Ways Liberal Democracy Destroys the Goodness of Humanity" argues as follows:

> Growing up in the west, especially in America, one is taught that you live in the most glorious time ever. . . . And while many of these truths may have proven true in the past, the excesses of modern liberal democracy have created weak men, shrill, out of shape, and damaged women, a decrepit culture, and declining values. America indeed has the *potential* to be great, but the western culture today destroys everything it touches. . . . This isn't to say that America is a bad place, or that it is intrinsically evil; if anything, it has the potential to become one of the greatest, wealthiest,

happiest, successful civilizations on the planet. But the current system of liberal democracy destroys all potential for this success.[43]

The evidence this article presents for America's intolerable cultural degeneration under liberal democracy is risibly weak: square dancing has been replaced by twerking, and sorority sisters no longer wear high heels. But even if it were proven that American society is in dramatic decline, how would that prove liberal democracy ought to be abandoned? Nowhere on Return of Kings or anywhere else in the Manosphere is there evidence that jumping from the alleged frying pan of liberal democracy into the fire of illiberalism would be an improvement.

Other Manosphere sites are even more radically misogynistic than returnofkings.com. Consider rooshv.com, with a monthly average of about 139,000 visits, 85,000 unique visits, and an average monthly engagement rate of 1.63 visits per unique visitor. There we find the following from an article entitled "How to Save Western Civilization":

It should be clear to you that women will always use their votes to destroy themselves and their nations, to invite invaders with open legs, to persecute their own men, and to ravage their economies with socialism. Because they don't operate on logic like men do, you will always have this destructive element within the political ranks of your nation as long as women have the right to vote. Giving them this right was a terrible mistake. I can now claim to have one political dream, and that is to repeal women's suffrage.[44]

One might think that depriving women of the vote, besides its blatant inegalitarianism, is about as atavistic a sentiment as could possibly be imagined. But mattforney.com, another Manosphere site, goes further still:

It's time to stop beating around the bush: *feminists want to be raped.* . . . Everything feminists do, from holding up "Refugees Welcome" signs at airports to passing affirmative consent laws, is geared around encouraging men to assault them. . . . Every feminist, deep down, wants nothing more than a rapist's baby in her belly. While more moderate women can be saved, no one will ever be able to convince the termagants of the left that they should be more afraid of Muslim rapists than white "racists."

There can be no compromise, no peace with these traitors inside the walls. They are our enemies, just as much as the dusky hordes planting their flags on our soil.[45]

But the most radically illiberal of the Manosphere sites was Chateau Heartiste, apparently named after the main setting in which the protagonist of the sadomasochistic novel *Story of O* underwent her abuse. The site had the largest audience of Manosphere sites, with about 298,000 visits and 47,000 unique visits on monthly average, and a high average monthly engagement rate of about 6.28 visits per unique visitor. Chateau Heartiste was operated by James C. Weidmann and dealt with "pick-up artistry" and "Alt-right politics, with an emphasis on racialism" in about equal measure.[46] The site was shut down by WordPress in May 2019 for unspecified violations of its terms of service. But Chateau Heartiste remains of interest because it had a large audience during the time period studied here, has its content preserved and still available at heartiste.org, and provides insight into the nature of contemporary illiberal misogyny.

The ideological offerings at Chateau Heartiste rejected political equality and demonized opponents as traitors. The site repudiated equality in a post entitled "Witnessing the Death of a Religion":

> The religion that is dying is Equalism, the doctrinal tenets of which are:
> - the races are biologically equal
> - the sexes are biologically equal
> - any inequality between the races and sexes is proof of heresy, cultural corruption, discrimination, and White male animus, but certainly not of innate, evolved biological differences.
>
> Modren [sic] White liberals (aka SWPLs aka shitlibs aka leftoids) are fervent disciples and proselytizers of Equalism. Their xenophilic devotion to the Word of ZOG is total.[47]

This quote requires some clarification: "SWPL" stands for "stuff white people like" and is used in this context to mean "white educated liberal bohemian";[48] "ZOG" is an anti-Semitic term that stands for "Zionist occupation government" and is used by illiberals of all stripes to refer to the American federal government, which has supposedly been taken over by Jews. There was a great deal of anti-Semitism on Chateau Heartiste, but the site was coy about that bigotry, and mostly preferred using the terms "special people" or "specials" when it defamed Jews.[49]

To avoid the appearance of flatly denying the political equality of all people, Chateau Heartiste used the neologism "equalism" to provide some protective coloration. But it turns out that "equalism," which is intemperately blasted again and again on Chateau Heartiste, simply means the American political proposition that "all men are created equal," which according to the website "is a *shameless* lie."[50]

In audience size and engagement, the Manosphere sites beat out many feminist sites, including msmagazine.com (about 64,000 visits, 47,000 unique visitors, and a 1.36 mean engagement rate), bust.com (about 104,000 visits, 85,000 unique visitors, and 1.22 mean engagement rate), and bitchmedia.org (about 209,000 visits, 150,000 unique visitors, and 1.39 mean engagement rate). In other words, despite their vulgarity and extreme illiberalism, the largest Manosphere sites have a bigger footprint on the web than do many sites with a conventional feminist orientation.

The Small Categories

The categories with the smallest audiences are Alt-South, Dark Enlightenment, and Alt-Catholic/Religious, with about 104,000, 117,000, and 220,000 visits on monthly average, respectively. The Alt-South sites are of interest primarily for their unique mixture of political inegalitarianism and secessionism. The largest of these sites is Abbeville Institute, named after the birthplace of the defender of slavery, nullificationist, and critic of Jeffersonian equality, John C. Calhoun. A post entitled "The Egalitarian Myth and Secession" follows Calhoun in rejecting the idea that all people are created equal. We are told that people who cite that iconic phrase of the Declaration "fatally misunderstand its meaning."[51] The founders supposedly knew better:

> Our Founders and Framers loathed egalitarianism. They knew—and foresaw—the ravages and destruction it would cause if ever imposed or enacted into laws of the republic. Equality does not exist in nature, does not exist under Natural Law, and attempts to legislate it are bound not only to fail, but cause tremendous and perhaps fatal consequences to the society where it is imposed.[52]

But the only people who misunderstand the Declaration's foundational phrase are illiberals of the Alt-South and other varieties. The rest of the

world knows that the equality referred to is political equality, not equality of talents and traits, nor equality of outcomes and possessions. What,
then, is the point of railing against an "egalitarian myth" that is irrelevant
to the Declaration's principles? The answer is that the writers at Abbeville
Institute and the rest of the Alt-South are following in the tradition of
their forefather John Calhoun and attacking the core liberal democratic
principle of political equality. The founders and framers most certainly
were egalitarians of that sort, otherwise they would not have signed and
revered the Declaration.

Of course, illiberals of all stripes reject political equality. What is distinctive about the Alt-South is its support for secession. The Confederacy's
case for secession was bogus for many reasons, not the least of which was
the whole purpose of exercising that alleged right was to deprive others of
their rights by maintaining slavery. Today the case for unilateral secession
is just as weak.[53] Under international law, the right to self-determination
applies to internal affairs and assumes the territorial wholeness of existing
states. Territories under foreign occupation and oppressed minorities can
have a right to secede. But regions of a larger state that make free political
choices, participate in and influence national policies, and pursue their
own social and cultural development, and where longstanding majorities do not express an unambiguous desire for separation, cannot invoke
a right to secede. Under such circumstances, Lincoln was entirely right
to say, "Plainly, the central idea of secession, is the essence of anarchy.
. . . Unanimity is impossible; the rule of a minority, as a permanent arrangement, is wholly inadmissible; so that, rejecting the majority principle, anarchy or despotism in some form is all that is left."[54] Put another
way, if the losers of an election secede, and secession continues after every
following election, the polity will eventually split into first a crazy quilt
of tiny polities and then eventually into an infinity of microscopic entities
or even individuals with nothing at all binding them together. Democracy
assumes that at some point the territorial integrity of the polity will be
taken as a given and the losers in the democratic process will opt for being
a loyal opposition rather than secessionists. In supporting secession of the
South today, the Alt-South is embracing anarchy, that is to say, a species
of illiberalism.

Another ideology disseminated by a few Hard-Core Illiberal Right
sites is Dark Enlightenment or Neoreaction, which RationalWiki defines

as follows: "The neoreactionary movement (a.k.a. neoreaction, NRx, the Dark Enlightenment) is a loosely-defined cluster of Internet-based political thinkers who wish to return society to forms of government older than liberal democracy. They generally present their views as a revival of the traditions of Western civilization, or a return to a natural order of things."[55] The movement is small, with none of its sites achieving a monthly audience of six digits in terms of visits. Yet the Dark Enlightenment is of some interest because it positions itself "Furthest Right" according to its largest site, amerika.org. That outlet certainly lives up to the challenge of being as reactionary as is humanly possible:

> The new form of society that we will adopt will place more focus on rewarding people and emphasizing a natural and divine order in the patterns of life and roles we all take. Its goal will be to produce more people of genius, instead of trying to find genius in the giant committee that is an electorate. . . . During this transition, we are likely to see a great deal of fear and doubt because most people do not want radical change and are afraid to admit that we have wasted many years and lives on liberal democracy, which was already known to be a failure 2,400 years ago.[56]

Some observers quip that conservatives can be classified by how far back in the past they would return to. Neoconservatives look back to the 1950s, libertarians to the 1890s, and some paleoconservatives, to the Middle Ages. But these exercises in political nostalgia are small change compared to the Dark Enlightenment, for whom everything has been downhill since the dawn of democracy in ancient Athens. Such extreme reaction does not deserve much comment except, perhaps, to point out that the democracy of the ancient world was not liberal democracy. Ancient democracy knew nothing of the political egalitarianism, human rights, rule of law, and republicanism that are all characteristic of modern liberal democracy, which hardly appeared on the scene until the founding of the United States. As the American founders famously argued, "The science of politics, however, like most other sciences, has received great improvement"[57] in the modern era, and so the defects of ancient democracy cannot be charged against modern liberal democracy.

The sites of the Alt-Catholic/Religious category also have relatively small visitorship but are of some interest for their practice of basing illiberal politics on theological arguments. The largest of these sites, barn hardt.biz, is edited by Ann Barnhardt, a hyperorthodox Catholic, and has the slogan, "Judge me, O God, and distinguish my cause from the nation that is not holy." The nation that is not holy is what Barnhardt refers to as "the former United States of America. FORMER."[58] Barnhardt's illiberalism often expresses itself in the form of an aversion to electoral democracy, as the following reflects:

> Democracy or representative democracy beyond the local level simply does not work. Stupid people should have say over their own lives and households, but stupid people should NOT have a say or vote over any system that affects other people. . . . Today, the world is literally being run by people who are mentally and functionally retarded, with many of them being sociopaths, psychopaths or at the very least malignant narcissists. The current political order will never, ever, ever fix any of this. Anyone who promulgates hope in "elections" is bearing false witness, no matter what their motivation.[59]

Alt-Lite

Alt-Lite sites are so named because they offer a watered-down version of Alt-Right ideology, one that usually avoids explicit denial of liberal democratic principles but indulges in all the rhetorical excesses, bad reporting, and political fetishes of the genuine article. Breitbart has by far the largest audience of the sites in the Alt-Lite category, with about 50.9 million visits and 5.5 million unique visitors on monthly average, and a very high engagement rate of about 9.32 visits per unique visitor on monthly average.

Main has already discussed Breitbart in his previous book, and that analysis remains valid today. Breitbart continues to engage in its stock-in-trade of xenophobia, race-baiting, and derision of immigrants, women, gays, and ethnic minorities. And its reliance on outlandishly nasty rhetoric continues in stories such as these:

> "Liberalism Is a Mental Disorder Which Feeds Islamic Terror" ("a deadly and largely incurable condition")[60]

"The Plotters and Their Plan to Destroy America" (" 'The Four Horse-women of the Democrat Apocalypse'—made up of Alexandria Ocasio-Cortez, Ilhan Omar, Rashida Tlaib, and Ayanna Pressley")[61]

"Tony Blair Is a Traitor. Where's Capital Punishment When You Need It?" ("In better times, Tony Blair would have been imprisoned in the Tower and then shot at dawn . . . been hung, drawn and quartered—his entrails burned in front of him—before his head was put on a spike at the entrance to the city of London *pour encourager les autres*.")[62]

All this is very much in the illiberal style and ostentatiously violates the liberal ethics of controversy requiring that one's adversaries be treated with respect, not demonized, and that common ground with them be sought.

Breitbart.com also frequently traffics in fake news, that is, news reporting that is based on unreliable sources and that is inaccurate or misleading. On July 1, 2016, the site published an article, "Palin on Paid Anti-Trump Protesters: 'Not Even President Yet and Our Guy's Already Creating Jobs,'" based on Sarah Palin's false claim that paid anti-Trump protesters were showing up at Trump rallies. One of the sources cited by the article was "ABC News," which turned out to be a fake news site that has illegally copied the network's trademarks to appear legitimate.[63]

"Planned Parenthood Teams up with Satanists to Promote Abortion in Missouri," published on September 13, 2017, was another fake news story in the classic breitbart.com style. The story was based on a tip to an email group that collected reports mocking political correctness and that then Breitbart contributor Milo Yiannopoulos belonged to. Planned Parenthood and the Satanic Temple did argue separate court cases against the state's restrictions on access to abortion, but subsequent journalistic investigation showed there was no "team up" or any form of collaboration between the groups.[64]

"Obama's new attorney general nominee Loretta Lynch represented Clintons during Whitewater," published on November 8, 2014, was another incorrect breitbart.com article. But the Loretta Lynch nominated by Barack Obama was not the same Loretta Lynch who represented Bill and Hillary Clinton. The mistake was first pointed out by Media Matters. Breitbart eventually acknowledged the mistake in a correction but nonetheless left the story up. Eventually the story was taken down, but not before the claim had spread to other rightest sites, including american thinker.com.[65] Many other cases of fake news reporting at breitbart.com are documented by MBFC.[66]

Other Alt-Lite sites of note are the web outlets for the political commentators Michelle Malkin, Ann Coulter, and Pat Buchanan. All three write columns that are printed in the Alt-Right outlet VDARE.com, and Malkin's and Buchanan's columns appear in the still more radical American Renaissance. Coulter is discussed further in chapter 4. Malkin for many years was an ordinary conservative commentator, although much given to the illiberal habit of branding her targets as traitors, including "treasonous Silicon Valley CEOs," Democrats with their "twisted and treasonous priorities," and, of course, "the Treason [*New York*] Times."[67] In recent years she has become more radical and has associated herself with Nicholas Fuentes, a young Alt-Rightist known for his anti-Semitic YouTube videos and defense of the storming of the Capitol on January 6, 2021.[68]

The traffic to Buchanan's website is not large, netting about 112,000 visits, 45,000 unique visitors, and an engagement rate of 2.47 visits per unique visitor on monthly average. But as a presidential speechwriter, candidate, and a best-selling author, Buchanan has been an influential right-wing figure. And his brand of discrete illiberalism deserves attention, as it features arguments against liberal democracy that turn up often not only in illiberal outlets but even sometimes on conventional conservative sites.

Buchanan's brand of illiberalism is expressed in his frequent disparagement of democracy. Typical examples are his columns with such titles as "Democracy—A Flickering Star?," "Is Democracy in a Death Spiral?," "Is Liberal Democracy an Endangered Species?," and "Is Democracy Another God that Failed?" Like other Alt-Lite outlets, Buchanan avoids being explicitly illiberal. He does so by framing his denigrations of democracy as questions. But upon reading his columns one finds that alleged evidence against democracy is piled on high with no counterbalancing material provided. Therefore, when Buchanan asks such questions as "Liberal democracy is in a bear market. Is it a systemic crisis as well?"[69] a negative judgment is implied. And in the end, he simply blurts out his illiberalism when he writes: "Democracy lacks content. As a political system, it does not engage the heart."[70] Further, Buchanan tells us that the framers of

America's government shared his negative evaluation of democracy: "Our Founding Fathers believed that democracy represented the degeneration of a republic; they feared and loathed it, and felt that it was the precursor of dictatorship. They may have been right again."[71]

However, another characteristic Buchanan shares with the rest of the Alt-Lite, and indeed all illiberal outlets, is bad scholarship. Among the evidence against democracy he provides are apparently telling quotations by the American founders, who are depicted as firmly anti-democratic. The only problems are that the quotes are frequently either bogus or taken out of context.

Buchanan has several times used spurious quotes from Jefferson ("A democracy is nothing more than mob rule, where 51 percent of the people may take away the rights of the other 49.") and Madison ("Democracy is the most vile form of government").[72] The Research and Education section of the web page for Jefferson's home, Monticello, characterizes the quote as "spurious,"[73] while the alleged Madison quote is nowhere to be found on the Founders Online database operated by the National Archives or on the JSTOR database of academic journals.[74]

Then there are the apparently anti-democratic quotes by the founders that are not bogus but that Buchanan takes out of context. He correctly quotes John Adams as saying "Democracy never lasts long. It soon wastes, exhausts and murders itself. There never was a democracy yet that did not commit suicide."[75] Adams was, as he himself expressed, writing under the influence of a document he had recently come upon, an "Alphabetical Dictionary of the Names and Qualities of Persons, 'Mangled and Bleeding Victims of Democratic Rage and Popular Fury' in France during the Despotism of Democracy in that Country."[76] His objection is thus to a "Despotism of Democracy"; that is, democracy unchecked by human rights, the rule of law, or any break in the will of the mob. Adams rejects all forms of government that are "simple," or without any checks and balances. Thus, he writes, "No simple Form of Government, can possibly secure Men against the Violences of Power. Simple Monarchy will soon mould itself into Despotism, Aristocracy will soon commence an Oligarchy, and Democracy, will soon degenerate into an Anarchy."[77] Thus it is simple democracy, or unchecked democracy, that Adams opposes, as he does all simple forms of government. Adams praises democracy when he speaks of American democracy, which, unlike that of revolutionary France, incorporates the necessary checks. He writes: "It is no wonder then, that every State upon the Continent has instituted a democracy, and that the people are universally fond of their new government. . . . [T]hese kinds of governments are the best adapted to their circumstances, but calculated to promote their happiness, their population, their agriculture, manufactures and commerce, as well as their defence."[78]

Besides bogus Madison quotes, Buchanan trades in quoting the father of the U.S. Constitution out of context. According to Buchanan, "Madison wrote in *Federalist* 10, 'democracies . . . have in general been as short in their lives as they have been violent in their deaths.' "[79] But the snippet Buchanan provides fails to indicate that Madison is talking about the pure democracies of ancient Greece, not modern liberal democracies like the United States. Here is a fuller and more accurate quote:

> . . . a pure democracy, by which I mean a society consisting of a small number of citizens, who assemble and administer the government in person, can admit of no cure for the mischiefs of faction. . . . Hence it is that *such* democracies have ever been spectacles of turbulence and contention; have ever been found incompatible with personal security or the rights of property; and have in general been as short in their lives as they have been violent in their deaths.[80]

The classically educated founders were most familiar with the pure or direct democracies of the ancient world, where not only was there no representation but also no human rights, no rule of law, and no barriers on the will of a momentary majority. Naturally the founders were at pains to explain that the government they intended for the United States would be nothing like the Greek pure democracies. When they wrote of democracy they were always clear that they meant pure democracy, which they contrasted sharply with the republican government of America. Thus, in *Federalist* No. 14, Madison explained: "in a democracy, the people meet and exercise the government in person; in a republic, they assemble and administer it by their representatives and agents."[81]

In short, the founders' criticisms of democracy were aimed at the ancient pure democracies and in no way demonstrate a hostility to modern democracies that feature representation, the rule of law, the protection of human rights, and a wide array of institutions to limit the power of the majority. Today, the founders' sharp distinction between (pure) democracies and republics has become largely otiose as pure democracies, already ancient when *The Federalist Papers* were written, have long ago ceased to be relevant. Virtually all modern democracies involve representation and so are also republics. And thus the very concept of democracy today implies representation and therefore republicanism; that is, representatives are chosen through elections to make political decisions. Joseph Schumpeter's definition of democracy is so frequently cited as to be quasi-official, and assumes representation and republicanism, for it asserts: "The democratic method is that institutional arrangement for arriving at political decisions in which individuals acquire the power to decide by means of a competitive struggle for the people's vote."[82]

Many illiberals, and even some mainstream conservatives, make a great fuss over the distinction between a democracy and a republic, and always with the intent of denigrating democracy, as reflected in the following question posed by Pat Buchanan:

> But did not the fathers create modernity's first democracy?
>
> No. They created "a republic, if you can keep it," as Ben Franklin said, when asked in Philadelphia what kind of government they had given us. A constitutional republic, to protect and defend God-given rights that antedated the establishment of that government. We used to know that. Growing up, we daily pledged allegiance "to the flag of the United States of America and to the Republic for which it stands," not some democracy.[83]

Assuming one works with a terminology that has been in standard use at the latest since the mid-twentieth century, it is perfectly correct to think of the United States as a democracy. To be perfectly clear, this book speaks of liberal democracy to emphasize that modern democracy incorporates republicanism and many other safeguards against the tyranny of the majority unknown to the ancients.

Buchanan is primarily of interest here for his frequent use of the now moot republic/democracy distinction as a shell game to disparage democracy without too openly displaying his illiberal ideology. Such coyness in various forms is characteristic of the Alt-Lite.

Conspiracy/Questionable

In organizing Hard-Core Illiberal Right sites into categories, when possible we relied on work by other investigators to avoid contaminating our findings with our own prejudices. We discovered that twenty of the sites in our sample had been placed by MBFC into the categories "Conspiracy/ Pseudoscience" or "Questionable."[84] We decided to accept that judgment. However, we combined the two categories into one because they both emphasized the untrustworthiness of the material they contained.

The twenty sites in the Conspiracy/Questionable category had the highest monthly average of visits of any Hard-Core category in this analysis, receiving about 126 million such visits. That represented about 67.7 percent of the visits to all Hard-Core sites during the time period. These sites received a mean of about 505,000 and a median of about 108,000 unique visitors. They had a high mean engagement rate of 4.92 visits per unique visitor and a median of about 3.56.

In the time period studied here, the first eleven months of 2019, the site with the largest audience in the Conspiracy/Questionable category, and indeed the largest audience of any Right Illiberal site, was drudgereport. com. The site received about 84.9 million visits and 4.1 million unique visitors on monthly average, and had a strikingly high average monthly engagement rate of about 20.5 visits per unique visitor. It was one of the most iconic outlets on the web, based on its huge audience along with the facts that the Drudge Report was one of the original political websites and experienced developments that would shape the nature of digital media.

In some ways, the position of the Drudge Report as one of the leading Hard-Core Illiberal Right sites is anomalous. It has been accurately described as mostly a news "aggregator containing selected hyperlinks to news websites all over the world, each link carrying a headline written by the site's editors,"[85] and sometimes contains a few articles written by its editor, Matt Drudge. MBFC described the site as conservative but less extreme than Breitbart News, American Thinker, and FrontPage Magazine. Unlike Hate, Alt-Right, Manosphere, Dark Enlightenment, and many other Hard-Core Illiberal Right sites, the Drudge Report does not run articles attacking political equality, liberal democracy, or racial and ethnic minorities. Moreover, in September 2020, MBFC changed its classification of the site from Right Biased and Questionable to Right Center "based on improved journalistic standards."[86]

Yet, in the time period of this study and for much of its existence, the site qualified as illiberal for its systematic violation of the ethics of controversy and spirit of informed debate needed for liberal democracy to function. Based on reviews conducted in July 2016 and October 2019, MBFC concluded that "Overall, we rate the Drudge Report Right Biased and Questionable due to promotion of propaganda and conspiracy theories, as well as for publishing fake news and the use of highly questionable sources."[87] It is this original Drudge Report that is particularly relevant to this study because by successfully evading a legal challenge to its shoddy editorial practices in the early days of digital journalism, it effectively undermined the status of online gatekeepers ever since. This legal episode will be discussed in chapter 6.

There is no doubt that the earlier Drudge Report was terrible journalism. But was it illiberal, and if so, in what sense? The Drudge Report was probably the least radical of the Hard-Core Right Illiberal sites, primarily because it seldom discussed ideology explicitly, so the attacks on liberal democracy characteristic of other Hard-Core sites did not come up at Drudge. Moreover, the site's rightist orientation was much less extreme than many of the sites we have examined here. Yet, Matt Drudge's outlet was illiberal because of the way it flung down and stomped upon the ethics of controversy essential to liberal democratic political culture. The site trafficked in outrageous falsehoods, thereby violating the commitment to facts required for democratic discourse. The Drudge Report unmistakably communicated a very right-wing account of politics, which in itself is neither here nor there. What was objectionable, and illiberal, was that its political positions were communicated not with arguments, but with shock-jock sensationalism. No reasons were given for the site's rightist view of the world. Rather, the reader was overwhelmed with factoids, lies, rumors, conspiracy theories, dirty stories, and nonsense. The Drudge Report pioneered the development of the fake-news site, stayed with the model for decades, and was instrumental in its spread throughout the internet. The earlier site was corrosive of democratic discourse and, for that reason, is accurately described as illiberal.

A qualified defense of the old Drudge Report is possible if the site is thought of as implicitly rather than explicitly illiberal. That is, during the time period considered here, Drudge disseminated lies, engaged in wild sensationalism, and was generally irresponsible, all of which undermined the liberal political culture of reasoned discourse. Drudge Report copiously indulged in an illiberal style of political reporting but did not articulate the case for it. Drudge practiced illiberal reporting but did not preach it. But other very popular Hard-Core Right Illiberal sites do cross that Rubicon. Zero Hedge is an example.

Zero Hedge, according to an article on Bloomberg.com, is a financial news and opinion site founded in 2009 by Colin Lokey, also known as Tyler Durden, a principal character from *Fight Club*; Daniel Ivandjiiski, a former hedge fund analyst who was barred by the Financial Industry Regulatory Authority (FINRA) in 2008 for insider trading;[88] and Tim Backshall, "a well-known credit derivatives strategist."[89] The site's name derives from a line in the movie *Fight Club* and also appears as a motto on Zero Hedge's home page: "On a long enough timeline the survival rate for everyone drops to zero." Overall, MBFC rates Zero Hedge "an extreme right biased conspiracy website" with a mixed record in factual reporting and a strong propensity for conspiracy theorizing.[90] Zero Hedge received about 22.2 million visits and 2.1 million unique visitors on monthly average and had a very high average monthly engagement rate of 10.7 visits per unique visitor.

What is of concern here is Zero Hedge's illiberal ideology, usually expressed in articles published under the pen name Tyler Durden. Often these articles take the form of long excerpts from other extreme rightist sources whose main target is liberal democracy. The site's attitude toward democracy as expressed in these articles ranges from excoriatingly critical to flat rejection.

An example of the former is "Our Hopelessly Dysfunctional Democracy," published March 22, 2017, under the Durden byline, but "Authored by Charles Hugh-Smith via OfTwoMinds blog."[91] According to the article:

> **Democracy in America has become a hollow shell.** The conventional markers of democracy—elections and elected representatives—exist, but they are mere facades; the mechanisms of setting the course of the nation are corrupt, and the power lies outside the public's reach.
>
> **History has shown that democratic elections don't guarantee an uncorrupt, functional government.** Rather, democracy has become the public-relations stamp of approval for corrupt governance that runs roughshod over individual liberty while centralizing the power to enforce consent, silence critics and maintain the status quo.[92]

Here, American democracy is about as awful as it possibly could be, "hopelessly dysfunctional," and as the article states elsewhere, "Beyond Reform." But is it only the American form of democracy that is done for, or is it democracy itself that is hopeless and beyond reform? Zero Hedge provides few hints as to what a positive form of democracy might be. But in some articles the message is clear: democracy itself is a fraud.

For example, "Guest Post: What Democracy?" pours on corrosive criticism of the Constitution, "the ruling establishment," and politics in general ("legalized harlotry"). Then we get to the bottom line:

> None of this is to suggest that a transition to real democracy is the answer. The popular adage of democracy being "two wolves and a lamb voting on what's for lunch" is undeniably accurate. A system where one group of people can vote its hands into another's pockets is not economically sustainable. Democracy's pitting of individuals against each other leads to moral degeneration and impairs capital accumulation. It is no panacea for the rottenness that follows from centers of power. True human liberty with respect to property rights is the only foundation from which civilization can grow and thrive.[93]

This is outright illiberalism of the right-wing anarchistic variety. But its invocation of the "popular adage of democracy being 'two wolves and a lamb voting on what's for lunch'" deserves comment. This tired trope can be found all over the internet, especially in its extreme right precincts. The Mises Institute—like Zero Hedge, an outlet of hyperorthodox Austrian economics—incorrectly attributes the quote to Benjamin Franklin.[94] The quotation is not only spurious but also irrelevant to modern liberal democracies, where minority rights are acknowledged and protected by the rule of law.

Another iconic, or rather infamous, site in the Conspiracy/Questionable category is infowars.com. The site had a monthly average of about 6.9 million visits, 1.4 million unique visitors, and a high engagement rate of 4.85 visits per unique visitor. The site is notorious as an outlet for the most bizarre and repellant conspiracy theories to be found anywhere on the internet. Under the direction of Alex Jones, infowars.com originated and circulated the noxious claim that the massacre of twenty-six people at the Sandy Hook Elementary School in 2012 was perpetrated by the U.S.

government for the purpose of discrediting the Second Amendment. In a December 2014 episode of Infowars, Jones summed up his mendacious claims about Sandy Hook: "The whole thing was a giant hoax. How do you deal with a total hoax? But it took me about a year with Sandy Hook to come to grips with the fact that the whole thing was fake. I did deep research and, my gosh, it just pretty much didn't happen."[95] Another notable conspiracy theory pushed by infowars.com was "pizzagate," which claimed that a child sex ring was being run by Democrats out of a Washington, D.C., pizzeria. In the same vein was a series of stories that refugees employed by the yogurt manufacturer Chobani had gang raped a young girl. As a result of legal action, Jones publicly retracted both the pizzagate and Chobani stories.[96] MBFC does not exaggerate when it categorizes infowars.com as "a crackpot, tin foil hat level conspiracy website that also strongly promotes pseudoscience."[97]

It is often said that Alex Jones and infowars.com are hard to characterize ideologically. RationalWiki describes Jones's political stance as "Notoriously hard to place ideologically (although clearly located to the right on most topics), Jones's views amount to some kind of high-powered mutant hybrid of libertarianism/paleoconservatism/evangelicalism/neoreaction/miscellaneous."[98] This is true if the comparison is to mainstream pundits or outlets that have a fixed perspective that endures, sometimes over decades. Jones, whose *modus operandi* is to chase after or cook up a bizarre rumor as opportunity permits, has a less stable identity. He indulges in the same paranoid fantasies about the annual Bilderberg meeting and the global elite that the John Birch Society did. But he adds his characteristic touch by suggesting the elite stay in power by ingesting DMT, a mind-altering drug supplied by the "clockwork elves":

> They believe they are communicating with entities they call the clockwork elves. . . . The elite, and most of those old men you see at Bilderberg, there is a reason they're all wacked out of their minds is they're taking DMT. You think they're all a bunch of old men? They're in power because they were into this seventy years ago. They were jacking DMT 70 years ago. They were injecting it.[99]

But through it all, Jones and infowars.com are clearly illiberal. The website often posts article excerpts from Austrian/libertarian and paleoconservative outlets denigrating democracy in the illiberal style. Typical titles include "What If Democracy Is Bunk?" "Is Western Democracy Real or a Façade?" and "Why Democracy Doesn't Give Us What We Want."[100] These articles, and many others, all make the same illiberal argument we have seen before. Democracy is equated with pure democracy and mob rule; liberal institutions are ignored or dismissed without serious argument; actual existing liberal democracies are therefore frauds; a leap of faith into one or another illiberal pipe dream is the only alternative.

Another long-running site that was instrumental in developing the Alt-Right style of rhetoric is frontpagemag.com. The site was established by David Horowitz, a former New Left intellectual and publisher of the radical magazine *Ramparts* who turned sharply right in the mid-1980s, and established a network of organizations and outlets that launched harsh attacks against almost the entire left half of the American political spectrum. His sites are gathered under the umbrella of the David Horowitz Freedom Center, established in 1988, whose website is also included in the Conspiracy/Questionable category. The traffic to the Freedom Center's web page is very small, but FrontPage Magazine has a healthier audience of about 684,000 visits, 264,000 unique visitors, and an engagement rate of 2.59 visits per unique visitor on monthly average. Moreover, Horowitz's sites are of interest because of his role as an early and influential developer of the illiberal rhetorical style.

Some of Horowitz's creations are useful up to a point. As mentioned above, Discover the Networks (DTN), one of the many platforms of Horowitz's Freedom Center, provides useful information on some Left Illiberal sites, even though it fails in its main task, which it says is to "bare the connections that tie today's left to the left of ages past."[101] But the main contribution of frontpagemag.com and Horowitz's other sites is a rhetorical style that would be widely taken up by the Alt-Right and illiberals in general.

If the maxim of the Alt-Right is "All People Are Not Created Equal," then "Politics Is War" is the maxim of FrontPage Magazine and Horowitz's other platforms. The magazine's sponsoring organization describes its mission as follows:

> The David Horowitz Freedom Center is unique among conservative think tanks whose emphasis is on public policy and institutional reform in that it sees its role as that of a battle tank, geared to fight a war that many still don't recognize.... The David Horowitz Freedom Center is best seen as a School

of Political Warfare. The Center's mission is to defend free societies which are under attack from enemies within and without, both secular and religious. The Center's focus and the School's curriculum have two agendas:

1. Identify the enemy and understand his nature
2. Devise ways to attack and neutralize him[102]

Horowitz and his outlets have insisted for decades that politics is war. In 1999, Horowitz published a handbook for Republican political operatives entitled *The Art of Political War: How Republicans Can Fight to Win*, in which he wrote that the first principle of political warfare is "Politics is war conducted by other means," or more simply, "Politics is War. Don't forget it."[103] Soon after Trump became president, Horowitz published *Big Agenda: President Trump's Plan to Save America*, which offers advice such as "conservatives must begin every confrontation by punching progressives in the mouth"; "Republicans must adhere to a strategy that begins with a punch in the mouth"; "the strategy is to go for the jugular"; "it's time to take the gloves off"; and "take no prisoners; stay on the attack."[104]

The salience, stress, and commitment Horowitz gives to this formulation show he is saying more than just "politics ain't bean-bag." The source he evokes with the phrase "Politics is war conducted by other means" is not Mr. Dooley but Carl von Clausewitz, the philosopher of war who famously wrote "War is a Mere Continuation of Policy by Other Means," which is often rendered as "War is politics conducted by other means."[105] By inverting Clausewitz's phrase, Horowitz utterly changes its meaning and arrives at a ferocious understanding of politics that cannot be squared with liberal democracy. The "politics is war" concept and the illiberal use made of it by Horowitz and others is discussed further in chapter 4.

If politics is war, then one's opponents must be not simply political adversaries, but enemies and traitors. And FrontPage Magazine does frequently portray garden-variety Democrats and progressives as traitors. The Democratic Party is "the Party of Plunder/Party of Treason."[106] Another article claims the nuclear arms control agreement the Obama administration negotiated with Iran "isn't just Chamberlain. It's Vidkun Quisling and Philippe Pétain. It's not bad judgment. It's treason." And not just treason but "Genocidal Treason."[107] Another article directly connects the concepts that politics is war and that opponents are traitors. In it, Daniel Greenfield announces that "The Civil War is Here" and then explains who the internal enemies are:

The left is a treasonous movement. The Democrats became a treasonous organization when they fell under the sway of a movement that rejects our system of government, its laws and its elections. Now their treason is coming to a head. They are engaged in a struggle for power against the government. That's not protest. It's not activism. The old treason of the sixties has come of age. A civil war has begun.[108]

But there is an obvious rebuttal to the notion that treason can be stretched widely enough to include violent street protests, arms control agreements, and militant opposition to the Trump administration. The Constitution deliberately defines treason much more narrowly than that. Article 3, section 3, reads:

Treason against the United States, shall consist only in levying War against them, or in adhering to their Enemies, giving them Aid and Comfort. No Person shall be convicted of Treason unless on the Testimony of two Witnesses to the same overt Act, or on Confession in open Court.[109]

Horowitz, of course, is aware of this constitutional definition but argues it is irrelevant. In an article about the Obama administration entitled "Acts of Treason," Horowitz writes:

But this legal definition of the crime is only one aspect of the issue, and in the end it is the less important one for understanding the significance of what has happened. There is also the common usage of the words "treason" and "traitor," which speak to the moral dimensions of the crime. It is these meanings that provide a proper guide to the seriousness and scope of what Obama, Biden, Comey, Brennan, Clapper and the others involved actually did.[110]

But why should common usage take precedence over the Constitution itself? The founders had a specific reason for defining treason narrowly, and it was not because, as Horowitz claims, they knew, "They were all guilty of it for rebelling against their king." Nor was their reason narrowly legal. It had to do with the sort of political culture they wanted to inculcate. In *Federalist* No. 43, Madison explained the founders' motives:

But as new-fangled and artificial treasons have been the great engines by which violent factions, the natural offspring of free government, have usually wreaked their alternate malignity on each other, the convention have, with great judgment, opposed a barrier to this peculiar danger, by inserting a constitutional definition of the crime, fixing the proof necessary for conviction of it, and restraining the Congress, even in punishing it, from extending the consequences of guilt beyond the person of its author.[111]

The founders defined treason as narrowly as they did to oppose a barrier to the "peculiar danger" of "new-fangled and artificial" definitions engineering violent factionalism and malignity to the detriment of free government. In using a looser definition, Horowitz is doing exactly what Madison and the founders warned against. But this is no surprise, as someone who insists politics is war will of course seek to pit violent factions against each other. In doing so, Horowitz breaks with the liberal democratic ethics of controversy implicit in the Declaration, which holds that adversaries are not to be treated like enemies or traitors short of literal, violent war.

Another site in the Conspiracy/Questionable category is american thinker.com. The site had 4.4 million visits, 895,000 unique visitors, and a very high engagement rate of 4.94 visits per unique visitor on monthly average. MBFC rated the site as "Questionable based on extreme right wing bias, promotion of conspiracy theories/pseudoscience, use of poor sources and failed fact checks."[112] The site contributed to the many conspiracy theories surrounding President Obama by publishing articles such as "Report: Obama said 'I Am a Muslim,'"[113] and "Obama and the Muslim Gang Sign,"[114] both of which relied on unconfirmed rumors to falsely accuse Obama of being a Muslim.

Another false story circulated by American Thinker was the claim that Seth Rich, a lower-level Democratic National Committee (DNC) staffer who was murdered during a robbery in 2016, was in fact assassinated for reasons related to the stolen DNC emails obtained by WikiLeaks.[115] This tall tale was convenient for Trump supporters and Hillary haters, as it suggested the source of the leaked emails was not Russian intelligence, but a DNC staffer. The well-respected *Columbia Journalism Review* characterized this false claim as "One of the first prominent 'fake news' conspiracy theories to metastasize from Internet rumor all the way to the [Trump] White House."[116] The theory was characterized by Snopes as "False" and was definitively debunked in the Mueller Report.[117]

American Thinker won its spurs as an outlet of pseudoscience for, among other things, its coverage of climate change. A typical example is a story on "The Hoax of 'Climate Change,'" which was described as not merely a hoax, but "the biggest hoax foisted on the human race."[118] Another anti–climate change article was "New Study Shows Sea Level Rise Has Been Slow and a Constant, Pre-Dating Industrialization," by the site's editor and publisher, Thomas Lifson. Several climate scientists took to the pages of the media watchdog site Climate Feedback to denounce Lifson's article as "factually inaccurate" and for having misrepresented its source.[119]

Contributors to americanthinker.com frequently attack democracy, usually by employing the common ruse of castigating the idea of pure democracy that was practiced by the ancient Greeks and concluding that modern representative, liberal democracies suffer from the same weaknesses. Thus an article on "The Dangers of Democracy" asserts "democracy, in its pure form, is nothing more than mob rule."[120] This is true of pure or direct democracy, but what of modern liberal democracy, where mob rule is checked by republicanism, human rights, the rule of law, an independent judiciary, and other liberal institutions?

Writers for americanthinker.com have come up with a way of dodging the obvious fact that the "liberal" in liberal democracy refers precisely to these firmly established provisions for preventing mobocracy. The dodge consists of claiming that the liberal component in liberal democracy refers not to constitutional structures that limit pure democracy, but simply to the progressive political agenda. This maneuver is executed in an article entitled "Towards a Conservative Democracy."[121] The title is very telling. If the desired opposite of liberal democracy is conservative democracy, then the term "liberal" is being taken to mean not liberal institutions that check democracy, but simply contemporary progressivism. And indeed, the author asserts, "The idyllic phrase 'liberal democracy' sounds the very essence of classic liberalism and Western democracy but is now, in fact, private code for socialism."[122] Yet, the only evidence offered to support the claim that liberal institutions no longer restrain democracy is that, over the long run, the United States has adopted much of the progressive policy agenda. This development is taken as ipso facto evidence that liberal institutions have broken down and mobocracy is now a reality. The possibility that liberal institutions are alive and well, and that progressive politics has continued to thrive within their limits, is not considered.

The fact that the Conspiracy/Questionable category is the largest of the Hard-Core sites in terms of visits says much about the nature of contemporary illiberalism. Obviously, sites that explicitly reject electoral democracy, political egalitarianism, and other core principles of liberal democracy are illiberal. But we should not forget other essential features of liberal democracy that relate to political culture rather than formal institutions. No set of institutions can guarantee the endurance of liberal democracy unless the citizenry wants it to endure and takes care to make it endure in their beliefs and practices. That is, to survive, liberal democratic institutions require a liberal democratic political culture. Tolerance, a democratic ethics of controversy, rejection of the friend/enemy conception of politics, and a respect for facts are all necessary features of the political culture of liberal democracy. The characteristic feature of the Conspiracy/Questionable sites is that they reject the elements of liberal democratic political culture in either principle or practice. Sometimes these sites do both, as in the case of Zero Hedge. But other sites focus on violating liberal democratic practice and come up with a distinctly illiberal rhetorical style. FrontPage Magazine and Breitbart practice the illiberal rhetorical style to the fullest but usually avoid openly repudiating liberal democratic principles. Infowars and the old Drudge Report are of this type too. Even though these sites trade in bizarre conspiracy theories and outrageously fake news, they are not politically harmless in the way supermarket tabloid stories about sightings of Elvis and Bat Boy are. Infowars and the old Drudge site report news and comment on politics in the illiberal rhetorical style, and thus degrade liberal democratic culture. So the main takeaway from this review of the Conspiracy/Questionable category is that contemporary illiberalism manifests itself not only as a political ideology, but also as a rhetorical style, both of which are inimical to liberal democracy.

Uncategorized Hard-Core Right-Illiberal Sites

Forty-five of the Hard-Core sites did not clearly fit into any category. These sites received, on monthly average, about 1.6 million visits. In terms of unique visitors, they had a mean of about 11,000 and a median of about 3,000. They had a mean engagement rate of about 2.93 and a median of about 1.92.

As might be expected from a collection of sites that defy easy categorization, these outlets are very eclectic: eagleforum.org, fgfbooks.com, revilo-oliver.com, and sobran.com feature the work of deceased right-wing extremists such as Phyllis Schlafly and Joe Sobran; hanshoppe.com, ilanamercer.com, laurensouthern.net, and propertarianism.com are platforms for Alt-Right–oriented libertarianism; hbdchick.wordpress.com, humanvarieties.org, mankindquarterly.org, and rlynn.co.uk focus on scientific racialism; and prowhiteparty.wordpress.com, stuffblackpeopledontlike.blogspot.com, whitedate.net, and whitebiocentrism.com are what you might expect.

The Political Impact of Illiberalism

Clearly illiberalism as it is defined here is radically opposed to liberal democracy and has a large and very engaged audience. But how much of an impact on American political life does illiberalism have? Do illiberal ideas find their way into mainstream political outlets? And do visitors to illiberal sites act on the ideas they find there and have a major impact on important political events? These questions are hard to definitively answer given the limitations of the data analyzed here. But some incidents suggest illiberalism is having an impact on American politics.

Among the many shocking images of the disorder following the death of George Floyd at the hands of police, one of the most shocking showed how, on June 4, 2020, a peaceful protester, 75-year-old Martin Gugino, was shoved to the ground by police in Buffalo, New York. Gugino cracked his head against the pavement and lay bleeding while many police officers walked past him. Viewers were almost universally appalled.[123]

On June 6, one of the websites in the Conspiracy/Questionable category, theconservativetreehouse.com, posted a story titled "Buffalo Officials Duped By Professional Antifa Provocateur—Arrest and Charge Two Police Officers—Righteous Police Team Stand Together and Walk Out." According to the story:

> During his effort Gugino was attempting to capture the radio communications signature of Buffalo police officers. CTH [Conservative Tree House] noted what he was attempting on Thursday night as soon as the now viral video was being used by media to sell a police brutality narrative. . . . The capture of communications signals . . . is a method of police tracking used by Antifa to monitor the location of police.[124]

The article offers no evidence for this claim other than its forced interpretation of Gugino's vague hand gestures.

MBFC placed the Conservative Treehouse in the questionable category "based on the use of poor sources, promotion of propaganda and conspiracy theories, a complete lack of transparency, and numerous failed fact checks."[125] Moreover, the site dispenses the same stale attacks on democracy that, as documented above, illiberal outlets specialize in. A typical post claims that "in an unvarnished democracy, unrestrained by a constitution, the majority can vote to impose tyranny on themselves and the minority opposition."[126] The solution, then, would seem to be a constitution to restrain democracy. But no, the post also says, "Constitutional democracies do not have the safeguards of the separation of powers and states' rights." So democracies unrestrained by a constitution are no good, and constitutional democracies provide no safeguards either. Thus the argument is that no sort of democracy is desirable. Both in terms of its promotion of fake news and its ideology, the Conservative Treehouse is a typical illiberal outlet.

The next step in the illiberal pipeline came when One America News Network (OANN) picked up on the Conservative Treehouse's unsubstantiated claim and, citing the website as its source, broadcast a news clip with the title "Report: Shoved Buffalo Protester an Antifa Provocateur." A news network that positions itself to the right of Fox News, OANN has been praised, and sometimes watched, by Donald Trump. MBFC places the website for OANN in the ordinary Right category, so in moving from the Hard-Core Illiberal outlet Conservative Treehouse to OANN, the phony story moved a step closer to the political mainstream. Interestingly, the reporter on the phony story about the Buffalo protester also writes for Sputnik, described by the *Washington Post* as "a Kremlin news service that U.S. intelligence agencies said was implicated in the Russian efforts to intervene in the 2016 election on behalf of Trump."[127]

Then the false story was picked up by Trump himself, who cited to the OANN segment in the following tweet from June 9, 2020:

Buffalo protester shoved by Police could be an ANTIFA provocateur. 75 year old Martin Gugino was pushed away after appearing to scan police communications in order to black out the equipment. @OANN I watched, he fell harder than was pushed. Was aiming scanner. Could be a set up?[128]

In the Treehouse story, we have a very interesting juxtaposition of Antifa and the Hard-Core Illiberal Right. The Treehouse, OANN, and Trump are all concerned about the influence of Antifa. But the numbers we have on the web audiences for these tendencies suggest the concern is misplaced. All Illiberal Left sites—which include antifa sites—received about 2.5 million visits, had a mean of about 11,000 unique visitors, and had a mean engagement rate of 1.76 visits per unique visitor. Meanwhile, the Treehouse alone had a much larger audience of about 3.2 million visits, 279,000 unique visitors on monthly average, and a strikingly high engagement rate of about 11.4 visits per unique visitor on monthly average. If we are to judge using the important criterion of web audiences, Antifa is vanishingly small while the Hard-Core Illiberal Right is relatively huge and is heard at the heights of American government. Thus from the Treehouse to the White House, here we have a clear example of how ideas developed in illiberal outlets can make their way through intermediate way stations to the highest levels of American politics and political culture.

For another example, the role of Nicholas J. Fuentes, his America First following, and other illiberal movements that were involved in the riot at the U.S. Capitol on January 6, 2021, are telling. Fuentes's website, nicholas jfuentes.com, was cited by our illiberal sources. It had an audience of only about 36,000 visits on monthly average, but Fuentes also reached audiences through his set of YouTube channels before he was banned from that service in early 2020. Fuentes then decamped to a video livestreaming service called DLive, which has a financial exchange system that enabled him to raise more than $61,000 between April 16 and late October of 2020.[129] Fuentes was banned from DLive on January 9, 2021.[130]

Before the Capitol riot, Fuentes was best known for his anti-Semitic videos, the conflict he got into with more mainstream conservative student groups, and the support he received from the Alt-Lite commentator Michelle Malkin.[131] Typical of his incendiary rhetoric was a comment he made in the course of pressing state legislators to overturn the results of the 2020 presidential election: "What can you and I do to a state legislator besides kill them? We should not do that. I'm not advising that, but I mean what else can you do, right? Nothing."[132]

Fuentes was among the protesters outside the Capitol on January 6. A video shows him exhorting a cheering crowd: "I say we should not leave this Capitol until Donald Trump is inaugurated president! We the American people will not let this fraudulent election go forward one more step!"[133] Videos show protesters near and inside the Capitol displaying flags with the "AF" logo of Fuentes's America First group, but Fuentes himself did not enter the building.[134] Shortly after the riot Fuentes recorded a video in which he boasted: "We stopped the counting of the Electoral College. We forced a joint session of Congress and the Vice President to evacuate."[135]

We know, therefore, that these participants at least were familiar with and had bought into illiberalism as it was expressed through Fuentes's outlet. And there were many other protesters who had apparently drunk the Kool-Aid. The Proud Boys are another extremist organization whose website, officialproudboys.com, was cited by our illiberal sources and whose logos were sported by some rioters.[136] Pepe the frog and the flag of the imaginary country Kekistan are both well-known Alt-Right symbols that were on display when the Capitol was stormed.[137] The Confederate flag, near and dear to the hearts of the Alt-South and hate groups was there too.[138] Most alarming perhaps were the nooses and gallows that referenced one of the most vicious documents to come out of the hate movements: *The Turner Diaries* and its fictional celebration of "The Day of the Rope," when Blacks and anti-racists are strung up en masse. Also present was the iconography of a host of movements not discussed in this book but known for their anti-Semitic, anti-democratic, conspiracy theory–oriented, and otherwise illiberal ideas, including QAnon, the Three Percenters, the Oath Keepers, and others.[139]

The Capitol rioters expressed their illiberalism not only in symbols but in words. Over and over again they shouted that the U.S. Capitol Police, members of Congress, and anyone who opposed them were traitors.[140] Some wore sweatshirts that read: "MAGA: CIVIL WAR January 6, 2021."[141] An analysis by *USA Today* found that "Calls for civil war intensified on the right-leaning social media platform Parler on Jan. 6 as President Donald Trump spoke and urged his followers to march on the U.S. Capitol."[142] And when Donald Trump Jr. communicated to his father's followers on the morning of the riot, he framed the issue at hand as follows: "Friend or foe, today, Republicans, you get to pick a side for the future of this party." In short, the rioters and their leaders expressed themselves in classic illiberal terms: opponents are traitors, politics is war, the world divides into friend versus foe. And, of course, the whole premise of the riot was illiberal in that it was based on an anti-democratic conspiracy theory. Wild stories of a nefarious plot convinced the protesters that they should overturn the results of an election that was obviously legitimate to anyone not trapped in the illiberal identity monad. The evidence is partly circumstantial but nonetheless compelling: the Capitol insurrection was illiberal ideas put into practice.

Further striking evidence on the spread of illiberalism comes from a poll conducted in 2017 by Reuters/Ipsos in conjunction with the University of Virginia Center for Politics. It found that "6 percent of respondents said they strongly or somewhat supported the alt-right . . . 8 percent expressed support for white nationalism [and] . . . 4 percent expressed support for neo-Nazism." Given that America has about 250 million adults, with at least 4 percent of them supporting a hard-core illiberal ideology—neo-Nazism—our nation has at least 10 million proponents of radical illiberalism.[143] That is larger than the number of adult Jews in America, of whom there are about 4.2 million, and larger than the populations of forty-three states and New York City, the nation's largest city.[144]

But why does illiberalism have such a large and engaged audience? Why can it penetrate mainstream American political culture? What are the intellectual origins of this ideology? And what can be done to stop and reverse the rise of illiberalism? The rest of this book will deal with these questions.

4
Identity

The Limits of Interest-Group Politics

Since Madison's defense of the American Constitution in *The Federalist Papers*, liberal democracy has often been conceptualized as a type of polity in which a multiplicity of interest groups—Madison's term is "factions"—compete for power, limit each other's ambitions, and so reduce "instability, injustice, and confusion" to make room for "liberty."[1] Madison argues that with a multitude of factions, "society itself will be broken into so many parts, interests, and classes of citizens, that the rights of individuals, or of the minority, will be in little danger from interested combinations of the majority."[2] Thus "in a free government the security for civil rights must be . . . in the multiplicity of interests."[3] Madison is often understood as the father of the pluralist account of liberal democracy, one that embraces the necessity of, and even celebrates, a plurality of factions or interest groups as the foundation of liberty.

The limitations of pluralist politics are well-known and most tellingly articulated in *The Logic of Collective Action* by Mancur Olson, published in 1965. There is no need to go into the details of Olson's critique here. His point is simply that some potential political factions organize much more easily than others and end up exploiting those others. Small, self-aware interest groups whose individual members have much immediately at stake organize more easily than large groups whose individual members have little at stake and are unaware of their interests. Further, such large, potential interest groups face a free-rider problem, as the costs of political organization are high for their potential members relative to the likely benefits, which accrue to the active and inactive alike. Thus in pluralist liberal democracies, the special interests benefit at the expense of the general interest, and public goods are underproduced.

There are three possible responses to this problem. One response focuses on interests. It seeks to reform the Constitution and the policymaking process in general, to discourage the formation of interest groups, reduce their number, and facilitate collective action. Many schemes for constitutional reform aim not at eliminating factions altogether, but at reducing the role they play in policymaking and weakening interest as a force in politics generally.

A second response focuses on ideas. If all groups knew the stakes involved in a particular public decision and if the demands of special interests could be checked by convincing evidence of the costs they impose on the general interest, then the power of interests could be counterbalanced by the strength of ideas and political action based on a sense of public spiritedness.

This chapter does not develop either of these responses to the collective-action problems of pluralism. They will be discussed in later chapters. The present focus is on a third response, one that involves identity. Madison observed that the dangers of factions could be eliminated "by giving to every citizen the same opinions, the same passions, and the same interests."[4] But he concluded this approach was "impracticable" because as long as people are at liberty to exercise their fallible reason, and have a diversity in their faculties, especially in those for acquiring property, there are "insuperable obstacle[s] to a uniformity of interests."[5]

But what if a uniformity of opinions, passions, interests, and faculties was practicable? Wouldn't the resulting homogeneity of the citizens create a nonpluralistic society with politics rooted not in factions, but in identity? This is precisely the response to the dilemmas of pluralistic politics that proponents of identity politics advance.

Identity as a Response to the Limits of Interest-based Politics

Identity and Unity

Creating a literal uniformity of interests among all citizens is the response of the most radical proponents of what is today called identity politics. But the strategy of overcoming a plurality of interests among the people by fusing them into a unity is old. It can be found in such foundational texts of political theory as Plato's *Republic* and *The Social Contract* by Jean-Jacques Rousseau. In the twenty-first century, this position has been updated and given fairly sophisticated expression by thinkers of the European New Right (ENR), such as Guillaume Faye with his concept of archeofuturism and Alain de Benoist's ethnopluralism. Therefore, the notion of a radical form of identity politics as a solution to the problems of pluralistic interest-group politics needs to be taken seriously and given a response.

Interest-cum-Identity Politics and Identitarian Politics

But before going further, an important distinction must be made. There are, indeed, radical forms of identity politics, such as those mentioned above, that are incompatible with political pluralism and, therefore, with liberal democracy. But there are also much less radical versions of identity politics that are really extensions, rather than repudiations, of political pluralism and, therefore, can be squared with liberal democracy.

Many political phenomena that are loosely called identity politics in fact represent no more than a desire to recognize and politically incorporate new ethnic, racial, sexual, gender, or other types of groups as distinct interests that can function within a liberal democratic political system. These weak forms of identity politics are not at all of the same character as the radical identity politics espoused by the ENR and other extreme forms of rightist nationalism or populism. Everyday forms of feminist, African American, and Latino identity politics—such as those of *Ms.* magazine, Black Lives Matter, and La Raza—are, whatever one finally thinks of them, no more than familiar interest-group politics expressed by relatively new interest groups. If women, African Americans, Latinos, or any other groups want to organize politically to better represent their interests, that amounts to no more than adding a few new interest groups to the already dense swarm that buzz about in American pluralistic politics and, as such, represents no fundamental challenge to liberal democracy, however much it may complicate the public sphere. On the other hand, this nonradical form of identity politics, precisely because it is really no more than a new flavor of interest-group politics, does not fundamentally address the collective-action problems of pluralist politics identified by Olson and others.

Therefore a distinction is in order. The most familiar form of identity politics is really a new extension of interest-group politics and might be called interest-cum-identity politics. The radical form of identity politics of Faye, Benoist, and other ENR thinkers, and of Far-Right nationalism and populism generally, can be called identitarian politics to distinguish it from the less problematic version. Identitarian politics represents an apparent cure to the maladies of pluralist politics, but one that is worse than the disease, as it is incompatible with liberal democracy.

Some observers deny or confuse the distinction between the interest-cum-identity politics of new ethnic and other groups and radical identitarianism. For example, William Voegeli, writing in the *Claremont Review of Books*, asserts that " 'identity politics' . . . is sometimes called 'identitarianism' " and the "claims put forward by identity groups go beyond those made by an interest group or voluntary association." For him identity politics are a form of multiculturalism and "multiculturalism . . . points to supplanting liberal democracy with a new, more radical order" and displays an "antipathy to republicanism—always implicit, now increasingly explicit."[6]

But Voegeli is unconvincing. First, as searches through prominent academic databases show, the terms "identity politics" and "identitarianism" are seldom used synonymously. Identitarianism is usually used pejoratively as, for example, when the prominent literary critic Gayatri Chakravorty Spivak writes: "I think identitarianism ignores what is most interesting about being alive, that is to say, being angled toward the other."[7] The literature that characteristically uses the term "identitarianism" is that of the illiberal right, which embraces the concept. Meanwhile the *Oxford English Dictionary* offers a quite anodyne definition of identity politics as "political positions that are based on the social groups that people see themselves as belonging to, for example, based on religion, race, or social background, rather than on traditional political parties."[8]

Further, in his review of proponents of identity politics, Voegeli cites none who reject liberal democracy or republicanism. The activists and scholars he quotes make a variety of demands but none that are radically beyond what might be expected from a conventional interest group. A gay activist group is cited as saying "Demanding corporate accountability and for wealthy people to pay an equitable share of taxes is LGBTQ2IA justice." Corporate responsibility and taxing the rich are boilerplate demands of a wide range of ordinary interest groups. A more explicitly radical demand cited is that of a trans author who calls for "a society that is radically changed by many kinds of people fighting many kinds of injustice, a society in which economic, social, political, and sexual relationships have been transformed." Certainly this is a sweeping claim but not necessarily more so than those of past union organizers, abolitionists, and progressive reformers whose demands were addressed, not only without undermining but also by positively extending liberal democracy and republicanism. And when one turns to the full essay from which this quote is drawn it turns out that the radical changes being called for hardly reject liberal democracy. The objection is to the fact that "LGBTQ2IA people are directly and disproportionately impacted by police violence, incarceration, unaffordable healthcare, homelessness, deportation, and economic inequality, among other things."[9] Wanting to correct these problems is not a radical rejection of liberal democracy. Admittedly Voegeli touches on an important issue when he criticizes some theorists of identity politics who celebrate marginality for its own sake. But as will be shown later this problem is mostly confined to illiberal identitarians who really do have a problem with liberal democracy. In the end Voegeli himself essentially admits there is a positive form of identity politics that is compatible with liberal democracy when he concludes: "Diversity is a fact, one that does make inclusion an imperative." Interest-cum-identity politics says no more than that, which, of course, is quite a bit.

The rise of interest-cum-identity politics is a result of inevitable shifts in the interests that make up American society. This version of identity politics, therefore, cannot be resisted; indeed, such resistance is likely to be harmful in various ways. But more importantly, garden-variety identity politics need not be resisted, as it simply represents the old wine of pluralism in a new or postmodern bottle and as such is no fundamental challenge to liberal democracy.

Identitarian Politics and Liberal Democracy

However, identitarianism is incompatible with liberal democracy. What makes identitarianism so pernicious is its radical perspectivalist ethics and epistemology. Identitarianism posits that every political group is a homogeneous monad with a culture, an entire worldview, that is alien to and incompatible with the cultures of other political monads. Identitarian monads, it may be said, are windowless. Real communication between different monads is impossible and, therefore, so are negotiation and ordinary politics. Monads interact only by clashing, that is, by making war on one another. At best, open war is suspended when a temporary equilibrium of power is reached, but no real peace is ever achieved. The problems of interest-group formation are "solved" by declaring a permanent state of emergency or war in which all interests except that of the whole must be suppressed, and then driving all other monads out of the political environment completely and with no holds barred.

But to make the charge that identitarianism is incompatible with liberal democracy, it must be proved that 1) the basic units of identitarianism really are windowless monads and real communication between them is impossible, and 2) with no possibility of communication, identitarian monads must wage endless war on each other.

The Windowless Monads of Identitarian Politics

What is meant here by a "monad," and the implications of saying that the basic units of identitarian politics are "windowless monads," must be explained. The terms are borrowed from Gottfried Leibniz, one of the great minds of Western philosophy and codeveloper of calculus with Isaac Newton. According to Leibniz, reality is a collection not of material atoms occupying positions in space and interacting with each other, but of immaterial monads, each of which is a disembodied mind or soul. Being immaterial, monads cannot bounce off of, connect to, or interact with each other in any way at all.

Another way to explain monads is to think back to the undergraduate dorm-room conversations of philosophy majors or anyone given to youthful speculation. "Suppose I am not a physical being at all but only a disembodied mind, dreaming not only that I have a body, but also the whole of reality surrounding that body?" This notion is solipsism: only the thinker's mind exists, and the world is his or her dream. For Leibniz, however, there is not just one solipsistic mind, but an infinite number, each one dreaming a dream that runs parallel to and is congruent with the others, but without the minds directly interacting causally with each other. Leibniz avoids solipsism because he posits there is a grand clock master, God, who has created every mind and programmed them all to dream dreams that reflect each other in every detail, but without any of those minds communicating or interacting with each other at all.

But what has all this to do with politics? The point is to illuminate the differences between interest-group politics and identitarian politics by drawing a very loose analogy between an atomic ontology and the monadology of Leibniz. In interest-group theory, the basic unit of politics is the faction, or a group of people who share an interest, economic or otherwise. In identitarian politics, the basic unit of politics can be likened to a monad, or a group of people who share a common worldview that dominates every facet of their consciousness. In interest-group theory, an individual can have several interests and so, belong to more than one faction simultaneously. Moreover, interest-group theory holds that a particular interest may shape but need not completely dominate one's political thinking. Different factions usually have at least some overlapping interests and can therefore understand and bargain with each other, and be split apart and organized into different coalitions or networks as seems appropriate to different occasions.

Identitarian monads are a quite different type of basic political unit than factions. While factions are made up of individuals, in identitarianism there really are no individuals. This striking implication is made explicit by some identitarian ideologues. Thus Brad Griffin (who usually writes under the pseudonym Hunter Wallace), editor of the American Alt-Right web magazine Occidental Dissent, explains one of the "hallmark characteristics" of that ideology:

> **Identity** . . . The Alt-Right's analysis of history and biology has led us to the conclusion that human beings ARE NOT primarily individuals. On the contrary, we are tribal beings who invariably divide the world into in-groups and out-groups, and those tribes have always been in a primordial struggle for DOMINANCE. . . . The timeless struggle for DOMINANCE between rival groups is why we have POLITICS.[10]

When monadic polities are spoken of here, what is meant is not that each member of the polity is a monad unto him- or herself, dreaming his or her own private dream. There are no individual members of society in identitarianism—or rather, there are such things, but they are unimportant in identitarian political analysis. A monadic polity is an entire community of people all programmed to dream the same dream or dreams that are congruent with each other but not at all with the collective dream of other polities. Thus each monadic people has a unique identity—indeed, a unique reality—that is indiscernible or incomparable with those of other peoples because there is no epistemological congruence or harmony between them.

Further, the members of a monad share not just a single particular interest, but an entire Weltanschauung, or worldview, that pervades the consciousness of each person. In identitarian theory, there is no such thing as an individual who has more than one Weltanschauung in the way that interest-group theory allows an individual to have more than one interest. A Weltanschauung is a worldview that dominates every facet of a person's thinking. There is, therefore, no possibility of an individual balancing or playing off one Weltanschauung against another. Moreover, since each member of a monad shares the same Weltanschauung, and different monads are defined by different Weltanschauungen, there is no way for members of one monad to sympathize with or even understand members of another, or of breaking up and reconstructing monads. In identitarian politics, monads cannot form coalitions or networks. A single monad fills up a given political space entirely, and such a polity is necessarily and completely homogeneous. On the other hand, in interest-group theory, a single polity can contain many heterogeneous factions.

The argument here is that the strains of identitarian thought identified above, although they do not use Leibnizian vocabulary, really do postulate a political environment that can fairly be described as a set of windowless monads entirely separate from each other and incapable of interacting or, at least, of communicating or understanding each other. Of course, this account is meant purely as an illustrative analogy; there is no deep philosophical overlap between Leibniz and twenty-first-century identitarianism. Moreover, even as an illustration, the analogy breaks down on one essential point. In Leibniz, all monads have been created by God, who has programmed every one of them to dream dreams that run parallel to each other and so make for what seems to be causal interaction. Things are as if I am a windowless monad dreaming that I am scratching your back and you are another windowless monad dreaming that your back is being scratched by me, all without us really interacting. This apparent interaction is the preestablished harmony imposed on all monads by God that makes for a coherent, intelligible reality. But, as this chapter shows, for far-rightist identitarians, there is no God to establish harmony among the worldviews of the monadic polities—a position that has striking consequences.

Radical Identitarianism: Faye

Why We Fight, *by Faye*

The most radical account of this identitarian monadology is found in the writings of the French ENR theorist Guillaume Faye. He is a prolific author and journalist whose works have been translated into English and made widely available through Alt-Right sites such as Counter-Currents Publishing, American Renaissance, and similar outlets. In this way, Faye has been a major influence on the thinking of both European and American far rightists, who have adopted much of his radical brand of identitarianism. His work merits attention here because of his importance to the ENR, direct influence on American illiberals, and the detail in which he develops the theory of radical identitarianism.

Perhaps the best introduction to Faye's ideology is *Why We Fight: Manifesto of the European Resistance*, first published in France in 2001 and then in English in 2011 by the Far-Right publisher Arktos Media. The work is particularly useful as a guide to far-rightist ideas, as much of it is devoted to a "Metapolitical Dictionary," which is a glossary of that ideology's key terms. The title of the book's first chapter urges sympathetic readers to "Unite on the Basis of Clear Ideas Against the Common Enemy," and declares, "The time has come for identitarianism, in the broadest sense, to reaffirm itself as the most lucid and ambitious form of thought."[11]

What, then, is identitarianism? Oddly enough, Faye's "Metapolitical Dictionary" provides no definition, lucid or otherwise, of this central term, so one has to be pieced together. "Identity" he defines as follows:

> A people's identity is what makes it incomparable and irreplaceable. . . . But **ethnic and cultural identities form a bloc: maintaining and develop-**

**ing the cultural heritage presupposes a people's ethnic commonal-
ity.** . . . Look: **identity's basis is biological; without it, the realms of
culture and civilisation are unsustainable.** Said differently: a people's
identity, memory, and projects come from a specific hereditary disposi-
tion. . . . The notion of identity obviously refers to **ethnocentrism** and
remains incompatible with "ethnopluralist" cohabitation.[12]

Identity, then, requires a people to be an ethnic and cultural bloc, that
is, ethnocentric. The opposite of ethnocentrism is "Chaos, Ethnic," of
which Faye writes:

An ethnically heterogeneous population—a kaleidoscope of communities—becomes an anonymous society, without soul, without solidarity,
prone to incessant conflicts for domination . . . ungovernable because
there's no shared vision of the world.[13]

Thus in ethnically heterogeneous populations, there is no shared vision
of the world, which results in ungovernability. So the key to governance
and ordinary politics is a shared worldview. Faye's term for worldview is
"conception-of-the-world," which he defines as follows:

The ensemble of values and interpretations of reality—implicitly or explicitly distinct to a specific human group . . . One speaks, almost indiffer-
ently, of a "worldview."
    The conception-of-the-world transcends—goes beyond—political
doctrines, as well as ideologies. . . . A conception-of-the-world comprises
the intellectual and spiritual, rational and intuitive facets. It's different
from culture, in which several conceptions of the world can coexist within
it. A conception-of-the-world implies a political and historical project,
along with a specific view of man's nature.[14]

Faye also provides a definition of "ethnocentrism":

The mobilising conviction, distinct to all long-living peoples, that they
belong to something superior and that they must conserve their ethnic
identity, if they are to endure in history.
    Whether it's "objectively" true or false doesn't matter: ethnocentrism
is the psychological condition necessary to a people's (or nation's) sur-

vival. History is not a field in which intellectually objective principles are worked out, but one conditioned by the will to power, competition, and selection. Scholastic disputes about a people's superiority or inferiority are beside the point. **In the struggle for survival, the feeling of being superior and right is indispensable to acting and succeeding. . . .**

History is above all a field of subjectivity, of struggle between subjectivities.[15]

From the above passages, a definition of identitarianism can be derived. As a theory, it holds that the political world is made up of peoples with incomparable identities. Those identities are ethnically based, or ethnocentric. An ethnocentric people share an all-encompassing worldview or conception of the world. All such conceptions of the world must deeply believe, on pain of paralysis and death, they are superior to all others, whether that belief is objectively true or not. Therefore all peoples that survive encase themselves in the impenetrable sphere of a subjective feeling of their own superiority, which is precisely why they are "incomparable," that is, they share no understanding or ideas that can be compared.

In short, identitarianism as Faye understands it is the theory that the basic unit of politics is an ethnocentric people, each with its own windowless conception of the world rooted in the invincible subjective belief of its own superiority, making objective comparison of these conceptions impossible. The building block of identitarian politics is a people locked in the windowless monad of a subjective belief in its superiority that pervades its entire conception of the world.

Why We Fight: *Faye's Identitarian Politics*

What, then, are Faye's identitarian politics like? That is, how do monadic peoples relate to each other? Faye writes:

Humanity cannot conceive of itself—this will always be the case—except in terms of the organic juxtaposition of its particularisms—and not as a universalism encompassing and overarching (allegedly secondary) particularities.[16]

Particular peoples are juxtaposed—no overlap or interaction between them is suggested—with nothing encompassing or overarching them. Faye thus rejects the possibility that there is any universal force or standard above identitarian peoples to establish harmony among them.

But if identitarian peoples cannot harmonize, doesn't that imply they must clash? Faye's answer seems to be yes. He writes:

> A dynamic, identitarian culture, buttressed by its native biological stock, is essential to the survival of a people or a civilisation. All political movements neglecting cultural struggle, all states rejecting a policy of cultural identity, operate in a void.
>
> Cultural struggle is not restricted to the defence of the patrimony, the maintenance of tradition, or dialogue with the historical memory. . . . We need a counter-offensive. . . .
>
> **Cultural struggle doesn't entail defending all cultures, only European culture, which it assumes is superior to other cultures."**[17]

Thus identitarian peoples engage in cultural struggle with each other, which is essential to their survival. The struggle involves both defense and offense, and the point at issue is who is superior to whom. It seems, then, that these monadic peoples are locked in an all-fronts competition with each other for domination and survival. That impression is confirmed in Faye's definition of "Competition, Struggle for Life":

> The clash of living-forms for supremacy and survival.
>
> Competition, or the struggle for life, constitutes the principal motor force of evolution in everything from bacteria to humans, as well as history. . . .
>
> For an individual or for a people, decay sets in once one starts believing that competition and the struggle for life are "unjust," that enmity toward the Other is "abnormal," that the state of peace is natural and war unnatural, and that the Garden of Eden is possible on Earth. Competition, the struggle for life, is the normal, permanent state of all living things. . . .
>
> There's no use complaining about enemies: we should instead take satisfaction in fighting and eliminating them, knowing that **they will always be with us.** . . .
>
> The enemy is never wrong, if he wins. A "superior people," a "superior

individual," a "superior group" (whether military, economic, religious, etc.) operates not with abstract, ontological principles, but on the basis of the concrete results that come from competition. This is the case for all living things. One is never "intrinsically superior" to others. One is superior only in successfully achieving supremacy.

It's the law of the strongest, the most capable, the most flexible that always dominates. *Vae Victis*, death to the vanquished, such is the law of life; there has never been born a philosopher who could prove otherwise.[18]

The internal logic of Faye's identitarianism leads to an exceedingly dark conclusion: The peoples of the world are locked in an unending war with domination or death being the only possible outcomes. Indeed, Faye himself confirms this will be his conclusion when, early on in *Why We Fight*, he answers the question implicit in his title:

The history of the world is a history of the struggle between peoples and civilisations for survival and domination. It's a battleground of wills to power. . . . The base of everything is biocultural identity and demographic renewal. . . .

Why do we fight? We don't fight for "the cause of peoples," because the identity of every people is its own concern, not ours, and because history is a cemetery of peoples and civilisations. **We fight only for the cause of our own people's destiny.**[19]

In this passage, too, Faye affirms that the peoples of the world are trapped in a life-or-death struggle for power, but here he provides a ferocious addendum: in this battle, each people cares only about its own survival and cares nothing at all about that of other peoples.

Is it possible that monadic peoples can coexist? It's hard to see how this logic, if taken seriously, results in anything short of a warrant for genocide. Can it be that Faye offers humankind no escape from this dour fate?

At one point, Faye tries to back off a bit from this frightening vision. He has written that history is a battle of the wills to power of different peoples for survival and domination. But when he defines "Will to Power," he seems to offer a qualification:

This Nietzschean concept has at times been misunderstood and abusively interpreted as "a tyrannical desire for brutal domination." . . . The will to power by no means implies crushing the weak, but rather protecting them. For it defies only the strong.[20]

The suggestion is that out of prudential considerations, a strong, victorious people will decline to exterminate a weaker people over whom it has achieved domination. Faye writes that "the will to power implies self-mastery and self-discipline. . . . It has to learn not to succumb to the stupor of its own hubris."[21] His point is that a dominant people should not overstretch its power lest it destroy itself through hubris. Thus it might follow that the Athenians should have listened to the Melians and abstained from slaughtering them because, as Thucydides relates, such overreaches of Athens's imperial power led to the Spartan victory in the Peloponnesian War.

But this apparent limit on the will to power of a superior people in fact amounts to no real limit at all. It allows a dominant nation to exercise its power without any check at all and to the fullest extent possible, holding back only when, in its own good judgment, going further would be counterproductive and thus not an exercise of power at all. For all peoples vanquished up to the point where the great nation has reached the outer limits of its power, the law of *vae victis* applies. So the Athenians were, in principle, correct when they told the defeated Melians that "the strong do what they can and the weak suffer what they must,"[22] but the Melians might have had a point when they suggested that destroying their city was imprudent. Before Athens decimated Melos, it considered wiping out Mytilene but was dissuaded from doing so when, during an assembly debate, Diodotus refuted the bloodthirsty arguments of the demagogue Cleon. But, hey, maybe before Melos, Athenian power had not yet reached its limit, so it would have been quite proper to annihilate Mytilene. By Faye's lights, why take chances? To say that the will to power of a dominant people is limited by its own self-discipline is like saying the greed of a burglar is limited by how much swag he thinks he can carry.

These considerations make clear that in Faye's radical brand of identitarianism, there can be no real peace or even coexistence between monadic peoples. Every people is free to strive to dominate others, with no limit to its ambition except its own judgment of what it can get away with.

Every successful aggression against another people is, by definition, right. Death is the just fate imposed on a vanquished people. There is no over-arching force above the peoples of the world and, therefore, no Hobbesian sovereign to put an end to their war of all against all. There is not even the possibility of a sovereign, Hobbesian or otherwise, because humanity thinks only in particularistic terms and cannot even conceive of such a universal standard or force.

In short, radical identitarianism, at least as Faye presents it, turns out to be incompatible not only with liberal democracy, but also with even the slightest bit of international peace. If this is the necessary upshot of identitarianism, that ideology not only offers no solution to the dilemmas of pluralist politics, but needs to be repudiated altogether.

Alain de Benoist: Moderate Identitarianism?

Faye versus Benoist

Faye's *Why We Fight* is an open polemic against a less radical vision of identitarian politics that draws back from the vision of history as the cemetery of peoples. Faye is alluding to this watered-down identitarianism when he rejects "the cause of peoples." The identitarianism with a human face that Faye scorns is "ethnopluralism," developed and most famously articulated by another French writer of the ENR, Alain de Benoist. Like Faye, Benoist is well-known to American illiberals and has been published in and discussed by U.S. Alt-Right outlets such as American Renaissance and Counter-Currents Publishing. Before concluding that identitarian politics leads straight to internecine war between windowless, ethnocentric peoples, we must consider whether Benoist's ethnopluralism somehow avoids that conclusion while remaining recognizably identitarian.

Alain de Benoist is a prolific French intellectual who is usually thought of as a founder of the ENR school of thought that originated in the 1960s. He is the author of more than 100 books and many articles, most of which have not been translated into English. The account of his thought given here is not meant to be comprehensive. For present purposes, Benoist is of interest because part of his project is to develop a moderate identitarianism that, while it rejects pluralism and liberal democracy, avoids the practically genocidal conclusions of radicals like Faye. Indeed, Faye developed his hard-core identitarianism precisely because he thought Benoist was refusing to face up to the ideology's obvious implications to make it palatable to mainstream audiences. The question of concern here is whether Benoist succeeds in developing a political theory that is genuinely identitarian and coherent but does not lead to the murderous conclusions of radical identitarianism. If Benoist is successful, then perhaps there is more to be said for identitarianism than has so far been granted here. But if Benoist either effectively abandons identitarianism or ends up implying the same grim conclusions that Faye and other radicals do, then the case against identitarianism developed here remains strong.

Benoist's Ethnopluralism

In Faye's monadic model of politics a key feature of each people's conception of the world is a conviction of its own superiority and a will to dominate, which makes history a series of life-or-death struggle between windowless, ethnocentric subjectivities, which leads to his practically genocidal conclusions. Benoist thinks this harsh conclusion can be avoided if all peoples resolve to live as isolated monads without interacting and, above all, without judging each other. This is Benoist's theory of ethnopluralism.

In works such as *Beyond Human Rights* and *The Problem of Democracy*, Benoist does not offer a direct definition of ethnopluralism. However, here is one offered in a British Alt-Right publication, Revolution Europea:

> Ethnopluralism is . . . a theory that doesn't subscribe to the lies of the great "melting pot" that the establishment have tried to fool us into believing in. The fundamental principle of this more realistic ideology, is the understanding that humans are not all the same. . . . These differences in turn account to some extent for the great differences in cultures between ethnic groups. . . .
>
> Different ethnic groups, or tribes, or however you want to refer to them, simply cannot coexist peacefully. What is a source of joy for one culture is dishonourable to another, what is acceptable to one is morally repugnant to another—there are simply too many differences.
>
> But, these differences are to be respected as true diversity. All ethnic groups should be allowed to develop their own cultures in their own

homelands, free from interference or negative influences from outside or in. This is the dignity with which we must build the world, a world where Europeans can be Europeans in their own homelands and Africans can be Africans in their homelands. We must say to the foreign ethnic groups in Europe, go home! Return to your homelands, develop them, enjoy them, live in peace and strive for prosperity. We will do the same. . . .

It is through this plurality of separate ethnic development that we will find peace, not through the false ideal that is multiculturalism. We must dismantle the multi-ethnic society that the elites have attempted to build, and forge a new ideal based on identity, communities and dignified celebration of difference.[23]

We can contrast Benoist's ethnopluralism to Faye's radical identitarianism as follows: Faye presents a world of monadic peoples locked in war to the death. Although he does not use the term, it is fair to describe Faye's vision, given its embrace of death to the vanquished, as militaristic. Benoist's ethnopluralism might be termed isolationistic. Benoist also presents an international scene of monadic peoples but thinks war can be avoided if peoples have nothing to do with each other.

But is it really true that there are simply too many differences between peoples for them to interact peacefully? Is it true that what is joy for one people is dishonorable for another and so on for every single issue such that there is no commonality at all between them? If so, then perhaps peaceful isolationism is best since if peoples interact, they will not understand each other, will inevitably judge each other negatively, and will end up at war with each other. But if peoples do share some common understandings about what is right and wrong, just and unjust, then perhaps they can understand each other, can come to shared judgments, and can interact through dialogue and politics rather than through war. Suppose we were to call such a set of shared understandings about how all people should treat each other human rights. Would not a shared understanding of what human rights are make it possible for different peoples to understand each other, engage in politics with each other, and interact peacefully with each other?

Benoist passionately rejects the idea of universal human rights. He writes that "the ideology of human rights . . . is universalistic insofar as it wishes to impose itself everywhere without consideration for relationships, tradition, and contexts," and that by this way of thinking, "Men are everywhere endowed with the same rights because, fundamentally, they are everywhere *the same*. In the final analysis, the ideology of human rights aims at subjecting all of humanity to a particular moral law reha- bilitating the ideology of the Same."[24] Benoist even goes so far as to say human rights facilitate war by making it possible for one people to judge another and therefore to justify hostilities. He concludes, "Theoretically founded on a principle of tolerance, the ideology of human rights thus reveals itself to be the bearer of the most extreme intolerance, of the most absolute rejection. The Declaration of Rights are not so much declara- tions of love as declarations of war."[25]

In the following passage from *Beyond Human Rights*, Benoist expands on his assertion that human rights amount to a rehabilitation of "the ide- ology of the same":

> The abstraction of human rights is what threatens most to render them inoperative. The principal reason for this is *that it is contradictory to affirm, at the same time, the absolute value of the individual and the equality of indi- viduals in the sense of a fundamental identity. If all men are equal, if they are fundamentally the same, if they are all 'men like others,' far from the unique personality of each of them being recognized, they will appear, not as irreplace- able, but on the contrary as interchangeable.* Not being different from each other by their particular qualities, only their more or less great number will make a difference. *Abstract equivalence, in other words, necessarily contra- dicts the proclamation of the absolute individuality of the subjects: no man can be at the same time 'unique' and basically identical to every other.* Inversely, one cannot affirm the unique value of an individual even while considering his personal characteristics as indifferent, that is to say, without specifying what makes him different from the others. A world where all are equal is not a world where 'nothing is worth a life' but a world where life is worth nothing.[26]

None of this has any bearing on the most fundamental of human rights, the right to political equality. The liberal democratic conception of political equality assumes that people may be very different and very unequal in the full range of human characteristics, except one: political status. Therefore, it is nonsense to claim "all men are equal" amounts to "all men are fundamentally the same." Mere common sense tells us that it is entirely possible for different people or things to be equal in some important sense but not at all fundamentally the same. Nadia Comaneci and Muhammad Ali might be said to be equal in the sense of being equally preeminent in their sports. But they were by no means "fundamentally the same." And when Benoist equates being fundamentally the same with being "interchangeable," he is entirely unconvincing. Comaneci and Ali are the same in both being Olympic gold medalists. But no one would conclude that the first person to score a perfect 10 in gymnastics could go fifteen rounds with George Foreman, or that the winner of the Rumble in the Jungle would cut a fine figure on the balance beam.

Benoist seems to think that universal human rights must be based on there being a universal, fundamental human nature so that saying all people have the same human rights requires saying all people have the same fundamental human nature. That seems to be his point when he writes of "the doctrine of human rights, defining rights as attributes inherent in human nature"[27] and that "the ideological bible of human rights stipulates explicitly that the rights of which it speaks are those of man in himself."[28]

There are a number of problems here. First, when Benoist argues that to say people have equal human rights is to say they are "fundamentally the same" or "basically identical," he never explains what he means by "fundamental" or "basic." When it is said that human rights are fundamental or basic, nothing more is necessarily meant than that human rights are extremely important as guides to international and domestic politics. But Benoist seems to think that claiming something is fundamental or basic to humans is to claim there is some kind of deep, ontological identity among them, one so primordial that it obliterates their individuality altogether. But supporters of human rights need say no more than that human rights are fundamental in the sense of being a very big deal indeed.

Further, Benoist's critique of universal human rights extends only to specious claims of universal human rights. It is true that one people may claim that, by some supposedly universal standard, another people has behaved unjustly, and then use that claim as an excuse to make war. But if that claim appeals to a standard that is not universal—not shared by at least both parties to the dispute—then it has no objective standing, is false, and does not justify war. Thus, if one people of a given religion makes war on a people of another religion based on solely theological grounds that its neighbor does not share, then that war is not justified by a universal standard, no matter what the aggressor thinks. On the other hand, if one people appeals to a standard that is shared by another and can demonstrate that its neighbor really has violated that standard, then war may truly be justified by that universal standard. Of course, determining in a given dispute who has behaved justly and who has not, and which side if any may legitimately resort to war, is hard to do, and the party that is found to have behaved unjustly will likely reject that determination. This only proves that adjudicating international disputes is difficult even when a universal standard really exists between the parties. The solution to this problem is to establish international forums in which such disputes can be resolved and whose judgments will be accepted by both sides. The solution is not to declare that universal standards are to be utterly rejected because they may be abused. Benoist's argument reaches only to false or insincere appeals to universal standards, and so it does not represent a critique of universalism at all.

The Failure of Identitarianism

To sum up, Benoist deserves credit for rejecting Faye's overtly militaristic geopolitics. But Benoist's isolationistic ethnopluralism offers no realistic prospect of peace. His denial of universalism, despite his arguments to the contrary, undermines the idea of an objective truth that stands above the ethnocentric worldviews of otherwise monadic peoples, makes communication and bargaining among them impossible, and sets the stage for interminable war. And Benoist naturally ends up opposing liberal democracy as well since human rights are a central component of that form of government. So in both its radical and moderate forms, identitarianism is incompatible with objective truth, human rights, peace, and liberal democracy.

The question now is, how did this illiberal and bellicose ideology develop and achieve a toehold in the international climate of intellectual opinion and American political culture? The political reasons for the rise of illiberal leaders and movements are discussed in chapter 7. This chapter on the penetration of illiberal ideas into American political culture develops an intellectual history that explains how illiberal ideas developed and proved to be useful to right-wing fringe groups when political and technological developments gave them an opportunity to increase their audience.

Intellectual Origins of Twenty-first-century Identitarianism and Illiberalism

Early Philosophies of Science

The story of how we got to our present situation goes as follows. From the beginning of the twentieth century through the early post-war years, the philosophy of science developed by pragmatists and modern positivists stressed that scientific objectivity was possible, but also that human values and politics played a role in the process of scientific inquiry itself. Modern positivists such as Otto Neurath recognized that the essential task of choosing hypotheses is always underdetermined by the facts and, therefore, human values come into play at this step of the scientific process. Deweyan pragmatists approached the problem rather differently. They held that since means and ends interact, scientific means of inquiry can be applied to the choice of ends. Therefore, choices of what ends to pursue—value and political choices—could be objective, and so there was no sharp break between value-neutral scientific means and value-laden moral or political ends. So either by injecting values into the scientific process or by applying the scientific process to the choice of values, the dominant philosophies of science of that time insisted that values—including very broadly understood political values—and science were inseparable. Don Howard's insightful essay "Two Left Turns Make a Right: On the Curious Political Career of North American Philosophy of Science at Midcentury" points out the following:

> When the philosophy of science as we know it today was first established, chiefly in German-speaking Europe in the 1920s and 1930s, many, if not most of its founders were motivated in large part by explicit social and political concerns, the dominant political orientation of those founders lying along a rather narrow spectrum of opinion, somewhere between Enlightenment liberalism and Marxist socialism. The companion movement in North America, at the center of which was the image of science crafted by John Dewey, was characterized by a liberal, social democratic politi-

cal orientation that tended in a direction similar to that of its Viennese contemporaries, even if it found expression in a political vocabulary more attuned to North American habits of thought. For many of these thinkers, the association between one's politics and one's interest in the philosophy of science was not accidental. On the contrary, a specific image of science was often promoted in the service of political ends, and those political ends in turn frequently determined, to some extent, the image of science that one promoted.[29]

What, then, were the political goals that pragmatists and modern positivists saw as the objectively defensible goals of science? It is a commonplace to say that science achieves progress, and philosophers of science of the mid-twentieth century did say this. But they did not only mean that, over time, science piles up more and more discoveries and ideas. Science was progressive in that it enabled people to achieve growth and to live broader, more complex, and less constrained lives.

This account of politics by philosophers of science was osmotically absorbed by other disciplines, trickled down to intellectuals, and finally crystalized as the public idea that scientific and social progress went hand in hand. Few people were concerned that thinking in this way amounted to a dangerous politicization of science in a purely ideological sense. It was in this way that science was both objective and progressive.

Later Developments in the Philosophy of Science

BERTRAND RUSSELL

But philosophers of science who came after the pragmatists, and eventually displaced them as the dominant experts on that subject, drove a wedge between science and values that had important consequences for the climate of intellectual opinion in the mid-twentieth century. Bertrand Russell, for example, was concerned that if human values were integral to the scientific search for truth, then "the concept of 'truth' as something dependent upon facts largely outside human control" would be undermined, and a "necessary element of humility" and "check upon pride" would be removed, thus "increasing the danger of vast social disaster."[30] Therefore, Russell separated values from the scientific process. Science can tell us what means to use to achieve a given end, but it is our values that tell us what ends to pursue. So science is now not necessarily progressive in any social sense. It can be put to bad uses or good uses. Driving values out of the scientific process proper not only deprives science of its progressive credentials, but also raises the question of how to ensure that science is used to good ends. Russell provides a very problematic answer to this question in his 1931 book, *The Scientific Outlook*.

Russell's strategy is "to depict the world which would result if scientific technique were to rule unchecked,"[31] that is, if science were used solely as a means to achieve active reorganization of the social environment. Used in this way, science merely seeks power over the world in the absence of any value judgments about the ends to which that power should be put. This picture of a purely "scientific society" is meant to be so shocking as to send the reader screaming into the arms of the values Russell endorses in the final chapter of his book.

How shocking is Russell's vision of the purely scientific society? So shocking that Aldous Huxley used it as the basis for his seminal dystopian novel *Brave New World*.[32] Many of the elements of Huxley's nightmare of a totalitarian technocracy are drawn from *The Scientific Outlook*, but Russell's account includes a detail that is especially relevant for the present argument. Russell does not use the word, but his scientific society is clearly racist. In that world, he tells us:

> The posts giving most power will presumably be awarded to the ablest men as a result of intelligence tests. For entirely inferior work negros will be employed whenever possible. . . . The society will not be one in which there is equality, although I doubt whether the inequalities will be hereditary except as between different races, i.e. white and coloured labor.[33]

Do not think that Russell is endorsing this horrific scenario, although he describes it with disturbing detachment. His point is to warn of what can happen if science as a powerful means and without any values to direct it toward a positive end is allowed free reign. Science gives power, yet "power is not one of the ends of life, but merely a means to other ends and until men remember the ends that power should subserve, science will not do what it might to minister to the good life." Indeed, without a sense of those ends, science will create the "cruel tyranny"[34] Russell has just frightened us with.

In this account of the relation between scientific means and social ends, Russell is executing a risky rhetorical strategy. He objects to the Deweyan position that scientific methods can be used to determine ends and, in turn, that the achieved ends will be progressive. Russell wants to sharply distinguish between science, which shows us means, and values, which determine ends. But then what ends should people value?

Russell is very reluctant to answer this question. "I do not think one man has the right to legislate for another on this matter."[35] But he stresses that it is absolutely essential to choose some ends or other, because failure to do so produces the cruel tyranny of the purely scientific society. So Russell denies that science is a value-laden enterprise but then, to convince the reader that values are nonetheless vital, terrifies with a picture of the world a value-free science would produce, so that humans will hold on to some values for dear life. But this leaves the reader with no account of how to decide what values to hold, what those values will turn out to be, and how to incorporate them in the process of changing the world through science. Russell has provided a compelling vision of the anti-democratic potential of science but only vague remarks on how to avoid them.

Analytic Philosophy in America

The next step in this process occurred when North American philosophers of science followed up on Russell's suggestions and began to purge their epistemologies of any taint of pragmatism or any methodology suggesting that the scientific process was value laden in any inherent sense.

It was for this image of science as intrinsically promoting some form of progressive political ends that Russell criticized Dewey. Soon other philosophers, especially the philosophers of science who were prominent in that field as it put down roots in American universities, followed Russell's example. Howard's account of "the eclipse of Dewey's vision of a socially engaged and socially responsible science" throughout the 1950s is complex and subtle, and cannot be recapitulated in detail here. But Howard convincingly shows how, during that decade, fears that what Russell and his followers regarded as philosophies of power would undermine the objectivity of truth—and disable it as a check of human hubris—became acute and eventually dominated the philosophy of science. Howard is persuasive when he argues that if philosophers of science were to institutionalize their discipline in American research universities, the need for these philosophers to professionalize themselves encouraged them to move away from discussions of the role of science in modern society and instead focus on technical analyses that only academic experts could follow.

What is of interest for the present discussion is the impact that these developments in the philosophy of science had on the production of public ideas and eventually on the intellectual climate of the early twenty-first century. First, by 1960, philosophers of science had discredited the ideas that science was inherently value laden and that the values with which it was laden were broadly progressive. Second, after having denuded science of its progressive credentials, philosophers of science retreated from the public sphere and allowed the nonexpert publics to draw their own political conclusions. Philosophers of science thus took themselves out of the process of producing public ideas—a move that had striking, unintended consequences.

When experts in the philosophy of science took themselves out of the process of interpreting their work, a broader group of public intellectuals—"secondhand dealers in ideas"—including journalists, people of affairs, and practitioners of other learned disciplines, were left to resolve a number of important issues on their own. If science was not inherently progressive, did it have any political implications at all? Undoubtedly the new generation of philosophers of science would have advised that, indeed, science had no inherent political orientation. Science, they would have said, simply tells how the world in fact is and so can guide people in achieving whatever ends, political or otherwise, they may value, but in itself implies nothing about what those values and ends should be.

Many public intellectuals, however, did not get this message, at least not as academic philosophers might have intended it. To intellectuals, especially those interested in public affairs, if science was not inherently progressive, did not this imply science was inherently conservative? In other words, when academic philosophers stripped science of its progressive credentials, they (however unintentionally) helped label it as conservative.

Mid-Twentieth-Century Philosophies of Science: Thomas Kuhn

Another development in the philosophy of science that had unintended consequences for political theory and the intellectual climate of the early twenty-first century was the publication of *The Structure of Scientific Revolutions* by Thomas Kuhn in 1962. Kuhn's stress on the importance of scientific communities is particularly relevant. Consider the following passage from *Structure*:

> The very existence of science depends upon vesting power to choose between paradigms in the members of a special kind of community. . . . What are the essential characteristics of these communities? . . . The group that shares them may not, however, be drawn at random from society as a whole, but is rather the well-defined community of the scientist's professional compeers. . . . Recognition of the existence of a uniquely competent professional group and acceptance of its role as the exclusive arbitrator of professional achievements has further implications. The group's members, as individuals and by virtue of their shared training and experience, must be seen as sole possessors of the rules of the game or of some equivalent basis for unequivocal judgments. [36]

Here Kuhn is stressing, as the modern positivists generally did not, that science is necessarily a social activity and impossible without a community of scientists, and that the judgments of that community are what pass for truth. Or rather, since Kuhn is skeptical that there is "some one full, objective, true account of nature,"[37] it is the judgment of the community of scientists that determines what developments in their work provide an "increasingly detailed and refined understanding of nature."[38]

Thus, by the mid-sixties the climate of opinion among intellectuals had incorporated two highly consequential public ideas about the nature of science. One was that, rather than being inherently progressive, science would, if pursued for its own sake, result in a totalitarian dystopia. The other was that what passed for scientific knowledge was determined by a "special kind of community." Another step was taken when intellectuals asked, if science is inherently conservative, what does that imply about the social orientation of the special kind of community that practices it?

Some passages of *Structure* that are hardly more than *obiter dicta* hint at what the social orientation of the scientific community might be. Kuhn makes a suggestion about the cultural roots of scientific communities when he writes:

> Only the civilizations that descended from Hellenic Greece have possessed more than the most rudimentary science. The bulk of scientific knowledge is a product of Europe of the last four centuries. No other place and time has supported the very special communities from which scientific productivity comes.[39]

So, scientific communities have their roots in a particular place and time: the modern West. And what is the relationship between these scientific communities and the rest of the society that supports them? Kuhn notes:

> The unparalleled insulation of mature scientific communities from the demands of the laity and of everyday life . . . Just because he is working only for an audience of colleagues, an audience that shares his own values and beliefs, the scientist can take a single set of standards for granted. . . the scientist need not choose problems because they urgently need solution. . . . In this respect, also, the contrast between natural scientists and many social scientists proves instructive. The latter often tend, as the former almost never do, to defend their choice of a research problem—e.g. the effects of racial discrimination or the causes of the business cycle— chiefly in terms of the social importance of achieving a solution.[40]

That is, not only do scientific communities share a set of values, beliefs, and standards that are supported only by Western culture, but also these communities are, by design and necessity, insulated from everyday life and almost never choose research problems based on their social importance. It sounds like scientific communities are Eurocentric and politically aloof, that is to say, conservative. And when Kuhn draws an analogy between scientific communities and a particular type of political community, he makes a very fraught choice:

> Inevitably those remarks will suggest that the member of a mature scientific community is, like the typical character of Orwell's *1984*, the victim

of a history rewritten by the powers that be. Furthermore, that suggestion is not altogether inappropriate. There are losses as well as gains in scientific revolutions, and scientists tend to be peculiarly blind to the former. On the other hand, no explanation of progress through revolutions may stop at this point. To do so would be to imply that in the sciences might makes right, a formulation which would again not be entirely wrong if it did not suppress the nature of the process and the authority by which the choice between paradigms is made.[41]

Of course, Kuhn is not saying that scientific communities establish what counts as scientific knowledge by torturing dissenters. But it is telling that when he searches for a political community that is loosely analogous to scientific communities, the polity he picks is a totalitarian dystopia in which might makes right.

The Dystopian Vision of Scientific Society

In thinking about the political conceptions of science that were prominent by the mid-1960s, it is very striking to note that two of the most influential philosophers of science of the century, Russell and Kuhn, ended up likening the practice of science to the most iconic dystopias in modern literature: *Brave New World* (Russell) and *1984* (Kuhn). This is in very striking contrast to earlier philosophers of science, who typically chose to compare scientific communities with liberal democracies. The entire two volumes of *The Open Society and Its Enemies* by Karl Popper can be thought of as drawing an elaborate parallel between the practices of science and those of democracy. And, of course, the close analogy between science and democracy was one of Dewey's central themes. But by the mid-1960s, the conception of science that was trickling down to public intellectuals was that science was anti-democratic in the sense that it depended on vesting power in an elite, Eurocentric, politically insulated community, and that if this community were given free reign, the result would be a soft, technocratic totalitarianism. This nightmarish vision received its fullest elaboration in Herbert Marcuse's *One-Dimensional Man: Studies in the Ideology of Advanced Industrial Society*, published in 1964. Inevitably a strong reaction to this worrisome characterization of science set in and was picked up by broader publics, as many developments in expert opinion are, and ultimately had an impact on the climate of opinion of the late twentieth century.

The Drive to Democratize the Philosophy of Science

Feminist Standpoint Theory

The pushback against the nearly reactionary description of scientific communities and the societies they build took the form of a search for ways to make those communities more democratic. Among philosophers of science and other academics—especially feminist scholars, whose numbers and presence were growing rapidly from the 1970s through the 1990s—this search went much further than calls for greater inclusion of women and minorities in science, or for science to address pressing social problems such as environmental degradation or issues in women's health. These scholars wanted to democratize not merely the profession of science, but the epistemology of science. In effect, they wanted to renew the progressive credentials of the scientific view of the world, which, since the decline of pragmatism, were no longer in good order. Feminist philosophers in particular had a radical agenda, and not only in the sense that many of them had a leftist political orientation born of their participation in the women's movement. They were also radical in the sense that they wanted to democratize science at its root, in its epistemology, in the whole way science was thought about by philosophers, other scholars, public intellectuals, and society overall.

How, then, did feminist philosophers and others pursue this agenda? The work of Susan Harding is particularly relevant here. Like other feminist philosophers, Harding started off from Kuhn who, she believed, "showed that all of natural science was located within social history."[42] This allowed Harding and other feminists to reclaim the insights of the modern positivists and pragmatists that since science is the work of people rooted in a particular society, the process is necessarily influenced by people's social values. As Harding wrote, "There is enough slack in scientific belief sorting to permit social values and interests fully to permeate these processes and their results."[43]

Kuhn had emphasized that the social values and interests allowed to permeate the scientific process need to be homogeneous throughout the scientific community. He held that "just because he [the scientist] is working only for an audience of colleagues, an audience that shares his own values and beliefs, the scientist can take a single set of standards for granted." But what if having shared values and beliefs, and a single set of standards, were the problem? Feminist philosophers, perhaps picking up on Kuhn's hints that scientific communities were Eurocentric and politically detached, wanted to know whose values, beliefs, and standards would guide the scientific process. Or, as Harding titled her important book published in 1991, *Whose Science? Whose Knowledge?* In that work and elsewhere, Harding argued, in effect, that a deep democratization of science involves democratizing the social values and interests held by members of the community of science:

> Scientific communities that are designed (intentionally or not) to consist only of like-minded individuals lose exactly that economic, political, and cultural diversity that is necessary to enable those who count as peers to detect the dominant culture's values and interests. The main problem here is . . . that the normalizing, routine conceptual practices of power are exactly those that are least likely to be detected by individuals who are trained not to question the social location and priorities of the institutions and conceptual schemes within which their research occurs. . . . Thus the sciences are left complicitous with the projects of the most powerful groups in society.[44]

Harding's project involves more than just bringing individuals from a more diverse range of economic, political, and cultural backgrounds into the scientific community. After all, female, Black, or gay scientists may have essentially the same values and interests as the current scientific community, and accept its routine conceptual practices. Democratizing science requires scientific communities to pay heed to people who are radically outside or marginal to those communities. Doing so is practicing "standpoint epistemologies," as Harding explains:

> Standpoint theories argue that if one wants to detect the values and interests that structure scientific institutions, practices, and conceptual schemes, it is useless to frame one's research questions or to pursue them only within the priorities of these institutions, practices, and conceptual

schemes. One must start from *outside* them to gain a causal, critical view of them. One important way to do so is to start thought from marginal lives.[45]

The development of standpoint theories represents the next step in the intellectual developments that, as we shall see, led to the crystallization of what has been called "postmodern conservativism" and facilitated the rise of illiberal ideologies in the early twenty-first century.

Marginal Lives

It is sometimes alleged that feminism and related postmodern theories want to politicize science in the sense of giving women, minorities, or other "politically correct" special-interest groups the power to set the research agenda for science, to forbid inquiry into issues they think are not in their interest, and to censor findings they find unpalatable. Harding mounts a convincing defense against this charge. She argues that her goal is not to ask women or any other special-interest groups what they want and then to make sure that science delivers what they ask for and not anything else. The values and interests that women or any other outsider group holds may themselves be colored by the assumptions of the dominant culture and so, not be able to provide a position that is outside those assumptions and capable of detecting them and their biases. Thus Harding writes:

> Moreover, to start from marginal lives is not necessarily to take one's problems in the terms in which they are expressed by marginalized people—and this is as true for researchers who come from such groups as for those who do not. . . . The dominant ideology restricts what everyone, including marginalized people, are permitted to see and shapes everyone's consciousness. . . . To start from marginal lives is not to take as incorrigible—as irrefutable grounds for knowledge—what marginal people say or interpretations of their experiences.[46]

So, starting a scientific inquiry from outsider or marginal lives does not necessarily involve the scientist being a member of such groups or uncritically accepting what such people say, think, or want. Harding herself asks, "What does it mean to 'start thought from marginal lives'?" and then answers:

> "Marginal lives" are determinate, objective locations in the social structure. Such locations are not just accidently outside the center of power and prestige, but necessarily so. It is the material and symbolic existence of such oppositional margins that keep the center in place: the rich can only be rich if there are others who are economically exploited; masculinity can only be an ideal if it is continuously contrasted with a devalued other: femininity.[47]

If marginal lives are "determinate, objective locations in the social structure," then starting an inquiry from that standpoint requires not necessarily being one of the people who occupy that location, but imaginatively or intellectually putting one's self in that location and then provisionally accepting, not necessarily how such people do in fact see the world, but how they would or ought to see the world if they were aware of their objective location in the social structure. It is at this point, after considerable effort to avoid sliding into mere "relativism" or "perspectivalism," that standpoint theorists run into problems.

Marginal Lives and the Problem of Dogmatism

The problems begin when one asks what exactly the central injunction "to start from marginal lives" means. C. S. Peirce and the other pragmatists were right to say that all thinking can start from only one point, "namely, the very state of mind in which you actually find yourself at the time you do 'set out' . . . laden with an immense mass of cognition already formed."[48] The call to start from marginal lives is no more useful than those to start from Cartesian doubt or from sense data. One, of necessity, starts where one is. So it is not possible to speak of starting from marginal lives. One has to start from the "immense mass of cognition" one already holds and then, if it seems to be a useful move in some sense, get to the standpoint of marginal lives. Harding, in effect, acknowledges that one cannot fundamentally start from marginal lives when she writes that "a standpoint is an achievement, not an ascription."[49] If a standpoint is an achievement, one must first get to it from some other position that is where one really started. Harding acknowledges this too when she writes: "One has to either live as a member of an oppressed group, or do the necessary work to gain a rich and nuanced understanding of what such life worlds are like, in order to think within that group's standpoint."[50] Harding has also noted that even members of oppressed groups may accept the values and assumptions of the oppressors, so even the oppressed will have to "do the necessary work" to achieve the standpoint of their group.

Standpoint Theory, Feminist and Marxist

At this point, feminist standpoint theory runs into the same problem as an earlier version of that theory. Feminist theorists freely acknowledge that their standpoint epistemologies draw on the efforts of Karl Marx, György Lukacs, and others in the Marxist tradition to develop a "standpoint of the proletariat." Harding observes that "the fundamental interest of mainstream Marxist theory and politics has been the difference created by the relationship between those who own the means of production and those who must sell their labor. Similarly, feminist standpoint theory, like much other feminist theory, has been fundamentally interested in the differences created by relationships between women's and men's lives."[51] Nancy Hartsock, one of the first theorists to write of "the feminist standpoint," acknowledged her debt to Marxist versions of standpoint theory when she described one of her earliest works:

> Following Lukacs's (1971) essay, "Reification and the Standpoint of the Proletariat," I wanted in my article to translate the notion of the proletariat including its privileged historical mission into feminist terms. I was arguing that, like the lives of proletarians in Marxist theory, women's lives in Western capitalist societies also contained possibilities for developing a critique of domination. By examining the institutional sexual division of labor, I argued that a feminist standpoint could be developed that would deepen the critique available from the standpoint of the proletariat and would allow for a critique of patriarchal ideology.[52]

Very much like Lukacs, Harding and standpoint theorists generally take a certain vision of class struggle as a privileged assumption. The claim is that marginal lives exist only because dominate lives have pushed them to the margin. Thus Harding tells us "the rich can only be rich if there are others who are economically exploited; masculinity can only be an ideal if it is continuously contrasted with a devalued other: femininity." Perhaps so, but just as there can be—whatever one thinks of them—ways of understanding poverty other than attributing it to economic exploitation, and ways of holding masculinity as "an" ideal (not "the" ideal) that do not necessarily devalue femininity, so, too, there are ways of understanding social development that do not focus on class struggle. And what might be a way of understanding social development that does not ground itself in class struggle? In a telling comment, Harding identifies a particularly significant alternative to class-struggle understandings:

> Standpoint theories, in contrast to empiricist epistemologies, begin from the recognition of social inequality; their models of society are conflict models, *in contrast to the consensus model of liberal political philosophy* assumed by empiricists.[53]

Thus when standpoint theories prioritize conflict models at the expense of consensus models, they do so to the detriment of liberal political philosophy. Or put another way, standpoint theories involve privileging nonliberal political philosophy. Of course, the nonliberal political philosophies that Harding has in mind are Marxism, radical feminism, and other leftist schools of thought. But this move would open the door to unforeseen and unfortunate consequences for public ideas and the climate of opinion in the early twenty-first century.

The Inversion Thesis

Lukacs and Harding both have answers as to why the standpoints of the proletariat and women, respectively, should be privileged. This discussion will not go into the deficiencies of Lukacs's answer[54] and only focus on the problems of feminist standpoint theory.

Harding's most powerful argument for the epistemologically privileged status of the standpoint of marginal lives begins with the claim that unless one examines the assumptions built into one standpoint—say, that of men—by at least provisionally accepting the assumptions of another standpoint—say, that of women—the assumptions of the politically dominant class will never be challenged or even detected. Harding further argues that the standpoints of marginal groups provide the most distance from the standpoints of dominant groups and thus are most useful in exposing latent biases. She writes:

> To start thought from marginal lives is scientifically and epistemologically preferable for all the reasons historians and social scientists value "stranger," "underclass," and "loser" perspectives on history and social life. What we do enables and limits the kinds of things we can know about ourselves and the world, and if one starts from the activities of those who are necessarily disadvantaged in a particular kind of social order one can come to understand objectively existing features of it that are much harder to detect when one starts from the activities of those who benefit most.[55]

So then, stranger, underclass, or loser perspectives get a preference relative to mainstream perspectives. This upshot of standpoint theory has been termed the "inversion thesis": "the thesis that certain kinds of epistemic advantage accrue to those who are otherwise (socially, materially) disadvantaged, in this case by systemic gender as well as class differences."[56] This thesis will turn out to have unforeseen and fateful consequences.

"The Nazi Problem"

Those consequences became clearer in the early twenty-first century. A 2011 article by Dan Hicks reviews feminist epistemologies and focuses on the work of Helen Longino, who, like other standpoint theorists, argued that strong objectivity is not possible until outsider groups are given a chance to provide alternatives to the assumptions of the dominant community. He quotes Longino as writing, "a community . . . must also take active steps to ensure that alternative points of view are developed enough to be a source of criticism and new perspectives. Not only must potentially dissenting voices not be discounted; they must be cultivated." Hicks does not use the phrase, but here and elsewhere Longino is advancing a version of the inversion thesis. Hicks then makes a key point: Longino's account of objectivity requires the active cultivation of historically excluded and marginalized groups.

However, this applies *mutatis mutandis* to views antithetical to those of feminists and other progressives and leftists: the exclusion of groups who hold misogynist and racist beliefs means certain feminist and anti-racist beliefs will be shared by all (or almost all) members of the community, and hence these beliefs cannot be subject to the critical scrutiny that objectivity requires; to prevent this, active steps must be taken to include members of these misogynist and racist groups. If Longino's account of objectivity requires the active cultivation of women and members of certain racial minorities in the scientific community, it also requires the active cultivation of misogynists and racists.[57]

Hicks explains why he calls this unwanted implication of standpoint theory "the Nazi problem":

> The arguments for the active cultivation of historically marginalized groups apply quite clearly to the . . . Nazi scientist. Without him and like-minded scientists, such background assumptions as the equality of sexes and races would acquire an invisibility that would render them unavailable for criticism. Hence, the community must take active steps to ensure that alternative, Nazi points of view are developed enough to be a source of criticism and new perspectives. Not only must potentially dissenting Nazi voices not be discounted; they must be cultivated.[58]

Hicks's formulation of his critique as "the Nazi problem" is unfortunate. It is very seldom useful to compare anything to the Nazis. Yet upon examination, Hicks's problem turns out to be more than just a mere "gotcha" thrust, for what if the standpoint of the dominant group incorporates liberal democratic values and assumptions? Harding implies this is the case when she writes that "paternal liberal political theory is challenged by feminist epistemology."[59] Feminist epistemology starts from marginal standpoints and challenges dominant standpoints. Therefore if feminist epistemology challenges liberal political theory, that theory must be part of the dominant standpoint that needs challenging. Further, Harding admits that democratic values and interests incorporated into a dominant standpoint must be challenged along with reactionary ones. She writes that "standpoint epistemology expands the competence of scientific methods so that researchers can detect the values and interests shared over entire social communities or even generations of them—androcentrism,

Eurocentrism, race or class values and interests, as well as prodemocratic ones."[60] Once it is admitted that the dominant standpoint incorporates liberal democratic values and assumptions, and then urged that marginalized standpoints are privileged in that they provide a necessary critical distance from the dominant standpoint, it would seem to follow that marginal illiberal and anti-democratic communities enjoy a certain epistemic advantage over liberal democratic establishments. Therefore Hicks, despite his unfortunate formulation, has identified a significant problem in standpoint theory.

To a considerable extent, feminism can be thought of as simply saying that the standpoint of women merits, but so far has not yet received, as much consideration as that of men or anyone else. "Feminist empiricism" is the term generally used to denote this idea. The problems begin when one considers whether some standpoints are somehow better than others, or "epistemologically preferable" or "privileged" as the feminist theorists say. One is tempted to respond, no: all one can do is incorporate into the community as many standpoints as seems useful without making any assumptions about which will turn out to be "better" than the others. But this answer is apparently unsatisfying, for what if there are an infinity of possible standpoints? How will one know which to incorporate and how many are enough? Feminist standpoint theory seems to offer an answer: Start with marginal standpoints because they offer the most critical distance from status quo standpoints. This is the inversion thesis, and it is with this plausible idea that feminist standpoint theory opens a can of worms.

Thus practitioners of standpoint methodologies would have to admit that thinkers working from "alien and possibly repugnant"[61] standpoints may deserve as much of a hearing as anyone else—and that it is precisely because some standpoints assume alien and repugnant values that they should be privileged over others.

An episode from art history illustrates this dilemma of standpoint theory. In 1924 the French poet Andre Bréton published the first Surrealist Manifesto, which defined surrealism as "psychic automatism in its pure state . . . dictated by the thought, in the absence of any control exercised by reason, exempt from any aesthetic or moral concern."[62] The problem with this position became apparent in the mid-1930s when Salvador Dali produced paintings such as *The Enigma of Hitler*, which showed "a dangerous fascination—even admiration"[63] for fascism. Bréton woke up and smelled the coffee. He "called a Surrealist tribunal on 5 February 1934 to condemn Dali for his fascist tendencies."[64] Apparently there were some moral concerns beyond which even surrealists were not supposed to go. Similarly, the Nazi problem should remind everyone involved in the useful effort to democratize the practice of science and the development of social knowledge that some marginal perspectives ought not to be cultivated.

As the inversion thesis began to spread through academia and then was reshaped by intellectuals into public ideas suitable for dissemination to broader audiences, some thinkers—who were not necessarily familiar firsthand or at all with the feminist literature—became aware of an opportunity. A new rhetorical strategy was now available to intellectual circles that had long been outside the mainstream of public discourse. If marginal or outsider standpoints enjoy an epistemic advantage, are to be privileged and cultivated, why not rush to the margins, declare oneself an outsider, enjoy that privilege, and get the hearing that one had for so long been denied? This was exactly the strategy that was deployed with considerable success by the American Alt-Right and other illiberal ideologies.

Illiberal Expropriation of the Inversion Thesis

Antonio Gramsci, Subalternity, and Metapolitics

This is not to say that the Alt-Rightists who twisted the inversion thesis to their own unlovely ends were familiar with or consciously applying the work of the feminist theorists who developed the original concept. Feminist standpoint theory comes up hardly at all in Alt-Right writings. But related schools of thought that also developed versions of the inversion thesis—especially post-modernism, multiculturalism, Critical Theory, and Gramscian Marxism—are mentioned often. One particularly striking example of Alt-Right appropriation of the inversion theory was published in 2013 by Counter-Currents Publishing, one of the most philosophically oriented and radical outlets of the movement. In the article " 'We Are the Real Subalterns,' " Mark Dyal discussed his conversations with members of the Italian neofascist organization CasaPound:

> "We are the real subalterns," I was once told by an activist at Casa-
> Pound. . . .
> A subaltern is someone who exists outside the normalized represen-

tational structures of society. He, she, or it, does not conform to the hegemony of the cultural norms of the state, living outside the universe of the state's moral obligation. The Left has normalized an understanding of the immigrant, racial/sexual minority, or colonial subject as the subaltern, and seeks to give voice to these voiceless souls through a well-developed language of guilt, evil, economic under-development, and outright racism. . . .

The lessons CasaPound offers the North American New Right are clear: become revolutionary. Become something that cannot be codified by the liberal state. Become something so active, so affirmative, and so different, that liberal sensibility is deterritorialized, never to capture our minds and bodies again. Become not only subaltern but also an enemy of the state.[65]

The term "subaltern" has two important references. One is in regard to Subaltern Studies, a school of sociopolitical analysis that was usually applied to Indian and Asian history, and that critiqued modern capitalist development from the point of view of marginal classes such as the peasantry, the lower castes, the extremely poor, rebel movements, and others. But the original source of the term is Antonio Gramsci. "Subaltern" was the code word he substituted for "proletarian" in his prison writings to disguise the Marxist nature of his work from his guards. In a vein similar to that of Lukacs, Gramsci argued that the standpoint of the subaltern, being outside of the dominant standpoint of the bourgeois, had a critical distance from the hegemonic culture and values of capitalist society. Or rather, Gramsci said the subalterns could develop such a counterhegemonic standpoint if they took advantage of their marginal status and developed their own "organic intellectuals" who would construct a revolutionary cultural outlook to challenge the dominance of the bourgeois. Gramsci believed that the revolutionary potential inherent in the economically exploited position of the subalterns would never come to fruition unless a set of intellectuals arose organically within that class and developed a revolutionary cultural consciousness that truly reflected their class position. Just as Harding and other theorists held that a feminist standpoint was an achievement, not an ascription, Gramsci believed that a counterhegemonic revolutionary culture was not at hand in whatever actual subalterns happened to think or feel, but had to be thought through and built up by subaltern intellectuals. Thus Gramscian Marxism, like feminist standpoint theory, deploys the inversion thesis: a marginal (subaltern) point of view, precisely because it is outside the dominant hegemonic point of view, is given a privileged epistemological status, making possible an understanding of the world that is hidden from status quo groups who cannot see their own biases and distortions.

While feminist standpoint theory is rarely mentioned in Alt-Right and other illiberal circles, Gramsci is invoked often. Thus Roman Bernard, a French New Right author who worked as a fundraiser and writer for Richard Spencer's Alt-Right web magazine, *Radix Journal*, correctly notes that "in the New Right in continental Europe and the Alternative Right in the Anglosphere, there has been much talk on 'right-wing Gramscism,' i.e. the need to first wage the metapolitical battle before winning the political war."[66] "Metapolitics" is a key term for both the ENR and the American Alt-Right. It refers to the strategy of developing a set of ideas among an intellectual elite that are slowly disseminated throughout the political culture and pave the way for more concrete political victories in the future. As I documented in my earlier book *The Rise of the Alt-Right*, representatives of that movement frequently declare their main political strategy is that of metapolitics—that is, changing political culture by dissemination of new ideas. But since Alt-Right metapolitics is rooted in Gramsci's articulation of the inversion thesis, metapolitics involves much more than simply communicating new ideas. Alt-Right metapolitics involves "starting from marginal lives." But the marginal lives Alt-Rightists and other illiberals have in mind are those of alienated, white, illiberal young men who regard themselves as outcasts from the American liberal democratic order.

Inverted Rhetoric

However, any intellectual current that makes use of the inversion thesis is basing its validity on its marginal status and therefore has to answer the question, how do you know you are marginal? The inversion thesis admits that the thinking or culture of any given, actual marginal group may, in fact, not have freed itself from the intellectual hegemony of the dominant group. Therefore, a thinker or analyst cannot demonstrate marginality just by noting that most workers (or women or whomever) agree with him or her. The problem is especially acute for illiberals, who are usually white, male, middle class, and right wing, and thus do not belong to any of the social groups that are typically thought of as being marginal. How, then, do the illiberal ideologues of the early twenty-first century manage to certify their marginal status and make a claim to epistemological privilege under the inversion thesis? Their answer is quite simple. Here are some expressions of it found in various Alt-Right outlets:

> If you feel angry and disenfranchised, good! You rage will be instrument [sic] of our salvation. . . . There are millions of Whites who are just as fed up and tired of a country where we, the architects of this nation, are marginalized and discounted. . . . We need merely to reawaken, because when we do, we will take the world by storm.[67]

> Rejectionism is . . . suitable for what Antonio Gramsci called a war of position, in which the ruling elite has basic popular legitimacy and we are far removed from any positions of power that would allow us to carry on an open struggle against it. In such circumstances . . . we should lead with a negative critique of the ruling elite and try to push most of our people into a state of radical disillusionment.
>
> Leading with negative attacks on the elite (i.e., before trying to convert our people to positive alternatives) widens the impact of our efforts, as more people can be converted to these positions.[68]

> We no longer accept the left's authority to decide who is and isn't a good person. . . . Want to win? Stop caring what they call you and start opposing them at every turn. . . .
>
> The alt-right is a safe space for crimethink. I recognize certain groups are double plus ungood, but as someone who's already at least ungood plus, I don't see any value in signaling that they're too extreme and hateful for me. The purpose of purges is to maintain respectability. . . . To be a safe space for crimethink, it means no purges. . . . The fact is, speaking within the left's moral framework has failed, so we're going to hang out down here in the pits with the rabble where we can speak freely.[69]

> We must move away from the judgementalism of the "political spectrum" towards a concept based purely on the facts of hegemony and marginalization, namely that of *center* and *periphery*. . . .

Let us imagine the "political terrain" as a fertile and well-cultivated expanse of land. . . . In the centre of the lands within the wall stands a ruling **Citadel**; on these inner lands from the Citadel to the wall subsist the teeming masses of the **People**; and on the marginal outlands beyond the wall there are various tribes of **Barbarians**. . . .

Given that a frontal attack through the voting system is still not possible in most of the West *the model for political action should be the Barbarian raid*: cheap, easy, negative attacks, which spread doubt about the Citadel and Tame Barbarians in the popular mind while winning notoriety for us. . . . *The main thing is to hammer the anti-Citadel message into the People's minds, a task in which repetition trumps finesse.*[70]

In a society that considers all genuine *ideas* to be subversive . . . the main goal must be to awaken people's consciences, raising traumatising problems and sending ideological electroshocks: *shocking ideas.* . . . Some people may regard many of my suggestions as *ideologically delinquent* in the context of the ruling ideology and pseudo-virginal chorus of the self-righteous. Well, they are.[71]

[C]ollege was an ideological training camp. . . . I saw the structural realities of power underneath every dialogue, every class, every student organization. I saw how the personal is political.

But more than that I saw they had it precisely backwards. *They* were the system. *They* were the structural inequality. Using what they taught me, I deconstructed the deconstructionists. I saw what a fighting politics could be: Left-wing techniques and social analysis mobilized for Right-wing ends.[72]

To summarize, the strategy developed by the Alt-Right and other illiberal ideological movements for establishing the bona fides of their marginal status and lay claim to epistemic privilege is to loudly declare their political adversaries are an oppressive status quo and then hurl abuse at them in the most offensive terms possible. The mainstream or status quo then responds with shock and rejection, thus pushing the illiberals to the margin, which is exactly where they think they need to be to claim epistemological privilege.

For Aristotle rhetoric was the best use of "the available means of persuasion." But the illiberal rhetorical style *deliberately does not seek to per-*

suade. It seeks to shock, outrage, attack, raid, hammer, disillusion, and, as we shall see, provoke to tears. Illiberals seek not to persuade, but, the very opposite, to alienate. This is not rhetoric but inverted rhetoric.

This strategy turned out to be more effective than one might think. Illiberals' abuse of the inversion thesis validated their position in their own eyes and, indeed, set up a self-reinforcing epistemic feedback loop. Illiberals, in effect, reasoned to themselves: the more shocking our ideas are, the more disgust and rejection they elicit from the mainstream, the more marginal our position must be, the greater our epistemic advantage must be, and therefore the more true what we have to say is. So, even if the illiberal abuse of the inversion thesis did not win many converts from the left, it steeled the spine of far-rightists and told them that the more disgust they provoked, the more correct they must be. In short, the Illiberal Right came to believe that even if it accepted the main premises of its adversaries' thought—indeed, precisely because it accepted its adversaries' premises—and offended everyone it communicated with, it must be right. Thus the premise that the illiberals felt they were now justified in using can be summed up as "immoderation is a virtue."

Resources for Justifying Immoderation

Obviously, this problematic conclusion does not necessarily follow from the iterations of the inversion thesis that were developed by feminist standpoint theorists. But other versions of left-oriented oppositional thought were less cautious and offered the illiberal celebration of immoderation some colorability. The Alt-Rightists who declare "we're going to hang out down here in the pits with the rabble" sound rather like Marcuse, who saw considerable revolutionary potential in groups related to the *lumpenproletariat* and in "a spread not only of discontent and mental sickness, but also of inefficiency, resistance to work, refusal to perform, negligence, indifference."[73] Postmodern thinkers generally put great store in the inversion thesis and can be incautious in doing so. Seyla Benhabib correctly notes, "If there is one commitment which unites postmodernists from Foucault to Derrida to Lyotard it is this critique of Western rationality as seen from the perspective of the margins, from the standpoint of what and whom it excludes, suppresses, delegitimizes, renders mad, imbecilic, or childish."[74] If Western rationality—and the liberal democratic world it helped create—can be usefully critiqued from the standpoints of the mad, the imbecilic, or the childish, why shouldn't critiques from the standpoints of the barbarians, the rabble, and the delinquents also have some legitimacy? Why can't the right-wing margins—the perspectives of the trolls and shitlords—also provide a standpoint for effective criticism?

Postmodern deployment of the inversion thesis raised these questions without seeing the bad use to which they could be put. Very presciently, Benhabib found

> baffling . . . the lightheartedness with which postmodernists simply assume or even posit those hyper-universalist, and superliberal values of diversity, heterogeneity, eccentricity and otherness. In doing so they rely on the very norms of the autonomy of subjects and the rationality of democratic procedures which otherwise they seem to so blithely dismiss. . . . As sons of the French revolution they have enjoyed the privileges of the modern to the point of growing blasé vis a vis them.[75]

In this way, Marcusean sympathy for the moral viewpoint of the *lumpenproletariat* and postmodern appreciation for the mad, imbecilic, and childish, combined with an insufficient appreciation for the liberal democratic heritage, gave the denizens of the right-wing margins an excuse to legitimize their own form of immoderation.

"Politics Is War"

There was another key premise that the immoderate right now felt it had justified. As mentioned above, any intellectual current that makes use of the inversion thesis must answer the question, how do you know you are marginal? Again, the inversion thesis admits that any given, actual marginal group may not have freed itself from the intellectual hegemony of the dominant group. Therefore, a thinker or analyst cannot demonstrate marginality just by noting that most workers, women, or whomever agree with him or her. Of course, Marxists and feminists could point to a good deal of scholarly work that documents the marginal status of the proletariat and women. But there are many variations on these schools of thought, some of which deny that others are the genuine article. And anyone can pick up a particular label. Therefore, any school of thought that invokes the inversion thesis has to provide some objective standard beside its practitioners' mere say-so to document that its thinking really does come from the margins.

Feminist standpoint theorists have no good answer to this question, which turns out to be a strength because, as we shall see, the most obvious solutions are not pretty. Lukacs, in explaining how to determine which ideas truly stem from the standpoint of the proletariat, gets right to the point:

> Lenin was the first and for a long time the only important leader and theoretician who tackled this problem at its theoretical roots and therefore at its decisive, practical point: *that of organization.* . . . The party, as the strictly centralized organization of the proletariat's most conscious elements—and only as such—*is conceived as an instrument of class struggle in a revolutionary period.*[76]

In other words (and to cite the title of the book chapter from which the above quote is taken), "The Vanguard Party of the Proletariat" determines what the standpoint of that class really is and which ideas genuinely begin from it. This answer is both highly illuminating and practically useless. That Lukacs's iteration of standpoint theory leads straight to Leninist democratic centralism is clarifying but only puts off the key question, because it does not reveal how to know when the party's thought really does derive from the standpoint of the proletariat.

How, then, was one to know when the vanguard party represents the standpoint of the proletariat and when they did not? Lukacs answers this question as follows:

> But does not the danger then exist that these "professional revolutionaries" will divorce themselves from their actual class environment and, by thus separating themselves, degenerate into a sect?. . . This . . . misses the core of Lenin's concept of party organization simply because . . . *Lenin's concept of party organization presupposes the fact—the actuality—of the revolution.*[77]

That is, the party cannot be separate from the consciousness of the proletariat because the party is presupposed to be an instrument of revolutionary class struggle, or actually engaged in revolution. If the party is not an instrument of actual revolution, then it has left the validating standpoint of the proletariat and is not a party at all. Thus, when the party is actively engaged in a revolution, it embodies subaltern consciousness; otherwise, it does not. Marxist versions of standpoint theory, in effect, weaponize Deweyan instrumentalism: ideas are true not when they are useful tools in remaking the environment, but when they are effective weapons in a war on hegemonic forces.

Since there is no independent standard for determining which ideas are effective weapons in a revolutionary war, this test cannot serve as a decisive measure of political legitimacy, but it does have clear implications for political rhetoric. One should expect that any marginal group wanting to validate its status as such will loudly proclaim that it is at war with the status quo. More importantly, a group that wants to invoke the inversion thesis to convince itself of the rightness of its ideas will think of itself, and present itself to others, as being at war with the status quo and at war with liberal democracy, if that is the nature of the status quo. In short, movements at the right-wing margins of a liberal democracy can justify their thinking—at least to themselves—if they accept the premise that politics is war. And this maxim is, in fact, often invoked, not only by the Alt-Right and similar illiberal movements, but also by less radical rightists, including the Alt-Lite, Breitbart, Fox News, advocates of Donald Trump, and right-wing populists generally.

Gamergate and the Crystallization of Illiberal Rhetorical Strategies

One of the purest examples of rightist rhetoric based on these two principles—immoderation is a virtue, and politics is war—is Vox Day's book *SJWs Always Lie: Taking Down the Thought Police.* Vox Day is a science fiction writer and video game reviewer. He was a central figure in the #GamerGate affair, which was a heated controversy about sexism in the communities of science fiction followers and the video game industry. Day loudly and intemperately defended himself and others charged with sexism, which led the *Wall Street Journal* to designate him "the most despised man in science fiction," a title proudly displayed on the cover of his book. Milo Yiannopoulos, an Alt-Right provocateur who disseminated the same school of thought on the popular right-wing outlet Breitbart News, provided a forward to Day's book. One might think that such a dustup at the margins of American popular culture would have no relevance to an account of recent intellectual history. But in fact, #GamerGate is frequently considered to be one of the formative events in the development of the American Alt-Right. According to one analyst of the Alt-Right, "Gamergate showed that an army of anonymous activists and trolls can have a substantial and lasting impact on real-world organizations. . . . The method of persistent, coordinated trolling has since been embraced by the Alt-Right and helped it break into the mainstream discussion."[78] Andrew Anglin, editor of perhaps the most radical and obnoxious Alt-Right outlet, the Daily Stormer, believes "the Gamergate provided a direct entry-point to what is now called the Alt-Right, as it was made-up of young White men who realized they were being disenfranchised by feminism and political correctness when aggressive SJWs began invading their space and making demands of them."[79] The "SJW," which stands for "social justice warrior," is what #GamerGaters called their critics. Day's book provides a detailed account of the rhetorical tactics he and other proto Alt-Rightists deployed against their detested adversaries, and so exemplifies the thought patterns and style of argumentation that soon spread through the American Illiberal Right in general.

Day explains his central point as follows:

> The basic idea is that if you can make the other person feel small or angry, you are winning at SJW rhetoric. . . . It doesn't matter what you actually say, and in fact, resorting to straight-up name-calling, the more ridiculous the better, is often the fastest and most efficient way to get through the conversational process with an SJW. . . . You know your rhetoric is effective when they block you online, or in person if their eyes widen with shock and their jaw drops. You will know you have mastered the art of rhetoric if you can make an SJW retreat in tears or cause a room full of people to gasp in disbelief before bursting out laughing at the SJW.[80]

Day's basic idea turns out to be the first premise the Illiberal Right pulled out of the inversion thesis: immoderation is a virtue. "Straight-up name-calling, the more ridiculous the better," is recommended as the best way to converse. What better way to immediately demonstrate that you have been marginalized, and so can claim epistemological privilege, than by causing "a room full of people to gasp in disbelief" at what you have just said?

But if you persistently marginalize yourself by offending everyone, won't you end up simply ostracized? Yes, but not to worry, for Day advises:

Accept your fate.

It is psychologically much easier to survive an SJW attack if you accept early on in the process that you are probably going to lose your job or be purged from your church, your social group, or your professional organization. . . .

This does not mean that you should despair or give up. Quite the contrary! It's only that you will be able to defend yourself much more effectively if you are not overly worried about the outcome. Ideally, you want to maintain the stoic state known as "Zero Fucks Given," or to put it in less vulgar terms, a state of total indifference as to the consequences.[81]

This passage marks an extraordinary turn in the conception of common sense in American political culture. From one end of the political spectrum, the progressive Dewey famously counseled his readers to "follow the pragmatic rule and in order to discover the meaning of the idea ask for its consequences."[82] At the other end, the central premise of the conservative Richard Weaver was (as one of his books is titled) *Ideas Have Consequences* and are to be judged by those consequences. But the rhetorical strategy of Alt-Rightism calls for "total indifference as to the consequences" of what one says. If this principle is taken seriously, how can anyone judge if what they are saying has any meaning at all?[83] Won't everyone, in the end, simply drift into meaninglessness?

But then, meaning turns out to be unimportant in the Alt-Rightist form of expression. Day tells us when dealing with SJWs:

Don't try to reason with them. . . .

There is no way you are going to be able to reason your way out of the situation. Most people who come under SJW attack have the causality backwards. They think the attack is taking place due to whatever it is that they did or said. That's not the case. The attack is taking place because of who you are and what you represent to the SJWs: a threat to their Narrative. . . .

The most important thing to accept here is the complete impossibility of compromise or even meaningful communication with your attackers. SJWs do not engage in rational debate because they are not rational and they do not engage in honest discourse because they do not believe in objective truth.[84]

"Meaningful communication" with SJWs is a "complete impossibility." They are not interlocutors at all, but "attackers." And why are they attacking? Not because of what you said, but "because of who you are." They are locked in their own "narrative," which you threaten precisely because you are who you are.

This passage represents a retreat into a radically monadic identitarianism with a vengeance. Simply because the others are who they are, they have their own narrative. I claim to base my own thought on "objective truth," but doubtless from the point of view of the others my group merely has its own narrative. There is no hope of settling whose claim to objective truth is correct, because no communication is possible. The result is two separate groups, each trapped in its own windowless narrative. With the possibility of rational debate and compromise foreclosed, the groups can interact in one way only: attack. In this way, Day ends up with the premise that politics is war or, perhaps more exactly, politics is impossible and so war is inevitable.

Day does not use the term identitarianism, but his account of discourse leads him to the same general vision that Faye's version of that ideology paints. Groups locked in windowless monads are fated to attack each other. To his credit, Day does not draw the dismal conclusions that Faye does. Faye's groups are racially defined peoples; Day's groups are ideologically based. Faye concludes that, more likely than not, monadic peoples will engage with each other in war to extermination. Day's ideological groups only hurl abuse and seek to drive each other to tears or unemployment.

Illiberalism Lite

The Illiberal Right's bad use of the inversion thesis comes in a spectrum of intensities. Radical identitarianism represents the genocidal hard core. Ethnopluralism offers an isolationistic version. Alt-Right and Alt-Lite outlets range between those two points. Day retains the irrationalist epistemology but drops the explicit racialism and presents a world not of endless war, but constant verbal abuse. Fox News commentators and similar pundits do not articulate the implications of identitarianism that are unsuitable for broadcast and stick to dishing out shrill polemics.

Two notable practitioners of such lite illiberal rhetoric are Ann Coulter and David Horowitz. In a 2004 book, tellingly entitled *How to Talk to a Liberal (If You Must)*, Coulter offers a set of simple rules on how to argue with a liberal, including her own formulation of the principle that immoderation is a virtue:

> You must outrage the enemy. If the liberal you're arguing with doesn't become speechless with sputtering, impotent rage, you're not doing it right.... If you are not being called outrageous by liberals you're not being outrageous enough. Start with the maximum assertion about liberals and then push the envelope, because, as we know, their evil is incalculable.... Nothing too extreme can be said about liberals, because it's all true.[85]

Here the whole point is to be as outrageous, extreme, outside the envelope—in short, as marginal—as possible.

Horowitz emphasizes the other premise illiberals derive from their misuse of the inversion thesis, that is, politics is war. Horowitz insists on this point in a 1999 handbook distributed to Republican candidates, *The Art of Political War: How Republicans Can Fight to Win*, which was incorporated in its entirety into his 2014 book, *Take No Prisoners: The Battle Plan for Defeating the Left*. In both publications, he presents "The Six Principles of Political Warfare," the first two of which are as follows:

1. Politics is war conducted by other means.
2. Politics is a war of position.[86]

Horowitz's first principle is a clear statement of the "politics is war" premise. His second principle suggests that he derives his conception of political warfare from Gramscian political theory. Gramsci frequently analogized his revolutionary strategy of developing a subaltern culture to challenge the hegemony of bourgeois culture to a war of position in which entrenched enemy camps besiege each other over the long term. Horowitz advises Republicans to recast themselves as "underdogs" and make their war against the dominant Left from that strategic position.[87]

Of course, Coulter and Horowitz do not invoke the open racialism, contempt for human rights, and irrationalism of Faye, Benoist, Day, and other illiberals and Alt-Rightists. Such fare cannot be offered to major political parties and mainstream publishers. But illiberalism lite is suitable for mass dissemination.

The Utility of Illiberal Rhetoric

By the end of the first decade of the twenty-first century, various schools of Far-Right thought had seized on the articulations of the inversion thesis by Gramsci, Marcuse, the postmodernists, and other left-oriented thinkers, then distorted them and, indeed, weaponized them to justify their extreme illiberalism. Lite versions of this ideology trickled down from these elite groups to broader audiences.

Of course, few sensible people—certainly no feminists, Marxists, or progressives—were now persuaded that the Alt-Right, neofascists, and other reactionaries deserved a new hearing. The Illiberal Right expropriated the inversion thesis to justify their anti-democratic ideologies to themselves. This was no small benefit. Throughout the latter half of the twentieth century, extreme rightists had been subject to well-deserved disgust and ridicule. All but the hardiest souls found this distain too much to bear, and so the appeal of the movement, even to anyone with latent extremist propensities, was limited. Such people had to express at least perfunctory support for democratic institutions, political egalitarianism, human rights, and so on, and not venture out on the rightist fringe too obviously.

When illiberals distorted the inversion thesis to their unlovely purposes, they developed what amounted to a highly effective stigma-management strategy. If one moves far enough to the margin, sets up a feedback loop that transforms any and all criticism into confirmation, and pays heed only to others on the margin, one has retreated into a window-less ideological monad. And being that it is the right-wing margin, this monadic ideology will of course take on a racialist cast. In this way, the small extremist remnant of the early twenty-first century was given heart to endure and redouble its efforts, and greater appeal to fence sitters. The intellectual leaders of the extreme right now had new rhetorical strategies to deploy, new vocabulary to express themselves with, new talking points to raise, and thus more resources of protective coloration and self-justification.

The formation of an elite group is crucial for any political ideology that seeks to penetrate a political culture. Such a group formulates the rich mixture of ideas and arguments that John Stuart Mill called "intellectual pemmican," which, in increasingly diluted versions, can be fed to publics further and further removed from the elite. In this way, long-brewing developments in specialized literatures, concepts familiar at first only to academic audiences, and debates among intellectual networks of only a few thousand people can finally have an impact on mass media, broad publics, and even elected officials.

Can Identity Politics Have Any Good Use?

Identity Politics in The Possessed

So far, this chapter has shown that interest-cum-identity politics is not about identity at all, and that no version of identitarianism—radical, moderate, Alt-Right, Alt-Lite, or otherwise—serves any positive purpose. Is it possible, then, for any sense of collective identity to function as a useful corrective to the propensities toward fragmentation and the resulting collective-action problems inherent in pluralistic liberal democracies? What would such a positive form of identity politics look like?

It is notable that Faye's identitarianism is in some ways similar to the political theory hinted at by one of the characters in *The Possessed* by Fyodor Dostoyevsky. In what is perhaps the greatest of all political novels, the author has Shatov, a former serf who briefly joins a nihilistic revolutionary cell and then, in horror, tries to flee from it, deliver the following words:

> Not a single nation has ever been founded on principles of science or reason. . . . The object of every national movement, in every people and at every period of its existence is only the seeking for its god, who must be its own god, and the faith in Him as the only true one. God is the synthetic personality of the whole people, taken from its beginning to its end. It has never happened that all, or even many, peoples have had one common god, but each has always had its own.
>
> . . . Every people is only a people so long as it has its own god and excludes all other gods on earth irreconcilably; so long as it believes that by its god it will conquer and drive out of the world all other gods. . . . If

a great people does not believe that the truth is only to be found in itself alone (in itself alone and in it exclusively); if it does not believe that it alone is fit and destined to raise up and save all the rest by its truth, it would at once sink into being ethnographical material, and not a great people. But there is only one truth, and therefore only a single one out of the nations can have the true God, even though other nations may have great gods of their own.[88]

Shatov speaks in theological terms, not in the vocabulary of contemporary political theory used by Faye and other illiberal thinkers. Nonetheless, up to a point, the similarities of their thoughts are striking. Dostoyevsky's character says that the members of a nation share not a pervasive conception of the world, but a "god who is the synthetic personality of the whole people." Faye holds that a nation's history is not a field of "intellectually objective principles," and similarly, Shatov claims that nations are not "founded on principles of science or reason." Faye argues that every nation or people must have an invincible conviction of its ethnocentric superiority, while Shatov says every nation must have "its own god" that "excludes all other gods on earth irreconcilably" and believe "that by its god it will conquer and drive out of the world all other gods."

That is, Shatov and Faye both advance a vision of politics in which the basic unit is peoples or nations, each encased in its own seemingly windowless monad of the subjective conviction of its right to dominate. But there are crucial differences.

First of all, in Faye, the conceptions of the world that distinguish each monadic people are rooted in their biologically defined ethnicity. Shatov says nothing of biology and disparages ethnicity. For him, the synthetic personality of a people is religious; it is the god they believe in. At some points, Shatov implies that a people's religion or god has nothing to do with ethnicity. He says that if a people no longer believes in its god, "it would at once sink into being ethnographical material, and not a great people." Ethnicity, then, in Dostoyevsky's novel is merely the residue left behind when a nation loses its identity, rather than the indispensable foundation of national identity. Significantly, Shatov affirms that "an atheist at once ceases to be a Russian" and that "a man who was not orthodox could not be Russian." These statements imply that religious belief is at least an indispensable part of what defines ethnicity, rather than ethnicity being the ground of a conception of the world. For Shatov, identity is based on religion, not biology.

Further, it is important to note that Shatov uses the words "religion" and "god" quite broadly, such that they may, but do not necessarily, refer to anything supernatural. He remarks:

> The Jews lived only to await the coming of the true God and left the world the true God. The Greeks deified nature and bequeathed the world their religion, that is, philosophy and art. Rome deified the people in the State, and bequeathed the idea of the State to the nations. France throughout her long history was only the incarnation and development of the Roman god ... Roman Catholicism.[89]

Thus Judaism and Roman Catholicism count as religions in this context and have their own gods, but philosophy and art were the religion of the Greeks, and the State was that of Rome. Therefore, Shatov's brand of identitarianism, though he often expresses it in theological terms, can be interpreted broadly, where what are usually considered nonreligious ideas and values can be the god that is the unifying force fusing together "the body of the people."

Second, Dostoyevsky's character acknowledges there is "the true God" that is quite different from the "great gods" of individual nations. The suggestion is that history is the story of the peoples of the world learning to put aside their great but false national gods and all coming to accept "the true God." So in Dostoyevsky, as in Leibniz, there is a grand clock master—God—who eventually harmonizes the worldviews of the monadic peoples and establishes a peace among them. In *The Possessed*, after Shatov has sketched out his vision, his interlocutor asks him a pointed question that leads to a crucial exchange:

> "I only wanted to know, do you believe in God, yourself?"
>
> "I believe in Russia. . . . I believe in her orthodoxy. . . . I believe in the body of Christ. . . . I believe that the new advent will take place in Russia. . . . I believe . . ." Shatov muttered frantically.
>
> "And in God? In God?"
>
> "I . . . I will believe in God."[90]

The point seems to be that while Shatov believes in the god of Russia, he is still struggling to accept the true God who transcends all national gods and in whom the hope for world peace rests. Without this final belief in something universal, Shatov's thought, as he himself admits, amounts to hardly more than "the rotten old commonplaces that have been ground out in all the Slavophil mills in Moscow."[91] If Shatov were to despair and abandon his struggle to accept the true God, he would end up either with the latest grind from Moscow's Slavophile mills—that is, Alexander Dugin's Eurasianism—or Faye's identitarianism.

Without necessarily recommending the brand of identity politics suggested by Shatov, one can still see it has certain merits that identitarianism does not. First, a tolerable identity politics must reject rooting identity entirely in biologically defined ethnicity. Collective identity must have, at least, a strong ideational element derived from sources such as the religion, philosophy, culture, or overall social and historical situation of a given group. Such an ideational basis for collective identity might be thought of as a standpoint. Second, a positive identity politics must acknowledge the reality of truths and values that overarch multiple identity groups and make it possible for there to be communication and political cooperation between them.

Egalitarian Standpoint Theory

Identity politics of this type would conceive of collective identity as being the shared bundle of already-formed cognition, largely shaped by the social situation of the community, that serves as the epistemic starting point of collective deliberation. Feminist epistemologists approached this position, but an acceptable iteration of identity politics would have to differ from their standpoint theory in some crucial ways.

Feminist standpoint theory took a bad turn when it invoked the inversion thesis to identify marginal standpoints as privileged standpoints, which unintentionally facilitated extremism and illiberalism. The inversion thesis must be abandoned, as must any effort to privilege *a priori* some standpoints over others. In principle, all standpoints must be regarded as potentially equally legitimate points of departure. What is needed is not feminist standpoint theory, but egalitarian standpoint theory.

To some extent, egalitarian standpoint theory simply makes a virtue of necessity, since no group can start its deliberations from anywhere other than where it actually is, and different groups are necessarily situated at different standpoints. But an advantage of egalitarian standpoint theory is that it removes the incentive of groups to make a claim to privileged standpoints and enforce that claim by hook or by crook.

Egalitarian standpoint theory acknowledges that every community has a set of assumptions and values that are already built into its standpoint and that can be hard to detect without the critical distance possible from another standpoint. But instead of the overly simple model of a single dominant standpoint open to critique only from marginal standpoints, an egalitarian epistemology sees all standpoints as potentially capable of providing critical distance on each other. Which standpoints provide the most useful critical distance from which others is an empirical matter to be judged, not *a priori*, but based on the fruitfulness of a given inquiry starting off from a particular standpoint relative to other inquiries with other starting points.

Egalitarian standpoint theory has the merit of acknowledging the reality of collective identities while leaving open the possibility of truths or values that are universal in the sense of being valid across many collective identities or standpoints. Universal truths or values are those that have withstood critique from multiple standpoints and can be accepted by the identity groups that work from those standpoints. That is, egalitarian standpoint theory meets the second requirement of a positive identity politics: it acknowledges the reality of truths and values that overarch multiple identity groups and make communication and political cooperation possible between them.

The Cognitive Nature of Group Identities

Egalitarian standpoint theory also meets the first requirement of a useful identity politics: it defines the nature of identity groups not in biological terms, but in cognitive terms. The standpoint that the members of an identity group share is not a set of reflexes hardwired into their nervous systems by their DNA, but the bundle of cognition they have come to share as a result of their common social position and history. The ideas, values, and assumptions making up that bundle can be shared with other identity groups much more easily than can genetic material and are open to debate in a way that biological realities are not. With these realizations, one can sketch out in more detail how communication and debate across identity groups is possible and how truths and values overarching different standpoints can be reached.

Group identities are based on standpoints that are bundles of cognition that, although deeply rooted, are nonetheless cognitive and, therefore, capable of being communicated. Further, in cases where groups have similar but not identical social and historical situations, these cognitive bundles can overlap. So identity groups can share common cognitive ground that provides warrants to their arguments and makes rational debate possible.

Moreover, since which particular cognitions get incorporated into a standpoint are socially and historically determined, they do not necessarily all logically imply each other. Standpoints are more like conglomerates of heterogeneous cognitive material than logically consistent and reinforcing sets of ideas. Therefore, the critical distance needed to critique the assumptions built into a standpoint can be found, not only from other standpoints, but also potentially from within a given standpoint itself. When the American colonists searched through the standpoint they shared with the British, rejected monarchism but tapped into the revolutionary potential of the Lockean political theory they found there, and then used it to make a convincing case for independence, they were using one aspect of a dominant but conglomerate standpoint to critique others.

If, then, group identities are conceptualized as standpoints, and standpoints are conceptualized as potentially overlapping and internally heterogeneous bundles of cognition, identity groups are not necessarily windowless monads, nor must they be invisible thought systems that offer their members no purchase for self-criticism.

Of course, in a given situation there can be no guarantee that communication between standpoints is possible because overlap exists between them. Nor is it necessary that self-criticism from within a standpoint is possible because it has sufficient internal variation. When different identity groups meet, or members of a single identity group reflect, all they can do is look for the communicative and critical possibilities that are available and hope for the best. But given the dangers of war and stagnation, hope is a reasonable presumption, to be abandoned only when extraordinarily strong evidence so compels.

One can say, then, that a group's identity is its standpoint and therefore speak of egalitarian identity politics. It makes communication, understanding, and bargaining possible among and within identity groups, thus facilitating the search for political solutions that transcend narrow interests and aid liberal democracies in addressing their collective-action problems.

But what would such a politics look like? In particular what would an American egalitarian identity politics look like?

The American Identity

One can begin to answer these questions by first considering whether there is such a thing as an American identity at all and, if so, what it is like. These are empirical questions about the way Americans today actually think, which cannot be resolved by analyzing foundational texts and elite literature alone.

However, there is plenty of good empirical work on these questions. Especially relevant is the research of Deborah J. Schildkraut.[92] She explains in recent scholarship:

> Group identities are largely considered to be social in nature, deriving their power from contexts and from the extent to which people consider their group based memberships to be an important part of how they conceive of themselves as individuals. . . . In this perspective, one's national identity is viewed as a social identity, which refers to the part of a person's sense of self that derives from his or her membership in a particular group and the value or meaning that he or she attaches to such membership.[93]

The key point is that scholars have been able to conceptualize group identify in social rather than racial, ethnic, or biological terms. Moreover, the content of such social identity is cognitive—what people believe, sense, value, or mean—not genetic.

In another vital finding, empirical research has demonstrated that a distinct American identity does exist. Schildkraut reports that "existing research documents a high degree of consensus across demographic groups regarding how American identity is defined."[94] Her own work is based on her analysis of data gathered in the "21st Century Americanism survey (21-CAS), a national random-digit-dial (RDD) telephone survey with oversamples of Blacks, Latinos, and Asians. It has 2,800 respondents: 1,633 white, non-Hispanic; 300 black; 441 Latino; and 299 Asian."[95] Data were collected from July 12 to October 8, 2004.

According to Schildkraut, "One of the most noteworthy findings of the survey is the little credence to the concern that ethnic minorities in the United States fail to think of themselves as American."[96] She further concludes, reviewing the literature overall in 2014: "The search for evidence to support the claim that America's increasing racial and ethnic diversity is eroding consensus on what being American means (e.g., Huntington 2004) consistently turns up little."[97] An American identity is not merely an abstract political concept or an unrealized cultural desideratum, but a documented reality.

Further, the scholarly consensus also finds that although a distinct American identity can be isolated, its content is heterogeneous. Schildkraut shows that the scholarly consensus embraces what is called "the multiple-traditions thesis":[98]

> Recent scholarship has identified complex and often competing components of American identity that are rooted in the widely accepted *liberal* tradition, the understudied *civic republican* tradition, the contested *ethnocultural* tradition, and the equally contested *incorporationist* tradition.[99]

The best known of these identity components is the liberal tradition. Gunnar Myrdal and Louis Hartz are the most famous expositors of the idea that American identity is largely a matter of adherence to the creed or foundational propositions of Lockean liberalism as expressed in the nation's papers of state and other iconic formulations. Before discussing the other components of American identity, a few words have to be said about the liberal tradition.

Alt-Rightists and other illiberals sometimes argue that adherence to the liberal tradition cannot serve as a group identity, or an element of such an identity, because liberalism is inherently antithetical to the idea of group identity. Thus Greg Johnson, editor of the radical Alt-Right outlet Counter-Currents Publishing, claims that "liberalism, therefore, is opposed to any political identities. . . . Collective identities are merely burdens to be cast off as soon as individuals are able to choose their own values and construct their own identities."[100] This is a mistake. At least some versions of liberalism are more substantive than just a set of neutral procedures that allow everyone to construct whatever identity they please. Stephen Macedo and others have argued convincingly that liberal democratic principles imply an underlying set of virtues that should be partly constitutive of whatever identities citizens of such a polity may choose. Johnson writes that a decent, liberal society "does not say 'Become who you are' to sociopaths and born losers."[101] Sociopaths and losers lack the self-discipline, respect for others, openness to discussion, sense of personal responsibility, and many other public virtues essential in citizens of a liberal regime. When Johnson claims that "to make liberal democracy the 'identity' of any society is basically to adopt a suicide pact,"[102] he fails to realize that liberalism is itself a distinct identity, or rather, a distinct identity type, within which wide but not absolutely open-ended variation is possible.

But the liberal tradition is not all there is to American identity. Schildkraut defines the other three elements of the American identity as follows:

> Civic republicanism emphasizes the responsibilities, rather than the rights of citizenship. Civic republicanism thus set boundaries on American identity by making demands on group members to be an informed and involved presence in public life, to prioritize the collective entity, and to see the community as a central component of their own identity. . . .
>
> Ethnoculturalism . . . is an ascriptivist tradition that sets rigid boundaries on group membership. In its extreme, ethnoculturalism maintains that Americans are white, English-speaking Protestants of northern European ancestry. . . .
>
> Incorporationism is . . . [the] notion that America's unique identity is grounded in its immigrant legacy and in its ability to convert the challenges immigration brings into thriving strengths.[103]

The details of Schildkraut's analysis need not be discussed here and are presented in the chapter appendix. A limitation of her work is that the data it is based on were collected in 2004, before the visible rise of illiberalism and the election of Trump. Perhaps the shared American identity has been weakened by those or other recent developments. But more recent work suggests not.

First, as noted above, when Schildkraut reviewed the literature on

American identity in 2014, she found no reason to change her conclusions based on data from a decade earlier. Further, in 2016 the Democracy Fund Voter Study Group gathered data for its VOTER Survey, and in December of that year the survey firm YouGov reinterviewed 8,000 respondents who had been interviewed originally in 2011 and 2012. The VOTER Survey did not exactly replicate Schildkraut's work but did include a battery of questions about the importance of a variety of factors related to "being truly American." The political scientist John Sides analyzed these data in his 2017 study, *Race, Religion, and Immigration in 2016: How the Debate Over American Identity Shaped the Election and What It Means for a Trump Presidency*. The factors relevant to being an American that respondents were surveyed about "speak to two conceptions of American citizenship—a 'civic' conception based on American ideals and institutions and a more 'ethnic' conception based on blood and soil." The survey found the following:

> [S]ignificant areas of consensus. Most Americans, including both Democrats and Republicans, said that three things are important: respecting American political institutions and laws, having American citizenship, and accepting people of diverse backgrounds. There was less consensus on speaking English, but majorities of both Democrats (75 percent) and Republicans (95 percent) still said this is important. On the opposite end of the spectrum, relatively few Democrats (16 percent) or Republicans (23 percent) said that it is important to be of European heritage.
>
> However, nearly one-in-three (30 percent) of Trump primary supporters said that European heritage is important. . . . Trump primary supporters stood out in this respect, although again, a substantial majority still did not consider European heritage important to being American. . . . [T]here were larger differences in terms of whether being Christian is important: 30 percent of Democrats, 56 percent of Republicans, and 63 percent of Trump primary voters considered this fairly or very important.[104]

These findings are consistent with Schildkraut's. "Accepting people of diverse backgrounds" is an incorporationist factor. "Respecting American political institutions and laws" amounts to an embrace of the liberal tradition. Refusing to consider European heritage important to being an American represents rejection of a racialist form of ethnoculturalism. But milder forms of that tradition show up among the majorities who think speaking English is important in being an American, as well as among the smaller number who think being Christian is important. Overall, the VOTER Survey found a civic conception of American identity based on ideals and institutions that predominated over an ethnic, blood-and-soil version. The finding suggests the American identity as it is understood by earlier work and this chapter endures.

Several broad points that are immediately relevant to the present analysis emerge from the empirical work on the American identity. The fact that American identity is a heterogeneous bundle of cognitions derived from several distinct traditions is very important. Focusing on a single tradition as if it were the only valid or overwhelmingly dominant source of American national identity is a mistake. In the past, the liberal tradition was held to be the predominant *fons et origo* of Americanism. Communitarians and some conservatives have lamented what they see as the hegemony of liberalism and have decried the rise of a purely "procedural republic" that supposedly resulted.[105] But whatever might be said about the nature of the contemporary policymaking process, the more community-oriented values of civic republicanism are a major part of how Americans understand their national identity. Whatever the pluses and minuses may be of the liberal tradition, they are, for good or for ill, counterbalanced in the American identity by those of civic republicanism.

It is also important to face the fact that ethnoculturalism is a significant part our national identity. Alt-Rightists are not incorrect when they point out that a sort of race consciousness or white nationalism continues to occupy a place in the American mind.[106] Their mistake lies in thinking that ethnoculturalism is or should be the *sine qua non* of American identity, all other aspects of which are excrescences to be rooted out. Ethnoculturalism is hardly the sole or even main feature of American identity. But it is a real part of that identity that has to be confronted and mitigated just like any dark aspect of a personality. The vital point is that there are tools for coming to grips with ethnoculturalism—or any other shortcomings in the American identity—already present in that identity itself. For example, incorporationism offers positions of leverage from which to address ethnoculturalism.

A capacity for self-criticism is a major virtue of having a national identity derived from multiple traditions and containing a mass of heterogeneous cognitions. National culture has been analogized to the water fish swim in, which is invisible to them.[107] But this need not be the fate of Americans, whose variegated but not absolutely schizophrenic national identity makes them more akin to amphibians, who can look back at the water they came out of, or out at the land they are going to. Americans can review one dimension of their identity from another, get critical distance on any particular point from various angles, and achieve, perhaps not a view from nowhere, but at least a view from more than a single perspective.

This internal capacity for, if not objectivity, then at least a degree of intersubjectivity is no small virtue. Positivist epistemologists, feminist standpoint theorists, Gramscian Marxists, Critical Theorists, postmodernists, and their illegitimate illiberal progeny have frightened us with a brain-spun dystopian vision. What if the modern world of science, technology, development, and liberalism is caught in a monadic Weltanschauung so invisible to its inhabitants that they are incapable of self-awareness and self-correction? The American identity provides at least some potential defenses against this pitfall. That identity is not a single standpoint, but a constellation of what might be called substandpoints. It is not a single subjectivity, but a collection of subjectivities, within which a certain amount of intersubjective checking and balancing is possible.

Of course, this is not to say the multifaceted bundle of cognition that is the American identity contains within itself the answer to all its shortcomings and challenges. All identity standpoints potentially can benefit from a critical perspective that can be achieved only from outside them. But the American identity provides internal resources for at least beginning the journey to a view from everywhere. Today's men and women of speculation might do well to look for answers to their philosophical problems in the hidden wisdom of American national identity.

Beyond Identity Politics: Identity Is Not Enough

Even if the garden-variety forms of identity politics are successfully incorporated into American political culture, and the pernicious forms of identitarianism are confronted and rejected, and the positive potential of an identity politics rooted in the American identity is appreciated, current challenges facing liberal democracy will remain. If new interest groups based on race, ethnicity, sex, gender, and so on, become part of the status quo, the limitations of interest-group politics will remain to be dealt with. And simply recognizing that the American identity can facilitate democratic discourse does not tell us how to do so, especially given the challenges of the digital age to the communication of public ideas.

But to know how to facilitate democratic discourse, we need to ask, what is the state of democratic discourse and the role of intellectuals in American political culture today? This question is taken up in chapter 5.

Appendix: Distinct Components of American National Identity as Analyzed by Schildkraut

Here is a table from Deborah J. Schildkraut, "Defining American Identity in the Twenty-First Century: How Much 'There' Is There?" *The Journal of Politics* 69, no. 3 (August 2007), p. 602. Table A4-1 shows what percentage of her entire sample responded that a given characteristic "should be" either "very important" or "somewhat important" "in making someone a true American." The characteristics she asked about were chosen to capture adherence to beliefs associated with one of the four national identity traditions developed in the literature.

Table A4-1. American Identity Survey Items

Intended tradition	Question	% very important	% somewhat important	N
Ethnoculturalism	Being born in America	24.2	27.1	2,768
	Being a Christian	19.3	15.6	2,745
	Having European ancestors	7.0	10.4	2,707
	Being white	3.8	6.1	2,747
Liberalism	Respecting America's political institutions and laws	80.9	15.9	2,764
	Pursuing economic success through hard work	69.0	21.7	2,760
	Letting other people say what they want, no matter how much you disagree with them	65.9	21.9	2,698
Civic republicanism	Doing volunteer work in one's community	44.3	41.9	2,773
	Thinking of oneself as American	68.9	24.3	2,763
	Feeling American	62.1	28.0	2,678
	Being informed about local and national politics	65.3	29.7	2,770
	Being involved in local and national politics	37.1	43.8	2,761
Incorporationism	Carrying on the cultural traditions of one's ancestors, such as the language and food	35.7	37	2,751
	Respecting other people's cultural differences	80.1	16.8	2,773
	Blending into the larger society	36.9	36.5	2,683
	Seeing people of all backgrounds as American	73.1	19.6	2,717
Contested/Multiple	Being able to speak English	71.0	23.1	2,787
	Having American citizenship	76.0	17.7	2,773

Note: Weighted results. "Don't know" and "no answer" excluded.

Ideas

From Identity to Ideas

Chapter 4 documented the existence of an American identity, understood as a bundle of cognitions that are widely shared and amount to an epistemic standpoint. That identity provides Americans with a standpoint from which to begin communication and inquiry. But the standpoint identity also contains enough internal variation that a good deal of critical distance can be obtained, even while working within it or perhaps from overlapping identity standpoints of other polities. Achieving the needed critical distance from the American standpoint identity does not require epistemically privileging standpoints marginal to or outside of it. Whether these available epistemic resources are sufficient to the issues facing the American people at any particular historical juncture can neither be assumed or rejected *a priori*. Nor can *a priori* judgments be made as to whether obtaining sufficient critical distance requires working from more distant identity standpoints that could accurately be described as marginal or outside. But the American standpoint identity provides a wide range of epistemic resources to exploit, to critique each other with, and from which to build bridges to more remote standpoints. This finding suggests that, in principle at least, the American polity has a built-in set of defenses, an autoimmune system, against the propensity to degenerate into an anti-democratic dystopia of the type imagined in *Brave New World* or *One-Dimensional Man.*

But if the American standpoint has such rich epistemic resources ready to apply to Americans' understanding of political life, what accounts for the rise of illiberal ideologies and the success of their misuse of the inversion thesis documented in chapter 4? To understand these developments, one has to look at the structure of ideational politics in America—that is, how public ideas, or widely held ideas about politics, are developed and disseminated. In the late twentieth century, American politics had developed a particular process for the production of public ideas. It was a process that won out over possible alternative systems and was still often challenged and critiqued after it had crystallized. By the turn of the millennium, this process was battered but unbowed, and it might well have continued for some time to set the terms of the debate and precipitate the climate of opinion within which Americans thought about public affairs. But in the early years of the new century, a perfect storm of social change hit the structure of American ideational politics, exposing and widening the cracks that were already present in it. The old structure was partly supplanted by not a new structure, but an alternative structure that was well developed and had been waiting in the wings for its chance. The new system proved vastly more conducive to the spread of illiberal ideas than the old system had been. The challenge that liberal democracy now faces is figuring out ways to work with, around, and against the new structure of ideational politics, and so continue to thrive in the twenty-first century. Before exploring that challenge this chapter looks more closely at the illiberal ideas that are now receiving wide circulation and about the nature of illiberal ideational politics.

Ideational Politics and the Divided Line

In the realm of ideational politics there are two types of ideas. One is expert ideas, which have been defined as "shared beliefs about cause-and-effect relationships, developed and disseminated by actors who are widely recognized as having special knowledge about a certain policy's target area—often, but not necessarily, as a result of academic training."[1] This definition requires some qualifications. The point that not all experts come to their ideas based on academic training deserves more emphasis. Special knowledge in a particular subject can be based on paraprofessional or on-the-job training, or on work or personal experience. In addition, simply living through unique life experiences makes each individual an expert in some senses regarding his or her own affairs. Thus, there is a distinction between formal experts whose knowledge derives mostly from academic training and informal experts whose knowledge is otherwise obtained.[2]

Then there are public ideas, which are usually derived from expert ideas but are simplified to be intelligible to nonexperts and suitable for mass dissemination. Public ideas have been defined by Mark Moore as follows:

> Most such ideas are not very complex or differentiated. There is no clear separation of ends from means, of diagnosis from interventions, of assumptions from demonstrated facts, or blame from causal effect. . . . Moreover, it is not clear reasoning or carefully developed and interpreted facts that make ideas convincing. Rather ideas seem to become anchored in people's minds through illustrative anecdotes, simple diagrams and pictures, or connections with broad common-sense ideologies that define human nature and social responsibility.[3]

That is, public ideas are simple, atheoretical beliefs couched in terms that are almost slogan-like and designed to have an immediate impact on public affairs and politics.

The book *The Rise of the Alt-Right* describes how an "ideational food chain" produces public ideas that, when the process is effective, not only can communicate policy options to the general public, but also can have a real connection to the complex ideas of formal experts. At the top of this chain are the formal experts, those who develop a scientific understanding of social problems at a high level of abstraction. Their work gets increasingly simplified as it passes down the chain by a series of secondhand dealers in ideas: intellectuals, policy entrepreneurs, media professionals, and finally, the public.

This top-down conception of the production of public ideas has its origins in the late 1940s, when Friedrich Hayek sketched its outlines and described how knowledge spreads through society as ideas developed by experts are simplified by intellectuals for mass audiences.[4] From the late 1980s to the century's end, some students of the American policymaking process developed the model in detail. Key texts included *Making Public Policy* by Steven Kelman (1987), *The Power of Public Ideas* edited by Robert Reich (1988), *The Transformation of American Politics* by David M. Ricci (1993), *The New Politics of Public Policy* edited by Marc K. Landy and Martin A. Levin (1995), and *Seeking the Center*, edited by Levin, Landy, and Martin M. Shapiro. These works and others describe *mutatis mutandis*, a process of intellectual trickle-down in which the scientifically rigorous concepts developed by experts are simplified and widely disseminated as described above.

But the food-chain metaphor is unfortunate. It connotes a predatory and entirely top-down process. Those further up the chain devour those further down, with no turnabout ever. A better metaphor is from the *fons et origo* of political theory, Plato's *Republic*. There, Socrates speaks of the process of thinking and knowing as a divided line.[5] At the top of a vertical line are the forms, or the most general ideas about reality that the human mind can grasp, knowable only through the intellection of the philosophers. Below the forms are the hypotheses or definitions, which are assumptions derived from the forms that are taken as given and serve as the warrants of arguments about the visible world, politics included. These arguments are applied to the next step down the line, to things: the world humans live in, experience through sensation, and seek to understand and change. At the bottom of the line are images, or pictures of and words about things that enable humans to communicate about those things.

In Plato's account, humans move up and down the divided line as they think. They begin with words and images that help them communicate about things. Then they get to know the things themselves, through experience and sensation. The next step in thinking is to make a leap from the world of the visible to the world of the intelligible, and to formulate a hypothesis concerning, or a definition of, the things people experience and communicate about—for example, "all people are mortal" or "human beings are rational animals." Once humans arrive at a hypothesis or definition, they can go down the line and apply the hypothesis to the world of things: yes, all people are going to die sometime, which means this or that particular person will eventually die; or if all humans are rational, perhaps they can reason with rather than fight each other. Such statements apply hypotheses and definitions from the intelligible world to the lower, visible world of things and people. Or, humans can go back up the line and ask, are these hypotheses or definitions good hypotheses and definitions? Are there perhaps other, more general principles that override or qualify them? What ideas of this higher level are the best, in the sense that they apply in all circumstances and explain the most of reality? This is the realm of the highest level of human knowledge, the forms, which are intelligible only to philosophers—those who have not only sharp minds and memories, but also a "natural connection or affinity with the ways of justice and all other beautiful things."[6] On rare occasions, once philosophers have reached the forms at the top of the divided line, they can try to direct their thinking back to the lower levels, to reframe inadequate ideas, apply their knowledge to the world of things, and correct the way people communicate about "the ways of justice."

The divided-line metaphor, if updated and democratized, can apply to the function of ideas in contemporary democratic discourse. In contemporary terms, at the top of the line there are experts, not philosophers. Experts may not have a natural affinity with the ways of all beautiful things, but they do have the education, training, or experience to illuminate the complex problems of public affairs with as much scientific objectivity as the nature of the subject matter allows. Expert discourse is framed at high levels of abstraction and is usually fully understood only by other trained experts.

At the next level down the line are intellectuals, who are not necessarily experts themselves, but who are professionals with the skills and inclinations necessary to understand at least some expert ideas and then simplify them to produce ideas that are immediately relevant to public affairs and can be communicated to mass audiences. In so doing, intellectuals distill and trade in public ideas, which are similar to the ideas found at the second level down on Plato's divided line, in that they derive from the more complex ideas in the category above them, and serve as the assumptions that are widely taken for granted and become the warrants of arguments about political life.

Intellectuals, as they are understood here, are a far larger group than Manhattan literati and ivory tower faculty. Anyone who follows public affairs avidly and has a "wide range of subjects on which he can readily talk and write, and a position or habits through which he becomes acquainted with new ideas sooner than those to whom he addresses himself"[7] counts as an intellectual. As was the case with experts, there are distinctions between formal intellectuals and informal intellectuals. Formal intellectuals usually have training in academic disciplines; hold positions at institutions of higher education, research, or prestige journalism; and write for well-educated, politically attentive audiences. Informal intellectuals include everyone else who is familiar with public affairs and communicates with others about them as part of their work. Such informal intellectuals include teachers, activists, organizers, members of the clergy, and local notables.

One step down from the intellectuals are policy entrepreneurs, whose profession is to take the public ideas developed by the intellectuals and apply them to concrete political issues. Textbook cases of policy entrepreneurs include Ralph Nader, who leveraged concerns about auto safety and the environment into passage of the Auto Safety and Clean Air acts, and Jack Kemp, who channeled the free-market thought of the 1980s into tax cut and tax reform legislation. Media professionals and organizations can also be policy entrepreneurs. Examples include the editorial page of the *Wall Street Journal* when it pushed for less restrictive immigration policy in the 1980s and 1990s, and Fox Business Network journalist Lou Dobbs, who pushed for the opposite policy in the early twenty-first century.

At the ground level of the divided line are most people: the mass audiences who consume the words and images produced at the higher levels of the line that point to the policy debates, public ideas, and expert ideas that are also produced there.

The divided-line metaphor is useful here because it accurately represents the structure of American intellectual life as it was in the late twentieth century but avoids the negative connotations of the earlier food-chain analogy. Experts do not devour the other participants. Ideas do not necessarily start with experts and trickle down but never up. Participants are not always locked into one position on the line. A given person can, in principle, occupy more than one level on the line. And thinking about public affairs ideally involves moving in one's thoughts up and down through all levels of the line. A participant in democratic discourse begins by being literate and familiar with the vocabulary of public affairs. He or she can then understand the basic point/counterpoint of particular policy and political debates. An attentive participant can then grasp the public ideas—the assumptions, hypotheses, and definitions—underlying and taken for granted in those debates. From there it is possible to either move down the line by applying the public ideas to policy debates or move up the line and achieve a deeper understanding of the public ideas by learning something about the expert ideas behind them. The fullest expression of democratic discourse happens when the participants move up and down the line, moving from the lower levels of abstraction, seeking greater understanding at the higher levels, and then moving back down as they apply the insights they have found to the issues of their daily lives.

Shocks to the Divided Line

As discussed in *The Rise of the Alt-Right*, this divided line crystallized in American politics in the early 1970s and functioned with a tolerable degree of legitimacy through the rest of the twentieth century. It was a source of public ideas that had an impact on deregulation, tax policy, welfare reform, immigration, environmental protection, special education, and other areas.

However effective this process for the production of public ideas might have been in the late twentieth century, it became increasingly dysfunctional after the turn of the millennium. A series of traumatic developments starting in 2001—including the events of 9/11, the Second Iraq War, the fiscal crisis of 2008, the Great Recession, economic restructuring, and visible demographic change—shook confidence in the conventional wisdom of American politics and made the public open to new ideas. Right-wing extremist groups spied an opportunity and were able to exploit it because the new technology of the internet gave them low-cost access to mass audiences they had previously lacked. Experts, intellectuals, policy entrepreneurs, and other cultural gatekeepers who had once been able to marginalize fringe elements thus had their positions undermined. These technological and social shocks of the new century hampered the production of useful public ideas and created an opportunity for illiberal ideas to spread.

But it is simplistic to attribute the spread of illiberal ideologies to the external shocks given to the ideational infrastructure of American politics. Consider the shock of the digital communication revolution. The power of cultural gatekeepers has much diminished during the twenty-first century and it would be easy to advance a *post hoc, ergo propter hoc* argument and fix the cause of that decline on the rise of digital media—a theory that is not all wrong. As discussed, digital media lowered the cost of mass communication and allowed previously marginalized extremists to start up their own inexpensive digital platforms and so make an end run around the once powerful editors, publishers, and broadcasters who had controlled access to the capital-intensive communications technologies of the predigital era.

Attributing the new century's dramatic shift in the climate of intellectual opinion to the digital revolution is true as far as it goes, but it misses a key point. External shocks such as jolting change in the economy, technology, or international relations are usually not enough in themselves to bring about such a major cultural change. For example, the facile argument is often made that World War I shattered the orderly cultural consensus inherited from the Victorians and ushered in the modernist world. But this analysis overlooks the fact that before the war, the certainties of Victorian culture had already been intellectually undermined by the developments of relativity and quantum physics, psychoanalysis, cubist and abstract art, Marxism, non-Aristotelian logic, experimental literature, and much else. Virginia Wolfe famously observed that the change in human character wrought by modernism had occurred "on or around December 1910," that is, well before the war began. World War I challenged the Victorian verities, but they might have remained in place had there not been a new set of ideas ready to take their place. It is telling that in the wake of America's catastrophic conflict—the Civil War—the nation's cultural consensus, of the North at least, remained in place. The reactionary ideology of the South had been defeated and no other plausible set of ideas was in place to challenge the Northern cultural consensus. The point is, war, other forms of catastrophe, or technological revolutions are not necessarily enough to precipitate the overthrow of a climate of intellectual opinion unless that climate has already been effectively undermined by an alternative set of ideas. An external shock will demolish a cultural consensus only if it has already been cracked by an internal shock.

What intellectual shock, then, had already cracked the ideational infrastructure of the twentieth-century gatekeepers such that the technological jolt of the digital revolution knocked them flat? What had happened is that the old model of ideational politics—the divided-line model—had been challenged for decades by a new, oppositional model that became increasingly radical and culminated in the extreme version of the inversion thesis developed by postmodernists. The legitimacy of the divided-line model had already been weakened, and an alternative to it had already been developed in detail when the technological, political, economic, and demographic shocks of the twenty-first century arrived. And so a particularly radical and problematic form of the oppositional model was able to assert itself politically in a way that it had not before.

Two Theories of Intellectuals

The divided-line account of ideational politics implies a theory of intellectuals: they are, as Hayek put it, "professional secondhand dealers in ideas." This is another unfortunate formulation, as it seems to disparage intellectuals as second-rate intellects. A better way of formulating Hayek's insights is to think of intellectuals as interpreters. They understand both the ideas of experts and the concerns of broader publics well enough to facilitate communication between them. That is the role the intellectuals played in the mid-to-late twentieth century, when they enjoyed more influence than is often appreciated and performed a positive function in American political culture. The conception of intellectuals as interpreters ensconces them in the middle of the process of the production and dissemination of public ideas. They are, in this account, an essential part of that process, a necessary link, integral to the spread of social knowledge. But there is another way to conceive of the intellectual's role, a rival account that is radically at odds with Hayek's theory.

In *Ideology and Utopia*, Karl Mannheim developed a theory of intellectuals that put them not firmly at the center of the production of public ideas, but necessarily detached from society overall. According to Mannheim, a climate of opinion or overall cultural outlook "is not likely to be developed by a class occupying a middle position but only by a relatively classless stratum which is not too firmly situated in the social order. . . . This unanchored, *relatively* classless stratum is . . . the 'socially unattached intelligentsia.' "[8]

Mannheim's claim was that the ideologies of all classes but one are totally determined by their social standpoints and therefore are incapable of a completely objective or scientific understanding of politics. But intellectuals, given their independence of the class structure, are able to overcome class interest and bias, and can more nearly achieve an objective or scientific understanding of politics than any other social group.

Without specifically mentioning Mannheim, American writers have often accepted his theory that for intellectuals to fulfill their role of providing an objective criticism of society, they must be relatively detached or alienated from that society. And these American theorists of intellectuals have often worried that, in one way or another, intellectuals were becoming incorporated into American society, thus losing their critical distance from it and becoming incapable of fulfilling their function of producing social criticism. In 1954, Irving Howe wrote the notable essay "This Age of Conformity," in which he both embraced the notion that alienation from society was necessary for intellectuals to be intellectuals and worried that intellectuals were losing their critical powers by being co-opted into the social mainstream. Howe argued that intellectuals' "alienation from the community . . . made possible their strength and boldness, precisely this 'lack of roots' gave them their speculative power." And he worried that "far from creating and subsidizing unrest, capitalism in its most recent stage has found an honored place for the intellectuals; and the intellectuals, far from thinking of themselves as a desperate 'opposition,' have been enjoying a return to the bosom of the nation. . . . We have all, even the handful who still try to retain a glower of criticism, become responsible and moderate."[9]

This same conception of intellectuals as a necessarily socially unrooted class and the fear of them losing that rootless status was expressed by Russell Jacoby in *The Last Intellectuals: American Culture in the Age of Academe* (1987). Jacoby argued that intellectuals must have their social and economic roots in bohemia to maintain a critical distance from mainstream society. He cites Robert Michels's account of bohemia as a demimonde inhabited by "surplus intellectuals. . . . floaters, outsiders, malcontents." Jacoby lamented the decline of bohemia with its "urban cafés and streets [that] sheltered marginal intellectuals"[10] and the movement of intellectuals into academia, where he feared their critical vision would be compromised by professionalization and co-optation. Jacoby worried:

> The decline of bohemia may entail not simply the decline of urban intellectuals and their audience, but of urban intelligence as well. To vary an old proposition, café society gives rise to the aphorism and essay: the

college campus yields the monograph and lecture—and the grant application.[11]

The 1930s and 1940s are generally thought of as a period when intellectuals were bohemian and felt highly alienated from American society. The 1950s are held to be a period when intellectuals were reincorporated into the mainstream by taking up positions in academia and government. This sense was made quasi-official in the famous *Partisan Review* symposium "Our Country and Our Culture," published in 1952, in which the editors noted "American intellectuals now regard America and its institutions in a new way. . . . Many writers and intellectuals now feel closer to their country and its culture. . . . For better or worse, most writers no longer accept alienation as the artist's fate in America; on the contrary, they want very much to be a part of American life." Richard Hofstadter charted this ebb and flow of intellectuals' proximity to mainstream society in his 1963 book, *Anti-Intellectualism in American Life.* He noted, with approval, the movement of intellectuals from the margins to the center of the nation's cultural life, although he also noted some ambivalence with this development.[12]

But intellectuals' satisfaction with their mainstream position, which was never without some qualms, did not last long. By the mid-1960s, the vision of intellectuals as radically alienated from the vital center of American life reasserted itself and intellectuals again began to conceive of themselves not merely as agents of critique and change, but often as revolutionists. For about a decade, one of the worst charges that could be leveled at intellectuals was that they had sold out to or been co-opted by the establishment. But again, this turn of the wheel did not endure, and through the mid-1970s and 1980s, intellectuals came to an uneasy peace with their positions in mainstream academic, governmental, and nonprofit institutions. And just as Irving Howe harshly criticized the mainstreaming of intellectuals during the 1950s and early 1960s, Jacoby made essentially the same complaint about the complete absorption of intellectuals into academia.

The point of this brief overview of intellectuals in recent American political culture is simply to document the dialectical relationship between two theories of the intellectual. One theory, descended from Mannheim, is that of the alienated intellectual whose function is to provide objective analysis and critique of society and who must be relatively detached from that society to have critical distance from it. The other theory is Hayek's, that of the intellectual as an interpreter of expert ideas to broad audiences.

Since intellectuals are a complex social phenomenon, neither of these theories by itself is able to satisfactorily capture their essence. Modern societies are extremely complex, and even if one assumes that the invisible hand of the market, left to itself, is able to provide a great deal of order, a tremendous amount of effort and understanding is necessary to keep societies functioning tolerably. (And of course, tremendous effort is also necessary to keep markets functioning.) No modern society can do without the work of experts of all sorts, and if the ideas of experts are to be broadly understood and applied, those ideas must be interpreted and disseminated by intellectuals. Therefore, some incorporation of intellectuals into the social mainstream as producers and disseminators of public ideas is inevitable.

On the other hand, a certain sort of alienation is indeed necessary for an intellectual to function. Consider the Hegelian concept of alienation, in which people, through their labor, produce goods and tools of all sorts that they can alienate themselves from in the sense of offering them up to be judged and valued by other people. The most obvious example of this process is people producing commodities of various sorts that are evaluated by other people through sale in the market. But ideas and purely intellectual products can also be alienated in this sense. Suppose someone comes up with a theory about how government or the economy functions. The theory itself cannot be sold on a market, but it can be communicated to other people who will then critique it, put it into practice, evaluate it, and set a value on it, though not necessarily a monetary value. In this account, alienation is a positive process, an essential process through which people come to understand themselves, others, and their world. All workers depend on this process of alienating the products of their labor, but in the case of intellectuals, what is alienated is their ideas. These ideas are evaluated not primarily by having a price attached to them, but by standing up to the critique of peers and the interested public. Intellectuals—whether they are situated in bohemian cafés, academic posts, or government jobs—must alienate themselves from their own ideas, learn how to see them as others see them, and dispassionately appreciate the critiques that are made of them. Further, intellectuals must be able to alienate themselves not only from their own ideas, but also from the ideas of their immediate audiences or patrons, whether they are aficionados, critics, scholars, or public officials.

The point is that alienation and incorporation are the yin and yang of intellectuals' status, and while in a given historical situation one tendency may be more salient than the other, neither can triumph completely and permanently over the other. What theorists such as Mannheim, Howe, Hofstadter, and Jacoby have documented is the various stages of this dialectic, none of which endure for very long. And one must understand the stage of this dialectic at the point when the potentially transformative shocks of the early twenty-first century hit to better account for the rise of illiberal thought at that time.

Intellectuals at the Dawn of the Twenty-first Century

The position of intellectuals at the dawn of the millennium was in some senses the worst of all possible worlds. As Jacoby noted, they were fully incorporated into the mainstream of academia and in terms of objective social position, were no longer marginal outsiders. But they were often uncomfortable in that position and intellectually embraced a particularly radical version of the alienated intellectual theory.

As discussed earlier, various versions of the inversion thesis had been embraced widely, though not universally, by academic intellectuals. The inversion thesis—like the accounts of intellectuals given by Mannheim, Howe, and Jacoby—held that intellectuals' force came from their marginal status. But the inversion thesis gave a particularly radical interpretation to marginality and why it was vital.

Marxist theorists such as Vladimir Lenin and others held that intellectuals had an objectively correct understanding of society based on Marxist social science, and that this knowledge drove them to a revolutionary stance that left them marginal to and alienated from mainstream bourgeois society. In other words, in the Marxist account, intellectuals played a valuable social role because they had substantive knowledge of society. Marginality in itself was not what made them significant. Intellectuals knew Marxist social science and could interpret it to the proletariat. Doing so made intellectuals a revolutionary vanguard and so placed them at odds with, and outside of, the bourgeois mainstream. But the strength of the intellectuals was in their knowledge. They knew something—or thought they knew something—and that was critical.

The various forms of the inversion thesis that had spread through the intellectual community by the late 1990s interpreted the significance of marginality in a different way. The marginal groups that the intellectuals of that era celebrated—women, Blacks, nonmainstream ethnic groups, the third world, sexual minorities, the criminal, the incarcerated, the mad, and so on—were usually celebrated not because they had substantive knowledge that mainstream groups did not. They were celebrated simply because they were marginal and therefore had critical distance from mainstream society. Marginality in itself was critical, and whatever previously unappreciated knowledge the marginal groups might have—if indeed they had any—was at best secondary.

Late twentieth-century intellectuals were ensconced in academia, had access to the expert knowledge generated there, and were themselves often experts in one field or another. But their embrace of the inversion thesis left them unable to effectively access this material. That is because the inversion thesis stipulated that having access to knowledge and having something to say about it were irrelevant to the vocation of an intellectual. Marginality, not knowledge, was important. This idea drove intellectuals to take increasingly more marginal positions and seek increasingly marginal groups to celebrate. It did not encourage intellectuals to tap into the expertise available to them, emphasize their own expertise, or base their legitimacy on their ability to interpret expertise from whatever source to others.

Thus intellectuals in the late twentieth century were in a precarious position. Based in academia and other mainstream institutions, they no longer could credibly claim to be alienated bohemians or revolutionary leaders. But in embracing the inversion thesis, they could no longer legitimate themselves on the basis of their own expertise or ability to interpret the expertise of others.

In fact, the inversion thesis ended up undermining the whole idea of expertise, for it privileged social position—marginal social position—rather than social knowledge. It cast into question all expertise, especially mainstream expertise. If thinkers are based in the social mainstream, all their expertise is open to doubt because it may incorporate biases and errors that are invisible from the mainstream standpoint. Expertise is therefore devalued relative to marginality and open to an assault from marginal standpoints, even if the thinkers occupying those standpoints had nothing substantive to say and no expertise of their own but were simply dispensing a sort of empty iconoclasm that was presumed to be somehow salubrious.

Therefore when the shocks of the early twenty-first century hit, intellectuals could not legitimate their gatekeeping function based on either their marginal position in bohemia, which they no longer occupied, or their expertise or proximity to it, for they had undermined the whole concept of expertise.

Intellectuals were therefore unable to perform their social function of gatekeeping. They were unable to legitimate themselves as gatekeepers to others or, more importantly, to themselves. When the perfect storm of social upheavals hit, the internal erosion of the intellectuals' position was already well advanced. It was the one-two punch of internal erosion and external shock that critically weakened the intellectual gatekeepers and presented a window of opportunity to illiberal ideologies.

Are Professional Intellectuals Necessary in a Digital Age?

One possible response to the weakened position of professional intellectuals is to simply say good riddance. It has sometimes been argued that the internet obviates the need for professional intellectuals since it not only can deliver critical information directly to the general public without the need for intermediation of intellectuals, but also allow a better-informed public to broadcast their views on public affairs. The argument is that digital media will enable a group of people much larger than that of professional intellectuals to make themselves heard in public discourse and thus generate greater public engagement. So, professional intellectuals will be demoted or decline, and their role will be played by "embedded" or "civic" intellectuals who will have less formal training but more immediate connections with mass audiences.[13]

The development of an "engaged public" capable of greater participation in democratic discourse is very much to be desired. But the internet and other digital media do not in and of themselves necessarily enable public engagement. An engaged public must have a grasp on material to engage with, and that material is the public ideas most salient in contemporary political debate. But where do those public ideas come from? They come from intellectuals whose role it is to distill expert ideas into simpler formulations that are relevant to political life. And public ideas need to be applied to topical public concerns by policy entrepreneurs. Distilling or simplifying expert ideas requires the training and skills necessary to grasp at the outlines of expert debate. And applying public ideas to current events calls for a detailed, insider's understanding of current public affairs. Most of the public lacks the inclination and aptitude necessary for that work. That leaves it to intellectuals and policy entrepreneurs to produce the public ideas and policy formulations that an engaged public is supposed to engage with.

But it is precisely those intellectuals and policy entrepreneurs whose function is undermined by the internet. The outlook is not optimistic that digital media will produce "engaged publics—speaking from alongside" and "more capable than intellectual authorities . . . speaking from above"[14] unless the positions of gatekeepers such as intellectuals and policy entrepreneurs are reinforced against the undermining forces of the internet so that the essential material of democratic discourse— ideas—continues to be produced at least as well as it was in the late twentieth century.

That reinforcement has to be partly in the form of new policies and practices that strengthen the power of digital gatekeepers to remarginalize the disinformation and anti-democratic ideologies that gatekeepers of predigital age once filtered out of mass circulation. More importantly, intellectuals must reconceptualize their role. They must bid farewell to the celebration of marginality for its own sake and yet maintain their critical distance from within the mainstream. They must exploit the possibilities for public engagement offered by the internet and yet still perform their function of reframing expertise and issues into the public ideas of democratic discourse. More immediately, they must first dissolve the illiberal discourse monad in which some significant percent of the American public is now trapped. Then intellectuals must shift the terms of political debate away from the ideological fetishes of both the Left and the Right, and toward a focus on democracy itself, as a goal in its own right, and on how to strengthen democratic institutions. And intellectuals must do so using terms of debate and drawing conclusions from anywhere within the liberal democratic ideological spectrum, considering only how useful they are to the task at hand. But all this reconceptualizing involves learning from those analysts who recognized the weakened position of intellectuals and other cultural gatekeepers early on.

Internal Shocks Documented Before External Shocks Hit

The internal shock to the ideational system of American political culture was noticed and documented well before the external shocks of the early twenty-first century hit. Many of these diagnoses came from conservative or neoconservative authors. Examples include *The Closing of the American Mind: How Higher Education Has Failed Democracy and Impoverished the Souls of Today's Students* (1987) by Allan Bloom; *Slouching Towards Gomorrah: Modern Liberalism and American Decline* (1996) by Robert H. Bork; and *The De-Moralization of Society: From Victorian Virtues to Modern Values* (1995) and *One Nation, Two Cultures* (1999) by Gertrude Himmelfarb. There were also leftist versions of this analysis, of which *The Revolt of the Elites and the Betrayal of Democracy* (1995) by Christopher Lasch is a striking example. And there are European examples such as *The Defeat of the Mind* by the French intellectual Alain Finkielkraut (1987).

These works all argued in various ways that developments in the late twentieth-century climate of opinion undermined the self-confidence and public authority of experts, and anticipated that these developments would be problematic for liberal democracy. On this intuition the authors were correct, but the specific arguments and evidence they advanced were often overdrawn and unconvincing. As a result, their conclusions were unduly pessimistic.

Perhaps the greatest shortcoming of such writers—termed "the Jeremiah school" by Richard Posner—is that they trace the origins of the internal crisis in ideational politics far into the past, sometimes all the way back to the beginnings of the Enlightenment and even further. For example, Bork writes that "current liberalism's rot and decadence is merely what liberalism has been moving towards for better than two centuries."[15] Bloom traces the current crisis in the American climate of opinion back to "the German invasion of the United States"[16] and the professionalization of the social sciences in the mid-to-late nineteenth century. Himmelfarb has argued that the trouble began with the publication of John Stuart Mill's *On Liberty* in 1859.

There is a long tradition of conservatives diagnosing the maladies of the modern intelligentsia and prescribing amputation of modernity itself. Richard Weaver, in the conservative classic *Ideas Have Consequences*, traced modern liberalism's crisis to "that world-wide and centuries-long movement against knowledge whose beginning goes back to nominalism."[17] Ayn Rand held that the problems began with Immanuel Kant, whom she described as "the first hippie in history."[18] The most recent articulation of this charge comes from Robert Curry of the Claremont Institute, writing in the Trumpian outlet American Greatness, who believes that the eclipse of the eighteenth century's Common Sense Realism has opened the floodgates to "irrationalist doctrines that came on in wave after wave beginning in the 19th century—romanticism, Hegelianism, Marxism, progressivism, existentialism, post modernism, and the like."[19]

Whatever else might be said of these diagnoses, they all share one shortcoming: they imply a fatal prognosis for liberal democracy. Modern democracies cannot simply chuck their entire intellectual heritage since the dawn of the enlightenment or the early modernism of the nineteenth century. Diagnosticians must work with surgical instruments, not a battle-ax. A brain transplant is impossible, but a bit of cognitive therapy is possible and likely to be effective.

The weakening of the position of intellectual gatekeepers was not the inevitable result of trends dating back to the rise of nominalism, the Enlightenment, or modernism. As discussed in chapter 4, the problem developed in the postwar years as thinkers of various stripes wrestled with the legitimate problem of how to structure intellectual communities to forestall an unhealthy homogenization of thought that would lead to a soft, technocratic tyranny. Feminist philosophers and others usefully argued that liberal democracies must take better advantage of the critical distance provided by marginal communities. But as often happens in the history of ideas, legitimate insights got pushed as far as they would go and then still farther, until they became counterproductive.

This process played out, not necessarily in the thinking of any one postwar thinker, but in the broad sweep of mid-to-late twentieth century social thought on the role of marginal groups in democratic discourse. At the beginning of the civil rights era, social critics and political theorists at last realized that marginal groups exist, were relevant to their studies, and were closely tied up with the fate of liberal democracy. The next step was to formalize a procedure whereby whatever knowledge was available from the perspectives of marginal groups was taken into account by the mainstream. The final step was to invest marginality itself with an epistemic privilege, regardless of whatever substantive knowledge was or was not held by marginal groups, and to search for ever more marginal groups to celebrate. Given that the feminist, multiculturalist, queer, postmodern, and other postwar thinkers who got caught up in this dynamic had come of age in the 1960s and were therefore quite critical of mainstream liberal democratic politics, this lurch to the margins struck well beyond the outer limits of liberal politics. But it may be that their sixties sympathies will provide the internal break that will eventually kick in with extremist dynamics. One suspects that the generation of 1968 and its epigone will follow through on the drive to the margins only so long as it leads further left. Now that there are groups on the right-wing margins of liberal democratic society that have exploited the inversion thesis to their own advantage, the celebration of marginality for its own sake has hit a wall. The intelligentsia is likely willing to rethink some of its recent operating assumptions as long as doing so does not involve rejecting the entire modern tradition since the Enlightenment. And in fact, it does not.

In pure logic, contemporary intellectuals need only move away from the various forms of the inversion thesis and adopt some variation on an egalitarian standpoint methodology. The search for, and celebration of, marginal perspectives that provide useful vantage points from which to critique the liberal democratic mainstream, or any other standpoint in need of critical inspection, can continue. A greater appreciation for the range of viewpoints within the wide liberal democratic political spectrum is in order, given that the alternatives outside that band have now boldly stepped forward in all their unloveliness. But a dogmatic embrace of liberal democracy is uncalled for, and still less so is such an embrace of the rightward-most versions of liberal democracy. At most what is called for is a conditional acceptance of liberal democracy as a kind of default position, subject always to reasoned critique in light of further experience and inquiry by all groups, however situated. And of course, the idea that intellectuals can regain their lost position only if they reject the whole development of critical thought since the nineteenth century, or the Enlightenment, or the development of nominalism, or the Socratic method, is absurd. The whole of Western thought—and non-Western thought—is a precious intellectual tool kit. The full range of the instruments it offers are to be put to use based solely on which of them seem most useful to the particular challenges the world now faces. This is true even for conservative hate objects such as Marxism, feminism, postmodernism, and all the rest. Neither can progressive bugaboos such as capitalism and the Western cannon be dismissed out of hand. Intellectuals can work within whatever school of thought seems most appropriate to them, so long as they acknowledge that, in the end, gold is where you find it and they are willing, like Socrates, to follow the lead of their arguments wherever they go.

Suggesting that intellectuals change the way they conceptualize their role in society is difficult in the same way that recommending changes in the U.S. Constitution is. Any change is hard, and radical change absent dramatic social upheaval is impossible. Therefore the trick is to recommend apparently small changes that have wide-ranging impact and that facilitate more dramatic changes down the road. The rest of this chapter will show how a shift in the climate of opinion away from the inversion thesis and toward egalitarian standpoint theory, while being an incremental rather than a radical change, will have a greater positive impact than might be apparent at first glance.

Intellectuals as Interpreters

Working with egalitarian standpoint theory rather than the inversion thesis frames intellectuals as interpreters rather than as alienated outsiders. Intellectuals can find the critical distance they need within the shared identity standpoint of their community and need not start their inquiries from outside that standpoint. Intellectuals can be reconceptualized as people who exploit the heterogeneous content of standpoints and the overlaps between standpoints as ways of moving from one standpoint to another, or of bringing standpoints into dialogue with each other. This idea is similar to the recent literature on intellectuals that understands them as "interpreters" because they make use of the "capacity of epistemic communities to link opposing sides . . . translate their interests in a way that facilitates communication and compromises among different involved parties."[20] Michael Walzer, working with a different account of how critical distance can be obtained from within a given cultural standpoint, has also developed the idea of intellectuals as interpreters.[21] His book *The Company of Critics: Social Criticism and Political Commitment in the*

Twentieth Century is particularly interesting because he shows that some of the most effective public intellectuals of that era—George Orwell and Albert Camus in particular—had their impact precisely because they offered their criticism from within a particular social standpoint rather than from outside it. So, the role of interpreter is already available to and used by contemporary intellectuals, but this approach deserves more widespread adoption than it now receives. Intellectuals need not, and should not, try to retrieve the ground they have recently lost by retreating to a position of prelapsarian dogmatism. Walzer's "stipulative definition of social criticism" posits a role for contemporary intellectuals that is in no way reactionary: "members [of a particular society], speaking in public to other members who join in the speaking and whose speech constitutes a collective reflection upon the conditions of collective life."[22]

Thinking of intellectuals as interpreters suggests various responses to their twenty-first-century predicament that are not available when one thinks of them as a classless, bohemian, or alienated stratum not firmly rooted in the social order—a definition that makes the fate of the intelligentsia look bleak. For decades, intellectuals have been increasingly incorporated into mainstream institutions such as government, media, and academia. Given the inevitable rise of an information economy in which the production of information is mostly performed by the public sector, this mainstreaming of the intelligentsia will only get stronger. So if classlessness, alienation, bohemianism, or any other marginal status is posited as a *sine qua non* of a true intelligentsia, that social function is doomed.

But a more positive prospect opens up if intellectuals are instead conceptualized as interpreters. Interpreters need not occupy any particular social position, whether inside or outside of the social mainstream. What is essential for an interpreter is the ability to move intellectually between one social position or standpoint and another. This ability does not depend on starting from or continuing to occupy any particular standpoint. So whether the intellectual begins at or stays embedded in bohemia or any other marginal position versus a position within the public mainstream is irrelevant. What is highly relevant is whether society can develop practices, policies, and institutions that allow intellectuals to perform their role as interpreters. An autonomous intellectual requires certain specific and hard-to-maintain structural conditions to fulfill his or her critical role. In the past the key structural condition was a mooring in bohemia, which has increasingly weakened and will continue to weaken as intellectuals move into the public mainstream. The issue, then, is what kind of structural conditions are necessary within academia and other public sector positions that intellectuals now increasingly occupy so that they can fulfill their function as honest-broker interpreters? Some of these conditions are well-known: tenure, peer review, high barriers to entry, independent financial status based in endowments. The problem is how to extend these conditions in the digital era.

Intellectuals, Expertise, and Objectivity

If intellectuals are to be interpreters, what are they to interpret and to whom? Yes, intellectuals are to interpret some sets of ideas, values, and arguments within a particular identity standpoint to people within that standpoint who work with other such sets. But we can be more specific than that.

Intellectuals can and should interpret the knowledge of experts to policy entrepreneurs and the general public. That is the role Hayek assigned to intellectuals when he called them professional secondhand dealers in ideas, and it is the role they occupied in the divided-line structure of the production of public ideas that functioned fairly effectively in the late twentieth century. It is the role that was undermined by the rise of digital communications technology. It is also the role that was undermined by intellectuals themselves when they embraced one or another version of the inversion thesis, thus calling into question the whole idea of expertise and also their role as interpreters of it. One cannot interpret what does not exist, and there is no point in interpreting what is hopelessly biased or irrelevant.

In other words, while it is not necessary and, indeed, would be destructive for intellectuals to reject, lock, stock, and barrel, the whole tradition of critical thought, to perform their functions as intellectuals they do need to work with a set of epistemological assumptions that make objective knowledge, and the expertise based on that knowledge, possible. The nature of objectivity is one of the most difficult of all philosophical issues and as such cannot be developed in much detail here. However, the question does come up in the literature on the twenty-first-century media environment and its impact on democratic politics. So, a few words have to be said about truth and objectivity within that specific context.

In their important book on past and present media regimes, *After Broadcast News* (2011), Bruce A. Williams and Michael X. Delli Carpini critique the concepts of objectivity and truth in a way that is typical of many analysts of digital media. The two claim that as a result of the multiplicity of visions of reality now available to the public—"multiaxiality"—and the resulting difficulty of distinguishing reality from representations of reality—"hyperreality—today "truth and objectivity are problematic concepts that have lost their authority."[23]

One can appreciate what Williams, Delli Carpini, and other authors writing before the rise of Donald Trump and illiberalism were trying to do. These authors were right to recognize that the era of broadcast news had come to an end, that a new media regime was forming, and that journalistic practices and standards would have to be rethought. Therefore it seemed plausible to draw on certain strains of postmodern thought in reconceptualizing journalism for a digital age. As Williams and Delli Carpini wrote:

> The notion of a clear distinction between objectivity and subjectivity has been thoroughly critiqued on an intellectual level, but it also is brought under attack by the new media environment; the sheer number and types of media easily available on virtually any subject coupled with the large proportion of time people spend with various media make reality itself an essentially contestable concept.[24]

One wonders, if they and other authors who questioned the relevance of truth, objectivity, and reality in the digital age had written during the Trump presidency, would they have found the postmodern critiques of these concepts still so compelling on an intellectual level? One can raise the same objections to the postmodern disparagement of truth that have been brought against Oscar Wilde's 1889 essay "The Decay of Lying." There, Wilde mocked America for "having adopted for its national hero a man, who according to his own confession, was incapable of telling a lie."[25] Writing in the wake of the Nixon administration, the literary critic Ihab Hassan observed, "Wilde could not have known then about Cambodia, Watergate, and the grisly antics of the CIA. Would the renascence of lying in America have cheered him? I think not."[26] Similarly, now that America and the world have gotten a taste of the fact-free political culture embodied by Trump and illiberalism, truth and objectivity have gotten a new lease on life. Yet it is still worthwhile to look at the charges brought against these concepts by the postmodernists and others to better understand what they mean, and do not mean, for democratic discourse today.

One can begin by distinguishing objectivity as a philosophical concept from objectivity as a journalistic practice. A way of understanding objectivity as a philosophical concept is to say it means some things exist independent of human consciousness and cannot be changed by human consciousness alone. This book is not a work of philosophy and therefore will not consider in detail the arguments that nothing exists except insofar as humans think about or perceive it. In my inexpert judgment, such arguments were exploded long ago and are irrelevant to the current issues of political knowledge, journalism, media regimes, and democratic discourse.[27] However, naïve critiques of objectivity as a philosophical concept are still found in the literature on media studies, education, and other disciplines and need to be rebutted. Here is an illuminating example from a recent textbook on social justice education for teachers in training:

> The concept of knowledge . . . [is] never purely objective, neutral, and outside human interests. . . . To illustrate the concept of knowledge as socially constructed and thus never outside of human values and subjectivity, consider an example of a tree—a seemingly neutral object whose existence is simply a physical fact that can be observed. Yet notice that how we *see* the tree is connected to our meaning-making frameworks (and thus is not neutral at all). First, consider our perceptions of its *size*. A tree that looks big to someone who grew up on the East Coast might not look big to someone who grew up on the West Coast. . . . In other words, humans can only make meaning of the tree from the cultural frameworks into which they have been socialized. And so it goes for history, physics, and all fields studied in academia.[28]

But can't the East Coaster and West Coaster resolve their differing judgments by simply measuring the tree and finding out how tall it really is? If the tree turns out to be 25 feet and 7 inches tall isn't that a purely objective, neutral piece of knowledge quite outside of any cultural framework? In other words, isn't it true that, at least in many cases, there exist procedures of inquiry by which people in different social positions can get outside of their own subjectivity and establish facts that have a strong claim to objectivity? One does not have to accept all features of Karl Popper's philosophy of science to agree with him that "scientific objectivity can be described as the inter-subjectivity of scientific method,"[29] which can be as simple as using a measuring tape or as complex as testing Einstein's theories. And so it goes, not only for history and physics, but for journalism, policy studies, and democratic discourse.

Thus, Saturn has rings around it and that is so regardless of what anyone thinks, feels, or knows. And in a July 25, 2019, phone call, Trump asked Ukrainian president Volodymyr Zelensky to look into allegations of corruption against Joe Biden and his son, Hunter, as was documented by an official White House transcript of the call. That is a fact even though 60 percent of self-identified Republicans believe otherwise.[30] Trump's remark to Zelensky about the Bidens remains a fact despite what 60 percent of Republicans think, or even what 100 percent of the human race may think, because Trump really did make that remark, as is documented by a reliable and undisputed record of the conversation. That is, Trump's remark is an objective fact. To say otherwise—or to deny that every day, countless numbers of objective facts about what happens in the White House, Washington, the United States, and the world are conclusively documented and disseminated through various means of communication to audiences small and large—is to fall headlong into a pit of nihilism. And that is exactly where Trump and illiberals generally want everyone to be. As the reporter who noted this depressing fact observed, "Virtually every day, Trump takes to Twitter to push ideas that are simply and provably false. . . . We are not just in an age in which the media is distrusted, we are in a moment in which facts are distrusted and in which the very idea of truth is under direct assault. . . . That's what Trump's presidency is doing."[31] Objectivity understood as a philosophic concept is thus indispensable to the practices of politics, social criticism, and democratic discourse and must be defended against the illiberal attacks on it.

However, objectivity understood as a set of journalistic practices is another matter. Williams and Delli Carpini summarize the literature on the subject as finding that "the doctrine of objectivity in American journalism . . . at a minimum . . . consists of five separate stylistic commitments: detachment, nonpartisanship, the inverted pyramid, balance, and facticity."[32] It is easy to see that, thus defined, objectivity as a journalistic practice is something much more contingent and contestable than objectivity as a philosophical concept. The limitations of balance, for example, which requires that plain statements of fact by one party be "balanced" by the gross falsehoods of another, have been obvious at least since the McCarthy era and are once again on glaring display in the Trump era. It is certainly true that the new, wide range of media and sources of information available to the public represent tumultuous change for the practice of journalism and are resulting in new stylistic commitments and professional conventions. So the journalistic doctrine of objectivity is being reconfigured from the ground up.

Public Intellectuals in Academia

To interpret expertise, one must have ongoing access to it and regular, professional engagement with it. In other words, an academic position, far from dangerously compromising the whole function of a public intellectual, is well suited to that vocation. Howe, Jacoby, and others have claimed that an academic position is the kiss of death to critical distance and the ability to function as a critical public intellectual. But this claim rests on the inversion thesis: marginal standpoints—whether in bohemia or radical politics—are preferable to mainstream standpoints—such as academic positions—as points of departure for intellectual inquiry. But the egalitarian standpoint approach applied here rejects all *a priori* assumptions about epistemic standpoints. The advantages and disadvantages of any particular standpoint for any particular inquiry have to be ascertained on the basis of experience.

Some of the advantages of starting inquiry from an academic position are noted above, but another is relevant here. Public intellectuals based in academia have access to a tremendous amount of expertise, scholarship, and research. Typically, even intellectuals based at second-, third-, and fourth-string academic institutions have access to digital databases, book collections, colleagues, and research support available to few nonacademics. Further, academics are themselves often experts, and even though they are seldom at the very highest levels of their fields, they have frequently mastered at least some small field. Moreover, since their education has taught them the most important skills, basic knowledge, and broad intellectual outlines of one discipline or another, academics are able to access the expertise they have not produced themselves in ways that few nonacademics can. So, once the prejudices against academic positions fostered by the inversion thesis are discarded, and once the function of interpreting expertise to broader publics is accepted as a legitimate and necessary role for intellectuals, the persistence of the notion that academia is fatal to the vocation of a public intellectual seems very wrongheaded.

Besides the supposed danger of losing critical distance, other criticisms of academia as a setting for public intellectuals have been made. For example, it is often alleged that academia is hopelessly biased against conservatives. But while empirical studies have shown that the majority of faculty at institutions of higher learning are progressive, the studies have not found bias in academic research or against conservative faculty and students.

Thus, a 2016 analysis of twenty-five years of data from the University of California, Los Angeles (UCLA) and its Higher Education Research Institute (HERI) triennial survey of college faculty, the largest pool of data on faculty ideology and views in existence, found that "while conservatives are a small minority among higher education faculty today and have been shrinking . . . there are minimal differences . . . with regard to job satisfaction which strongly suggests that the feelings of oppression and discrimination may be overstated despite the regular reports of hostility and bias."[33] The most comprehensive study of academic conservatives is the 2016 book *Passing on the Right: Conservative Professors in the Progressive University* by Jon A. Shields and Joshua M. Dunn Sr. The authors summed up their findings as follows:

> As two conservative professors, we agree that right-wing faculty members and ideas are not always treated fairly on college campuses. But we also know that right-wing hand-wringing about higher education is overblown. After interviewing 153 conservative professors in the social sciences and humanities, we believe that conservatives survive and even thrive in one of America's most progressive professions. . . . The vast majority of conservative professors we spoke with said the right-wing campaign against the university overstates its politicization. . . . Conservative professors do not say the university is implacably hostile to their ideas and values. In

fact, about half the professors we interviewed began drifting toward conservatism while in the academy itself. . . . Finally, movement conservatives should deescalate their rhetorical war against the progressive university. Such polemics, after all, may inadvertently solidify progressives' troubled rule over academia by discouraging young conservatives from becoming professors.[34]

In his 2001 book, *Public Intellectuals: A Study of Decline*, Posner makes a criticism of academically based intellectuals that is in some ways the inverse of the claim that academia is a poor setting for intellectuals due to its political bias. His analysis is that when scholars produce work for academic forums, such as peer-reviewed journals and tenure committees, their contributions are high quality because they must be able to pass professional oversight. But when academics write for broader audiences through popular outlets—that is, when they take on the role of public intellectuals—the quality of their work declines because there are no equivalents of the academic reviews to maintain standards.[35]

Posner backs up his analysis with a review of the work of academics in their capacity as public intellectuals commenting on such issues as the impeachment of Bill Clinton, the 2000 presidential election deadlock, the 9/11 attacks, and the Second Persian Gulf War. Posner succeeds in showing that the work produced by academics writing as public intellectuals for popular outlets did not meet scholarly standards. However, that work stands head and shoulders above the material offered up by the online political magazines from 2015 to the present. This is especially true of the content found on the illiberal outlets reviewed in chapter 3. If it was true at the dawn of the twenty-first century that the media in which public intellectuals published "perform virtually no gatekeeping function," then we must conclude that the online outlets of fifteen years later really performed no gatekeeping function at all. But that is not quite strong enough. The combination of cheap access to mass audiences and what has been called "the campaign against established knowledge," far from filtering out substandard work, is positively encouraging the "unqualified and unqualifiable" to boldly step forward in all their illiberal dullness. Jose Ortega y Gasset has a not-entirely deserved reputation as a reactionary and so his work should be drawn on with caution. But he sounds as if he is describing the sort of people who contribute to illiberal and far-right magazines, blogs, posting boards, and comment sections when he laments the intrusion into public affairs by the sort of person "who, in the face of any problem, is satisfied with thinking the first thing he finds in his head."[36] The mid-to-late twentieth century, when intellectuals were often experts or academics, or at least had some close connection with academia or other sources of expertise, looks like a golden age compared to the present when, to quote Ortega again, "the intellectually vulgar" "proclaims and imposes the rights of vulgarity, or vulgarity as a right."[37]

The point here is that whatever the deficiencies of public intellectuals were when they, in one way or another, tapped into expertise and disseminated it to broader publics, the situation had virtues that were unappreciated at the time. If intellectuals gave up on the strategy of legitimating themselves by marginalizing themselves and reworked the strategy of interpreting and applying expertise to the broad public arena for a digital age, they might be able to regain some of the authority they have lost.

Here, then, we have the first institutional implication of public intellectuals reconceptualizing themselves as interpreters of expertise to broader publics: public intellectuals should be based in academia, or at least have a strong relationship with academic institutions, and be informed consumers of the research they produce. Further, academic institutions should give scholars professional credit for their work as public intellectuals and develop a set of appropriate standards and processes for evaluating such work.

The Decline of Think Tanks

A second institutional implication follows from conceptualizing intellectuals as interpreters of expertise: if academia today is a position favorable to the pursuit of such work, think tanks generally are not.

The story of the rise and decline of think tanks as developers and disseminators of public affairs expertise is well-known. Particularly useful accounts include *The Idea Brokers: Think Tanks and the Rise of the New Policy Elite* by James A. Smith (1991); *The Transformation of American Politics: The New Washington and the Rise of Think Tanks* (1993) by David M. Ricci; *Think Tanks, Public Policy, and the Politics of Expertise* (2004) by Andrew Rich; and *Think Tanks in America* (2012) by Thomas Medvetz. While Medvetz's account differs to some degree from the others, collectively the story these works tell is as follows.

The origins of contemporary think tanks date back to the beginning of the Progressive Era, with the establishment of the Russell Sage Foundation and the Bureau of Municipal Research in 1907. Both these institutions, as Rich writes, "placed a premium on the promise of objective social science and the contributions of experts in devising solutions to public problems."[38] The National Bureau of Economic Research and the Brookings Institution, founded in 1920 and 1927, respectively, were begun after the Progressive Era but still reflected the ideals of that period.

By mid-century, several institutions developed so that experts could contribute their knowledge to government decisionmakers, and think tanks also began playing that role. Franklin Roosevelt consulted with his brain trust, and in 1946 the Council of Economic Advisors was formed. In 1948 the RAND Corporation—originally a subsidiary of Douglas Aircraft that had done systems analysis work for the Air Force—became an independent entity that was supported almost entirely by government research contracts. The Brookings Institution also developed into almost a quasi-official source of expertise for government—so much so that in 1966, President Lyndon Johnson would say, "After 50 years of telling the Government what to do, you are more than a private institution. . . . You are a national institution, so important . . . that if you did not exist we would have to ask someone to create you."[39] The Progressive Era confidence that expertise could solve social problems remained and perhaps was even fortified as think tanks and similar research centers became part of the Washington establishment.

This close identification with the Washington establishment of the Great Society era created a crisis for the established think tanks, but not for think tanks as an institution. When the Vietnam War was lost and the economic slowdown of the 1970s began, the experts at the Council of Economic Advisors, the RAND Corporation, and the Brookings Institution lost some credibility.

The result was not so much that faith in experts and the institutions that housed them was entirely lost, but rather that a new set of experts got a hearing that they had previously not achieved and developed a new set of institutions to work from. The rise of a network of conservative think tanks during the 1970s, their incorporation into the Washington establishment during the Ronald Reagan administration, and their ongoing influence up to the present is related in all the works cited earlier.

Indeed, Medvetz argues that the research organizations founded prior to this period are not true think tanks at all. He claims that earlier research organizations were primarily conduits through which academic expertise flowed to government decisionmakers. The think tanks founded or reoriented after 1970 were more ideological than their predecessors, as they were intended to rebut the Keynesian/Great Society consensus that was seen as failing. They were funded by business interests and smaller foundations that expected an immediate policy impact in return for their investment. And these think tanks were established at a point where the power of electronic media was established and well understood. As a result, Medvetz convincingly argues, the new think tanks, instead of facilitating a two-way exchange between academics and government, now had to balance a four-way set of forces: academia, journalism, the market, and politics.

For some years, this new structure went largely unnoticed and new think tanks seemed to carry on much as older ones had, making academic expertise available to government. This was because after World War II, an impressive network of more conservative academics and traditional public intellectuals had developed and provided the new think tanks with a steady supply of research and public ideas to transmit to public decisionmakers. In a compelling essay on the history of free market–oriented think tanks, Fred Block traces their success back to the ideas developed by the Mont Pèlerin Society—a scholarly society established by Friedrich Hayek—and other academic networks:

> Hayek and the Mont Pèlerin Society were extraordinarily successful in moving from extreme marginality in the 1940s to global hegemony in the 1970s and 1980s. And think tanks play a role in this triumph. Friedman and Hayek cultivated links to proto and actual think tanks that invested vast resources in disseminating their ideas. But the Mont Pèlerin Society itself was nothing like a think tank; it was basically an academic debating society that forged strong international links among a network of likeminded economists. But without this debating society and the systematic elaboration of a set of ideas by Friedman, his Chicago colleagues, and others in the international network, the right-wing think tanks would have had no effective ammunition and no legitimacy in their attacks on Keynesianism and the welfare state.

In a word . . . ideas really matter, and in the triumph of market fun-
damentalism, the work of university-based intellectuals loomed large in
making right-wing think tanks powerful and effective. Even if one has
little respect for the modal Chicago School article that demonstrated with
mathematical precision that each benevolently designed government initiative inevitably exacerbated the problem it was designed to solve, these
were products of a social scientific research program elaborated by autonomous intellectuals.[40]

In the early 1980s, I worked briefly for one of the new conservative
think tanks. An executive there handed me a copy of Hayek's essay, "The
Intellectuals and Socialism," describing it as the organization's mission
statement. The executive told me the organization was primarily devoted
to communicating ideas rather than original research, because all the research had already been done by academics and all that was necessary to
have an impact on policy was to disseminate those ideas to journalists,
decisionmakers, and the general public. He was more right than he knew
since, besides the body of work accumulated by neoclassical economists,
there was also the work of neoconservative political scientists and sociolo-
gists, and a wide range of material developed by the academics and public
intellectuals of many stripes who turned rightward for a time as they responded to the shortcomings, real and perceived, of progressive thought.

But just as progressivism and Keynesianism had their heydays and
then came under increasing critical scrutiny, so, too, did the neoliberalism
and neoconservatism that the new think tanks specialized in disseminating. By the mid-1990s, the academic ammunition had run out, and the
new think tanks, which had never developed their own research capacity,
ended up with no connection to academia, which was no longer producing
enough ideas useful to a traditional conservative agenda. With academia
gone as one of the four supporting legs of the new think tanks—which
by the early twenty-first century were no longer new—those organizations now found themselves catering entirely to their remaining bases of
support: journalism, the market, and politics. None of these sectors, as
they are now configured in the United States, provides the long-term au-
tonomy that is necessary for legitimate public intellectuals to thrive. The
new think tanks lost their base in academia, and academia lost a major
conduit for its expertise into public affairs. Medvetz describes the result

as follows: "Thus, the main conclusion of this study is that the growth of think tanks over the past 40 years has played a pivotal role in undermining the relevance of autonomously produced social scientific knowledge in the United States by fortifying a system of social relations that relegates its producers to the margins of public debate."

Medvetz's judgment is not idiosyncratic or ideological. Rich comes to the same conclusion: "The role of think tanks in the policy process often has become one focused more on providing skewed commentary than neutral analysis. With these efforts, think tank influence is diminished, and the reputation of think tanks and experts generally among some policymaking audiences is damaged."[41] In a detailed review of the role of public ideas in the governing of four democracies, John L. Campbell and Ove K. Pedersen found little to praise in America's "knowledge regime":

> The U.S. knowledge regime . . . facilitates great diversity in the types of analysis and policy recommendations it generates. . . . The downside is that the ideas that come from the private policy research organizations, particularly the advocacy oriented ones, if not some of the state [i.e., governmental] organizations, may be so infused with political ideology as to be of little use for well-reasoned and civil policymaking debate. This, of course, is exacerbated by the big role private funding from wealthy individual and organizational patrons plays in this knowledge regime and the fact that the weight of this funding tends to tilt toward more conservative policy research organizations in line with the rising level of political and ideological partisanship in Washington. Insofar as this has contributed to political gridlock recently where policymakers seem unable or unwilling to agree on much of anything, we are not enthralled with this system.[42]

Campbell and Pedersen's analysis is particularly significant because it identifies other systems for the production of public ideas that the United States can emulate and suggests reforms that can take the country in the right direction. While they acknowledge there is no one best knowledge regime, they admire "the comparatively uniform and high level of analytic sophistication of the German knowledge regime; and the nonideological and inclusive nature of the Danish knowledge regime as well as its increased emphasis on analytical sophistication."[43] In their final chapter, the authors suggest several strategies for improving the American knowledge regime, all of which involve making think tanks become conducive to the work of academic experts. For example:

> Proposition 5: Knowledge regimes that are dominated by policy research organizations favoring scholarly empirical analysis will more likely exhibit high-intellect learning and produce analysis and recommendations that, if adopted by policymakers, lead to successful political-economic outcomes than knowledge regimes that are dominated by policy research organizations oriented more toward politically partisan advocacy work.[44]

How, then, to reform American think tanks so they are more disposed to favor scholarly empirical analysis? Such analysis is produced by academically trained experts who have the independence to adhere to professional as opposed to ideological norms. Campbell and Pedersen's final suggestions involve how think tanks can achieve this necessary independence:

> Proposition 10: Private policy research organizations whose funding comes from a large number of small donors are more likely to operate with independence than organizations whose funding comes from a small number of large donors.
> Proposition 11: Policy research organizations managed by professionals with advanced degrees are more likely to operate independently than other organizations.
> Proposition 12: Policy research organizations with close connections to universities are more likely to operate independently than other organizations.

And another conclusion that follows from Campbell and Pedersen's analysis is that policy research organizations whose funding comes to a large extent from endowments are more likely to produce socially useful analyses than organizations wholly dependent on soft money from politically interested donors.

But what has this discussion of think tanks to do with the rise of illiberalism? Illiberal ideas came into previously unachieved prominence for several reasons. One was the loss of confidence of intellectual elites in the possibility of producing expert ideas that were not hopelessly contaminated by prejudices and unwarranted assumptions of mainstream society. These elites responded by celebrating marginality for its own sake, thereby opening an intellectual loophole for marginalized, and often self-marginalized, illiberals to claim as much epistemic privilege as any other marginal group. The way to close this loophole is for intellectuals to cease depending on a marginal or alienated stance to legitimate their work, and to reconceptualize themselves as possessors and interpreters of expertise. That expertise is produced primarily by trained, independent professionals insulated from influences irrelevant to their work. Today these conditions are found in academia but seldom in the world of think tanks.

The upshot of this analysis is straightforward. The donors that are supporting the network of ideological think tanks are mostly wasting their money. The products of these institutions are generally not high quality because they are produced to back up an ideological position rather than to objectively analyze social problems. That these products are exercises in advocacy, not analysis, is well-known, and so they have little power to persuade. Private funders therefore need to insist on the reforms identified by Campbell and Pedersen or find other ways to have an impact on public affairs. And people aspiring to a career as public affairs analysts are better off pursuing an academic career.

An Engaged Public versus a Phantom Public

Even if an intellectual class has reconceptualized and reorganized itself as recommended above, it cannot entirely by its own efforts reestablish itself as an effective ideational gatekeeper and successfully respond to the rise of illiberalism and other challenges democracy faces in this new century. Intellectuals occupy only one segment, albeit an important segment, of the divided line of ideational production. A key characteristic of the divided line is that individual citizens can, in principle, move up and down the line in thinking about public affairs. Intellectuals can and should move up the line to the level of experts and grasp the highly abstract and complex ideas about political life to be found there. And then intellectuals can address themselves to the policy entrepreneurs and general public further down the line, and interpret for them the knowledge of the experts. But all the actors along the divided line can move up and down it in such fashion. This is true and especially significant for the general public. Members of the public must have the intellectual skills necessary to move up the divided line, understand the policy proposals advocated by policy entrepreneurs as well as the public ideas developed by the intellectuals, and apply those ideational resources to the political problems they encounter in their everyday life. And members of the general public must be able to communicate their political concerns to the policy entrepreneurs, intellectuals, and experts further up the line, so that the work done by these actors is relevant to the political realities of the body of citizens. That is, a renewed ideational regime, one capable of meeting the illiberal challenge and other challenges of the twenty-first century, requires an engaged public along with a reconceptualized intelligentsia.

This point leads to the long-standing debate about whether an engaged public is at all possible in modern society. The debate was opened in the 1920s by Walter Lippmann in his books *Public Opinion* (1922) and *The Phantom Public* (1925) and then taken up by John Dewey in *The Public and Its Problems: An Essay in Political Inquiry* (1927).

In this debate over the nature of the public, Dewey was more nearly correct. Lippmann was right to recognize the importance of experts and to realize that they cannot be dispensed with. But it is not possible to have a democratic polity with all the thinking done by experts and a completely passive public. The reason is that an expert class is too susceptible to becoming a homogeneous, scientist, monadic community incapable of self-criticism. The critical distance necessary to maintain a democratic polity has to come not from a single or a few marginal communities, but from a broad public with the cognitive resources necessary to provide critique through democratic discourse. To facilitate that discourse, experts are needed. But so, too, are intellectuals who rework expert ideas into public ideas that serve as the warrants of political debate; policy entrepreneurs who apply the public ideas to specific policy issues; and a public with the basic knowledge and critical thinking skills needed to use those ideational resources in democratic discourse to the best of their ability. But the *sine qua non* of healthy democratic discourse is a public capable of engaging in it. Therefore one must ask, how prepared is the American public for democratic discourse and what practices and policies are necessary to prepare them?

One theory suggests that civic education is the key to preparing a public for democratic engagement and that the decline of civic education is a cause of the rise of Trump and illiberalism. In an insightful critique of identity politics, the distinguished political theorist Mark Lilla laments how Trump's voters "were generally clueless about how our democratic institutions work, and about all the informal rules and norms that keep them working well" and notes "the urgent need for civic education in an increasingly individualistic and atomized nation."[45] The same connection was drawn by another notable social critic, the iconoclastic rock musician Frank Zappa, who argued that "after all the student rebellions in the '60s, civics was banished from the student curriculum and was replaced by something called social studies. . . . And so, if you don't know what your rights are, how can you stand up for them?"[46]

One wishes that the answer to the decline of America's democratic political culture was as simple as more civic education. But unfortunately for that diagnosis, the public is no more or less knowledgeable about politics than it has been since World War II. The definitive book on the public's political knowledge remains *What Americans Know About Politics and Why It Matters* by Michael X. Delli Carpini and Scott Keeter, published in 1996. The authors summarized decades of research on this issue as follows: "A consensus has emerged concerning contemporary levels of political knowledge. Studies . . . suggest that knowledge is at best no greater than it was two to four decades ago, and it may have declined on some measures. Our research generally confirms these findings, although we found some evidence of greater knowledge today. . . . It appears that over fifty years, the level of public knowledge has remained remarkably stable."[47] The most recent national survey of Americans' political knowledge was published by the Pew Research Center in 2007 and came to much the same conclusion:

> The coaxial and digital revolutions and attendant changes in news audience behaviors have had little impact on how much Americans know about national and international affairs. On average, today's citizens are about as able to name their leaders, and are about as aware of major news events, as was the public nearly 20 years ago. . . . Despite the fact that education levels have risen dramatically over the past 20 years, public knowledge has not increased accordingly.[48]

In a personal correspondence, one of the authors of the Pew study wrote, "I doubt that anything in the past 12 years would change the conclusion we reached in 2007."[49]

While the level of the public's political knowledge has been steady since the 1940s, that level has been low. The 2007 Pew study was based on the answers of 1,502 respondents to twenty-three questions about public figures and news events. The results of the survey are shown in table 5-1. The report notes that "using a common school grading scale in which 90% correct is the minimum necessary to receive an A, 80% for a B, 70% for a C, 60% for a D and less than 60% is a failing grade, Americans did not fare too well. Fully half would have failed, while only about one-in-six would have earned an A or B."[50]

These data do not support the theory that the rise of Trump and illiberalism in the United States have been caused by a decline in civic education. That theory assumes less civic education results in fewer well-informed citizens who are thus easier marks for illiberal demagogues. But whatever the trend in civic education has been, it did not result in a less informed citizenry, and thus there was no decline in citizen knowledge that could take the blame for Trump and his style of politics.

Of course, given the low level of Americans' political knowledge, one could argue that more civic education is required in any case, because a better informed and more engaged public is always desirable. And even if there was no decline in political knowledge to take the rap for the crisis in America's political culture, perhaps an increase from the low level of what the public now knows would be salubrious.

However, the evidence on the potential of civic education or other

Table 5-1. How Americans Scored on the Pew Knowledge Quiz

Correctly answered at least . . . *	% of respondents
20 questions	10
15 questions	35
12 questions	52
10 questions	66
7 questions	83
5 questions	92
1 question	99

*Out of twenty-three core questions. A total of twenty-six questions were asked, including three that did not test knowledge of political and world affairs. N = 1,502.

Source: Pew Research Center, "Public Knowledge of Current Affairs Little Changed by News and Information Revolutions: *What Americans Know: 1989–2007*," April 15, 2007, p. 5.

sorts of government intervention to have a large impact on public knowledge is mixed. The long-term stability of public knowledge despite radical expansion in education at all levels and in the availability of media suggests that significant improvement in what the public knows about public affairs will be hard to achieve. Delli Carpini and Keeter admit as much but are cautiously optimistic:

> In spite of numerous changes in their political, social, economic, and technological environments, Americans are essentially no more nor less informed about politics than they were fifty years ago. This . . . demonstrates how difficult it is for society to raise its aggregate level of political knowledge. Viewed most pessimistically, it may indicate inherent limits to how informed the general public is willing and able to be. . . . Although what Americans know about politics has changed very little, there is some evidence that it is *changeable,* and although Americans appear less politically educated than one might hope, there is evidence that they are *educable.*[51]

But if there is evidence that Americans are educable about civics, exactly how to educate them so as to make a big difference remains a matter of debate. In 2003 the Center for Information and Research on Civic Learning and Engagement (CIRCLE) identified "six promising practices of civic education pedagogy." A 2011 report cosponsored by CIRCLE rechristened these as "proven practices" and presented some evidence that taking a civics class raised students' political knowledge somewhat. But in general, research on civic education has found, as one researcher put it, silver linings but no silver bullets.

It may be that trying to improve citizens' civic practice by improving their civic education is putting the cart before the horse. In *Do Facts Matter? Information and Misinformation in American Politics,* Jennifer L. Hochschild and Katherine Levine Einstein found, as have most observers of public political knowledge, that Americans are often very ignorant of basic facts about civics and public affairs. Even worse, the authors found that much of the public is not merely ignorant of but positively misinformed about political issues, that many of these citizens base their political behavior on their mistaken beliefs, and that disabusing these "active misinformed" citizens is extremely difficult. In their conclusion, the authors review a number of practices for improving public political knowledge and enlightening the active misinformed. While research and education are considered, the authors conclude that "relying mainly on education to produce informed and active citizens is unwarranted; too many efforts yield only disappointment."[52] Nudging, ignoring the active misinformed, superimposing expertise, changing political actors' incentives, shaming, and punishment are also examined, and authors evaluate all these strategies as "plausible, hopeful, but indeterminate."[53] None are particularly successful in increasing the public's political knowledge. Overall, the literature on civic education does not support the idea that this strategy will strikingly increase what citizens know about politics and create an engaged public more resistant to illiberal misinformation.

However, at the very end of their book, Hochschild and Einstein take note of a remarkable instance in which public engagement had a dramatic impact on political knowledge: the civil rights movement. Before that movement, the authors point out, most white Americans accepted as true a great number of falsehoods about Black Americans. A 1944 survey showed that 84 percent of white Americans thought that "Negroes in this town have the same chance as white people to get a good education," half thought Black Americans had an equal chance to "make a good living," and a third thought "Negro blood" was "different in some way" from white blood.[54] By the end of the 1960s, most of these false beliefs about the absence of discrimination and the imagined biological differences between the races had been dispelled through the hard work of the civil rights movement.

In other words, the civil rights movement is an example of a successful effort to improve public political knowledge, but it is not an example of how more civic education led to better informed citizens and then to a more engaged public. The process worked the other way around: an engaged public—not the whole public, but the most immediately concerned public, the Black public—set out to change political reality and, in the process, informed the rest of the public and, as it were, gave all Americans a civic education, perhaps the most consequential civic education enterprise in modern American history.

Civic education does not produce an engaged public; civic education enlightens an already engaged public. Thus understood, civic education is much more than the type of courses taught in school, although academic learning is part of civic education. Civic education is all efforts to provide an engaged public with the knowledge it needs to achieve its democratic ends. To a considerable extent, an engaged public is an autodidact in civic education, for the public is the best judge of what it needs to know and which sources of knowledge are the most useful to its purposes. And intellectuals must function as such useful sources, tapping into expert knowledge, reformulating it as public ideas, and communicating those ideas in terms that are broadly relevant to the American political identity and the needs of an engaged public striving toward democratic ends.

The Already Engaged Public

If civic education will not produce an engaged public, then one needs an already engaged public to educate. And as it turns out, an engaged public is ready at hand. Polarizing presidential candidates boost levels of public political engagement as measured by interest in and concern about election results, political knowledge, and participation in the political process. Alan I. Abramowitz has argued that before Trump, George W. Bush was the most polarizing presidential candidate in postwar political history and the size of the engaged public increased dramatically when he ran for reelection in 2004. Abramowitz writes:

> As the leaders and the Democratic and Republican parties have become increasingly polarized along ideological lines, interest in politics and participation in political activities have been increasing among the public. In 2004, with the public deeply divided over the presidency of George W. Bush and the war in Iraq, voter turnout increased dramatically, as did participation in other election-related activities. In 2008, Bush was no longer on the ballot, but Barack Obama and John McCain presented Americans with sharply contrasting positions on almost every major domestic and foreign policy issue. Polling data and turnout in the presidential primaries and general election indicate that public interest in the 2008 presidential campaign was even higher than in 2004. Some Americans may be turned off by the sharp ideological divisions between the parties, but more Americans appear to be excited and energized by the choice between a consistently liberal Democratic Party and a consistently conservative Republican Party. As a result, the size of the engaged public has been increasing.[55]

Among many other dubious achievements, Trump has surpassed George W. Bush as a polarizing president and, as a result, greatly stimulated public political engagement. For example, voter turnout in the midterm elections of 2018 achieved the highest level of any midterm election in a century. Voter turnout was 50.3 percent of the voting eligible population, which represented the largest increase from a previous midterm in American history (36.7 percent of eligible voters in the 2014 midterms).[56] Michael McDonald, of the United States Elections Project, noted the dramatic rise and attributed it to Trump. Noting that the next highest midterm turnout was in 1966, when 48.7 percent of eligible voters went to the polls, McDonald commented: "1966 is the middle of the civil rights movement. We had Vietnam going on. It's a tumultuous time in our politics. If you look at 2018, that's your parallel. . . . The country's doing well economically, but Trump is really driving the conversation. He's impassioned people both for and against him . . . Trump's not going away in 2020. . . . I wouldn't be surprised to see record turnout."[57] Voter turnout among young voters (aged eighteen to twenty-nine) also increased dramatically in 2018, up from 13 percent of eligible young voters turning out in the 2014 midterms to 28.2 percent four years later.[58]

Other forms of participation in the political process are attending a protest or rally, or working for a cause or candidate. A 2018 Kaiser Family Foundation poll found 20 percent of Americans had attended a rally since 2016 and another 26 percent were "nuts and bolts" activists, having worked for a party, campaign, or political group, or engaged in other forms of activism. Half of rally-goers reported being more active in attending events in the past two years, and 19 percent said the first rally they attended had been in the last two years, which shows an increase in activity during and since the 2016 election.[59]

And of course McDonald was right to anticipate record voter turnout in 2020. In that year's presidential election about two-thirds—66.3 percent—of the voting eligible population actually voted. That was the highest voter turnout in 120 years, beating out the previous high turnout year since 1900, which was 1908, when 65.7 percent of the eligible population voted.[60]

The increase in public political engagement under Trump should not be overstated. By some traditional measures, public engagement remains unimpressive. The public continues to show low awareness of important national news stories and figures.[61] But in terms of the most essential feature of political engagement, voting, the public engagement is literally at historically high levels. One might say that the public is engaged but not as informed as might be hoped and is possible.

This situation presents intellectuals with an obvious opportunity. The members of the public are, for the moment, engaged but not informed. Their approach to political practice is something like "ready, fire, aim." They are active and the majority of them know what they do not want, which is the illiberalism lite offered by Trump and the Republican Party, but are feeling their way forward to determine what they do want. Intellectuals can facilitate that process by being interpreters between experts and the public, applying expert ideas to public problems, and communicating the concerns of the public to experts. This is a process that is not likely to be effective if intellectuals deliberately take up intellectual standpoints that are as marginal as possible to the mainstream of political activity, under the mistaken assumption that only from there can critical distance be achieved. Intellectuals have to navigate a course that covers many standpoints, including all those that are part of the American national identity and the wide range of standpoints occupied by intellectuals of different disciplines and schools of thought. Their object must be to help make democracy work, by facilitating democratic discourse on what the goals of democratic politics should be, the best means of reaching them, and how democratic institutions can be structured to make implementation of those means possible. This involves abandoning popular ideological fetishes and making democracy itself the focus of political life.

How Ideas Matter Now

Again, the American public is more politically engaged than it has been in a long time, and that engagement manifests itself mostly as opposition to Trump and his watered-down version of illiberal ideology. The 2018 midterm elections saw record turnout and so did the presidential race of 2020, which, given the anti-Trump sentiments of the majority of voters, was mostly bad news for Trump and illiberalism-lite. Trump lost handily, but not in a landslide realigning election that some analysts had predicted and hoped for.

A realigning presidential election in 2020, one along the lines of 1932 or 1964, would have been tremendously helpful. A sharp repudiation at the polls would have checked the vogue for illiberal and identitarian ideologies and driven the Republican party back within the bounds of the liberal democratic political spectrum. Moreover, a landslide victory putting Democrats in control of both the White House and Congress would have created a moment of syzygy—assuming a conservative Supreme Court could have been brought to heal—and made possible bouts of both nonincremental legislative change and constitutional reform to address government dysfunctions. The latter would have been especially important. The cause of much of the public sector failures that have created a breeding ground for illiberal movements is our overly fragmented constitutional system, which is in sore need of updating and rationalization. A repudiation of anti-democratic ideologies and the reinvigoration of liberal democratic political institutions would have dealt illiberalism a formidable one-two punch.

Many observers predicted this rosy scenario would unfold. The most detailed sketch of this hope was *R.I.P. G.O.P.: How the New America Is Dooming the Republicans*, by polling analyst Stanley B. Greenberg. He believed "Trump's Tea Party-Evangelical GOP can't just be defeated. It must face a repudiating, shattering defeat,"[62] and asserted that "the 2020 election could produce a historic result on an even greater historic scale" than the strong Democratic victories in the 2018 midterm elections.[63] Of course this did not happen and the question now is how to address the ongoing illiberal threat given this much-less-than optimal outcome.

If the goal is a realigning presidential election, reaching it is largely a matter for activists and politicians. Obviously more red states will need to be flipped blue, and so two of the states where that happened in 2020—Arizona and Georgia—provide models that need to be replicated elsewhere. Georgia is especially interesting for the successful effort of Stacy Abrams to build a grassroots network of activists who got out Black, Hispanic, and Asian-American voters to throw the state to Biden. Why not build similar networks in other battleground states and so produce the desired realigning election?

This strategy is articulated in the most detail by Steven Philips in *Brown Is the New White: How the Demographic Revolution Has Created a New American Majority*. Phillips's argument is that America is moving toward being a minority-majority nation and that process has created a

New American Majority. He writes that "Obama's ascendance marked the political emergence of a New American Majority consisting of the overwhelming majority of people of color and a meaningful minority of Whites who are progressive," and that "The United States remains a nation in demographic transition, and, despite Trump's election, those changes are continuing apace. . . . The swelling ranks of people of color comprise the cornerstone of the New American Majority."[64] Philips lists the minority groups that, in sum, add up to a slim majority of the electorate: African Americans, Latinos, Asian Americans, Native Americans, Arab Americans, Iranian Americans, and progressive Whites. His political prescription is straightforward: 1) make sure all potential voters in these groups actually vote by investing in grassroots networks that will get them to the polls, and 2) give nonvoters a reason to vote by fielding candidates from these groups who support a strong progressive agenda. There is no point, Phillips argues, in making appeals to voters outside these blocs because those outside—such as the white working class—are shrinking in size. The goal is simply to ensure that the groups making up the New American Majority end up dominating politics.

Given the striking success of Stacy Abrams in delivering Georgia to Biden in 2020, Phillips seems to be essentially correct. Certainly more of what he calls "frontline states," such as Texas and Florida, can be flipped blue through greater on-the-ground organizing of minority voters who would bring the needed realigning election much closer. Phillips is convincing when he argues that Democrats should direct more money into such efforts and less into television advertising. But his vision of politics as war between two sets of identity groups that is won by whichever set assembles 50 percent plus one of the electorate oversimplifies the matter.

It has been pointed out that over time the percentage of people of Hispanic, Asian, and Black backgrounds who identify as white might well grow. In the 2010 Census, 53 percent of Latinos, and more than half of Asian Americans of mixed background, identified as white.[65] Very possibly members of these groups will assimilate as more established ethnic groups have done and increasingly think of themselves as white. Whether people of Hispanic, Asian, and Black backgrounds who identify as white will vote progressive and function as part of Phillips's New American Majority is not clear.

Further, Phillips uses the percentage of each identity group that voted for Obama in 2012 as a proxy for how progressive it is. In that election, 93 percent of Blacks voted for Obama. Therefore Philips assumes 93 percent of the Black electorate is progressive and will remain so in future elections. But there will never again be another first Black president, so it is not certain whether 93 percent of Blacks can be relied on to vote as progressive Democrats through the foreseeable future.

Also uncertain is whether it is safe to assume that because 39 percent of whites voted for Obama in 2012 therefore a solid 39 percent of whites will reliably vote progressive in years to come. Researchers have found that whites express more conservative opinions when they are exposed to information about the ongoing majority-minority demographic shift. This phenomenon is termed "group status threat" in a 2018 study entitled "Racial and Political Dynamics of an Approaching 'Majority-Minority' United States," which explains:

> Given the rise in group status threat in response to exposure to the "majority-minority" shift information; . . . the known influence of group status threat on political identity; . . . and support for racial exclusionary policies designed to protect whites' political, economic, and social privileges . . . it is, again, unsurprising that highlighting this shift affects whites' political behavior. . . . Indeed, whites for whom the impending racial demographic changes of the nation are salient (1) endorse more conservative positions on a variety of policy issues, . . . (2) express more support for the Tea Party, . . . and (3) reported greater support for Republican presidential candidate Donald Trump (if they also reported having higher levels of ethnic identification . . .).[66]

Very interestingly this study found that exposure to information about the growth of America's Hispanic population not only made whites express more conservative views, but had the same effect on other minority groups, including Blacks, Asian Americans, and Native Americans. So emphasizing the arrival of a New American Majority of which Hispanics are a prominent part might drive other potential members of that potential majority into the conservative coalition.

In short, Phillips's analysis is static and assumes that how people think of themselves and how their self-conception effects their politics will stay as they were circa 2012. But a deeper problem lies in its assumption that the

problems confronting America can be solved by overthrowing the old conglomerate faction that governs America and substituting a new one. Here
we bump into the limitations of the benign identity politics of new ethnic
and racial groups organizing as interest groups to get their fair share out of
the nation's pluralistic political system. A new set of interest groups, even
if it amounts to a progressive New American Majority, is still subject to
all the limitations of pluralistic politics identified by Olson in *The Logic of
Collective Action*. Smaller, narrow, self-aware interests with sizeable costs or
benefits at stake will still have an easier time organizing into effective lobbies than will large, indifferent groups whose members each have relatively
little to gain or lose on any particular issue. If it gained power, Phillips's
New American Majority would produce a burst of, and ongoing support
for, progressive legislation that is much to be desired. But even so, special-
interest groups would go on exploiting the unorganized public interest,
public goods would still be underproduced, collective action to address
common dangers such as pandemics and climate change would not necessarily be facilitated, Congress would go on being dominated by lobbyists,
public finance would still be a shambles, compensating people damaged by
globalization and economic restructuring would remain difficult, and the
bureaucracy would continue malfunctioning. Simply adding new interests
to America's political scene and reconfiguring the coalition of interests
that adds up to a majority faction may do a lot of good, but it will not
address the shortcomings inherent in the pluralistic politics of liberal democracy. And without a better functioning government the public-sector
failures that illiberals exploit to their advantage would remain.

Phillips's analysis, and any analysis that focuses primarily on demographic change and the creation of new interests as the solution to the
rise of illiberalism in America, overlooks two key concerns. One is the
need for constitutional reform to improve the functioning of government.
This issue is dealt with in chapter 7. The other is the need to once again
make it possible for ideas to check the power of interests by reinvigorat-
ing the production of public ideas. Here intellectuals and the ideas they
disseminate have a role to play, one that is ignored by political observers
who believe demographics is destiny. Inevitable social trends do not automatically produce the desirable political outcomes that they portend. And
because ideas are an independent political resource, realizing the potential of a New American Majority requires not only organizing by activists

but also work by intellectuals. Intellectuals must interpret the significance of demographic change so that people respond to it in ways that reinforce rather than undermine liberal-democratic institutions and political culture. There are various ways they can do so.

Very importantly, a study on the racial and political dynamics of a majority-minority America found that when whites were exposed to information about the majority-minority "threat" but were also "assuaged" with information that their social status would not be undermined, they did not express increased support for conservative positions, movements, and candidates. The authors conclude that to avoid the emergence of a reactionary white identity politics, "it is entirely likely that some effort to assuage the identity threat and broader concerns of white (Christian) Americans is going to be necessary, but any efforts to do so will also need to avoid privileging the continued and guaranteed racial dominance of whites."[67] The study offers some suggestions on what this assuaging could look like:

> So what can be done to avoid the likelihood of increased racial tension, discrimination, and perhaps violence in the wake of the increasing diversity of the nation? One possibility is that altering the way the demographic change information is framed could reduce its most divisive effects. Consider, for instance, the "majority-minority" construct. Is there any compelling reason to think of all Americans who are not in the "non-Hispanic white" category as one group to be contrasted against non-Hispanic whites? This "us vs. them" framing is certain to facilitate the zero-sum thinking that promotes racial conflict. Similarly, it may be useful to rethink who is counted as "white" in these estimates. . . . Indeed, recent research suggests that creating a definition of white that includes, rather than excludes, anyone who identifies as having a white parent can alleviate some of the social and political effects typically found when the growing diversity of the nation is made salient.[68]

The finding that the us-versus-them framing of demographic change stokes white opposition and racial tension is important. As the review of illiberal identitarianism in chapter 4 showed, the us-versus-them or friend-versus-foe conception of politics is central to that ideology. The friend-versus-foe concept is a cornerstone of illiberalism precisely because it promotes white identitarianism. Proponents of a demography-is-destiny analysis who fall into an us-versus-them framing of the New American Majority are unintentionally playing into the illiberals' hands.

Phillips could have usefully incorporated these suggestions in his analysis. He engages in an us-versus-them framing of the New American Majority when he describes conservative states as "occupied territory" and progressive states as "liberated zones" and sees politics as "electoral struggles between the proponents of hate and the champions of love."[69] Further, instead of working with an expansive definition of white, he expansively defines African American and Asian American by including in those categories all people who in the 2010 Census identified themselves as being both white and African American or white and Asian American. Phillips also opts for the us-versus-them framing when he assumes there are no commonalities between the New American Majority and the rest of the country. He scoffs at the idea of "explaining historical events through commonalities and shared ideals of the American people" and asks "which shared ideals existed between Native Americans and the people who massacred them and what the commonalties were between Black people held in slavery and the owners who whipped them."[70] He approvingly cites the idea of framing "the story of the United States as 'identity politics'—a series of conflicts over power and control between various groups."[71]

Thus the first imperative for intellectuals in interpreting the significance of ongoing demographic change is to challenge any us-versus-them formulation of it. Doing so involves finding and emphasizing whatever real commonalities exist between groups in the new and the old American majority. Of course there are situations where there is no such commonality, as evidenced by the historic injustices against Native Americans and enslaved people cited by Phillips. But as chapter 4 demonstrated, there is an American identity in the sense of a bundle of cognitions about what it means to be an American that people of many different backgrounds hold in common. This chapter has discussed the importance of intellectuals in interpreting expert ideas to a broad public. But the American identity provides another set of ideas that need interpreting by intellectuals. Intellectuals can contribute to the forging of a New American Majority by interpreting, insofar as possible, that development as congruent with or at least not contrary to the key elements of the American identity.

One feature of that identity clearly lending itself to this purpose is incorporationism, which is defined, as noted earlier, by Schildkraut as the "notion that America's unique identity is grounded in its immigrant legacy and in its ability to convert the challenges immigration brings into thriving strengths."[72] She further notes that "the incorporationist conception of American identity . . . centers on the immigrant legacy of the nation, emphasizes the immigrant experience as a shared one, and sees American society as a multiethnic one that occupies a space somewhere in between the two extremes of cultural erasure and separatism." Incorporationism is not multiculturalism, which, in its "hard" versions, is an "extreme scenario of complete cultural divisions or the promotion of a corporatist or consociational society; it does not call for placing ethnicity prior to citizenship . . . [or] call for the state to provide ethnically based group rights[;] that particular perspective has never gained much currency beyond academic and activist circles."[73]

Incorporationism can be expanded to include once marginalized groups such as women, Blacks, gays, and others who are not immigrants but who also have only relatively recently started to be incorporated in the mainstream of American politics. One must be careful here. Nathan Glazer and Daniel Moynihan made a bad slip when, in their seminal work *Beyond the Melting Pot*, they interpreted African Americans as an ethnic group rather than a racial group in order to categorize their experience as essentially similar to that of immigrants. Obviously, the unique experiences of Blacks, women, and gays are very different from the immigrant experience. Incorporationism should not involve seeking some simplifying common denominator among very heterogeneous groups. Doing so would be the extreme cultural erasure that incorporationism rejects. But it is possible to draw on America's experience of mass immigration and the nation's ability to finally convert its challenges into strengths and draw a loose analogy between that process and the current rise of a New American Majority. Certainly, the analogy will not hold in all respects and real differences and new issues will have to be acknowledged. The point is that thinking about current demographic change in terms of incorporationism frames that change in terms that are familiar to and consistent with a major feature of the American identity. Doing so potentially can assuage the group status threat that whites and other groups may feel and so forestall a backlash that would undermine the creation of a new majority.

If incorporationism is a feature of the American identity that offers an obvious resource to intellectuals in helpfully interpreting current demographic change, another feature, ethnoculturalism, presents an obvious problem. To cite Schildkraut again, "Ethnoculturalism . . . is an ascriptivist tradition that sets rigid boundaries on group membership. In its extreme, ethnoculturalism maintains that Americans are white, English-speaking Protestants of northern European ancestry. . . ."[74] If the possibility of a majority-minority America is interpreted in extreme ethnoculturalist terms, we end up with the Alt-Right position that a New American Majority is an existential threat to the "real" America and must be resisted at all costs. Therefore intellectuals have to oppose the increasing salience of extreme ethnoculturalism in American politics, which is a challenge given that for much of the population ethnoculturalism is a fixed part of the American identity.

One strategy would be to separate the "ethno" and "cultural" elements of this part of the American identity and emphasize its shareable cultural aspects over its ascriptive ethnographic side. A good symbol of this approach is Khizr Khan, the Pakistani immigrant and Gold Star father who, while speaking before the Democratic presidential convention of 2016, pulled from his pocket and held aloft a copy of the Constitution of the United States. As *The Rise of the Alt-Right* discusses, despite the many racist practices of American history and today, the ideas of the American founding are not inherently ethnocentric and can be shared by all Americans in a way that ethnicity and race cannot. And the founding ideas are really more than ideas; they are ideals, cultural norms that are deeply embedded in the American identity. Illiberals despise the idea that America is a propositional nation, one where citizenship is based prominently on shared ideals rather than ethnography. The propositional nation concept breaks off the cultural aspect of ethnoculturalism, discards the ethnographic element, and thus domesticates the element of the American identity that illiberals place their hopes on and want to elevate to the exclusion of all others.

Ethnoculturalism can be defanged and white group status threat can be assuaged if the development of a New American Majority is interpreted as posing no necessary danger to the preeminent status of the founding ideals in American political culture. Doing so should not involve covering up the gap that has always existed between the founding ideals and social reality. Nor should the imperfect expression of those ideals by the founders themselves be papered over. The goal is not to paint a highly airbrushed account of the founding ideals and then berate newly rising ethnic, racial, and other groups into worshiping them. Rather, the object is to establish a continuity between earlier expressions and manifestations of the founding ideals and the developing New American Majority that will, as past generations have done, find its own way of articulating and implementing them. It is entirely possible to be honest about the limitations of the founders and the founding and yet see their ideals as part of a unifying American identity both old and new groups can share. In fact, it is probably best to make sure that even such blemishes on the foundational ideals as Jefferson's and Lincoln's disparaging remarks about the abilities of Blacks are known to all. When these shortcomings are hidden, illiberals can uncover and flaunt them to create the specious impression that these uncharacteristic expressions of racism represent the only truth about what the founding means for race. Being honest about these blemishes inoculates people against this rhetorical maneuver. It also makes it possible for intellectuals to interpret the newly emerging America as the latest generation struggling—imperfectly as past generations have—to more fully realize the founding ideals, and thus is consistent with the established American identity.

Do Ideas Really Matter?

But is it really true that the developing New American Majority needs to be midwifed by intellectuals who seek to forestall backlash by interpreting it as essentially consistent with the American identity? There is a school of thought among some writers on race and ethnicity that ideas are purely secondary phenomena. It is held that seizing political power and enacting policies come first, and then ideas are cooked up to justify those developments. By this account ideas do not anticipate or precipitate political developments and so changing the ideas people hold is a useless strategy for social change. If this is true, there is little role for dealers in ideas, or intellectuals, to play in the transition to a new majority.

Ibram X. Kendi develops this account of ideas as epiphenomena in *How to Be an Antiracist* and other writings. He repudiates his earlier approach to racism in which he ". . . became a college professor to educate away racist ideas, seeing ignorance as the source of racist ideas, seeing racist ideas as sources of racist policies, seeing mental change as the principal solution, seeing myself, an educator, as the primary solver."[75] His research led him to what he considers a more sophisticated view:

> The source of racist ideas was not ignorance and hate, but self-interest. The history of racist ideas is the history of powerful policy-makers erecting racist policies out of self-interest, then producing racist ideas to defend and rationalize the inequitable effects of their policies, while everyday people consume those racist ideas, which in turn sparks ignorance and hate. . . . Educational and moral suasion is not only a failed strategy. It is a suicidal strategy.[76]

In his earlier book, *Stamped from the Beginning: The Definitive History of Racist Ideas in America*, Kendi emphasizes that overcoming racism involves not only education, but ". . . Americans committed to antiracist policies seizing and maintaining power. . . ."[77]

From all of this one would expect Kendi to give up on being an educator and college professor and become purely a political activist seeking to seize power and make policy. But not a bit of it; Kendi writes about establishing a university antiracism center and how "My research in the history of racism and antiracism revealed that scholars, policy experts, journalists, and advocates had been crucial in successfully replacing racist policy with antiracist policy."[78] How, one wonders, did these scholars, experts, and others go about formulating antiracist policies unless they developed and articulated them as ideas? Before racist policies can be replaced, doesn't someone have to come up with an idea of the antiracist policies to replace them? And in that case, won't the ideas come first and the policies second and not the other way around, as Kendi claims is always the case?

If Kendi is arguing that ideas all by themselves will not create policy change, he is right. Other political resources such as votes, organization, money, and authority will have to be mobilized to implement the ideas. But if he is arguing that ideas never preceded or provoked policy change, he is wrong. The literature on the generative role of ideas in the policy process is large and documents many situations in which ideas come first and policies second.[79] In fact, despite Kendi's de-emphasis of the role of education in overcoming racism, he writes that one part of the work done at his antiracist university center will be to "Disseminate and educate about the uncovered racist policy and antiracist policy corrective."[80] So it seems that as an operational matter of fact, education and ideas will play an important role in Kendi's efforts to replace racist policies. He is, after all, the author of two influential books on antiracism, one of which is explicitly a history of ideas, so ideas really are his stock-in-trade. Why then Kendi works with a methodology that relegates ideas to an entirely secondary role is not clear.

Kendi's de-emphasis of ideas leads him to reduce the role of what he calls "mental change" or "educating for the sake of changing minds," that is, persuasion. He believes people in political power are driven entirely by self-interest and that "Power cannot be persuaded away from its self-interest."[81] But in fact there is a large literature questioning the assumption that political actors are driven primarily by self-interest,[82] and there is also more-focused work that shows people in privileged positions are not motivated solely by self-interest and can be persuaded to change their minds.

The most recent work that is directly on point for the issue of self-interest in identity politics is a dissertation by Vladimir E. Medenica, "How the Few Persuade the Many: Overcoming Marginality in the Fight for Public Opinion." Medenica sets out to answer "why American society has witnessed substantial progress on issues fraught with conflict and controversy, often in a historical eye blink and, almost by definition, at some non-zero cost to the majority group."[83] The issues he examines are same-sex marriage, voter identification laws, and support for the United Farm Workers (UFW).

Regarding same-sex marriage, there was a dramatic change in public opinion from only 12 percent of respondents to the General Social Survey (GSS) who were in support of the idea in 1988 to 57 percent support in 2014, one year before the Supreme Court upheld the right of same-sex couples to marry in *Obergefell v. Hodges*. The idea that there was such a right was first articulated in 1983 by Evan Wolfson, a Harvard Law School student who wrote his thesis on the subject. After graduating, Wolfson tried to establish that right through litigation, but by the late 1990s that strategy had bogged down. Therefore, Wolfson "decided to leave litigation and build a mass opinion movement. Changing hearts and minds, Wolfson believed, would help create the popular support necessary for a successful legal strategy."[84]

But were the efforts of Wolfson's Freedom to Marry activist group and others really successful in changing hearts and minds? Perhaps the dramatic shift in public opinion was not due to attitude changes but to demographic changes, including older people against gay marriage passing away and a new generation favorable to the practice coming of age. Medenica tests this hypothesis by decomposing opinion trends on the issue using repeated cross-sectional data from the GSS. He found that "While 27% of attitude change is attributable to cohort replacement, over 70% is due to individual-level opinion change." That is to say "the bulk of attitudinal change since 1988 is driven by individuals changing their minds. . . ."[85]

But how were individuals brought to change their minds? The way activists framed the issue was crucial. Given the failure of the early court-oriented, litigation strategy, Medenica suggests that "framing the issue of same-sex marriage rights as one of 'equality' may not have worked in generating support."[86] What framing of the issue did work? Medenica explains:

> In their quest to build a mass opinion movement, Evan Wolfson and Freedom to Marry considered and employed a number of potential messaging strategies with one message standing above the rest: Gay people didn't want to redefine marriage or simply profit from its legal benefits, as opponents asserted; they wanted to join it as an expression of love. Much of Freedom to Marry's messaging strategy was predicated on emphasizing the love and commitment that same-sex couples share and the idea that these couples want to marry for the very same reasons as different-sex couples. . . . Freedom to Marry's messaging strategy . . . is aimed at highlighting similarities between two otherwise distinct groups. . . .[87]

Thus the experience of a major anti-discrimination cause, same-sex marriage, directly contradicts the theory that policy always comes before ideas and that dominant groups are motivated only by self-interest. In fact, that movement broadly parallels the ideational model of political change discussed earlier. First there was expert analysis, Wolfson's thesis, making the case for gay marriage. Then that analysis was simplified into a public idea—"Freedom to Marry"—that nonexperts could grasp. Then there were policy entrepreneurs, for Freedom to Marry was not only a slogan-like public idea, but an organization of activists who disseminated the idea to policymakers and mass audiences. Wolfson thus functioned at three different levels of the divided line of ideational politics: as an expert doing the original research, as an intellectual distilling the expertise to a public idea, and as a policy entrepreneur who sold the concept to broader publics. The long sought-after policy change—a Supreme Court judicial breakthrough—came after the experts, the intellectuals, the policy entrepreneurs, and the public had done their work. Justice Kennedy was explicit that the pathbreaking decision *Obergefell v. Hodges* came after this long ideational process when he wrote that the court's arguments "reflect the more general, societal discussion of same-sex marriage and its meaning that has occurred over the past decades."

Moreover, the majority-heterosexual public did not change its mind based on self-interest. In fact, heterosexuals had little to gain from same-sex marriage. What changed the dominant-heterosexual majority's mind was, Medenica found, "personal evaluations, namely moral considerations and feelings of warmth," toward gays. That is, the majority was moved when confronted with minority activists who persuasively argued that gays and heterosexuals shared many commonalities, such as the needs for love and union. The literature describes this approach as "analogic perspective taking," whereby members of a majority group "are encouraged to draw equivalencies to the experiences of" marginalized groups.[88] In other words, the majority was persuaded to change its mind when gay marriage was interpreted through the lens of ideals it deeply held.

Medenica also looks at how the mostly Hispanic UFW union won support from non-Hispanics and how white voters think about voter identification laws. He found that in order to win vital support from white consumers for its grape boycott, "the UFW strategically altered their message framing when appealing to distinct target audiences, highlighting their connection to the American labor force in English-language media while emphasizing their quest for social justice in Spanish-language appeals."[89] According to Medenica, appealing to a shared identity was crucial to the boycott's success:

> [T]he English boycott coverage was largely framed as a continuation and part of earlier American labor movements that benefitted large swaths of Americans and that were favorably perceived in the national conscious-

ness. . . . The UFW was able to communicate their struggle in a way that created a shared sense of identity among Americans who otherwise did not have much in common.

The case of the UFW can be instructional for other minority groups who face structural disadvantages but wish to effect policy change. In order to effectively appeal to majority opinion, groups must devise frames and construct narratives strategically to appeal to parts of the majority group's identity and highlight strong similarities between two or more otherwise distinct groups. . . . [P]ersuading others to join them as allies in their fight against growers and boycott grapes meant establishing clear connections and linkages to the American public by highlighting shared aspects of their identities and struggles.[90]

Regarding voter ID laws, Medenica's findings speak to the question of how to change the minds of majority group members about a contentious policy issue with racial overtones. White people were more likely to oppose voter ID laws when they were exposed to information on the issue from an advocacy group with a distinct racial identity as opposed to information provided without any such context. Thus whites were more likely to oppose voter ID laws when they received information from "Black Americans for Voting Rights" or "Hispanic Americans for Voting Rights" as opposed to information not identified with any group. Medenica suggests that:

[T]he mere presence of an advocacy group lobbying for opposition to ID requirements seems to influence opinion. . . . Stripping away the abstraction and human detachment with which many issues are discussed in politics and reminding voters that there are people who stand to be affected by policy decisions may be powerful enough to move opinion, at least on the topic of voter ID laws.[91]

The key point to take away from Medenica's work is what he concludes about identity and collective action:

[S]trategic appeals targeting majority identity can be particularly powerful. . . . [I]dentity matters for collective action. Indeed, much of the work in that area suggests that the existence of a collective identity is a necessary precursor to participating in collective action. . . . Collective identities allow people to see themselves as "linked by interests, values, [or] common histories" . . . When people see themselves as sharing a common identity, their "solidarity and motivation to work together" is enhanced.[92]

The "majority identity" to which the marginalized groups in Medenica's study appealed was the American identity. It is true that the ideals to which these minorities appealed were not exactly those identified by Schildkraut as the essential elements of that identity. Gays appealed to love and commitment, the UFW to union and solidarity, the voter ID messages to sympathy and humanization. But the point is that minds were changed when those seeking change sought common ground with those they were seeking to convince. And, in fact, such common ground did exist. As Schildkraut has documented, a great deal of common ground among a wide diversity of interests exists in the form of the American identity. Intellectuals must take advantage of this precious epistemic resource if the emerging New American Majority is to realize its potential.

Transition from Ideas to Interests

A main thesis of this book is that the rise of illiberalism is in large part due to the suboptimal performance of liberal democracies in coordinating collective action to address social problems and produce public goods. This problem is especially acute in the United States, whose separation-of-powers Constitution and fragmented policymaking process make taking public action notoriously difficult. The classic solution is a realigning election—such as those of 1932 and 1964—that temporarily creates a unified government, opens a window of opportunity for nonincremental change, and makes possible the creation of a new political and policy baseline. So if at some point through the work of activists and intellectuals and the general public America finally achieves another realigning presidential election, American government will improve its performance, address the problems that are driving the illiberal surge, and save liberal democracy, right?

Not hardly. First of all, periods of unified government are, as noted earlier, "relatively brief and infrequent interludes."[93] The new collective-action problems now facing America include climate change, maintaining peace in a multipolar world, globalization, demographic shifts, capitalist creative destruction on a grand scale, and maintaining economic growth in the face of uncertain technological development. These new challenges are on top of many hardy perennials among political problems, such as public finance, maintaining a welfare state, rationalizing government bureaucracies, and redistributing wealth while avoiding moral hazard issues. All these issues (and more) are of a scale and endurance that they are unlikely to be resolved by infrequent and fleeting windows of opportunity.

Moreover, as of late, even when moments of unified government arrive, they have turned out to be less effective than in the past. The election of 1932 was the most consequential of the post–Civil War realignments, for it established the welfare state as a permanent fixture in the American polity and inaugurated the long-lasting political baseline of the New Deal. But elections that resulted in united government since then have had less dramatic results. The election of 1964 created a united government that accomplished much: Medicare and Medicaid, the Voting Rights Act of 1965, and the expansion of the Food Stamp Program, among other things. But it did not result in a long-term political realignment, and just four years later Richard Nixon would figure out a way to defeat the New Deal electoral coalition. And some of the Great Society initiatives, such as the War on Poverty, met with ongoing opposition and had mixed success. On balance, it cannot be said that the unified government created by the 1964 election had nearly as much permanent impact as the unification achieved in 1932. Other episodes of unified or almost unified government under Reagan, George W. Bush, Obama, and Trump had important consequences but did not result in the dramatic political realignment or the permanent restructuring of the American state that was achieved under the New Deal.

It is true that Americans have found ways to implement nonincremental change even in the absence of unified government, as discussed in *The New Politics of Public Policy* and *Seeking the Center*. The Clean Air Act of 1970, the Education for All Handicapped Children Act of 1975, the Tax Reform Act of 1986, and the Personal Responsibility and Work Opportunity Act of 1996 are examples. In all these cases, policy entrepreneurs were effective at reducing an expert consensus on a complex issue into a simple public idea, such as "broaden the base; lower the rates," or "end welfare as we know it." And in a competitive political environment with a divided government, various political actors fought to claim credit for turning these ideas into law, which resulted in a legislative bidding-up process and eventually, the passage of nonincremental legislation. This ideational/entrepreneurial model of politics achieved major changes in situations where experts thought gridlock would prevail. But in the twenty-first century, this model for achieving change has not been evident, partly because the process of translating expert consensus into public ideas has broken down as a result of the digital revolution in communications. With the new technology, the value of real expertise has been diminished, the position of intellectuals has been weakened, and the quality of public ideas, reduced.

In other words, the efficacy of realigning elections and ideational/entrepreneurial politics has been reduced. These strategies were the main work-arounds that American politics had relied on to make change possible despite a highly fragmented constitutional structure and policy process. As a result, the United States must face up to a problem that it has been kicking down the road for decades. Nonincremental change is simply too hard to achieve in our constitutional system.

The difficulty of achieving major change and addressing salient social problems under the American Constitution are well-known and may be summarized as follows: In a parliamentary system, the chief executive is chosen by the legislature, so a unified government is guaranteed. But in America's separation-of-powers system, the presidency and the congressional majority may well owe allegiance to opposing parties. Indeed, America is often plagued by a divided, even antagonistic, government. Legislators—with no responsibility for picking the president or carrying out his agenda—are left free to pander to their constituents. Citizens expect no less and withhold their votes if their representatives fail to deliver the goods. Congress is thus held hostage by well-organized lobbies.

Congress is parochial in the sense that it is controlled by local interests and so feels no broader mission or purpose. Moreover, it is a powerful institution. Congress—being closer to the people—has the whip hand over the president, who is required to take a national perspective. It is difficult for government to act, and when it does act, it often produces weak, slapped-together, patchwork policies that are incoherent and ineffective. The latest example of this dysfunction is Obamacare, which is a dizzyingly complex, jerry-built structure that no one working from scratch would have contemplated. And so, too, are many policies that govern education, taxation, welfare, energy, and much else.

It would be a mistake to think that the dysfunctions of Congress are necessarily overcome by unified government. Obamacare was passed under a unified government, but doing so required the president to cave in to a swarm of demands from congressional representatives under pressure from effective interest groups. Even under united government, constitutional design empowers lobbying groups and thus determines the incentives that legislators face. The confusion and ineffectiveness of the American policymaking process is mostly an institutional phenomenon and cannot be decisively solved by electing to office the right sort of people, whether that is taken to mean conservatives or progressives.

In short, though a dramatic realigning election is much to be desired, one will not be enough to enable a dysfunctioning government to optimize its performance over the long run, respond to the crises that are encouraging the rise of illiberalism, and reassert liberal democracy as the dominant model of politics for the foreseeable future. To achieve all of that, the well-known limitations of the U.S. Constitution have to be addressed at last. How to do that is the subject of chapter 7.

6
Irony

Ideas and Irony

Chapter 5 discussed ideas, how the process of producing public ideas has been damaged and requires repair, and how the professionals who deal in ideas—intellectuals—have an important role to play in the emergence of a New American Majority and a much-needed political realignment. The next step in the argument could be to discuss the constitutional changes that are needed if the New American Majority, once it gets its moment of opportunity in a united government, is to be able to take effective collective action and achieve the nonincremental reforms that will undermine the rise of illiberalism. That step is taken in chapter 7, on interests.

But before moving on from ideas to interests, there are still some issues regarding ideas to be addressed. More needs to be said about how new digital media have altered the entire tone of public communication. That tone is highly ironic, so much so that it undermines clear communication on digital media, to the point where knowing exactly who is saying what to whom is often impossible. The absence of gatekeepers on new media raises "the difficulty of distinguishing irony from earnestness in public conversation online"[1] to an axiom of communication on the web. This chapter discusses how to deal with this problem through better regulation of the internet to promote greater candor among its users.

The Irony Wars

Almost immediately after the 9/11 attacks, there was a sense in many quarters that an old cultural climate had come to an end and a new one had begun. This sense often invoked irony in its expression. Graydon Carter, the editor of *Vanity Fair*, declared "the end of the age of irony." The *New York Observer*'s editor, Peter W. Kaplan, said that "irony is on the junk heap now," and a New York City book publisher announced that "somebody should do a marker that says irony died on 9-11-01." Other cultural leaders disagreed. The editor in chief of *New York* magazine, Caroline Miller, said, "I don't think a year from now we are going to be taking our experience straight up. We will still have a limited tolerance for earnestness." And a *Salon* magazine writer insisted, "As jingoists call for a New Sincerity, we need irony—the serious kind—more than ever."[2]

Perhaps readers find it as odd as I do that in the debate over how to interpret America's greatest military catastrophe since Pearl Harbor, the concept of irony should play such a prominent role. The reason is that, by the turn of the millennium, irony had come to be a proxy for postmodernism, while seriousness was seen as the essence of modernism. Thus one literary scholar noted, "Some critics have directly linked postmodernism's alleged demise with 9/11 . . . arguing that on that day 'any reign of irony ended' . . . replaced instead by 'a return to feeling, an upwelling of unironized emotion that writing has attempted to honor, represent, and contain.'"[3] The postmodernist critic Alan Wilde writes that the "modernist response to chaos" is "the artistic ideal of perfect, epiphanic moments," while postmodern irony, being "chary of comprehensive solutions, doubtful of the self's integrity . . . confronts a world more chaotic (if chaos admits of gradations) than any imagined by its predecessors." Thus postmodern irony generates a cultural climate where "a world in need of mending is replaced by one beyond repair."[4] With irony thus linked to postmodernism and postmodernism linked to visions of a world beyond repair, it is not hard to see how some commentators, anticipating the start of one of the biggest repair jobs in American history, felt the country could do without irony.

Pushback against the end of irony thesis came quickly, and by 2013 it was held to have "largely been laughed out of court."[5] In his useful history of the role of irony in early twentieth-century American literature, Matthew Stratton surveyed the victory of the pro-irony forces:

> Of course, by now the ostensibly empirical question of whether or not irony "died" on 9/11 is long settled; even if you haven't read *The Onion* or you somehow missed the ascendancy of Jon Stewart and Stephen Colbert from comedians to respected and influential political analysts, a slew of critical studies and popular pundits have reassured us that irony is indeed still alive and kicking, performing its ancient function of critique and entertainment. . . . Thus scholars working in philosophy, cultural studies, and political theory have produced intellectually robust defenses of irony . . . that demonstrate how irony continues to be a salient feature of manifold cultural discourses and articulate myriad reasons why democratic societies don't just seem to like irony but *need* irony. . . . Such defenses plainly outnumber continuing complaints about the "anti-democratic implications" of the supposed fact that "we have in recent decades been building a towering Fortress of Irony." Moreover, such defenses of irony have proved more convincing than novelists or critics pining for "a post 9/11, postironic novel" that would "move beyond irony and youthful nihilism."[6]

In 2021, it remains the case that irony plays a prominent role in American culture. Things could not be otherwise, of course. Irony can no more "die" than can metaphor, symbolism, analogy, or any other trope. And for one currently prominent cultural movement, irony is a central rhetorical strategy. The only problem is that this movement really does exploit the anti-democratic implications of a certain type of irony and does indeed put that form of expression in the service of youthful nihilism. That movement is illiberalism, which has weaponized postmodern irony to persuade a new generation that the liberal democratic order really is beyond repair.

Illiberalism and Irony

Wayne C. Booth, author of *A Rhetoric of Irony*, the most comprehensive work on the subject by an American, identified one use of irony that contemporary illiberals employ to the utmost: "Self-protection. Whenever we use irony we are disguising a truth, usually a hostile or embarrassing truth, one that we don't dare speak right out."[7] Illiberals, who certainly believe plenty that they do not dare speak right out, rely a great deal on irony for self-protection and are not afraid to say so. Here is Nick Fuentes, a young Alt-Rightist best known for his Holocaust-denying YouTube programs, blurting out what he is up to:

> Irony is so important for giving a lot [of], like, cover and plausible deniability for our views. . . .
>
> Earnestness, this sort of academic filibustering, obfuscating, this is not effective political communication. Especially not when you're dissident and especially not for young people. What is required is someone who is tactical with their language. Tactical, OK? Use irony because, you know, when it comes to something like Holocaust revision, I mean this is something where you cannot deviate from the popular consensus on. But you also, you also can't like, I also think you can't tell the truth if you adhere to that.
>
> So, it's sort of like getting in the middle. It's being provocative, it's being, I can't explain this in a very explicit way. You're going to have to just, sort of get what I'm saying here. When it comes to a lot of these issues you need a little bit of maneuverability that irony gives you.
>
> "Oh well, what does that mean?" "Well, I was joking." "Well it's whatever." "Well, you don't understand the tone." "Well, you don't understand humor."
>
> And that's true. And it is true to a great extent. You know if you sat me down with a fucking lie detector and asked me to go through all my views completely earnestly and sincerely, I'd probably come across a lot more moderate than you'd imagine.
>
> But irony is like a very important, like, linguistic and rhetorical weapon so that we can be subversive. And that is what they don't understand. We are dissidents.[8]

The most striking thing about these remarks is how Fuentes deliberately lets the cat out of the bag about how he and his movement hide their nasty ideas behind a fog of irony. Note also how he openly denies the truth of the "popular consensus on" the Holocaust—which is simply that the Holocaust really happened, was mainly directed against Jews, and claimed the lives of millions of people—and defends Holocaust revision.

Greg Johnson, editor of Counter-Currents Publishing, one of the most radical Alt-Right websites, also acknowledges the utility of irony in disseminating illiberal ideas, but he stresses the need to finally "close the deal" and convince neophytes to straightforwardly embrace illiberalism:

> There's a place and a role for irony. People are not overly eager to commit to new things, especially if they are radical and marginal. This is why we have changing rooms at clothing stores, so you can try clothes on and see if they look good on you before you buy them. This is why we let people test drive a car before they commit to buying it. This is why merchants have 30-day money back guarantees. If you don't have to fully commit upfront, then you're more likely to try something, and if you try it, then you are more likely to buy it.
>
> Ironic spaces where people can encounter White Nationalist ideas and memes perform an important function for our movement. They allow people to try on radical ideas for size before committing to them. Irony gives them deniability if mom looks over their shoulder. They can just jump back and say, "Whoa! I'm just playing around here! Don't take this seriously! I'm not committed to this. I disavow! I was just being ironic!" If more people feel safe trying on our ideas without committing to them, more people will ultimately come on board.
>
> But we must never lose sight of the fact that, in the end, we have to close the deal. The salesman who lets you take a test drive can't let you remain non-committal. The shop girl who lets you try on a shirt can't let you remain non-committal. When people are exploring our ideas, we can't let them remain non-committal either. This is not a game. We are not just playing with ideas, we are fighting for the survival of our race against cunning and ruthless enemies who are out to exterminate us. If you are detached and bemused about that, you haven't gotten the message. This is war, and there is no room for ironists in foxholes.[9]

This passage is interesting for several reasons. First, it confirms how illiberals use irony as a means of acclimatizing potential recruits. And it indicates that irony is only a stepping-stone to serious commitment to white nationalism, which is Johnson's brand of illiberalism. Also striking is the open acknowledgement that illiberals regard those who disagree with them, not as adversaries, but as "cunning and ruthless enemies" with whom they are at war. As for ideas, they are merely things to play with.

However, some illiberals go a step further with their use of irony and turn it into not merely a convenient way station on the path to full illiberalism, but a complete Weltanschauung that cuts them off from the liberal democratic society around them and immunizes them against any criticism. Here again it is Fuentes, who apparently cannot stop himself from spilling the beans about what illiberals are up to, who states explicitly how illiberals turn irony into a vision of life:

> As a young man, as somebody in Generation Z, we look around at the world that we live in, and especially as a young person it can be very disorienting, very discombobulating to see, like everything that you ever know turns out to be a lie and evil and wrong. That's something that's a very jarring process, the so called red pilling. I think they call it a defense mechanism, but I think defense mechanisms have utility. Ironic detachment as a defense mechanism is, I think, something that helps people cope, for better or for worse, with that disorienting feeling.
>
> But being disoriented by the collapse of the world that you know, because you grow up and you realize "Oh, wait a minute. American history is a lie. Racism is a lie. World War II is a lie. The cold war is a lie. Judeo-Christian is a lie. Illuminati is a lie (like you know what it really means). Everything is a lie. And if you hit the Catholic pill it's like, oh, no, legit, everything is a lie because the founders were Masonic and Protestant. You just don't know what to believe any more. We're just in this limbo, space.
>
> And so I think ironic detachment helps people to kind of insulate themselves from the fact that everything they attach meaning to is either wrong or uncertain. That's the age of anxiety, the renewed, that we're living in. And I think the irony helps. And also its fun, you know. If we can't have an empire, if we can't have piety, at least we can laugh, right? So.[10]

Here we have Fuentes celebrating the "irony and youthful nihilism" that was once charged against postmodernists but is now the stock-in-trade of illiberals. With this, Fuentes is more radical than even Johnson, who wants irony to stop once potential converts achieve the putative certainty of white nationalism. However, Fuentes is not only more radical than Johnson, but more consistent. If your standard of truth is so high— or so dysfunctional—that you judge American history, racism, World War II, the cold war, and Judeo-Christian culture to be lies through and through and without any exceptions or conditions (for Fuentes acknowledges none), then how can you commit to white nationalism? If you find nothing worth believing in the Declaration of Independence and the Constitution, in the work of Frederick Douglass and Martin Luther King Jr., in the oratory of Franklin Roosevelt and Winston Churchill, in the Universal Declaration of Human Rights and the writings of the Russian dissidents, in the Old Testament or New, what warrant do you have for believing the sorry collection of lumpen scholarship, phony history, and mere hate that is white nationalism? To paraphrase C. S. Lewis, once you become a nihilist, it is not that you believe in nothing, it is that you will believe in anything—Holocaust denial, white nationalism, and illiberalism included.

Fuentes and his illiberal followers have fallen headlong into a pitfall that Booth recognizes in *A Rhetoric of Irony*:

> Irony in itself opens up doubts as soon as its possibility enters our heads, and there is no inherent reason for discontinuing the process of doubt at any point short of infinity. . . . Pursued to the end, an ironic temper can dissolve everything, in an infinite chain of solvents.[11]

Certainly Fuentes and his followers seem to be linked into "an infinite chain of solvents." Young illiberals on that slippery slope are fated to end up in a position that even undergraduates in bull sessions recognize as a jejune self-contradiction: "Everything is a lie."[12]

Irony and Ambivalence

But so what if some illiberals have, by their own admission, backed themselves into an epistemic limbo from which nothing positive can come? It is true, as chapter 3 showed, that the illiberal audience is larger and more influential than is generally understood. But can it really be that the illiberals' radically nihilistic irony has significantly penetrated into mainstream American political culture? The answer is yes. In fact, illiberals' weaponized irony has spread widely through the internet and can even be considered the internet's characteristic style of discourse.

Whitney Phillips and Ryan M. Milner, the authors of a sometimes-insightful book, *The Ambivalent Internet: Mischief, Oddity, and Antagonism Online*, describe a popular maxim about irony on the internet:

Poe's Law [is] an online axiom stipulating the difficulty of distinguishing irony from earnestness in public conversation online. By posting something obnoxious to an internet forum, for example, a person might be messing with their audience for a laugh. On the other hand, they might sincerely hold an absurd or outright contemptible opinion. Both options are equally plausible, and in most cases involving unknown strangers, equally unverifiable. . . . Poe's Law is . . . particularly potent in public conversations online, where observers have far fewer opportunities to consider para linguistic signals alongside a particular statement, and just as importantly, rarely have access to the full relational context of a given interaction.[13]

There is very little literature on how frequently a typical internet user runs into real-life examples of Poe's Law.[14] But Phillips and Milner chronicle enough case histories of how difficult it is to distinguish irony from seriousness online that it seems likely Poe's Law identifies a real phenomenon. Moreover, the mere possibility that examples of Poe's Law are common has an impact on how people interpret discourse on the web. What, then, can be done when an entire medium of communication, one that is perhaps the characteristic medium of the early twenty-first century, fosters such potentially paralyzing doubt about what people are saying to each other?

Phillips and Milner say nothing can be done—get used to the fact that online communication is "ambivalence all the way down."[15] Here is what happens when these authors try to conclude what the ambivalent internet implies for democratic discourse:

Our position is simple. We are staunch advocates of the democratic process and think that problematic speech should be countered with more speech. Except actually maybe not, because not all speech, and not all voices, are given equal weight, and that position privileges those whose voices already carry further and louder than others. So okay, we're staunch advocates of the democratic process and think that the only voices that should be silenced are the voices that silence others. Except actually maybe not because sometimes those silencers are silencing silencers, and that's good, except when it isn't. . . .

So okay, we're staunch advocates of the democratic process and think it's actually good for things to get a little heated sometimes, because that's how we know that democracy is working. Yes. Except actually maybe not because underrepresented populations disproportionally bear that burden. . . . So, okay, we are staunch advocates of the democratic process . . . [ellipses in original] as our voice trails off and we stare blankly into the distance.[16]

The consequences of Phillips and Milner's bottomless ambivalence are the same as Fuentes's ironic detachment: you just do not know what to believe and end up believing nothing, or rather anything. Next stop, illiberalism. The point is that a completely ironic or ambivalent medium enormously facilitates the spread of irrationalism. And in contemporary America, the form of irrationalism most on offer is illiberalism.

If this is the intellectual atmosphere facilitated by a medium as dominant as the internet, then liberal democracy faces a serious problem. An internet that is ambivalent or ironic all the way down is not good for liberal democracy, not only because it facilitates the spread of illiberal ideologies but also because it hinders democratic discourse or, indeed, any kind of discourse at all.

The Rhetoric of Irony

Again, what can be done? A response should take two parts: first a theoretical response, a way of thinking about irony and democratic discourse in a digital age, and second a policy response, a way of regulating the internet to discourage weaponized irony and absolute ambivalence, and promote dialogue among its users.

Booth puts a name to what is needed theoretically. As to how to put an end to the "infinite chain of solvents" that irony evokes, he writes:

It is not irony but the desire to understand irony that brings such a chain to a stop. And that is why a rhetoric of irony is required if we are not to be caught, as many men of our time have claimed to be caught, in an infinite regress of negations.[17]

Thus what is needed to stop the infinite regress of weaponized irony into epistemic limbo is a rhetoric of irony—that is, a much better understanding of how irony works and how it is that, as slippery as it can be to interpret irony, "learning where to stop" is possible so long as people are frank with themselves about how irony is actually used. And since irony is the characteristic style of speech on the internet, a rhetoric of irony will lead to a rhetoric of the internet and suggest a way that democratic discourse on this medium can lead to some conclusions more helpful than trailing off and staring blankly into the distance.

To be useful in the context of the internet, the first point a rhetoric of irony must recognize is that a discourse of irony and nothing but irony will be merely an infinite regress of negations. Booth correctly notes that "when ironies are piled on ironies—when ironic moments, each presumably delightful in itself, are multiplied—suddenly all readers discover that they are bored."[18] But one can go further. No one trope can express all the limitless thoughts the human mind can form, and designating any one style of expression as primary sets an arbitrary limit on thinking that people are bound, in practice, to find tedious and will eventually strive to move beyond. When, in the end, limitless irony leaves someone bored or stymied, it must be balanced with another kind of attitude—one that is its typical counterpoint: candor. A certain type of candor puts an end to the infinite regress of doubt that an ironic temper is prone to and makes irony meaningful rather than paralyzing.

Although he does not often use the term, candor plays a significant role in C. S. Peirce's account of inquiry, in which Peirce follows the Declaration of Independence, which assumes there is no point in submitting its facts to anything other than "a candid world." He issues the following warning to skeptics:

> There is a strong tendency in us all to be skeptical about there being any real meaning or law in things. . . . I applaud skepticism with all my heart, provided it has four qualities: first, that it be sincere and real doubt; second, that it be aggressive; third, that it push inquiry; and fourth, . . . that it stand ready to acknowledge what it now doubts, as soon as the doubted element comes clearly to light. . . . But you know there is such a thing as a defect of candor of which one is not oneself aware. . . . [I]f . . . you were to turn your gaze away from an idea that shines out clearly in your mind, you would be violating your principles in a very much more radical way.[19]

Skepticism is worthwhile only if one has the candor to admit when one's doubts have been satisfied and a well-founded belief has been established. The same can be said of irony, ambivalence, or whatever frame of mind threatens to paralyze one with endless doubt. Peirce goes on to point out that people do overcome doubt and go on to hold many beliefs that seem to them to be well founded. The only point at issue is whether someone has the candor to admit there are some things he or she regards as absolutely true. In "The Essentials of Pragmatism," Peirce writes:

> Do you call it *doubting* to write down on a piece of paper that you doubt? If so, doubt has nothing to do with any serious business. But do not make believe; if pedantry has not eaten all the reality out of you, recognize, as you must, that there is much that you do not doubt, in the least. Now that which you do not at all doubt, you must and do regard as infallible, absolute truth. Here breaks in Mr. Make Believe: "What! Do you mean to say that one is to believe what is not true, or that what a man does not doubt is *ipso facto* true?" No, but unless he can make a thing white and black at once, *he* has to regard what he does not doubt as absolutely true.[20]

The illiberals' ironic detachment is exactly the sort of paper—or digital—doubt that has nothing to do with any serious business and is based on a defect of candor. Fuentes claims everything is a lie, but then he lets slip that he believes in Holocaust revisionism. This young man is not being candid with himself, which is understandable because thinking of yourself as an ironic subversive who believes in nothing is more flattering to your ego than realizing you are a neofascist, anti-Semitic dupe.

The Rhetoric of Assent

Real candor about one's beliefs can be hard to achieve. In developing his rhetoric of irony, Booth acknowledges that difficulty:

> Remember . . . it will not do to say, "Of course I can doubt that if I put my mind to it." In this game you are allowed to doubt only what you cannot *not* doubt, only what you have persuasive reason *to* doubt. . . . I know from my own experience how hard it will be for some of us not to claim doubt except when we *really* doubt.[21]

The next step in developing a rhetoric that keeps irony in its place is to appreciate what happens when not just one person, but a whole community of people, however defined, are candid about their beliefs and especially candid that they do in fact have certain beliefs. This realization opens up a possible escape hatch from the epistemic limbo of an endlessly ambivalent or ironic internet. Booth, again, is useful here as he moves beyond a rhetoric of irony to a rhetoric of assent:

> Suppose we say that we "know"—that is, have good warrant to assent to—whatever *everyone in this hall* really believes, regardless of whether we can think of abstract arguments about why his belief is not proved by other tests. Instantaneously our domain of knowledge is immeasurably increased. . . . Our knowledge is of "whatever we have good reason to believe" in the sense of "having no good reason to doubt." There will of course be gradations of such knowledge. . . . When any belief seems self-evident and we find empirically that we can think of nobody who in fact doubts it, we will be sure about it; when we find, as we usually will, that some men deny what we all agree to, we will be less sure but still able to act on our knowledge with confidence, so long as we think we could persuade any reasonable person. But when we find ourselves or the postulated experts disagreeing, we will become more tentative in proportion to their qualifications and our own sense of where the good reasons lead us.[22]

This principle that "we know whatever we can agree together that we have no good reason to doubt . . . [and] what we believe together with sureness is given 'the benefit of a doubt'" is what Booth calls "systematic assent."[23] Booth thus transitions from a rhetoric of irony to a rhetoric of assent, which is the transition we should seek to accomplish with the internet. When Booth developed his rhetoric of assent in the early 1970s, his main target was scientistic epistemologies that privileged mathematical and scientific knowledge as "true" knowledge and disparaged other forms. Whatever one makes of that debate, the rhetoric of assent is useful in the twenty-first century in a new context: it provides a way to think about the hotly debated issue of gatekeepers on the internet, as well as a theory of gatekeeping that serves as the foundation of new approaches to internet regulation.

Gatekeeping

To start at the individual level, the fact that, as Booth notes, "nobody ever gives every voice equal weight"[24] means that everyone is, in a certain sense, a gatekeeper. Each individual must and does make decisions—not all of them fully thought through or even conscious—about which of all the voices, experiences, and other evidence that bombard him or her every day will garner attention and fix his or her beliefs. This process of fixing beliefs based on some, but not other, material is what can be called gatekeeping. Without gatekeeping there is no belief, and if people are candid enough with themselves to acknowledge that they do have some beliefs they do not doubt, then they must also candidly admit the indispensability of gatekeeping to inquiry.

Gatekeeping is no less of an indispensable reality at the social level than it is at the individual level. Suppose an individual were to resolutely screen out everything that did not support beliefs to which he or she tenaciously clings. This is certainly gatekeeping, though of a primitive form that Peirce terms "the method of tenacity," which has sharp limits:

> But this method of fixing belief, which may be called the method of tenacity, will be unable to hold its ground in practice. The social impulse is against it. The man who adopts it will find that other men think differently from him, and it will be apt to occur to him, in some moment, that their opinions are quite as good as his own, and this will shake his confidence in his belief. This conception . . . arises from an impulse too strong in man to be suppressed, without danger of destroying the human species. Unless we make ourselves hermits, we shall necessarily influence each other's opinions; so that the problem becomes how to fix belief, not in the individual merely, but in the community.[25]

There is, then, communal or social gatekeeping, just as there is individual gatekeeping. But now the question arises as to who shall be the gatekeepers. Booth does not use the term "gatekeeper," but his principle of systematically giving provisional assent to whatever "we" all believe opens the question of who this "we" is that performs the gatekeeping function:

What is demanded by the principle of systematic assent is more rigorous thought than is customary about who "we" are, the group of relevant judges, the axiological experts whose shared experience confirms what we know together. Nobody ever gives equal weight to every voice. What satisfies us in practice, though the practice always can and should be refined, is the discovery that a given belief that fits our own structures of perception and belief is supported by those qualified to know.[26]

This touches on an issue that greatly preoccupies illiberals: figuring out who "we" are. As discussed in chapter 4, the illiberal answer to this question is that "we" are members of the same race, whose interests and thoughts are determined by race, and who are locked in a zero-sum struggle with other races for power and survival. This solution puts adherents on the road to either genocide or monadic isolationism. Moreover, as Peirce recognizes, the racialist answer to who the gatekeeping "we" are will collapse due to its lack of candor and the strength of the social impulse, in even the most epistemically homogeneous societies:

> [There are] men [who] possess a wider sort of social feeling; they see that men in other countries and in other ages have held to very different doctrines from those which they themselves have been brought up to believe. . . . Nor can their candor resist the reflection that there is no reason to rate their own views at a higher value than those of other nations and other centuries; thus giving rise to doubts in their minds. . . . The willful adherence to a belief, and the arbitrary forcing of it upon others, must, therefore, both be given up.[27]

Peirce's theory of inquiry can be developed to provide a better answer to who are the "we"—the relevant judges and axiological experts—that are a society's epistemic gatekeepers.

The most important point to remember is that there need not be, and should not be, a single gatekeeping class. Gatekeeping is part of the process of testing and fixing beliefs, which Peirce calls "inquiry." In principle, anyone who rationally seeks the truth participates in inquiry. But there are inquiries about many things: What caused COVID-19? Are there any Earth-like exoplanets? How can the Jets become a winning team? Who should be president? No one set of persons could possibly process all the material relevant across these and the infinite number of inquiries—great and small, consequential and minor—that are ongoing in any society, every day. The answer to "who shall be the gatekeepers?" depends on the nature of a given inquiry and who possesses the knowledge and skills relevant to advancing it. Knowledge and skills relevant to a given inquiry are expertise, which, as discussed in chapter 5, should be interpreted broadly and not be limited to only formal experts with academic or professional training. So part of the answer to the question of who shall be the gatekeepers is all experts—formal and informal—with the knowledge and skills relevant to the inquiry at hand.

But something more than expertise is necessary to be a gatekeeper in a liberal democratic polity. Also needed are a set of virtues—intellectual and moral habits—that sustain inquiry. Many authors have written about virtues of this type. For Steven Kelman, the key virtue needed in a democratic policymaking process is public spirit. Lawrence Mead has identified high-mindedness as essential in making policy in potentially divisive fields. Stephen Macedo lists some of the liberal virtues in his book of the same name: "broad sympathies, self-critical reflectiveness, a willingness to try and accept new things, self control and active, autonomous self-development, an appreciation of inherited social ideals, an attachment and even an altruistic regard for one's fellow liberal citizens."[28] More to the immediate point is a compelling article by Robert B. Talisse that applies Peirce's account of "The Fixation of Belief" to politics, and identifies "the virtues of inquiry" as follows:

> Open mindedness, willingness to listen to others respectfully, ability to change one's mind when considerations so require, and, most generally, the disposition to *critically engage* in cooperative and constructive dialogue—*these* are the virtues of inquiry, the marks of epistemic responsibility more generally, and the constituent traits of the deliberative-democratic way of life.[29]

It is important to note that while expertise is something necessarily exclusive, the virtues of inquiry are not. Not everyone is or can be an expert on professional football, tax economics, animal husbandry, the needs and concerns of a particular community in rural Tennessee, or whatever. Certainly no one can be an expert in everything. But there is no reason in principle why everyone cannot exemplify the virtues of inquiry to the best of his or her ability. In this way, even people whose expertise does not extend beyond a knowledge of their own personal affairs and thoughts can participate in liberal-democratic communal gatekeeping. They can strive to exemplify the virtues of inquiry themselves and be judges of the extent to which others exemplify them. So, the answer to the question of who makes up the "we" whose beliefs are to be provisionally embraced depends partly on who has the expertise relevant to the inquiry at hand, but also on who exemplifies the virtues of inquiry. The first question is likely to identify a relatively small group of people, but the second will identify a much larger group—potentially everyone in a liberal democratic polity who is at all engaged in a public discourse.

Gatekeeping on the Internet

How does all this fine talk apply to the intractable problem of regulating internet speech? Interestingly, Talisse's 2004 article on the Peircean politics of inquiry features an early critique of political discourse on the internet. Already the bloom was off the rose of the democratic potential of the internet, and Talisse mocks writers who "tell of an inevitable brave new world in which direct internet democracy will render government obsolete."[30] He goes on to criticize not only the internet and other media, but also the entire concept of politics as a win-or-lose struggle between competing ideological or identity camps:

> In the name of fairness and balance, mainstream media present a corrupt vision of the democratic process by reducing political decision to a Super Bowl of Left versus Right. The Internet, once seen as the savior of civil society, has revealed itself as a filtering device which allows citizens to hear "more and louder echoes of their own voices." . . .
>
> A pragmatic deliberativism cannot be a politics of policy advocacy or a politics of the "Left" or "Right"; it must go beyond these categories, for they are blocks to inquiry. On the Peircean view, the question of how to repair democracy is the question of how to *cultivate reasonableness.*[31]

With its lack of paralinguistic signals, anonymity, absent gatekeepers, irresponsible service providers, and unclear contexts, the internet today weaponizes irony, discourages candor, and positively undermines reasonableness. The question now is, what policies and practices will facilitate a more reasonable and "democracy friendly"[32] form of public discourse?

The problem with today's largely unregulated and discoursively polluted internet is a variation on a well-known problem of collective action known as the tragedy of the commons. In this scenario, a town keeps a tract of land (a commons) open to all citizens for grazing their sheep. If all of the citizens graze all their sheep there as often as they like, the grass will quickly be eaten up and the common grazing area will be overrun and eventually destroyed. All know this, but there is no gatekeeper to limit access to the commons and thus preserve it. Everyone thus has an incentive to get as much use of the commons as possible before its inevitable demise, and anyone who does not do so is simply a sucker.

Today's internet, with its lack of gatekeepers, is in some ways much like the tragic commons. True, the internet cannot be physically destroyed through overuse like a commons can be. A more exact analogy would be a river into which the town dumps its sewage and to which everyone has limitless access. With no gatekeepers, all can dump their sewage without let or hindrance no matter how polluted the river becomes. Without gatekeepers to enforce good behavior, anyone who incurs the expense of reducing his or her own pollution will simply be replaced by some other polluter and the river will still eventually become thoroughly foul.

Today's giant internet platforms—such as Facebook, Google, YouTube, and other service providers—are much like a commons or river with no gatekeepers. Users incur no cost no matter how much, and for what, they use the internet. The issue of "for what" is key. Disseminating disinformation, hate speech, coarse vulgarity, radically illiberal ideologies, and similar material through the internet is like taking a whiz into a river: impolite but satisfying and harmless up to a point. But if the practice catches on and becomes a mass phenomenon, problems will develop.

Of course, unlike a commons that can be destroyed or a river that can become impotable, the internet endures no matter how much nasty material is uploaded into it. Moreover, access to a given individual site can be controlled by its editors and so people can avoid immediate contact with the polluting material by accessing only those sites with gatekeepers. But these gatekeeping sites can be breeched through their comments sections or when offensive material is spread so widely through the unregulated internet that the regulated sites eventually have to take notice. In this way, hate speech, disinformation, and invective eventually intrude on people who would rather avoid them. Moreover, while sheep will die if they have no land to graze on and polluted water is sickening, an internet disproportionately shaped by illiberal and inquiry-blocking material will not kill anyone, at least in the short run. All that will happen is, over time, a dominant medium of communication will become increasingly democracy-unfriendly, to the detriment of American political culture overall.

One might say that the analogy of a commons to the internet fails in an important respect. As an economist would observe, there is a simple answer to the tragedy of the commons, which is enclosure or privatization. The commons will be overused and eventually destroyed only if it is a public resource and no one has an interest in preserving it and the right to do so. A private owner with property rights will protect his or her long-term interest by rationing access to the commons, in the form of charging for its use. This is a correct answer in classic microeconomic terms. Are not Facebook, Google, YouTube, and the rest all privately owned platforms? Can they not regulate access to their services, just as a private owner of grazing land can?

Regulating the Internet

The answer to this question is complicated, but for the moment just one aspect is relevant. It is true that, as private organizations, internet service providers are within their rights to regulate access to their platforms. Put aside for a moment the practical challenges of doing so. Another issue, and one relatively easy to deal with, is that under the current regulatory regime, private internet service providers have the right to but no interest in regulating access. This is because of current legislation regulating the internet—especially Section 230 of the Communications Decency Act of 1996—and the interpretation of that legislation by the courts in cases such as *Blumenthal v. Drudge*.

The early Drudge Report has been accurately described as a news "aggregator containing selected hyperlinks to news websites all over the world, each link carrying a headline written by the site's editors."[33] Matt Drudge established his outlet back in 1996, when he was working in the gift shop of CBS TV in Los Angeles. He started off emailing friends with bits of gossip he picked up and later posted them on the web. In the summer of 1997 he posted, without any effort at verification, an inaccurate rumor that Sidney Blumenthal, then an incoming aide at the Clinton White House, was a spouse abuser. Drudge quickly retracted the story, but Blumenthal filed a $30 million lawsuit against him and his website's carrier, America Online (AOL). But AOL argued it was immune from being sued because it had no role in Drudge's posting of the claim and had merely been its carrier. The company based its claim on Section 230 of the 1996 act. A law review article described the court's findings:

> The court agreed [with AOL] and held that AOL was merely a provider of an interactive computer service that carried the Drudge Report, and noted further that Congress made clear that "such a provider shall not be treated as a 'publisher or speaker' and therefore may not be held liable in tort." . . . The court followed the statutory language of Section 230 holding that AOL was immune from suit and granting its motion for summary judgment.[34]

Thus at the very dawn of internet journalism, online gatekeepers had their legs cut out from under them. Online service providers were legally immune no matter what they carried, so long as they themselves had not produced it. So who needed gatekeepers?

As for Drudge himself, the court ruled that although he was a California resident, he could be sued in Washington, D.C., as Blumenthal was doing. In a footnote, the court also questioned whether Drudge deserved the legal protections usually due to journalists: "Drudge is not a reporter, a journalist, or a newsgatherer. . . . He is, as he admits himself, simply a purveyor of gossip."[35] Yet, Drudge managed to garner support from a range of sources concerned about the First Amendment implications of the case, and in the end Blumenthal dropped his suit. It was the origin of another bad precedent for online gatekeepers. Purveyors of lies and other nasty material who violated all cannons of good journalism were nonetheless able to garner political support by draping themselves in the mantel of the First Amendment.

The height of mainstream support for the Drudge Report was when its editor was invited to give an address at the prestigious National Press

Club of Washington, D.C., in 1998. Drudge presented himself as creating a new paradigm for communication, one free of gatekeepers:

> Clearly there is a hunger for unedited information, absent corporate considerations. . . . We have entered an era vibrating with the din of small voices. Every citizen can be a reporter, can take on the powers that be. The difference between the Internet, television and radio, magazines, newspapers is the two-way communication. The Net gives as much voice to a 13-year-old computer geek like me as to a CEO or speaker of the House. We all become equal. . . . Now, with a modem, anyone can follow the world and report on the world—no middle man, no big brother. And I guess this changes everything. . . . I envision a future where there'll be 300 million reporters, where anyone from anywhere can report for any reason. It's freedom of participation absolutely realized.[36]

Much of Matt Drudge's credibility rested on his breaking of the Clinton-Lewinsky scandal, but that scoop was much less than it seemed at the time. Drudge learned that *Newsweek* had fully researched and confirmed the facts but was delaying publication of the explosive story until every last detail was in place. Drudge reported that *Newsweek* had the story but was holding back and so the dam burst earlier than the magazine's editors intended. In other words, all the work had been done by a traditional journalistic outlet, and the story would have come out in due course. Drudge had done nothing to uncover the facts of the case, which had been developed by professional journalists, not adolescent computer nerds. All Drudge had done was pick up on a media rumor, incautiously roll the dice, and luck out.[37]

The Drudge Report remains a huge news aggregation site, but neither it nor the unfiltered mode of journalism it pioneered have lived up to the expectation that they would change everything for the better. Since Lewinskygate, Drudge's imagined workforce of 300 million reporters has not unearthed another major story, but it has generated an endless supply of rumors, conspiracies, far-fetched speculation, and the like.

The point is that due to Section 230 of the Communications Decency Act of 1996 and the court's interpretation of it in *Blumenthal v. Drudge*, internet services are not responsible for libelous material disseminated on them unless they themselves created that material. Owners of private grazing land will limit access because the cost of overuse falls on them. But the owners of private web services face no cost when they provide access to libelers, haters, liars, and peddlers of disinformation.

It therefore seems that one answer to the question of how internet regulation can make this iconic medium of the twenty-first century more democracy friendly is at hand: Section 230 could be rewritten so that providers of internet services are responsible for damage caused by libelous and other hurtful material they disseminate. As things now stand, Section 230 analogizes internet services to magazine stands or bookstores that are not legally responsible for libelous material in the publications they sell. It would be better if these services were held to be like newspapers and publishers who can be sued for liable if plaintiffs meet the high standards of proof courts demand in such cases.

The point of discussing the impact of Section 230 is to help illustrate how the internet today, despite being dominated by privately owned service providers, is nonetheless much like a tragic commons. Facebook, Google, and the rest have the right to moderate the content they carry but not as much incentive to do so as could be desired. It is true that Section 230 specifically gives providers the option to moderate content if they wish to do so, and it even stipulates that if they exercise that option, the providers do not thereby become legally responsible for that content. Therefore a complete repeal of Section 230 could result in less rather than more content moderation. Moreover, repeal of the section would not by itself give service providers an incentive to block illiberal ideologies, hate speech, fake news, and other content that degrades democratic discourse. Dissemination of such material is held to be protected by the First Amendment, so service providers face no legal liability regardless of whether there is a Section 230. Therefore, other approaches to encourage better gatekeeping by service providers must be found.

The Politics of Internet Regulation

A detailed analysis of internet regulatory policy is beyond the scope of this book. But formal regulation is not the only way to give providers an incentive to moderate their content. Political and consumer pressure have had considerable impact. An insightful article by Jack Goldsmith of Harvard Law School and Andrew Keane Woods of the University of Arizona College of Law points out that the unregulated internet of the late twentieth and early twenty-first centuries has been greatly tamed—and not by government regulation, but because as the negative results of a totally unmoderated environment became obvious, informal pressure had driven providers to self-regulate. Goldsmith and Keane Woods write:

> Ten years ago, speech on the American Internet was a free-for-all. There was relatively little monitoring and censorship—public or private—of what people posted, said, or did on Facebook, YouTube, and other sites. In part, this was due to the legal immunity that platforms enjoyed under Section 230 of the Communications Decency Act. And in part it was because the socially disruptive effects of digital networks—various forms of weaponized speech and misinformation—had not yet emerged. As the networks became filled with bullying, harassment, child sexual exploitation, revenge porn, disinformation campaigns, digitally manipulated videos, and other forms of harmful content, private platforms faced growing pressure from governments and users to fix the problems.
>
> The result a decade later is that most of our online speech now occurs in closely monitored playpens where many tens of thousands of human censors review flagged content to ensure compliance with ever-lengthier and more detailed "community standards" (or some equivalent). More and more, this human monitoring and censorship is supported—or replaced—by sophisticated computer algorithms. The firms use these tools to define acceptable forms of speech and other content on their platforms, which in turn sets the effective boundaries for a great deal of speech in the U.S. public forum.[38]

The transition from a free-for-all to monitored playpens is a highly ambivalent development. The authors note that "digital surveillance and speech control in the United States already show many similarities to what one finds in authoritarian states such as China."[39] But Goldsmith and Keane Woods also note that given the alarming growth of harmful content, "Significant monitoring and speech control are inevitable components of a mature and flourishing internet, and governments must play a large role in these practices to ensure that the internet is compatible with a society's norms and values."[40] Quite rightly the authors come to an open-ended conclusion: "We are about to find out how this trade-off will be managed in the United States."[41]

This trade-off is real and cannot be avoided. But there is good reason to hope that the outcome will be much better than it is in China. The fact that, in America, internet services are provided by the private sector is crucial. Like all governments, that of China is a monopoly and a dictatorship at that. From its judgments, there is no appeal and no alternative. In America, some of the internet platforms dominate their markets, but none is an absolute monopoly. Users can vote with their feet, or their fingers, and move to a new platform if the policies of another are stultifying. Moreover, America's private sector internet is subject to regulation by a democratic government. It is sometimes said that the market power of Facebook and other providers is so overwhelming that they cannot be treated like private sector actors. However, America has plenty of experience with apparent technological monopolies, such as the railroads, telephone networks, and broadcasters. But in such cases, dominant providers of these transformative technologies were eventually brought to heal by government regulation. Therefore, if internet providers more actively moderate the content they disseminate, the chance that they will become totalitarian censors beyond the reach of democratic control is remote.

A better regulatory regime for the giant tech platforms might be similar to that imposed on broadcast media in the 1960s, which empowered them to ban offensive material but, through the fairness doctrine, required them to give air time to a diversity of opinions. It is true that given the billions of communications made through the major digital services every day it is unrealistic to hold the tech platforms responsible for vetting each and every one of them. It may be that, just as employers are not responsible for every indiscrete remark made by their employees but are held liable for a toxic work environment, the tech giants, while they cannot edit every user, can be expected to take action about major bad actors who consistently and to a wide audience generate a toxic communication environment.

The Tide Begins to Turn

In the months before the presidential election of 2020, the major digital platforms were under increasing public pressure to exercise the discretion that Section 230 grants them and moderate the material they disseminate more forcefully. Twitter's reaction to a particularly egregious piece of fake news promoted by Donald Trump may have represented a turning point.

On May 23 and 24, 2020, Trump disseminated two tweets that restated a baseless conspiracy theory against Joe Scarborough, a former Republican congressman and now a news anchor critical of Trump. The claim was that a young staffer who died in Scarborough's Florida congressional office of natural causes was likely the victim of foul play. In fact, Scarborough was in his Washington office at the time of the staffer's death, police found no evidence of a crime, and the coroner concluded the staffer had an undiagnosed heart condition that caused her to faint and fatally hit her head.[42] Here is Trump's May 24 tweet:

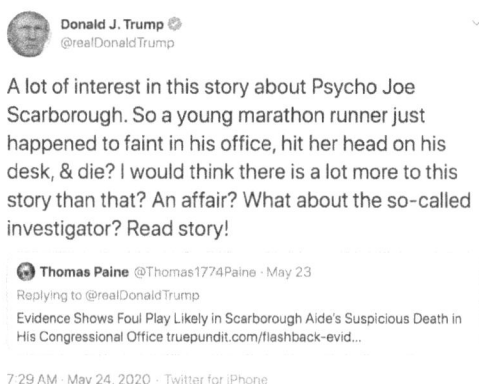

> Donald J. Trump ✓
> @realDonaldTrump
>
> A lot of interest in this story about Psycho Joe Scarborough. So a young marathon runner just happened to faint in his office, hit her head on his desk, & die? I would think there is a lot more to this story than that? An affair? What about the so-called investigator? Read story!
>
> 🌐 Thomas Paine @Thomas1774Paine · May 23
> Replying to @realDonaldTrump
> Evidence Shows Foul Play Likely in Scarborough Aide's Suspicious Death in His Congressional Office truepundit.com/flashback-evid...
>
> 7:29 AM · May 24, 2020 · Twitter for iPhone

The source Trump cites for this phony story is truepundit.com, which used the Twitter handle "Thomas Paine." That website was not mentioned in any of the link lists or blog rolls of the illiberal sources consulted for this book. However, Media Bias/Fact Check (MBFC) categorized the site as Conspiracy-Pseudoscience and concluded the following: "Overall, we rate True Pundit not only Questionable, but also a far-right conspiracy site that rarely publishes credible news. This is a far-right conspiracy source that cannot be trusted for accurate news reporting."[43] Here, then, is another example of how fake news, cooked up by the illiberal right, is picked up by a more established outlet—in this case, Trump's Twitter feed—and penetrates mainstream political discourse.

Trump had repeatedly tweeted this false story going back to 2017. Finally Timothy Klausutis, the widower of the unfortunate staffer, had had enough. He wrote a letter to Jack Dorsey, CEO of Twitter, calling for action:

Nearly 19 years ago, my wife, who had an undiagnosed heart condition, fell and hit her head on her desk at work. She was found dead the next morning. Her name is Lori Kaye Klausutis and she was 28 years old when she died. . . . There has been a constant barrage of falsehoods, half-truths, innuendo and conspiracy theories since the day she died. I realize that may sound like an exaggeration, unfortunately it is the verifiable truth. . . . The frequency, intensity, ugliness, and promulgation of these horrifying lies ever increases on the internet. These conspiracy theorists, including most recently the President of the United States, continue to spread their bile and misinformation on your platform disparaging the memory of my wife and our marriage. . . .

My request is simple: Please delete these tweets.

. . . I've reviewed all of Twitter's rules and terms of service. The President's tweet that suggests that Lori was murdered—without evidence (and contrary to the official autopsy)—is a violation of Twitter's community rules and terms of service. An ordinary user like me would be banished from the platform for such a tweet but I am only asking that these tweets be removed. . . .

I understand that Twitter's policies about content are designed to maintain the appearance that your hands are clean—you provide the platform and the rest is up to users. However, in certain past cases, Twitter has removed content and accounts that are inconsistent with your terms of service. . . .

I'm asking you to intervene in this instance because the President of the United States has taken something that does not belong to him—the memory of my dead wife—and perverted it for perceived political gain. . . . My wife deserves better.[44]

Just how abusive were these tweets by Trump? Peter H. Schuck of Yale Law has argued convincingly that Trump likely committed the tort of intentional infliction of emotional distress against Mr. Klausutis and that "Mr. Scarborough might succeed in a defamation suit against Mr. Trump for reputational harm."[45] In the predigital age, no responsible or even irresponsible publication would have run Trump's allegations. Gatekeeping editors and lawyers would have chucked the whole thing in the trash, not only out of respect for the cannons of professional journalism, but also as an act of self-preservation against legal action. Thus, libel is among the unlovely material that the unregulated internet pumps into American political discourse.

Twitter did not take down the tweets but did say the following: "We've been working to expand existing product features and policies so we can more effectively address things like this going forward, and we hope to have those changes in place shortly."[46]

Apparently Mr. Klausutis's letter had hit a nerve, or perhaps Twitter really was on the verge of changing its policy. On May 27 the company added information to two tweets by Trump that contained inaccuracies about mail-in voting and false claims that the upcoming presidential election would be "rigged." A company spokesman explained that Trump's tweets about mail-in voting "contain potentially misleading information about voting processes and have been labeled to provide additional context."[47] And the company also began attaching fact-checking labels to hundreds of tweets. Twitter, which had for years taken a mostly hands-off approach to moderating the content on its platform, was shifting to a more active policy. In a series of tweets, Jack Dorsey announced, "We'll continue to point out incorrect or disputed information."[48]

Trump responded furiously to Dorsey's change of direction and signed an executive order that threatened to strip internet service providers of the protections they enjoy under Section 230. Apparently the president did not understand that doing so would push the platforms to protect themselves by moderating content more, not less. And Mark Zuckerberg of Facebook, clinging to the techno-libertarianism that dominated discussion of the internet in its early days, rejected Twitter's newfound sense of responsibility: "I just believe strongly that Facebook shouldn't be the arbiter of truth of everything that people say online."[49] Dorsey shot back: "This does not make us an 'arbiter of truth.' Our intention is to connect the dots of conflicting statements and show the information in dispute so people can judge for themselves. More transparency from us is critical so folks can clearly see the why behind our actions."[50] After the mob assault on the electoral vote count that Trump fomented through his Twitter account and other means, the tech platforms had had enough. Twitter suspended his account permanently and Facebook banned him at least through the remainder of his term.[51]

Twitter's decision to ban Donald Trump permanently shows that better content moderation by web service providers is possible. That action came only after Trump had for years regularly used the service to disseminate lies, culminating in his big lie strategy to overturn the legitimate results of the 2020 presidential election. Many observers expressed legitimate concern over a private company being powerful enough to deny access to a president of the United States. Certainly, regulation should be promulgated that will give people who are banned avenues of appeal and will encourage the development of alternative platforms. But the fact that disinformation about the election on Twitter declined by 73 percent after Trump was banned shows that, if done properly, deplatforming notoriously bad actors can be effective.[52]

Another interesting development is the shift of the Drudge Report away from its former bad journalistic practices and questionable status to greater responsibility and less extremism. Why this change took place is not clear. Some reports speculate that Matt Drudge no longer works on or even owns his creation. Another theory is that Drudge, after sedulously supporting Trump in 2016, became disenchanted when Trump as president failed to build the southern border wall. In any case, the Drudge Report, once notoriously irresponsible, has considerably cleaned up its act. Perhaps this transformation of what was once among the largest of the illiberal outlets studied here is a sign of a change of direction for digital discourse.

Whatever one makes of these developments the key point is that a long chain of abuse by a crypto-illiberal president provoked public pressure that resulted in a major internet platform abandoning the anarcho-digital vision of the internet and facing up to the need for responsible gatekeeping. The realization that gatekeeping should be done and the determination to actually do it are more important right now than being sure exactly how to do it.

This is an experimental stage, with everyone feeling their way toward solutions. As C. S. Lewis quipped, "Anything worth doing is worth doing badly." Through trial and error, new standards, practices, policies, and technologies will be developed to strengthen the hand of gatekeepers. Over time, a better balance between openness and moderation will be struck. This book seeks only to suggest some factors that must be weighed in that balance. Various sorts of harmful internet content have been recognized, including "bullying, harassment, child sexual exploitation, revenge porn, disinformation campaigns, digitally manipulated videos." To this list can be added illiberal ideologies and the nihilistically ambivalent speech environment that facilitates them. Let those factors, too, be part of the balance when the trade-off is struck.

7
Interests

The Limits of Interest-Group Politics, Again

To recapitulate the dilemma of liberal democracy this book seeks to address: That form of government features an interest-based, pluralistic form of politics that has well-known collective-action problems. The political freedoms protected by liberal democracy encourage the formation of a wide range of interest groups. As James Madison argued, that multiplicity of factions in turn reinforces political freedom. But because no one faction is concerned with any interest except its own, such polities have trouble taking collective action and generating public goods. Further, as Mancur Olson has pointed out, not all interests are equally capable of organizing into politically effective groups. As a result, pluralistic polities are prone to some typical maladies: the exploitation of large, unorganized interests by narrow, better organized ones; difficulty in redistributing the results of economic growth; increased economic inequality; suboptimal performance in creating public goods such as a clean, sustainable environment; ineffective responses to the dislocations of creative destruction wrought by global capitalism; and other problems. And recent experience adds another collective-action problem experienced by American liberal democracy: weak responses to public health dangers such as pandemics.

The American Constitution consciously facilitates the crystallization of interest groups and therefore unintentionally enables the pathologies associated with pluralistic democracies. Over time, these long-standing problems have become more acute. Theoretically, the problems that constitutional structure has promoted could be mitigated by constitutional reform. There is no shortage of proposed constitutional changes intended to temper the propensity toward fragmentation brought on by the Constitution's combination of separation of powers, checks and balances, federalism, strong bicameralism, adversarial court system, and other features. But amending the Constitution is, by design, very difficult, and even attempting to do so is discouraged by the quasi-religious veneration that Americans give to the document. Thus the deep structure behind the collective-action problems of American democracy seems beyond remedy and therefore never gets onto any serious political agenda.

Addressing these collective-action dilemmas and the social problems they cause involves fixing our fragmented policymaking system. Doing so requires not only a new appreciation of how the American identity facilitates democratic discourse and a new climate of intellectual opinion, but also formal constitutional reform. Such reform will not be possible until a realigning election ushers in a new bout of presidential/majoritarian change. But before that political development materializes, intellectuals must pave the way for constitutional reform by making a strong case for it. At the very least, America needs to stop assuming that such reform is just impossible. It is important to advance the idea that useful constitutional change is possible and that the American people can be trusted with that task. In the not-too-distant future, the need for and possibility of constitutional reform will have to get on the mainstream American political agenda. Toward the end of his long career, Robert Dahl, one of America's premier political scientists and a theoretician of pluralism, described his strategy for moving constitutional change into the realm of the possible. He wrote of "the possibility . . . of a gradually expanding discussion that begins in scholarly circles, moves outward to the media and intellectuals more generally and after some years begins to engage a wider public."[1] This chapter aims to facilitate that expanding discussion and to set the stage for constitutional reform.

To that end, and acknowledging that immediate, radical constitutional change is unrealistic and undesirable, this chapter advances proposals for incremental constitutional changes that, if passed, would have a dispro-portionate impact, but that in any event would stimulate much-needed public awareness and civic self-education. Of the two proposals I advance, one focuses on making it easier to change the Constitution and the other, on reducing fragmentation by strengthening the presidency. The first is an amendment, patterned after similar provisions in many state constitu-tions, that would require, in one way or another, real opportunities for constitutional amendment to be put regularly before the American elec-torate. The other proposal is an amendment that would allow the presi-dent to submit a legislative agenda directly to Congress, which would be required to promptly vote the whole package up or down, without amend-ments, on a strict majoritarian basis. But before presenting these propos-als, the case that some constitutional change is desirable must be made.

Since about the turn of the millennium, several political science books have argued for sweeping constitutional reform. These include Daniel Lazare's *The Frozen Republic: How the Constitution Is Paralyzing Democracy* (1996), Dahl's *How Democratic Is the American Constitution?* (2001), Sanford Levinson's *Our Undemocratic Constitution* (2006), Larry J. Sabato's *A More Perfect Union: 23 Proposals to Revitalize Our Constitution and Make America a Fairer Country* (2007), and William G. Howell and Terry M. Moe's *Relic: How Our Constitution Undermines Effective Government and Why We Need a More Effective Presidency* (2016). Part of Tom Ginsburg and Aziz Z. Huq's *How to Save a Constitutional Democracy* (2018) is also devoted to the sub-ject. Other writers have developed critiques of key features of the Con-stitution, including judicial review (Mark Tushnet, Jeremy Waldron), the presidency (Richard M. Pious, Andrew Rudalevige, Dana D. Nelson), the Electoral College (George C. Edwards III, Robert Richie), and the Senate (Richard N. Rosenfeld, Frances E. Lee and Bruce I. Oppenheimer). In his 2012 book, *On Constitutional Disobedience*, Louis Michael Seidman goes to perhaps the greatest critical length when he argues that the Constitution should simply be ignored when that suits present purposes. And today's constitutional critics are only the latest avatars of a critical tradition that reaches back through the Anti-Federalists, the Abolitionist Movement, and the Progressive Era.

The concern for effective governmental action is an especially impor-tant value for this argument. In *Political Order and Political Decay*, Francis Fukuyama makes the case that twenty-first-century American government has become repatrimonialized: that is, after a long but successful effort throughout the nineteenth and early twentieth centuries to develop an effective federal bureaucracy, government has, with the increasing dominance of special interests in the policymaking process, slid back into a kind of spoils system, where favors are handed out, not to loyal party workers, but to generous political donors. Such a system of governance is not only undemocratic, but also ineffective, as is demonstrated in detail by Peter H. Schuck in *Why Government Fails So Often* and more succinctly by John J. Dilulio Jr. in *Bring Back the Bureaucrats*.

The case, then, for wholesale government reform is strong, but its political prospects have been weak. What is needed is a nonideological but broadly neoprogressive movement to revitalize American governance. But just as the original progressive movement was long delayed and almost derailed by America's constitutional system of checks and balances and multiple veto points, so, too, are contemporary reform plans unlikely to make it through this highly fragmented process. For example, Dilulio posits a creative strategy for cutting back on an outsourced but bloated governance system, which he terms Leviathan-by-Proxy, by hiring more federal employees while cutting back on contracting-out properly governmental functions. However, this strategy, which involves hiring one million more full-time federal bureaucrats, is politically unrealistic.

Thus, as during the Progressive Era, governmental reform requires a certain amount of constitutional reform, and constitutional reform requires responsible constitutional criticism. The pity is that contemporary constitutional criticism, as discussed above, is so often unrealistic, wrongheaded, and narrowly ideological. What is needed is a brand of constitutional criticism that is purged of utopianism, partisanship, and irresponsibility, and focused on making only such changes as are necessary to revitalizing American government. Beginning to develop such a style of constitutional criticism is the goal of this chapter.

Thomas Jefferson and James Madison represent the poles between which constitutional criticism ranges. Jefferson, as quoted by Levinson, urges that "when we find our constitutions defective and insufficient to secure the happiness of our people we can assemble with all the coolness of philosophers and set it to rights." At the other end, urging veneration of the Constitution, is Madison, who argues in *Federalist* No. 49 that a "nation of philosophers is as little to be expected as the philosophical race of kings wished for by Plato. And in every other nation, the most rational government will not find it a superfluous advantage to have the prejudices of the community on its side." Given the present situation in the United States, responsible constitutional criticism must shift toward the Jeffersonian pole. Madison correctly showed that Jefferson's scheme of revising the political order every nineteen years would produce instability. But no sensible person can argue that revising the Constitution 232 years after it was ratified would be hasty. Those who argue against constitutional change today are like the (probably mythical) communist Chinese official who, when asked for an opinion about the French Revolution, is alleged to have replied, "It's too soon to say." Some of the shortcomings of the Constitution discussed here and in the literature mentioned above have been known, not merely for decades, but centuries. The Electoral College is only the best-known example. The United States is now almost in the position where it must face up to the necessity of change or acquiesce to the dogma that the Constitution is as eternal and unalterable as fundamentalists claim holy scripture to be.

But before looking at constitutional changes that can improve the ability of the American polity to take effective collective action, one must look at the evidence that shows the rise of illiberalism really is related to the weak capacity of the policymaking process to take such action. A classic example from local policymaking illustrates the sort of problem that today plays out with far-reaching consequences at the national and global levels.

A Case History of Redistribution in a Democracy: New York City's Fire Companies in the 1960s

The difficulty that democracies face in advancing the general welfare through redistribution of resources is well-known. An example from local politics illustrates the problem. In the mid-1960s, New York City's progressive Republican mayor—yes, there were progressive Republicans back then—called in the RAND Corporation to rationalize the placement of fire companies throughout the four largest boroughs. At that time, fire companies were scattered about haphazardly based on historical and political reasons as well as informal, back-of-the-envelope calculations. The result was that many neighborhoods plagued with frequent fires had few fire companies, which resulted in unacceptably long response times to fire alarms, while other neighborhoods with fewer fires had an overabundance of fire companies and, therefore, response times that were shorter than was absolutely necessary. The whiz kids at RAND saw an opportunity to work a public sector miracle through the magic of systems analysis: Simply relocate some of the fire companies from the over-serviced neighborhoods to the under-serviced ones. Response times in the former would be longer but still well within good fire-fighting practice, while response times in the high-need neighborhoods would fall, in some cases dramatically. Thus average response times for the large boroughs as a whole would fall without any neighborhoods being made significantly worse off and without any increased spending.

Unfortunately, politics got in the way of smart policy. The low-need neighborhoods with few fires were relatively affluent and white; the high-need neighborhoods were relatively poor and Black or Hispanic. Residents of the better-off neighborhoods had the time, savvy, and resources to lobby the city council for more fire companies. People in the worse-off neighborhoods, who were struggling just to get by, were less effective lobbyists. The richer neighborhoods successfully fought the relocation of "their" fire companies, and so a golden opportunity to solve an important problem, at no real cost to anyone, was muffed. The result? Because of this failure and other shortcomings of RAND's analysis, the South Bronx and other poor neighborhoods nearly burnt to the ground over the next decade. This disaster benefitted no one, including the people in the richer neighborhoods, who held on to fire companies they really did not need but had to pay for the devastation in the form of higher taxes to aid the hard-hit poor, as well as in reduced quality of life as the pathologies of homelessness and disorder eventually spilled over onto their doorsteps.[2]

New York City's experience with allocating fire companies in the 1960s and 1970s illustrates a well-known problem with policymaking in a pluralistic, liberal democratic setting. Better organized and resource-rich interests beat out less rich and less organized interests, with the result that even basic public goods are underproduced or inefficiently distributed, and the overall public interest is not served. New York City eventually pulled out of the death spiral it seemed to be in until the early 1990s. Interestingly for the argument of this chapter, it was New York's strong mayoral system and a relatively weak legislature that enabled determined leaders such as Ed Koch, Rudy Giuliani, and Mike Bloomberg to get the city back on the right track. But on the national level, the United States continues to exhibit dysfunctions typical of pluralistic polities. The issue of globalization is a good example of this type of problem.

Globalization, Collective Action, and Illiberalism

One can think of economic globalization as "international economic exchange and the flow of goods, services, people, information, and capital across national boundaries."[3] There is considerable evidence that disruption of labor markets brought on by globalization increases electoral support for populist parties, including illiberal populist parties. Dani Rodrik, of the Harvard Kennedy School, summarizes the literature on the link between globalization and support for right-wing populist movements as follows:

> Globalization had a big upside. It greatly expanded opportunities for exporters, multinational companies, investors, and international banks, as well the managerial and professional classes who could take advantage of larger markets. It helped some poor countries—China in particular—rapidly transform farmers into workers in manufacturing operations for export markets, thereby spurring growth and reducing poverty. But the decline in global inequality was accompanied by an increase in domestic inequality and cleavages. Globalization drove multiple, partially overlapping wedges in society: between capital and labor, skilled and unskilled workers, employers and employees, globally mobile professionals and local producers, industries/regions with comparative advantage and those without, cities and the countryside, cosmopolitans versus communitarians, elites and ordinary people. . . . People thought they were losing ground not because they had taken an unkind draw from the lottery of market competition, but because the rules were unfair and others—financiers, large corporations, foreigners—were taking advantage of a rigged playing field. . . . A number of empirical papers have linked the rise of populist movements—Trump and the right-wing Republicans in the US, Brexit in Britain, far-right groups in Europe—to forces associated with globalization, such as the China trade shock, rising import penetration levels, deindustrialization, and immigration.[4]

If the losers in the process of globalization could be placated in some way, then presumably they would not turn to populist illiberalism to redress their grievances. One theory says the solution to the unevenly distributed costs and benefits of globalization is to redistribute some of the benefits from the winners to the losers. There is great debate about how much redistribution would be required to fully compensate the losers, and about whether the losers really are a concentrated and easily identified group as the compensation solution implies. But in any case, no one doubts that the losers in the process of globalization ought to be compensated. Yet in fact they seldom are. The Trade Adjustment Assistance (TAA) program in the form of expanded unemployment insurance, subsidized vocational retraining, and other support to impacted workers is one of the few attempts at compensation but is far too small to make up the losers' total losses.[5]

So, why do liberal democracies seldom make use of compensation? Rodrik has reviewed the literature on this issue, too, and concludes:

> But perhaps the more serious difficulty with compensation is the political one, and it relates to credibility and time consistency. As long as reversing trade agreements is costly, governments always have the incentive to promise compensation, but rarely to carry it out. The winners need the losers' assent for the agreement. But once the agreement is passed, there is little reason for the winners to follow through. This is largely the story of TAA in the US. Practically every trade agreement that the US has signed has had a compensatory arrangement attached to it in some form or another. Yet there is widespread agreement that TAA and similar measures have not proved very effective. It is not implausible to think that the reason is the lack of political incentives ex post to render them effective. . . . In view of such economic and political difficulties, genuine compensation rarely occurs.[6]

In other words, in making economic policy, it is a lot easier for liberal democracies to bestow benefits than it is to withdraw part of them to compensate people hurt by a particular policy. This is true even if, after the compensation, everyone is better off than they would have been had the policy not been implemented.

But what is the evidence that the failure of liberal democracies to protect and compensate people vulnerable to the shocks of globalization in fact drives those people to support illiberal leaders and policies? Pippa Norris and Ronald Inglehart have subjected this hypothesis to rigorous quantitative tests. They develop a complex but convincing account of the recent rise of illiberalism, one that stresses the importance of a cultural backlash that has occurred in most affluent democracies as a long-term shift toward post-materialist values and lifestyles has reached a tipping point. However, economic restructuring also plays a major role. Their analysis of postwar European democracies demonstrates the following:

> Support for authoritarian values and populist attitudes were indeed concentrated among the "losers" from processes of economic globalization, the manual workers, and low-income families on many indicators. In particular, authoritarian and populist values are consistently stronger among less prosperous people, who are most likely to feel a sense of economic insecurity.[7]

Regarding American politics and the election of Trump in 2016, Norris and Inglehart find the following:

> Trump's . . . strategy to reach the White House exploited cultural wedge issues about race, religion, and nation that have divided American party politics for decades. . . . When economic measures were included in the analysis, several, but not all of them were significantly related to votes for Trump. Those who felt worse off were more likely to vote for Trump.
>
> We found support for both the economic grievances theory and the cultural backlash theory. They seem to reinforce each other—but the cultural factors clearly played the dominant role in people's decision to vote for Trump or [Hillary] Clinton.[8]

The cultural factors that induced people to vote for Trump manifested themselves as the various forms of identity politics and are discussed in chapter 4 of this book. It is important to recognize that the increasing popularity of illiberal ideologies and movements cannot be entirely attributed to rational dissatisfaction on the part of people who have been economically hurt. The cultural developments discussed in chapter 4 are also important. In this chapter the point is to note that economic grievances work hand-in-glove with those other forces but can, in theory, be addressed by redistributive and compensatory policies. As Norris and Inglehart note:

> Western societies have increasingly become winner-take-all economies dominated by a small minority, while the overwhelming majority have precarious jobs. If left to market forces, this tendency will prevail. But government can be a countervailing force that reallocates resources for the benefit of society as a whole. . . . High–income countries can use taxation policies and public spending to expand employment, educational opportunities, and public services addressing material inequalities.[9]

Ganesh Sitaraman comes to much the same conclusion in his contribution to an anthology entitled *Constitutional Democracy in Crisis?* Sitaraman does not look at the cultural factors that Norris and Inglehart consider, but he does include a wider array of economic problems that, by being unresolved by liberal democracies, have facilitated the rise of illiberalism.

> Globalization—and liberalized trade, in particular—promises to increase the wealth of all societies. But one of the central challenges of globalization is that the gains from trade have not been distributed evenly within countries. In developed economies such as the United States, for example, the industrial Midwest suffered from the downsides of trade liberalization over the last two generations. Under economic theory, the gains from trade should exceed the downsides, thereby allowing the winners to compensate the losers. But in political reality, such compensation rarely happens—and when it does it is limited and largely ineffectual. Technological change is similar. As automation reduces the need for human labor, workers are displaced, left jobless, or forced to downgrade to lower wage work. Here too, retraining programs have not been effective at mitigating the downsides of economic change.[10]

But redistribution, even when it can serve to make everyone better off, is difficult under the American constitutional system. Indeed, any major change is difficult under this system. But why exactly is change so difficult? The answer lies at the heart of the American Constitution: separation of powers, and checks and balances.

Political Change Under Separation of Powers

One of the most comprehensive reviews of the impact of constitutional design on political outcomes is the anthology *Do Institutions Matter? Government Capabilities in the United States and Abroad*, edited by R. Kent Weaver and Bret A. Rockman. They write, "In parliamentary systems centralization of legislative power presumably decreases the alternatives open to interest groups and party discipline makes appeals to individual legislators an almost hopeless strategy in terms of changing policy outcomes."[11] If citizens from a particular locale do not like a bill being considered by parliament, there is little point in them lobbying their representative in parliament against it. If the local parliamentarian is in the minority, he or she cannot help as he or she will simply be outvoted; if in the majority, he or she most likely will not want to help, because effective party discipline means backing party policies. If the local parliamentarian and enough others of the majority party vote to defeat a bill supported by a prime minister of their party, then not only does the bill not pass, but the prime minister no longer has a majority. The result may well be a national election to select a new parliament to pick a new prime minister. In parliamentary systems, nominations to run for parliament are made by the party itself, not through primaries as in the United States. Therefore, if the parliamentarians who defied their party's prime minister want to run for reelection, they will have to ask the party they threw out of office to renominate them to run for their old seats, which is unlikely to happen. Thus, in a parliamentary system, refusing to support the prime minister of one's party to please a constituent or lobbyist is a career-threatening move that most members of parliament will seldom risk.

The incentives facing legislators in a separation-of-powers system are quite different. When the chief executive is elected independently of the legislature, constituents and lobbyists have a much easier time influencing legislators. If, for the sake of satisfying a given interest, legislators vote against a bill supported by a president of their party, their unfaithfulness is likely risk-free. The president remains in office regardless of how the legislature votes, so breaking ranks with him or her has few consequences. When an uncooperative legislator is up for reelection, his or her nomination to run again depends on winning a primary, not on the decision of the party or the president. In short, separation of powers strengthens the legislature relative to the executive because it makes defiance of the executive much less risky. But separation of powers also weakens the ability of legislators to resist lobbyists, and therefore strengthens lobbies and encourages their formation. Legislators—with no responsibility for picking the president or carrying out his or her agenda—are left free to pander to their constituents. Citizens expect no less and withhold their votes if their representatives fail to deliver the goods. Congress is thus held hostage by well-organized lobbies.

The U.S. Congress is an intensely parochial institution in the sense that it is controlled by local interests and has no institutional sense of a broader mission or purpose. Moreover, it is a powerful institution. Congress—being closer to the people—has the whip hand over the president, who is more likely to take a national perspective. It is very difficult for American government to act in situations where such a national perspective is needed, and when it does act the result tends to be weak, jerry-built policies that are incoherent and ineffective.

The political science literature abundantly documents this dysfunctional dynamic. Perhaps the most recent example is the Patient Protection and Affordable Care Act (ACA), also known as Obamacare, which has accurately been described as "an incredibly complex patchwork that no one would have favored or designed if working from the ground up."[12] The same has been said for recent policy in education, taxation, welfare, and energy.

And yet the ACA, for all of its faults, is an example of the constitutional system functioning at its best, for the ACA was passed using one of the three mechanisms the American policymaking process has for temporarily overcoming its propensity for incoherence: by exploiting one of its increasingly infrequent moments of unified government. This is the presidential/majoritarian model of policymaking.

In a parliamentary system, the chief executive is chosen by the legislature, so a unified government, in the sense of the executive and legislature being controlled by the same party, is usually guaranteed. But under America's separation-of-powers Constitution, the presidency and the congressional majority may well owe allegiance to opposing parties. Indeed, America is often plagued by divided, even antagonistic, government. Divided government often leads to gridlock, making nonincremental change impossible. So, American politics must take maximum advantage of its infrequent moments of unified government, such as after the 2008 election that produced Democratic control of both Congress and the presidency under Obama. Thus the ACA was passed—but only after a good deal of horse trading, logrolling, and interest-group appeasing deprived it of most traces of rationality. Thus, even under the presidential/majoritarian model, America's separation-of-powers Constitution struggles to function effectively.

Given the infrequency of unified government, the American policy-making system has developed other pathways for achieving major change. One is the ideational/entrepreneurial model. This approach depends on developing a consensus of expert opinion on some thorny policy problem, such as pollution control, tax reform, or welfare reform. The building up of such a consensus can take decades, but when it crystallizes, policy entrepreneurs can put it to good use. Their task is to translate the expert consensus into a public idea that makes a complex issue comprehensible to nonexperts and yet remains faithful to the essence of the experts' insight. Phrases such as "the right to clean air," "broaden the base, lower the rates," and "end welfare as we know it" are examples of public ideas that were disseminated through the mass media and created a climate of opinion in favor of change that no political actor wanted to defy. The result is a bidding-up process between the legislature controlled by one party and the executive controlled by another that leads to legislation that makes a clean break with baseline policy.

The ideational/entrepreneurial model was effective from the early 1970s through the late 1990s but has been less so since the turn of the millennium. This model depended on the development of an expert consensus that all parties respected. But with the well-documented death of expertise,[13] an authoritative consensus is much harder to develop or, even if it finally crystallizes, to popularly exploit. Every interest group now has its own experts and think tanks, and digital media make it possible for everyone, however unqualified, biased, or ignorant, to get a hearing for their ideas. The days are gone when faculties, editors, publishers, broadcasters, and other gatekeepers can effectively spike ideas or advocates that lack relevant bona fides. The new media and intellectual environments have weakened, not only the value of ideas as a political resource, but also the effectiveness of the ideational/entrepreneurial model as a means of producing nonincremental change.

Another mechanism for achieving major change under the fragmented American Constitution is the judicial breakthrough model. In the American separation-of-powers system, not only are the legislature and the executive independent of each other, but the judiciary is also independent of both. This means lobbies that receive no support from the executive or the legislature can, quite literally, take their case to court. The status of the American judiciary as a fully independent third branch of government and its powers of judicial interpretation and review offer interest groups yet another access point into the policymaking process and thus encourage the formation of interest groups that feel they can exploit that opening.

This is what happened when the civil rights movement reformulated its political demand for unsegregated schools into an assertion of a right under the Fourteenth Amendment and achieved a victory at the Supreme Court in *Brown v. Board of Education* that had proved elusive in state legislatures and Congress. The pro-choice movement used the same strategy when it articulated its political demand for legalization of abortion into the claim of a right to choose, which it successfully litigated in the case of *Roe v. Wade*. *Obergefell v. Hodges*, which upheld the right of same-sex couples to marry, is the latest example of the judicial breakthrough model in action.

As a mechanism for achieving nonincremental change, the judicial breakthrough model has produced mixed results. This approach typically requires creative reinterpretation of the constitutional text, which can sometimes be convincing but other times is less so. The court's unanimous decision in *Brown* to abandon the strained interpretation of the Fourteenth Amendment in *Plessy v. Ferguson* and embrace the interpretation of "separate is inherently unequal" has stood the test of time. On the other hand, when the court relied in *Roe* on "penumbras" and "emanations" of not obviously germane constitutional provisions to get to a right to privacy and then took another leap to a right to an abortion, it was less convincing. Thus millions of American women find an essential element of their control over their own bodies hanging by a thread of strained constitutional interpretation. Right or wrong, such creative construal of the Constitution provoked a reaction in the form of the originalist school of interpretation, which now seems to have a majority on the Supreme Court. What the upshot of this development is for the capacity of the

American political system to produce nonincremental change is hard to say. If the originalist majority applies its principles honestly, the creative judicial interpretations that the judicial breakthrough model relies on will end, the model will cease to function, and an important avenue for producing major change will shut. On the other hand, despite their avowed principles, originalists are also capable of overly creative constitutional interpretation. In *Citizens United v. Federal Election Commission*, an originalist majority unconvincingly teased out of the First Amendment's freedom of speech the right of corporations to spend unlimited amounts of money on political communications. If the current originalist majority hands down a series of landmark decisions based on its own form of creative constitutional interpretation, it is unlikely that many people outside of conservative ideologues will be happy about the continuing viability of the judicial breakthrough model as a mechanism for producing nonincremental change. It is therefore doubtful that judicial breakthroughs will in the future be productive avenues for achieving long-blocked change.

Then there is the most obvious route to nonincremental change in American politics, which is simply bipartisan cooperation. But in an interesting book on governing, *The Disappearing Center*, Alan I. Abramowitz correctly notes: "Given the current level of partisan-ideological polarization among political elites and engaged partisans, successful efforts at bipartisan cooperation and compromise are unlikely."[14]

The remaining mechanism the American political system has for making the kind of major changes that would be necessary to meet the challenges of globalization, economic restructuring, environmental threat, and many others is a realigning election to usher in a period of presidential/majoritarian change. But there are two problems with resting hope for needed change on such a development. The first is all too obvious in the wake of the blue landslide that failed to materialize in the election of 2020: realigning elections, which have always been rare, now are harder than ever to produce. The second problem is pointed out by Abramowitz: realigning elections, even when they occur, can be stymied from producing change by America's fragmenting Constitution. Let us take up the second, less obvious, problem first.

Polarization, Responsible Government, and Constitutional Structure

Ideological polarization of voters and politicians is often presented as the main obstacle to the effective functioning of the U.S. political system, but in fact, polarization has its virtues and need not necessarily impede effective government action. As discussed in chapter 5 a polarized political environment makes for high-stakes elections and, thus, for an engaged public, and an engaged public, as Dewey argued, is overall a great plus for a democratic policy.

Polarization can result in effective government if it is conjoined with something like responsible two-party government—that is, a system in which the parties are clearly split ideologically and elections produce either a unified government capable of implementing the winning party's ideological agenda or at least a clear mandate for the president-elect's agenda. American politics has usually not embodied the responsible party model and has often featured parties that were each ideologically heterogeneous. But a case can be made for the responsible party model and, indeed, was made in a 1950 report by the American Political Science Association (APSA).[15] Whatever the pros and cons of a responsible party model might be, it is a potentially workable model—one better than the current gridlocked system the United States now has, and one that acknowledges and works with the country's ineradicably polarized climate.

The problems with responsible party government set in when a polarized majority wins a high-stakes election, brings a unified government to power, and nothing happens. Abramowitz explains the major obstacle to responsible party politics in America today:

> On the electoral side, the conditions for responsible party government in the United States have largely been met. The Democratic and Republican parties today offer voters a clear-cut choice between coherent policy packages, one liberal and one conservative, and most voters appear to have little difficulty choosing the party whose package is more to their liking. . . . Participation in the electoral process has been increasing because voters perceive more to be at stake in elections as a result of partisan-ideological polarization. . . . But although the conditions for responsible party government have largely been met on the electoral side, with ideologically defined parties offering voters a clear choice between alternative sets of

policies, the institutions of American government remain a major obstacle to effective party governance. The theory of responsible party government is based on a strongly majoritarian view of democracy. This theory assumes that after an election is over, the winning party will carry out the will of the majority by implementing the policies on which it campaigned. However, many features of the American political system were deliberately designed to thwart the will of the majority. Divided party control of the legislative and executive branches, the presidential veto, the bicameral structure of the legislative branch, the overrepresentation of less populous states in the Senate, and the cloture rule in the Senate all have important antimajoritarian consequences.[16]

In other words, even if the 2020 presidential election had been a realigning election that produced a unified, neoprogressive government and a clear mandate for change, it is possible that little would have been achieved. America's constitutional system makes it unnecessarily difficult to achieve anything at all, and without a great deal of change, the problems that have facilitated the rise of illiberalism will remain, and so will illiberalism.

Some political analysts who understand the need for a decisive, realigning election on the scale of 1932, 1964, or at least 1980, and who believed that 2020 would hit that mark, failed to appreciate the limitations of the presidential/majoritarian model of achieving change, given the constraints of the American Constitution. For example, in *R.I.P. G.O.P.: How the New America is Dooming the Republicans*, polling analyst Greenberg asserted that "the 2020 election could produce a historic result on an even greater historic scale" than the strong Democratic victories in the 2018 midterm elections.[17] Of course, as discussed in chapter 5, Greenberg, along with many other analysts, was wrong. Moreover, at the very end of his book, Greenberg runs into another problem:

What if the GOP's last heave leaves it shattered, fractured, illegitimate, and ashamed?

What if the GOP is off the battlefield, figuring out how to be relevant again?

What if the politics is not linear and the past no longer predicts the future?

What happens the day after?[18]

Excellent questions, but Greenberg provides only an interesting suggestion by way of an answer. He analogizes the 2018 midterms to those of 1910, which also were a great Democratic victory that gave the party control of the House, and suggests that after the blue tsunami of 2020 that never materialized, another progressive age could have been ushered in. He also briefly notes that constitutional reform—that is, the Sixteenth, Seventeenth, and Nineteenth Amendments—was part and parcel of the progressive agenda.

The point to note here is that realigning elections—even when they finally materialize—will not produce a wave of nonincremental change absent constitutional reform. Transformational elections do not happen very often. When they come, long-delayed legislative reforms must be achieved. But legislation is not enough. Historic windows of opportunity must also be used to ease the constitutional constraints that make vital legislation so hard to pass.

The original progressives were acutely aware of the need for constitutional reform to make effective government easier to achieve. Woodrow Wilson was the greatest expositor of progressive thought, and he made constitutional reform central to its logic. He took pride that "we of the present generation are . . . the first Americans to . . . ask whether the Constitution is still adapted to serve the purposes for which it was intended; . . . the first to think of remodeling the administrative machinery of the federal government, and of forcing new forms of responsibility upon Congress."[19]

Wilson was among the first analysts to critique separation of powers—which he called the Constitution's "radical defect"[20]—for enabling gridlock. He put the matter thus:

> Moreover, it is impossible to deny that this division of authority and concealment of responsibility are calculated to subject the government to a very distressing paralysis in moments of emergency. There are few, if any, important steps that can be taken by any one branch of the government without the consent or cooperation of some other branch. Congress must act through the President and his Cabinet; the President and his Cabinet must wait upon the will of Congress. There is no one supreme, ultimate head—whether magistrate or representative body—which can decide at once and with conclusive authority what shall be done at those times when

some decision there must be, and that immediately. Of course this lack is of a sort to be felt at all times, in seasons of tranquil rounds of business as well as at moments of sharp crisis; but in times of sudden exigency it might prove fatal—fatal either in breaking down the system or in failing to meet the emergency. Policy cannot be either prompt or straightforward when it must serve many masters. It must either equivocate, or hesitate, or fail altogether. It may set out with clear purpose from Congress, but get waylaid or maimed by the Executive.[21]

The point is, the severely limited capacity of the American constitutional system for necessary collective action—whether in an emergency or seasons of tranquility—has been understood for a long time and remains a major problem today.

Progressivism 1.0 used its window of opportunity to achieve long-delayed legislative victories such as the Clayton Antitrust Act and the establishment of the Interstate Commerce Commission, the Federal Trade Commission, the Food and Drug Administration, and the Federal Reserve System. But the twentieth-century progressives were also acutely aware of the need for, and did in fact achieve, major constitutional reform. Twenty-first-century neoprogressivism, if it ever gets its window of opportunity that failed to appear in 2020, must follow suit and not only achieve a collection of legislative reforms to service its various constituencies, but also enact constitutional reforms to make it easier for those interests and future winning coalitions to also make a difference.

A similar understanding of the need for systemic, constitutional reform is mostly lacking among the anti-Trump and neoprogressive forces of today. In an analysis of the resistance to Trump, political scientist Kenneth M. Roberts introduces the useful concept of "metaresistance." He writes that "on one level," resistance to "exclusionary populism . . . entails opposition to specific policy initiatives, particularly those that are exclusionary in their treatment of certain interests or groups in society." Opposition to discriminatory immigration policies, curtailment of women's rights, voting disenfranchisement, welfare state rollback, limitations on access to healthcare, and inegalitarian tax policies are indeed the meat and potatoes of the resistance to Trump. But Roberts also writes that "at another level" there is the metaresistance, which "seeks to buttress an institutional edifice that not only allows societal actors to have input in the policymaking process, but also one that recognizes their very right to resist."[22] He notes that metaresistance is "surely unfamiliar to most contemporary social movement activists. . . . [They] are accustomed to mobilizing . . . within an 'opportunity structure' afforded by democratic institutions; they are not accustomed to mobilization aimed at the defense of those very institutions."[23] But not only are leaders of protest movements not used to defending the opportunity structure of liberal democracy, they are also unused to questioning aspects of that structure that really do need change. Hence today's social activists often underestimate the importance of constitutional reform.

If we want to halt the rise of illiberalism, a realigning election and a window of political opportunity will not suffice. We must, at long last, address the need for constitutional reform. But before dealing with constitutional reform there remain issues concerning polarization.

When Is Polarization a Problem?

In itself, polarization, defined as a wide ideological gap among voters and/or political elites with little overlap, is not necessarily a problem. Or at least it is not necessarily a problem immediately relevant to the main concern of this book, which is the threat to liberal democracy represented by the current rise of illiberal ideologies and movements. It is entirely possible for a secure liberal democracy to have a political environment of two parties that offer voters a clear choice between sharply differing bundles of policies associated with distinct ideologies. Such was the political environment of many European democracies for decades, and such was the vision offered by the American Political Science Association's controversial 1950 report, "Towards a More Responsible Two-Party System." Over many decades, the pluses and minuses of this system have been fully thrashed out. On the positive side, a polity polarized in this sense may facilitate a clearer expression of popular will: the public knows what it is voting for, the winning party can claim a mandate from the people, and at reelection time the public knows which party is responsible for the state of the polity and can vote accordingly. On the negative side, polarization can encourage incivility, a propensity to break the rules, and a party strategy of pandering to the party's base while neglecting to reach out to other interests.[24] But whatever one makes of this debate, the point here is that polarization in itself is not necessarily a threat to liberal democracy. Whether polarization becomes or contributes to such a threat depends on how the political environment is polarized and what it is polarized over.

American politics today is not polarized in the way many postwar European democracies were polarized or in the way the APSA report envisioned. In those polarized systems, all parties took liberal democracy as an unquestionable foundation. Parties were polarized within the standard spectrum of liberal democratic politics, stretching from mainstream conservatives on the right through to social democrats on the left. Communists, if they played a role, watered down their ideology enough to stay on the spectrum, and fascists played practically no electoral role at all.

Moreover, the twentieth-century versions of polarization were symmetrical polarizations. The distance from the middle of the political spectrum out to the positions of the parties of the left and right was about equal. A reactionary right wing devoted to the divine right of kings did not square off against garden-variety progressives, nor did a radical anarcho-syndicalist left contest with a status-quo-oriented right. Thus, elections did not present voters with a one person/one vote/one time scenario. With the winning party being not so very far from the political center, the minority party could, with some ease, play one of the most important of all roles in a democracy: that of the gracious loser.

American politics today is polarized, but not in the benign sense discussed above. American polarization is not symmetrical. In a review of the literature on current polarization, Jacob S. Hacker and Paul Pierson conclude, "One of the most striking and consequential features of growing polarization [is] its asymmetric character. Overwhelmingly, the evidence suggests, the growth of partisan polarization is a result of GOP moves to the right, rather than an equal retreat of Democrats and Republicans from the center."[25] Similarly, an analysis of party presidential platforms found that from 1980 on, Republican platforms began to diverge strikingly from those of the Democratic Party, such that by 2012, it was found that "Republicans are the primary source of polarization in the American system."[26] This imbalance means that insofar as polarization itself causes problems such as incivility, dirty fighting, and pandering to a base, the solution lies disproportionately in pulling the Republicans back toward the center. The often-healthy American tendencies to hold "both sides" responsible, and to "split the difference" will not work when the responsibility and difference lie primarily with just one side that has to make big changes while the other does not.

More importantly, polarization in American politics is not safely contained within the familiar liberal democratic ideological spectrum. If the endpoints of a continuum are fixed, one can move only so far away from the center before brushing up against and passing one endpoint or another. In the present case, it is the Republicans who are all too close to trespassing where liberal, small "d" democrats fear to tread.

Of course, Republicans holding or running for elective office usually do not explicitly reject liberal democracy and openly embrace illiberalism. Republicans manifest their illiberal propensities less overtly. As discussed in chapter 3 the Illiberal Right has created its own intellectual food chain, with radically anti-democratic outlets at the "top" and a series of less radical platforms passing by step up to the gates of the mainstream right. On the left there is nothing analogous to this set of stepping-stones from the Illiberal Left to the progressive wing of the Democratic Party. Therefore, on the right, the border between illiberalism and mainstream conservatism is fluid. Further, rightist illiberals have developed a rhetorical strategy that communicates their radically reactionary ideology in situations where it is prudent to not be too explicit. Their deliberately offensive and alienating rhetoric conveys the message that the current political status quo—which is a liberal democratic status quo—deserves only contempt. And, the implication is, so do all institutions and constituencies associated with the liberal status quo: nonwhites, the welfare state, Jews, the news media, gays, the rule of law, moderate Republicans, the Constitution, Democrats, the federal government, women, and finally even the United States of America itself as it now exists. The Right Illiberal food chain produces not only public ideas that can be articulated by others further along the chain, but also a whole illiberal rhetorical style and worldview that can be marketed by mainstream Republican politicians and mass media conservative outlets for whom too much explicit rejection of liberal democracy is unwise. Trump and his Republican followers are the main practitioners of this "illiberalism lite" style. This mainstreaming of illiberal ideas and rhetoric is one sense in which the Republican Party can fairly be charged with straying beyond the legitimate liberal democratic spectrum.

It is also true, as Roberts has pointed out, that the structure of the American party system facilitated the takeover of the Republican Party by a suitably discrete illiberalism. In Western Europe, parliamentary institutions and proportional voting encouraged illiberal movements to organize as new, independent parties. Mainstream conservative parties could co-opt the illiberal parties by adopting some of their key issues—such as opposition to current levels of immigration—or forming alliances with the illiberals in parliament. Illiberal parties thus gained some influence, but their hard edge was moderated, and they never managed to install their own head of government.

The American two-party, winner-take-all, presidential system discourages the formation of third parties. Proto-illiberals who ran for president on third-party tickets—such as George Wallace, Ross Perot, and Pat Buchanan—achieved no political power. In America, any movement that aims at governing influence has to attach itself to one of the two major parties and seek leverage within it. Illiberals in both their lite and hard-core versions naturally pitched camp in the rightward-most party, and when a series of long-term social trends, a perfect storm of political events, and the defects of the American presidential election system came to a head in 2016, a candidate with strong illiberal propensities became chief executive.

The real problem with America's polarized politics is that the polarization has been accomplished by one party breaking with the liberal democratic baseline and embracing an anti-democratic ideology. The challenge is to rebut the rise of illiberalism, prevent it from ensconcing itself in our political culture and practice, and reform the policymaking process to address the problems that gave illiberalism the opportunity to grow. As to whether this goal is best achieved by reviving bipartisan cooperation or by achieving responsible party government, support for my view that responsible party government is the most feasible option is discussed below.

The Case for Responsible Party Government

As has been noted, responsible party government accepts and works with the highly polarized political climate of America today, which is an important point in its favor. But more can be said.

Populists often claim that they represent the political will of the people as opposed to the corrupt elites who represent only their own self-interest. A quintessential statement of this charge was made by Trump—or more likely, his ghostwriter—in an op-ed article for the *Wall Street Journal* published during the 2016 presidential campaign:

> The only antidote to decades of ruinous rule by a small handful of elites is a bold infusion of popular will. On every major issue affecting this country, the people are right and the governing elite are wrong. The elites are wrong on taxes, on the size of government, on trade, on immigration, on foreign policy.
>
> Why should we trust the people who have made every wrong decision to substitute their will for America's will in this presidential election?[27]

This op-ed complains about the arcane rules of presidential primaries that supposedly block the process from revealing the popular will. But it raises deeper questions: do democratic elections ever reveal the popular will and, if so, under what circumstances?

Political scientists have known for decades that elections are, at best, very imperfect tools for expression of the popular will. Indeed, seminal work by Kenneth Arrow and other social choice theorists has called into question the whole concept of popular will. In the early 1980s, William H. Riker published a book with the prescient title *Liberalism Against Populism*, which summarized the implications of modern political science theory for these two political philosophies. In Riker's account, populism, "proposition 1" of which is "What the people, as a corporate entity, want ought to be social policy," does not hold up well:

> The social amalgamations of individual values are . . . often inadequate—indeed meaningless—interpretations of public opinion. . . . The notion of popular will is itself unclear. . . . An election tells us at most which alternative wins; it does not tell us that the winner would also have been chosen over another feasible alternative that might itself have a better claim to be the social choice. Hence falls proposition 1 . . .
>
> Populism as a moral imperative depends on the existence of a popular will to be discovered by voting. But if voting does not discover or reveal a will, then the moral imperative evaporates because there is nothing to be commanded. . . . Populism fails, therefore, not because it is morally wrong,

but merely because it is empty. . . . I believe that in the next generation populist claims will be rejected simply because it will be recognized that, however desirable they might be, they are based on a flawed technique that renders populism unworkable.[28]

Riker's social choice critique of twentieth-century populism is devastating. But he underestimated the ingenuity of later populists. Since elections cannot credibly be held to express the popular will, populists now utilize charisma, demagoguery, prejudice, and similar devices to support their specious claims to be its true representatives.

Unlike populism or, more specifically, the twentieth-century version of populism that Riker refutes, liberalism holds up under social choice analysis. But it is a very narrow form of liberalism that survives:

> The essence of the liberal interpretation of voting is the notion that voting permits the rejection of candidates or officials who have offended so many voters that they cannot win an election. This is, of course, a negative ideal. It does *not* require that voting produce a clear, consistent, meaningful statement of the popular will. It requires only that voting produce a decisive result: that this official or this party is retained in office or rejected. . . . The kind of democracy that thus survives is not, however, popular rule, but rather an intermittent, sometimes random, even perverse, popular veto. . . . Liberal democracy is simply the veto by which it is sometimes possible to restrain official tyranny.[29]

A form of liberal democracy that frankly acknowledges the "sometimes random, even perverse" nature of its electoral outcomes may win a purely theoretical contest against a brand of populism that is entirely "meaningless" and "empty." But how well will such liberalism do in the real politics of the twenty-first century now that populists have wised up and trick themselves out in rousing nationalist and identitarian rhetoric? Liberal democracy needs to find some way to make a better claim than illiberal populists can to representing the public will.

Chapter 3 discusses one way that liberal democratic politics can make a legitimate claim to representing the popular will: to root democratic discourse in the national identity—that is, to use the bundle of cognitions that make up the epistemic standpoint of the polity such that when a political consensus develops, it is seen by the citizens to have developed organically out of that identity and is thus a real expression of the public will. Ideally, a shared national identity that sets some parameters on political discourse and, so, limits the range of policies that receive serious consideration can be an effective response to the weakness of liberal democratic elections as expressions of public will.

Another way that elections in a liberal democracy can make a more convincing claim to representing the public will is when there are politically responsible parties and a constitutional structure that enables majority parties to enact the political agenda they ran on. It is true that such a political environment is subject to all the limitations identified by social choice theory and that elections in that environment will remain very uncertain expressions of the public will in terms of that theory. But liberal democracy today needs to justify itself, not against the critique of social choice theory, but against the critique of illiberal populism. Its claim to represent the popular will is entirely specious, being based in demagoguery and identitarianism, but it can be convincing when matched against the almost self-deprecating case that has been made for liberal democracy in the twentieth century and up to the present. A liberal democracy that offers voters clear electoral choices, produces decisive results, and enables winners to deliver as promised will have a much stronger claim to representing the public will than bombastic illiberalism does. But if liberal democracy is to offer such a choice, enable social action, and overcome gridlock, constitutional reform is necessary.

A Strategy for Constitutional Reform

The consensus among students of the "American Magna Carta" is that the chances of major constitutional reform are slim. At the beginning of the twenty-first century, Robert Dahl concluded, "My reflections lead me to a measured pessimism about the prospects for greater democratization of the American Constitution. . . . Public discussion that penetrates beyond the Constitution as a national icon is virtually nonexistent."[30] Dahl expressed this judgment in 2001, but today—when recent impeachment hearings against a crypto-illiberal president signal that the country is in the midst of a constitutional crisis—perhaps the prospects for a serious discussion of the limitations of the Constitution are better. Even so, it is still necessary to be realistic about the prospects for constitutional reform and to distinguish between changes that are mere pipe dreams and those with better chances for realization. But what are the criteria for making this decision?

The distinguished Yale constitutional scholar Akhil Reed Amar makes an excellent suggestion for separating fantasies from possibilities:

> The state constitutions provide road-tested exemplars of constitutional reform and therefore define a sensible American reform agenda. . . . In general—albeit with some notable exceptions—stuff that the states have done is a plausible basis for a proposed constitutional reform and stuff that the states have not done is not.[31]

There are a number of much-needed reforms of the federal Constitution that meet the criterion of having been extensively road tested at the state level.

The Electoral College, despite its misfires in 2000 and 2016, continues to have supporters in some right-wing precincts.[32] More convincing are writers who acknowledge the system's obvious defects but argue that opposition from small states makes constitutional change impossible. Both camps overlook the fact that direct election of the chief executive has been the rule in the states for centuries, with no unfortunate results. Direct election of the president is a constitutional reform that has received as much road testing in the states as is humanly possible and so ought not to be dismissed as entirely unrealistic. Besides, the growing national popular vote initiative—in which states voluntarily agree to require that their electoral votes will go to the winner of the national popular vote—provides a mechanism less onerous than a formal constitutional amendment for achieving this reform.

Reforming the malapportioned Senate is another constitutional change that is often labeled hopelessly unrealistic. Yet, malapportionment in state senates was resolved in the early- to mid-1960s in the one person/one vote decisions made by the Supreme Court. States have suffered no ill effects. And Nebraska has no senate at all yet seems to do well enough. Therefore, reapportioning the Senate is another reform that has been thoroughly tested by the states. True, Article V of the Constitution states that no amendment changing equal representation of the states in the Senate is permitted. But Amar has pointed out various ways around this provision, including an amendment that would preserve equal state representation in the Senate, but transferring all legislative powers to a new, more fairly apportioned chamber. The chances of pulling off that particular maneuver are remote. But in general, Amar convincingly argues that throughout American history, ways have been found to work around and eventually overcome the formidable obstacles that Article V imposes on constitutional reform. For example, before the Seventeenth Amendment was passed, reformers found various ways to circumvent the constitutional provision that senators were to be chosen by state legislatures. In the early twentieth century, Oregon and Nebraska passed laws that based the choice of U.S. senators on the popular vote. Before then, ten states had nonbinding, popular vote primaries for Senate candidates that functioned as advisory referenda for the state legislatures.

Nonetheless, the federal Constitution remains unnecessarily difficult to change and is far more difficult to change than any other democratic constitution in the world. This observation brings us to the most interesting constitutional reform—one that, while it is often dismissed as either utopian or dangerous, has been implemented in all the states, with mostly positive results. All state constitutions are much easier to change than the federal Constitution, all have been changed much more often than the federal Constitution, and many have formal provisions requiring periodic opportunities for change in various forms. Constitutional change is a recurring fact of life at the state level. Why should this not also be so at the federal level? If American electoral politics ever again serves up a realigning presidential election and a neoprogressive movement achieves unified government, it should make constitutional reform a part of its agenda, and the most important reform it could support would be an amendment modeled after those of the states that makes constitutional change much more achievable than it is now. And when change is less difficult, changes that improve the capacity of the federal government to achieve coherent collective action should be implemented.

Constitutional Change in the States

State constitutions are vastly more malleable than the federal Constitution. In a 2009 review of state constitutional change, Bruce E. Cain and Roger G. Noll summed up the U.S. experience as follows:

While the U.S. Constitution has been amended only twenty-seven times, states have replaced and amended their constitutions much more frequently. Only nineteen states still have their original constitutions, and most states have adopted three or more. Collectively, states have held more than 230 constitutional conventions and have adopted 146 constitutions. They have added over 5,000 amendments (over 100 per state) and have been the first to adopt important innovations in government structure and political rights, including women's suffrage, the line-item veto, direct democracy, balanced budget requirements, and the direct election of upper houses in legislatures.[33]

Many state constitutions have provisions for automatic, periodic evaluations of whether changing them would be desirable. As Cain and Noll summarize, "Most states offer several ways to amend their constitutions. While the hurdles for successful amendments are not trivial, they are lower than for amending the U.S. Constitution and not much higher than the hurdles for passing ordinary statutes."[34] Two mechanisms are especially relevant here: regular state referenda on whether to call a constitutional convention; and mandatory, periodic empaneling of constitutional commissions whose proposals are presented directly to the voters.

The constitutions of fourteen states require that the question of whether to call a constitutional convention be automatically referred to a statewide ballot with no requirement that the state legislature vote to put the question before the voters. The states are Oklahoma, Alaska, Hawaii, Iowa, New Hampshire, Rhode Island, Michigan, Connecticut, Illinois, Maryland, Missouri, Montana, New York, and Ohio.[35] Spurred by the Supreme Court's one person/one vote decisions, there was a wave of state constitutional conventions in the 1960s and 1970s. Between 1963 and 1976, thirteen states revised their constitutions. But in recent decades, state constitutional conventions have been infrequent—so much so that some scholars have concluded that states are gripped by a "conventionphobia." Between 1960 and 1985, automatic convention calls were approved only in New Hampshire, Rhode Island, and Alaska.[36]

Conventionphobia stems partly from acceptance of the maxim "if it ain't broke, don't fix it." After being forced by the Supreme Court to acknowledge that the malapportioned upper houses of their legislature were, indeed, a problem, the states in effect decided that their constitutions were not in need of any further repair. But another factor in the decline of state constitutional conventions in recent decades is democ-racyphobia. As cynicism about politics spread and as Congress declined in public esteem, there was little enthusiasm for holding constitutional conventions that would likely be subject to the same special-interest lob-bying as other deliberative bodies.

For example, in 2017, New York State had a vote to call a constitu-tional convention, known as Proposition 1. However, early support for the proposal vanished when well-organized anti-convention forces raised the specter of a convention dominated by corrupt special interests. The *New York Times* reported that "advertisements paid for by the New York State AFL-CIO and the Communications Workers of America—two major players in state politics—depict supporters of the convention as money-hungry lobbyists, slimy salesmen and martini-swilling elitists seeking special deals, a motley collection depicted in another anti-Proposition 1 ad as 'the bar in *Star Wars*.' "[37] Even traditional good government groups and reform supporters came out against the convention on these grounds. The *Times* editorialized:

> There's every reason to believe we would basically end up with the same politicians and factotums who now shape (or misshape) state policy. . . . You have to wonder if New York democracy is failing the electorate, or the other way around. Voters complain endlessly about Albany's fecklessness, yet they send the same people back to the State Senate and Assembly year after year.[38]

The argument that constitutional conventions ought not to be held because they are as susceptible to interest-group corruption as legislatures cuts both ways. After all, when politicians, factotums, and the scum of the political universe dominate the legislature, people do not conclude that the legislature should not meet, or that it should meet as infrequently as possible. One solution is to decrease the disproportionate influence of well-positioned interest groups in all facets of political life. And one way of doing that is to amend the Constitution.

When confronted with a reform proposal that is hard to deny but un-pleasant to accept, convention skeptics who are aware of the need for con-stitutional change often deploy an argument famously used by Oxbridge dons. This maneuver has been called the Principle of Unripe Time: the idea is good, but the time is not yet ripe.[39] Just before the vote on Proposition 1 in New York, the progressive outlet *Dissent* ran an article that relied on this principle. In "New York Isn't Ready for a Constitutional Convention," the writer argued:

> Historically, such conventions have only been successful at creating real change when backed by a new political movement. No such movement exists in New York today—at least not on the scale necessary—making a constitutional convention more of a liability than an opportunity for the left.[40]

The problem with this argument is not that there is no such thing as a particular time being ripe or unripe for a given change. (If and when a realigning presidential election occurs, that will be a time ripe for non-incremental reform.) Problems set in, however, when established interests resort to the Principle of Unripe Time so often that change ends up happening almost not at all, and the assumption that change is impossible itself achieves a quasi-constitutional status. But if change is impossible, then democracy is impossible, for democracy is nothing if not periodic, contested elections that give citizens a chance to change who is in office. Cynicism about constitutional change therefore often boils down to cynicism about democracy or, more exactly, about the *demos*. The *New York Times* quip about the electorate failing democracy is telling. If the people do not take advantage of certain mechanisms of change, shouldn't the conclusion be that other mechanisms ought to be offered? Moreover, the assumption that all political ills can be changed by simply voting the "right" people into office is naïve. A polity's constitution—broadly understood as how procedures for collective decisionmaking are constituted—determines to a considerable extent what choices, including choices of leaders, are put before the people. It is therefore entirely plausible to argue that needed political change may be best achieved through constitutional reform rather than by ordinary elections.

But even if constitutional change should be more generally on offer, perhaps mandatory referenda on constitutional conventions are not the best way to achieve it. Proposition 1 was voted down overwhelmingly by Empire State voters. Scholars of state constitutional politics saw the handwriting on the wall for such mandatory, periodic ballots on constitutional conventions. One expert concluded that "conventions are not likely to be called as a result of a mandatory convention question. Experience in New York and comparative analysis show that this process is a very uncertain route to constitutional change."[41] But there are other, more effective provisions in state constitutions for achieving regular consideration of constitutional reform that might be workable at the national level as well.

Constitutional Commissions

Constitutional commissions are an alternative to constitutional conventions for responding to concerns about the influence of entrenched special-interest groups. Constitutional commissions began as bodies of experts that would advise constitutional conventions or legislatures that were considering possible constitutional reforms.[42] New York, in 1872, was the first state to make significant use of this type of constitutional commission. New Jersey followed suit in 1873, with a constitutional commission that formulated twenty-eight amendments that were added to the state constitution in 1875. In more recent decades, many states have made use of constitutional commissions, including Mississippi, Oklahoma, Georgia, Kentucky, California, and Utah. Prior to the 1997 referendum on whether to call the constitutional convention that was mandated by its constitution, New York State established a constitutional commission to educate and advise the public on reform options. But Florida is the state that has most thoroughly incorporated constitutional commissions into its political process.

In 1968, Florida adopted a constitution that required automatic, periodic review of the state constitution through commissions of constitutional revision. The Florida Constitution Revision Commission (FCRC) was to be called ten years after the adoption of the constitution and then every twenty years thereafter. These commissions had the power to submit recommended amendments or revisions directly to the electorate. At the time, this was a unique feature in American constitutional history.[43]

The first Florida commission called under the new provision met in 1977, and although its recommendations for constitutional change were "important and well considered," they were all rejected by the state's voters. Observers felt this was because the commission met too soon after Florida had already adopted a new constitution and because of the pres-

ence of a controversial item on casino gambling on the same ballot. However, many of the changes proposed by the commission and rejected by
the voters in 1978 were eventually incorporated into the state constitution. "These included amendments adding a right of privacy to the Declaration of Rights (adopted 1980), extending impeachment to county judges
(1988), providing uniform rules for the judicial nominating commissions
(1984), extending the widows' exemption to widowers (1988), allowing the
legislature to classify inventory for property tax purposes (1980), and providing various changes in the bonding power (1980, 1984)."[44] Later constitutional commissions had more immediate impact. The FCRC of 1997
saw eight of its nine proposals approved by the voters. These included
amendments that created the Florida Fish and Wildlife Conservation
Commission and restructured the state cabinet. The 2017 constitutional
commission saw all seven of its proposals that appeared on the ballot approved by the voters, including a ban on offshore oil and gas drilling, and
a prohibition on public officials lobbying for compensation while in office
and six years afterward.[45]

Interestingly, when, in 1980, the legislature referred to the voters a
constitutional amendment to abolish the FCRC, the amendment was
voted down. And in 1988, voters approved a proposal to create a Florida
Taxation and Budget Reform Commission, which, like the FCRC, meets
every twenty years and can refer constitutional amendments related to
taxation and the budgetary process directly to the voters. In 2006, Florida
voters approved an amendment that required referred amendments to
obtain a 60 percent supermajority of votes to be approved, rather than the
previous requirement of a simple majority. It is also worth noting that, in
total, Florida has five different mechanisms for changing its constitution.
A citizen's initiative process was used to put a constitutional amendment
on the ballot in 2018 to restore voting rights for people with prior felony
convictions, except those convicted of murder or a felony sexual offense,
upon completion of their sentences. In short, Floridians have made well-
regulated constitutional change a regular part of state politics, and the
results have been mostly positive. Why shouldn't the federal government
follow suit?

Making Federal Constitutional Change Easier

The reason why constitutional change has been taken up in this chapter is because of its relevance to this book's main concern, which is the preservation and extension of liberal democracy in the United States and the world in the face of the current rise of illiberalism. To respond to the illiberal challenge, liberal democracies must more effectively perform a function that is essential to all governments: taking coherent collective action to produce public goods and redistribute resources. That capacity is especially needed now to mitigate the impact of capitalist creative destruction, which is intensified by globalization. Improving the ability of American government to take collective action requires reform of its hyperfragmented constitutional structure, and it is for this reason that amending and otherwise changing the Constitution should be made easier.

There are various proposals for constitutional reform intended to satisfy one or another progressive constituency. Certainly, if a much-needed progressive wave to repudiate illiberalism and produce unified government occurs in the foreseeable future, then progressive interests will have to believe they will get something out of that development. Feminists are now trying to revive interest in the Equal Rights Amendment, and some African American citizens are supporting reparations, which would not necessarily involve a constitutional amendment but would be a high-profile concession to a central progressive interest.

Perhaps almost any constitutional amendment that is not positively pernicious would be desirable, if only because it would demonstrate constitutional change is possible and so, open the door to other vitally needed changes. But if a progressive governing coalition materializes in the near future, it should beware of supporting constitutional amendments or other dramatic proposals that are mostly symbolic. Ibram X. Kendi's sweeping proposal for "an anti-racist amendment to the U.S. Constitution that . . . would make unconstitutional . . . racist ideas by public officials (with "racist ideas" and "public officials" clearly defined) . . ." addresses a deep problem but is unworkable.[46] The definitional issues Kendi acknowledges are formidable and the absence of road testing at the state level suggests that the amendment would lack political support. If progressives get another window of opportunity in the twenty-first century, then whatever else they do, they must make maximum use of that chance for constitutional reform to improve government functioning.

Here is how the process could work. Assume that eventually there is a realigning election that brings with it unified progressive government. Constitutional reform should be high on the progressive agenda, and several desirable amendments would have a realistic opportunity to pass. Obvious candidates include the abolition of the Electoral College and the establishment of a right to vote. But progressives ought to also take advantage of this opportunity to make the Constitution easier to change. The best approach would be to incorporate Florida's constitutional commission system into the federal constitution. The Florida model need not be followed exactly, but if its broad outlines were followed, the federal constitution would be amended to require a constitutional commission that meets every twenty years. Commission members—there are thirty-seven in Florida's case—would be appointed by the president, the president pro tem of the Senate, the speaker of the House, and the chief justice of the Supreme Court. The commission would set its own rules and procedures. The 2017 Florida commission created ten standing committees to cover all the articles of the Florida constitution. The commission had from March 20, 2017, to May 10, 2018, to hold public hearings and was required to submit its proposed amendments at least 180 days before the general election of November 6, 2018.

The Florida commission submits its proposed amendments directly to the voters, and since 2006 a supermajority of 60 percent of votes cast has been required to approve an amendment. Given the extraordinary stasis of the U.S. Constitution over well more than two centuries and the great store of plausible reforms extensively tested at the state level, more constitutional experimentation at the federal level seems highly desirable. But even a commission process that refers proposed changes to the states rather than the federal electorate would be an improvement over current practice, which, as a practical matter, amounts to a near ban on any significant constitutional change at all.

Passing a constitutional commission amendment would be the first step in a process of progressive constitutional reform. As such, this change would have to happen under the current Article V amendment process, which, as discussed, is daunting. But fairly recent history does provide an example of a realigning election that nearly produced the conditions necessary for constitutional reform under Article V. A successful amendment needs 290 votes in the House, 67 votes in the Senate, and approval by 38 state legislatures. In 1964 such dominance was almost achieved when Democrats not only won the White House but ended up with 295 votes in the House, 68 in the Senate, and control of 32 state legislatures while 10 were split. Chapter 5 discussed how intellectuals and activists working together could replicate that outcome in the twenty-first century. The point here is that historical precedent and the abundance of analogous practices at the state level make it plausible that a constitutional commission amendment could overcome the obstacle course created by Article V.

Then What?

If constitutional change is made easier and if more radical changes—ones that are not necessarily thoroughly tested at the state level—become possible, then amendments that directly address the issue of improving government performance will become possible. Indeed, if the hoped-for victory of progressive forces is large enough, and if appreciation of the need for constitutional change is strong enough, it may be possible to make more radical amendments sooner rather than later, and even under the cumbersome Article V process. At that point, what will be needed is a constitutional amendment with maximum bang for the buck, a relatively small change that leaves the main structure of the Constitution in place but creates a significant improvement in the federal government's ability to take coherent collective action.

Professors William G. Howell and Terry M. Moe offer a good suggestion in their recent book, *Relic: How Our Constitution Undermines Effective Government—and Why We Need a More Powerful Presidency.* They support a constitutional amendment that would allow the president to submit a legislative agenda directly to Congress, which would be required to promptly vote the entire package up or down, without amendments and on a strict majoritarian basis. The essence of their idea is to strengthen the agenda-setting power of the president, whose new role would be somewhat closer than it is now to that of a prime minister under a parliamentary constitution.

Given the difficulty of amending the Constitution, wholesale revision—like switching to a parliamentary system—is impossible. Howell and Moe thus propose their very limited but highly consequential constitutional amendment. As they summarize it, "the president would propose. Congress would decide, up or down."[47] The process would not allow constituency-pleasing amendments to the president's legislative package, and the entire agenda would become law if Congress did not act within ninety days. Such a change would do no more, the authors show, than extend to all policy matters the fast-track authority that presidents now enjoy in trade deals.

The authors' idea follows neatly from their diagnosis: They rightly see that the problem is a localistic Congress with powerful incentives to serve narrow interests, and convincingly argue that the solution is a stronger president who is ready to implement a national agenda. "Presidents," they write, "are the champions of coherence and effectiveness in a fragmented, parochial political world."[48]

The case for constitutional reform in *Relic* is the best—certainly the most realistic—in many years. Yet some caveats apply. *Relic*, as its title suggests, lays great stress on how different the founders' world was from the current one and how outdated their work must now be. That the eighteenth and twenty-first centuries are radically different is indisputable but not relevant to the argument. At issue is not the Constitution's age but its effectiveness, and *Relic* documents ample contemporary pathology. Moreover, one may question the authors' claim that "the founders did *not* believe that all men are created equal."[49] Recent scholarship shows the famous lines of the Declaration of Independence were indeed meant to extend to all people, and incautious suggestions to the contrary today only play into the hands of illiberals.

Howell and Moe's proposed amendment is relevant here because it goes directly to the heart of the primary constitutional cause of American government's collective-action problems: separation of powers. As discussed earlier, separation of powers not only empowers the legislature relative to the executive, but also makes it easy for legislators to disagree with the executive and please pork-seeking constituents, which in turn makes the legislature easy to lobby. And by making lobbying easy, separation of powers guarantees a plethora of lobbies and interest groups. In parliamentary systems where the legislature picks the executive, legislators who oppose their executive are a threat to the ruling government and, hence, party discipline is strong. Thus, pandering to constituents happens less often, which is to say, lobbying the legislature is hard and, hence, fewer lobbies form. So separation-of-powers constitutions, such as America's, facilitate the interest group swarm that fragments political decisionmaking and discourages collective action, while parliamentary systems mitigate that problem.

Obviously, a shift to a parliamentary system is unsuited to American tradition and political culture, and therefore impossible. But Howell and Moe's proposal is a small step toward taking a cue from parliamentary systems by making Congress harder to lobby than it is now. Under their plan, once the president's legislative agenda is submitted to Congress, no lobbyist-pleasing amendments could be added to it. So the coherence of the president's agenda would be preserved, although Congress could still service pork-seeking interests through other legislation. And the ability to advance a coherent legislative agenda is exactly what is needed to improve the collective-action potential of American government and make effective action against the social problems discussed above a more real possibility. Under those circumstances, the developments that stoke the growth of illiberalism could be addressed and American liberal democracy rendered more secure.

Tom Ginsburg and Aziz Z. Huq, in their otherwise insightful book *How to Save a Constitutional Democracy*, oppose Howell and Moe's proposal. But on balance, Ginsburg and Huq are not convincing. First, they are not persuaded that *Relic's* plan is "an effective response to public discontent with national politics" or that "public discontent with Congress is a simple result of legislative deadlock."[50] But in his exhaustive overview of the causes of government failures, Peter H. Schuck documents convincingly that "the public's dissatisfaction is well founded, amply justified by the government's record of poor performance" and that "Congress is the single greatest *institutional* source of government failure."[51] So addressing congressional dysfunction is a rational approach to reducing public discontent.

Moreover, since Ginsburg and Huq admit that Howell and Moe's proposal "would facilitate policymaking . . . reduce gridlock and the concomitant discontent with government sclerosis,"[52] it certainly sounds like the fast-track amendment is worth a shot. The social problems reviewed in this book have to be dealt with in any case, even if doing so does not lessen public discontent with politics. But is it reasonable to suppose the public is obdurate and will be unmoved if policymaking is facilitated, gridlock reduced, government sclerosis overcome, and serious social problems thereby addressed? If so, what motives do politicians have under any circumstances to produce good government and advance the national interest?

However, Ginsburg and Huq have their qualms with the concept of the national interest or, to use their phrase, the national good. *Relic*'s plan, they write:

> Implies . . . the existence of a single, supervening national good. In this way, it stands in tension with a key background assumption of pluralistic democracy—the existence of extensive reasonable disagreement that must be negotiated but never suppressed.[53]

But is it true that the concept of the national good "stands in tension" with "extensive reasonable disagreement"? In the recent past, there was a school of thought that believed not. Those thinkers argued thus:

> Indeed, there are even political scientists who, disgusted by the whole business, insist that the phrase ["the public interest"] be discarded, along with its equivalents, "the common good," "the common weal," "the public welfare," "the national interest," etc. . . . But we do believe that the term, or one of its synonyms, is not to be escaped from.[54]

And they concluded:

> The public interest is not some kind of pre-existing platonic ideal; rather it emerges out of differences of opinion, reasonably propounded.[55]

The above were the sentiments expressed by the editors in the first issue of and the prospectus for the classic neoconservative journal *The Public Interest*. Of course, neoconservativism is very shopworn today. And *The Public Interest*, by the end of its long run, had become sharply ideological, despite its early promise to "be animated by a bias against all such prefabrications."[56] But the initial insight remains valid and can be separated from the later ideological baggage.

If the aim of politics is not to approach some sort of a national good—

or public interest or whatever term one prefers—what is it that is being "negotiated" in a pluralistic democracy? What, exactly, is the "extensive reasonable disagreement" about? If the debate is entirely over "who gets what, when, how," as Harold D. Lasswell famously held, then how will satisfactory resolutions to the disagreements and negotiations be recognized? If the response is that negotiation will go on until a Pareto or Kaldor–Hicks optimal distribution of resources has been achieved, then one has embraced a conception of the national good, although a narrowly economistic one that, by itself, likely will not have wide appeal in the American political environment.

An account of liberal democracy without a compelling vision of the public good is in danger of becoming the caricature that illiberals accuse it of being: a discussion without end or point. Consider the following very telling quote in an article from Counter-Currents Publishing, one of the most radical Alt-Right outlets, which deploys against liberal democracy an argument by the Nazi political theorist Carl Schmitt:

> So, if—according to Carl Schmitt—Liberal Democracy is characterised by government by "discussion" and by "openness," what are the defining characteristics of non-liberal Democracy? It is that of an identity of the ruled and ruling, where there is a shared common good—achievable through homogeneity of the populace.[57]

There will be a shared sense of common good in every polity, and if people believe it cannot be approached through discussion, they will seek it in race or something equally illiberal. Ginsburg and Huq rightly reject the prospect of a notion of the national good being imposed on everyone without discussion. The solution is not to reject the idea of a public interest, but to insist that it emerge out of reasonable discourse and not out of racial homogeneity or illiberal identitarianism.

The Perils and Promise of Presidentialism

Ginsburg and Huq offer another criticism of *Relic*'s proposed fast-track amendment, one that broaches larger issues about turning back the rise of illiberalism:

Worse, Howell and Moe's proposal is likely to exacerbate the risks of democratic erosion, because a strong executive is the principle (although not the only) locus of such risk. Under their system, a charismatic president may be able to make national policy without significant legislative debate. Given sufficient partisan degradation, indeed, it is possible that fast tracking would accelerate the ongoing systemic drift to a wholly presidentialist form of government, one that had a far higher risk of charismatic populism than current arrangements.[58]

To respond to this criticism, one must think about how presidential systems can be susceptible to illiberal encroachment. The analysis of Juan J. Linz in his famous article on "The Perils of Presidentialism" is highly relevant. He argued that presidential systems are more likely to degenerate into authoritarianism than parliamentary systems because the separation of powers in presidential systems makes them prone to gridlock between the executive and legislature branches, which encourages coups and other anti-democratic maneuvers to break the stasis. Thus Linz noted, "It is therefore no accident that in some such situations in the past, the armed forces were often tempted to intervene as a mediating power."[59] But in another passage, Linz described a dynamic more relevant to the American situation:

> One need not delve into all the complexities of the relations between the executive and the legislature in various presidential regimes to see that all such systems are based on dual democratic legitimacy: no democratic principle exists to resolve disputes between the executive and the legislature about which of the two actually represents the will of the people. . . .
>
> In such a context, a president frustrated by legislative recalcitrance will be tempted to mobilize the people against the putative oligarchs and special interests, to claim for himself alone true democratic legitimacy as the tribune of the people, and to urge on his supporters in mass demonstrations against the opposition. . . .
>
> Even more ominously, in the absence of any principled method of distinguishing the true bearer of democratic legitimacy, the president may use ideological formulations to discredit his foes; institutional rivalry may thus assume the character of potentially explosive social and political strife.[60]

Parliamentary systems, Linz showed, were less susceptible to this form of democratic erosion because their unity of the executive and legislature discouraged gridlock and facilitated effective government.

Howell and Moe do not mention Linz, but their analysis is congruent with his. If presidential systems are more prone to illiberal degeneration than parliamentary systems, then wouldn't a move toward parliamentarianism reinforce a presidential democracy against that syndrome? If presidentialism begets dangerous gridlock, then wouldn't making the president a bit more like a prime minister discourage gridlock and the anti-democratic stratagems it can foster?

If Linz's analysis is applied to recent U.S. political history, it shows that anti-democratic scheming in the executive branch to break through gridlock with Congress is more frequent than one might think. Of course, the centuries-long stability of the American constitutional system wards off overt coups, but less bald-faced schemes to overcome standoffs with the legislature are not unknown. The Iran-Contra episode was such a maneuver. So, too, was the notorious mendacity of the George W. Bush administration in its relations with Congress. Trump's overall contempt for Congress is a similar phenomenon. Indeed, the whole "unitary executive" theory of the presidency amounts to no more than a carte blanche for chief executives to play the hardest hardball possible with Congress on the grounds that otherwise they will accomplish nothing. One critic of the unitary executive theory accurately summed up its thrust as follows:

> The unitary executive offered an aggressive brief for . . . avowedly adversarial relations with Congress. . . . This preemptive model of presidential powers aims to counteract the difficulties presidents face in the era of politically divided government. At the same time it highlights a growing contempt . . . for Congress's supposed "inefficiency" and for the way it roadblocks "leadership." . . . This model . . . looks for ways to end-run the Congress, whose weakness and so-called legislative imperialism it scorns.[61]

None of these devices are justifiable, nor are they effective, and for the same reason: They all end up excusing presidential skullduggery, and even criminality, which is good for neither democracy nor effective government.

All such activity needs to be uncovered, opposed, and where appropriate, prosecuted. But the constitutional structure underlying this misbehavior needs to be addressed. If the president's hand with Congress were strengthened constitutionally, in a clearly prescribed manner and for specified purposes, the excuses for excesses would be removed. Moreover, if presidents had the power to present Congress with legislative agendas that had a real chance of being passed in a coherent form, the executives would find their energy better compensated in that endeavor than in running arms, fudging testimony, and similar tricks.

In other words, a weak president with few powers relative to Congress—which is the current scenario—is tempted to overreach. That is, the president is likely to conclude that his or her legitimate powers are not enough to deal with Congress and therefore, illegitimate measures are necessary and justified. It is better to eliminate the propensity to overreach by explicitly increasing the constitutional powers granted to the president as the *Relic* proposal does, in a focused and responsible manner. Thus the fast-track amendment will actually diminish, rather than exacerbate, the risks of democratic erosion.

The Need for Constitutional Change

An anthology I edited on the pros and cons of constitutional change was published in 2013.[62] It included an article by the constitutional scholar Jeremy Rabkin that made a comprehensive case against constitutional reform.[63] His arguments have not held up over time.

For example, Rabkin wrote that despite "the freakish result of the presidential vote in 2000 (where the winner of the electoral vote got fewer popular votes than his opponent) . . . the clamor for reforming the Electoral College died down rather quickly in the aftermath." Unfortunately, with the ascension in 2016 of another popular-vote loser to the White House via the Electoral College, the results of 2000 can no longer be called freakish.

More importantly, Rabkin's optimistic evaluation of the functioning of the American constitutional system is much less convincing now. "Why Fix It if It's Not Broke?" Rabkin asked.[64] But as Schuck showed in his exhaustive review of the problems facing American government, "most Americans today believe that our government is failing to deliver what it promises, and they have lost confidence in its effectiveness." As to why Americans feel this way, Schuck documents in great detail that "the most straightforward answer is that *the federal government does in fact perform poorly in a vast range of domestic programs.*"[65] Rabkin correctly pointed out voter discontent is not so high that "they [voters] would have supported violent rebellion or a military coup."[66] But that is the very least one could ask for. Otherwise, things really are quite bad.

In *Federalist* No. 14, Madison implored America not to reject constitutional change, in these words:

> Hearken not to the voice which petulantly tells you that the form of government recommended for your adoption is a novelty in the political world; that it has never yet had a place in the theories of the wildest projectors; that it rashly attempts what it is impossible to accomplish.

After more than two centuries of political history, during which practices that were once novelties have been widely tested and the theory of government has become greatly more sophisticated, one might say that the opponents of constitutional reform today are petulant voices against experience in the political world and the theories of the soundest projectors. Constitutional reform must now soberly attempt what has been possible to accomplish in not only other countries, but also the American states themselves. When the time comes that activists and intellectuals produce the episode of united government and political realignment needed to produce a spell of nonincremental change, constitutional reform must be part of their agenda.

8
Conclusion

Here, then, in summary is this book's prescription for turning back the illiberal tide. A crucial part of the answer is to improve the capacity of America's liberal democracy to take collective action on the problems that generate the legitimate concerns illiberals take advantage of.

To do that, America must make its peace with identity politics. Garden-variety identity politics in the form of new ethnic, racial, and gender interest groups wanting their piece of the pie must be accommodated and embraced. Radical identitarian politics in the form of Alt-Right, European New Right, and other illiberal forms of racial consciousness must be rejected. And the American political identity that is already widely embraced by Americans of all sorts has to be recognized as an invaluable resource that makes democratic discourse possible while maintaining a healthy heterogeneity of political values.

Further, the ability of American democratic discourse to fruitfully address important political problems has been diminished by the shocks of the early twenty-first century to our political system. The intellectual gatekeepers who upheld the ethics of controversy during the mid-to-late twentieth century have been undermined by the rise of digital media and other social developments. These gatekeepers no longer have the power to play the role of intellectual antibodies that maintain a healthy climate of opinion by isolating illiberal ideologies. Nothing can fully restore the power these gatekeepers once enjoyed. Intellectuals do not need just technological fixes, but an intellectual strategy for rebutting the encroachments of illiberalism into American political culture. Illiberals have embraced, irresponsibly exaggerated, and weaponized rhetoric strategies that were once used by some serious thinkers to address real problems but have long outlived their usefulness. The assumption that outsider standpoints are always epistemically privileged standpoints and the reflexive use of irony to gain a hearing for unprepossessing ideas have been captured by the illiberal right and no longer serve democratic purposes. A new intellectual rhetorical strategy is needed—one that acknowledges the indispensability of objectivity and liberal democracy, and yet is comfortable with the entry of new voices and technologies into public discourse.

And then a new approach to interest-group politics is needed. It must be one that accepts and even celebrates the arrival of new interest groups into liberal democratic politics. But it must also recognize that adding more interest groups into an already hyperpluralistic political environment cannot in itself solve the problems of collective action that all pluralist polities are subject to. Collective-action problems have to be addressed at the constitutional level. This is especially true of the problems that illiberal movements and politicians are taking advantage of.

To seriously address the illiberal challenge, America must come to terms with identity politics; reorient its intellectual life away from glorifying transgression and toward appreciating rational discourse; make better use of the ideals central to the American identity to facilitate the development of a New American Majority; and reform its political institutions to make government action more effective. All of this is possible. Whether it is accomplished is now up to the America people.

Will It Work?

Is the above agenda, even if it were fully implemented, enough to repair America's damaged political culture and dramatically improve the capacity of American government for collective action? In his important book *Why Government Fails So Often and How It Can Do Better*, Peter H. Schuck provides a comprehensive account of all the obstacles to improving the public sector's effectiveness. His conclusion is sobering:

The most striking feature of this failure—other than its sheer frequency and pervasiveness—is how deep and structural its causes are. They are grounded neither in Democrats' abiding commitment to an activist domestic policy agenda nor in Republicans' traditional opposition to it. . . . Nor is failure due to insufficient resources or lack of official commitment. . . . This relationship between government's growing ambition and its endemic failure is rooted in an inescapable, structural condition: officials' meager tools and limited understanding of the opaque, complex social world they aim to manipulate. . . . The lesson of this book is that the chasm will remain too wide for policy makers to bridge except under the most favorable circumstances. . . . These conditions are less likely to materialize in the future than they did in the past.[1]

Writing in 2014, Schuck did not see the rise of illiberalism and the election of Trump. The importance of achieving more-favorable circumstances to produce more effective government and so stem the tide of illiberalism is now clear.

Chapter 5 of this book sketched out a strategy for bringing about circumstances favorable to structural change. It is a strategy of political organizing to empower a New American Majority and work by intellectuals to facilitate that development by interpreting it as consistent with the American identity leading to a realigning presidential election in the not-to-distant future. That outcome, it is true, would be a victory for Democrats, but the most important reason the outcome would be desirable is not because it would give Democrats a chance to enact their partisan agenda. Rather, the most important results would be political realignment and a moment of constitutional syzygy that would temporarily overcome one of the deepest structural problems Schuck and many other analysts have identified: the propensity toward fragmentation and gridlock inherent in a separation-of-powers government. Much will depend on whether non-populist conservatives, Republicans, and independents recognize the need for an episode of unity and reform, and throw their backs into achieving it, even though doing so temporarily empowers their traditional adversaries.

Much will also depend on whether, if realignment is achieved, the Democrats do not devote themselves entirely to paying off the factions that supported them and do recognize the need for systemic change. Con-

stitutional change of the sort advocated in chapter 7 and the good government reforms advocated by Schuck and others sometimes have limited
appeal to the disadvantaged interest groups that Democrats represent. But
the long-term prospects for a more effective government that can ditch
the illiberals and leave them without a constituency depend on whether a
unified government that emerges from a realigning election has the fore-
sight to institutionalize that unity in appropriate constitutional change.

A fragmenting and ossified Constitution and a dysfunctional Congress
are two of the most powerful structural barriers to effective government
identified in Schuck's exhaustive analysis. If the window of opportunity
provided by a moment of presidential/majoritarian change can be leveraged to address these two issues, the basic structure of American politics
will be changed. A new era in American politics will open up—one in
which the constraints on effective government action will be much reduced.

The Role of Ideas

Schuck focuses most of his relatively pessimistic analysis on structures
and says almost nothing about ideas. But under certain circumstances,
ideas can facilitate political change such that when they are taken into
consideration, the prospects for effective government look better than
when only structural factors are considered.

As was discussed in chapter 5, an ideational/entrepreneurial model
of policy change functioned from the early 1970s up to the end of the
twentieth century in America. It was a model that made nonincremental
change possible even in policy areas that political scientists had believed
were impervious to reform, such as environmental, tax, immigration, and
welfare policies.[2] A particularly interesting contribution to the literature
on the ideational/entrepreneurial model was "The Politics of Rapid Legal
Change: Immigration Policy in the 1980s." The article noted that "until
late 1986, the prospects for *any* meaningful immigration reform, restrictive or expansionist, seemed decidedly bleak. Experts viewed immigration
policy as the Vietnam of domestic politics, an arena of bitter, protracted
warfare from which no one could emerge unharmed."[3] Yet "long-stale-
mated immigration reforms were finally enacted." But why? The author
wrote:

Ideas, I argue, were crucial to the triumph of expansionist immigration reform. . . . Ideas can *precede* interests as well as *promote* them. They not only help political actors fulfill their existing political agendas; they also affect how those actors construct their agendas in the first place. Ideas can alter how people perceive the world, how they decide what to value, and how they organize to attain their goals. In this way they redefine ends and means and may even supply new ones.[4]

The article shows convincingly how experts and policy entrepreneurs distilled a powerful public idea, "Close the back door and open the front door," and how this and other "ideas flooded TV and radio talk shows, congressional hearings, and the editorial pages of major newspapers."[5]

The author of this convincing analysis of the role ideas played in immigration policy was Schuck, who by 2014 produced the almost entirely structural analysis of policymaking referenced above—one in which ideas are mentioned almost not at all, and the prospects for positive change are very limited. But there is no contradiction in this. Schuck does not discuss his change of emphasis, but he does not have to. As chapter 5 in this book has shown, the internal contradictions in intellectuals' understanding of their role in society, the rise of social media and their undermining of the power of gatekeepers, and the many social shocks of the early twenty-first century all worked to dismantle the ideational/entrepreneurial model of political change. Thus, American politics was deprived of an important tool for resolving social problems through effective government action.

The challenge, therefore, is how to revive and renew the ideational/entrepreneurial model for the digital age. A key question is how digital media can be reconfigured to reinforce the position of intellectual gatekeepers. That question raises issues about communications technologies and regulation that are outside the competence of this author. But the important point is that a campaign to do so is already underway. The libertarian fantasies entertained by the early literature on the internet, about how the new, unregulated medium would spontaneously produce a golden age of direct democracy, have been falsified. Of course digital media have had many positive effects that no one wants to deny or give up. But the internet has also enabled a tidal wave of trafficking, harassment and bullying, pornography, fraud, disinformation, rumor, and other negative material.

This sort of stuff had always been around. By the late twentieth century, much of it was not legally censored. There was no need. In the days of predigital media, nasty material was mostly filtered out of mainstream outlets and relegated to relatively marginal platforms that people uninterested in it could easily avoid. Given the ubiquity of computers in modern life, what the unregulated internet has done is intrude this unlovely content into every home, workplace, and phone, where it cannot be avoided even by those who want no part of it. No doubt the benefits of digital media have outweighed these costs. But the costs are considerable, and there is no reason why regulation should not seek to achieve a better bottom line.

Now we must add illiberal ideologies to this list of problematic content. Here breaks in the anti-regulation absolutist: "What? You call for mere censorship of ideas you don't like!" No. As is well understood, censorship is governmental prohibition of the production and dissemination of particular material. Nothing of the sort is called for here. What is called for is the creation of a media ecology analogous to that of the late twentieth century, where there was no censorship but anti-democratic ideology was marginalized through the efforts of private media, independent intellectuals, and an educated public.

But is social marginalization of this sort merely de facto censorship? Again, no. First, there is a world of difference between de facto and de jure. Consider that while it is true much de facto segregation exists in the United States and it is a serious social problem, few people would argue there is no difference between de jure and de facto segregation. Similarly, legal censorship is problematic because it involves the police power of government and raises constitutional issues in ways that informal measures do not.

Moreover, what one thinks about social marginalization depends on what is being marginalized. Black people are rights-bearing citizens and contributors to American society. Marginalizing them is enormously costly; bringing them into the social mainstream is a great achievement.

Do illiberal ideologies deserve to be socially marginalized? Consider a recap of some material from illiberal outlets that were discussed in chapter 3 and ask whether it merits a place in mainstream political culture.

- What about sites such as national-socialist-worldview.blogspot .com, kkk.com, and a site whose racist URL I will reference here as nwordmania.com?

- What about sites like the Daily Stormer, whose editor, in his official style book, asserts "the Daily Stormer is . . . designed to spread the message of nationalism and anti-Semitism to the masses. . . . The basic propaganda doctrine of the site is based on Hitler's doctrine of war propaganda outlined in Mein Kampf. . . . I actually do want to gas kikes"?[6]

- How about Manosphere sites that say, "It's time to stop beating around the bush: *feminists want to be raped*. . . . Every feminist, deep down, wants nothing more than a rapist's baby in her belly"?[7] And here's another: "It should be clear to you that women will always use their votes to destroy themselves and their nations, to invite invaders with open legs, to persecute their own men, and to ravage their economies with socialism. . . . I can now claim to have one political dream, and that is to repeal women's suffrage."[8]

- What about Alex Jones and Infowars, which spread the lie that the Democratic Party was operating a satanic child pornography ring out of a Washington, D.C., pizza parlor, which resulted in an armed attack on that establishment?[9]

Again, the question is not whether sites of this sort should be censored; they should not be. The question is whether they should be informally marginalized; they should be. The important question of what regulatory scheme will best promote such marginalization is an issue for writers who, unlike myself, have the relevant expertise.

The marginalization called for here should be informal in the sense that it is not achieved by direct government policy, but primarily by private sector actors. And despite their great size and influence, the main digital service providers—such as Google, Facebook, YouTube, and Twitter—still count as private sector organizations. In their insightful article on internet speech, Jack Goldsmith and Andrew Keane Woods noted that the ongoing global trend toward greater regulation of digital media was being accomplished in China through its authoritarian government but through private organizations in the United States. This difference is like that between lightning and the lightning bug. China's authoritarian dictatorship is not subject to democratic control or an independent judiciary, so there is no way of contesting its regulation of the internet. America's giant internet companies are beasts of another kind entirely. None of them is a complete monopoly, so they are subject to some market competition and customers can always vote with their feet if they do not like how they are treated. All of the U.S. internet companies are subject to democratic control via government regulation and interest-group pressure. And they can be hauled before an independent judiciary when they violate the law. Thus, equating the level of management Facebook and similar organizations impose on the material that is posted on their platform to Chinese censorship obscures vital distinctions. There is no doubt that America's giant internet companies yield enormous social influence and face limited market competition. In this way, they resemble the railroads of the nineteenth century. But that is the point: just like the railroads, today's internet titans are and should be subject to government regulation in a way that dictatorial governments cannot be.

The point of this digression into internet regulation is simple: Reviving the ideational/entrepreneurial mechanism of political change involves strengthening the hand of private gatekeepers through regulation of the internet. But the private gatekeepers themselves, that is to say, intellectuals, must be up to the task. Therefore most of chapter 5 was devoted not to the details of internet regulation, but to rethinking the role of intellectuals so they will be able to perform their gatekeeping functions when greater opportunity to do so develops. When that happens (and it will), intellectuals must function as interpreters of expertise; take advantage of the resources and independence afforded to them in academia; extend an epistemic privilege to no standpoint, marginal or otherwise; work with an appreciation for liberal democracy and its institutions, subject always to critical scrutiny; and point the way toward political change that is consistent with the American identity.

Identity Again

What does the issue of identity have to do with a central issue of this book, which is how to improve the capacity of government for collective action and so meet the illiberal challenge? First, identity is the concept that illiberals have made the lance point of their movement. Their argument is that liberal democracy destroys identity; that without identity, politics has no object and life has no meaning; that the resulting spiritual void creates decadence and facilitates tyranny; and that only race can provide an identity, fill the void, and produce . . . Well, it is not always clear what illiberalism will produce. But the white race, or at least some portion of the white race, will be in charge and liberal niceties such as human rights, political egalitarianism, the rule of law, electoral democracy, and tolerance will be dispensed with. So, one point of taking up identity is to meet this argument head on by challenging its conception of identity.

The long discussion of identity in chapter 4 showed, hopefully, that illiberal appropriation of the concept of identity is easily rebutted. Many authors have worked themselves into a state of confusion trying to explain how the illiberal white identity politics they oppose are to be distinguished from the Black, Latinx, feminist, gay, and other forms of identity politics they approve of. But the answer is simple: The identity politics of the latter sort are merely old-fashioned interest-group politics of newly active interests. In principle, they are congruent with America's Madisonian political environment, even if, as has always been the case, some groups have a harder time fitting in than others, for historical and cultural reasons. In the end, all can fit in and should be helped to do so. And so these ordinary versions of identity politics square easily with liberal democracy.

Illiberal identity politics, or identitarianism, is another thing entirely. It posits race alone as wholly determinative of identity, sees politics as entirely a struggle of the races for dominance, and holds the white race as superior to other races. Hard-core identitarianism sees the argument through to its logical end and endorses genocidal war with "death to the vanquished." Softer versions counsel racial isolationism, but how this is to be achieved in multiracial countries and what will happen when racial groups bump into each other are not convincingly explained. And, of course, all versions of identitarianism reject liberal democracy root and branch, which is another good reason for rejecting them.

But another response to illiberal's appropriation of identity politics is possible, one that raises larger issues. Illiberals argue that liberal democracy is hostile to not only identity, but also the whole idea of the public good. Here is Greg Johnson, editor of Counter-Currents Publishing, on the issue:

> Liberalism is a modern political philosophy that proclaims that the common good doesn't exist, or it can't be known, or if we can know it,

it doesn't matter, or if we can know it, we can't pursue it, and therefore basically, we just have to set up mechanisms whereby people can pursue private interests and somehow we have to hope that it all works out. I say phooey to that.[10]

And here is Alain de Benoist making the same claim:

Liberals insist particularly on the idea that individual interests should never be sacrificed to the collective interest, the common good, or the public safety, concepts that they regard as inconsistent.[11]

But liberal democracy does recognize the concept of the common good and to see why that is so we must note that liberal democracy also recognizes the concept of identity.

As was demonstrated in chapter 4, America already has an identity in the sense of a set of widely shared notions about what it means to be an American. The American identity is a composite of components from several traditions: liberalism, civic republicanism, ethnoculturalism, and incorporationism. Each of these traditions has contributed its own set of ideas, beliefs, habits, traditions, arguments, and other cognitions to the American identity. The American identity is the American standpoint, the necessary starting point that is provisionally taken as given when Americans discuss politics.

The liberal democratic conception of the common good requires the existence of such a standpoint identity. As was shown in chapter 7, the liberal democratic notion of the common good is that it "is not some kind of pre-existing platonic ideal; rather it emerges out of differences of opinion, reasonably propounded." So liberal democrats hold that the public good is to be discovered through reasonable inquiry. But inquiry must begin somewhere, from a baseline standpoint that is provisionally accepted as true until proven otherwise. The American identity is that beginning standpoint that makes rational inquiry possible. And if rational inquiry is possible, inquiry into the nature of the public good is not futile.

The liberal inquiry into the public good is not, as illiberals claim it to be, an aimless, endless discussion where everything is always up for grabs and no resolution is possible. Liberal political inquiry begins from a particular standpoint identity. When the president presents a budget proposal to Congress, he asserts a powerful influence over the direction and resolution of that chamber's debate. Similarly, the American identity grounds, establishes the starting point of, sets limits to, and provides standards for resolving the polity's inquiry into the public good. The liberal elements of the American identity point to an enormously rich set of ideas, practices, and institutions for conducting and resolving political debate. Liberalism, civic republicanism, and incorporationism each imply certain public virtues that are necessary for their realization and that can guide political practice. Even ethnoculturalism can play a useful role in facilitating liberal inquiry into the public good. It provides the polity with a warning of particular vices to be avoided, of injustices to be overcome, of negative propensities to be rechanneled, if possible. Just as an individual's struggle against neuroses can be liberating, so too can the struggle to prevent ethnoculturalism from amounting to pure racism be productive. Liberal democratic discussion of the public good does not start *ex vacuo* and proceed with no roadmaps or landmarks. Its structure rules some things in and some things out while indicating a very wide set of possible public goods.

In short, liberal democracy does have a substantive, if flexible, conception of the public good. And liberal democracy does have a concept of identity, one that makes possible the reasonable inquiry into exactly what public good is in a given situation. Now the question is whether America can make the best use of these resources in responding to and turning back the rise of illiberalism.

Notes

Chapter 1

1. Sarah Posner, "How Donald Trump's New Campaign Chief Created an Online Haven for White Nationalists," Mother Jones, August 22, 2016, www .motherjones.com/politics/2016/08/stephen-bannon-donald-trump-alt-right -breitbart-news.

2. Joseph Bernstein, "Data Shows Tucker Carlson Is the Daily Stormer's Favorite Pundit," BuzzFeed News, November 28, 2018, www.buzzfeednews .com/article/josephbernstein/tucker-carlson-fox-news-daily-stormers-favorite -pundit.

3. Chris Kahn, "Half Of Republicans Say Biden Won Because of a 'Rigged' Election: Reuters/Ipsos Poll," Reuters, November 18, 2020, www.reuters.com /article/us-usa-election-poll/half-of-republicans-say-biden-won-because-of-a -rigged-election-reuters-ipsos-poll-idUSKBN27Y1AJ. The poll was conducted from November 13–17, contacted 1,346 respondents nationwide (598 Democrats and 496 Republicans), and had a confidence interval of five percentage points.

4. Joel Rose, "Even If It's 'Bonkers,' Poll Finds Many Believe QAnon and Other Conspiracy Theories," NPR, December 30, 2020, www.npr.org/2020/12 /30/951095644/even-if-its-bonkers-poll-finds-many-believe-qanon-and-other -conspiracy-theories. The poll questioned 1,115 Americans, was conducted from December 21–22, and has a confidence interval of 3.3 percentage points for the overall sample.

5. Gregory Stanton, "QAnon Is a Nazi Cult, Rebranded," Just Security, September 9, 2020, www.justsecurity.org/72339/qanon-is-a-nazi-cult-rebranded/.

Also see, Hatewatch Staff, "What You Need to Know About QAnon," Southern Poverty Law Center, October 27, 2020, www.splcenter.org/hatewatch/2020/10 /27/what-you-need-know-about-qanon?fbclid=IwAR0XBdSz3vKPFfQTuJuM1 GWJ0TCaQiF0ZqkmnK3Nlxa3L5aZEgWlxuhMU-0.

6. Thomas Jefferson, letter to Charles Yancy, 1816, in *The Writings of Thomas Jefferson, Memorial Edition, 1903–1904*, vol. 14. Washington, D.C.: Thomas Jefferson Memorial Association, p. 384.

7. Kelly Hooper, "Trump Wins Title of Americans' Most Admired Man in Annual Survey," Politico, December 29, 2020, www.politico.com/news/2020/12 /29/trump-gallup-most-admired-452126.

8. Marist Poll, "PBS NewsHour/Marist Poll Results & Analysis: Insurrection at the Capitol," January 8, 2021, p. 8, http://maristpoll.marist.edu/pbs -newshour-marist-poll-results-analysis-insurrection-at-the-capitol/#sthash .AYe9ptLF.UEci6KEJ.dpbs.

Chapter 2

1. "Declaration of Independence: A Transcription," National Archives: America's Founding Documents, www.archives.gov/founding-docs/declaration -transcript.

2. Joseph Schumpeter, *Capitalism, Socialism, and Democracy* (New York: Harper and Row, 1956), p. 269.

3. Locke writes: "The great end of men's entering into society, being the enjoyment of their properties in peace and safety, and the great instrument and means of that being the laws established in that society; the first and fundamental positive law of all commonwealths is the establishing of the legislative power. . . ." By "entering into society" Locke means establishing a government so "the great instrument and means" of government achieving its ends is the rule of law. John Locke, *Second Treatise of Government*, Chapter XI, "The Extent of Legislative Power," Project Gutenberg, 2010, p. 42, https://english.hku.hk/ staff/kjohnson/PDF/LockeJohnSECONDTREATISE1690.pdf.

4. In *The Road to Serfdom*, Hayek, though he does not use the term, in substance endorses a limited welfare state when he writes that government should guarantee a ". . . security which can be achieved for all, and which is therefore no privilege but a legitimate object of desire. . . . security against severe physical privation, the certainty of a given minimum of sustenance for all . . . there can be no doubt that some minimum of food, shelter, and clothing, sufficient to preserve health and the capacity to work, can be assured to everybody. . . . Nor is there any reason why the state should not assist the individuals in providing for those common hazards of life against which, because of their uncertainty, few individuals can make adequate provision. . . . [T]he case for the state helping to organise a comprehensive system of social insurance is very strong. . . . [T]here is no incompatibility in principle between the state providing greater security

in this way and the preservation of individual freedom." But in a later work, *The Constitution of Liberty*, Hayek took back much of what he said when he turned against the "kind of welfare state that aims at 'social justice' and becomes 'primarily a redistributor of income.'" F. A. Hayek, *The Road to Serfdom* (London: George Routledge & Sons, 1945), pp. 89–90. F. A. Hayek, *The Constitution of Liberty: The Definitive Edition* (University of Chicago Press), p. 376.

5. Brink Lindsey, "Why Libertarians and Conservatives Should Stop Opposing the Welfare State," Niskanen Center, August 9, 2017, www.niskanencenter .org/libertarians-conservatives-stop-opposing-welfare-state.

6. I have argued that a welfare state is a necessary element of liberal democracy. See Thomas J. Main, "The Future of the Welfare State and Liberal Political Theory," *Perspectives on Political Science* 35, no. 4 (2006), pp. 219–24. But there is not an overwhelming consensus on the issue.

7. ABC News, "Read Joe Biden's Full Inaugural Address: 'End This Uncivil War,'" January 20, 2021, https://abcnews.go.com/Politics/read-joe-bidens-full -inaugural-address-end-civil/story?id=75351694. Tucker Carlson, "Joe Biden Declares War on 'White Supremacy.' What Does He Mean by That?" Fox News, January 20, 2021, www.foxnews.com/opinion/tucker-carlson-joe-biden -inauguration-war-on-white-supremacy.

8. Heather MacDonald, "Words of Division," City Journal, January 20, 2021, www.city-journal.org/bidens-inaugural-speech-words-of-division.

9. *Oxford English Dictionary*, definition of white supremacist, www-oed-com .remote.baruch.cuny.edu/view/Entry/421024?redirectedFrom=%E2%80%9C white+supremacist%E2%80%9D&.

10. Jared Taylor, "The Truth About 'All Men Are Created Equal,'" American Renaissance, June 23, 2017, www.amren.com/features/2017/06/truth-men -created-equal, at 5:43 and 7:29.

11. Davis Carlton, "The Idolatry of Equality, Zionism, and Pluralism in the Contemporary Southern Baptist Convention," Faith & Heritage, July 22, 2017, http://faithandheritage.com/2017/07/the-idolatry-of-equality-zionism-and -pluralism-in-the-contemporary-southern-baptist-convention. Pastor Mark Downey, "The Truth About Lies, Part 1," December 30, 2011, Kinsman Redeemer Ministries, http://kinsmanredeemer.com/truth-about-lies-part-1.

12. Tyler Durden ("Submitted by James Miller of the Ludwig von Mises Institute of Canada"), "Guest Post: What Democracy?" Zero Hedge, August 5, 2012, www.zerohedge.com/news/guest-post-what-democracy.

13. Paul Craig Roberts, "In America Democracy Destroyed Democracy," December 8, 2020, www.paulcraigroberts.org/2020/12/08/in-america-democracy -destroyed-democracy. Emphasis in original.

14. Alain de Benoist, *Beyond Human Rights* (London: Arktos Media, 2011), pp. 23–24.

15. Guillaume Faye, *Why We Fight: Manifesto of the European Resistance* (London: Arktos Media, 2011), p. 229.

16. Examples of articles by and about Benoist and Faye published by illiberal web outlets include: Kevin MacDonald, "Alain de Benoist on the West," Occidental Observer, April 22, 2011, www.theoccidentalobserverl.net/2011/04/22/alain-de-benoist-on-the-west; Andrew Joyce, "Review: View from the Right: A Critical Anthology of Contemporary Ideas, Volume I," Occidental Observer, May 25, 2018, www.theoccidentalobserverl.net/2018/05/25/review-view-from-the-right-a-critical-anthology-of-contemporary-ideas-volume-i; Alain de Benoist, "On Identity," Occidental Observer, November 2, 2013, www.theoccidentalobserverl.net/2013/11/02/on-identity; Andrew Joyce, "A Race War Prophecy," Occidental Observer, September 8, 2019, www.theoccidentalobserverl.net/2019/09/08/a-race-war-prophecy; Charles Jansen, "Guillaume Faye: Seven Mistakes that Explain the Failure of the European New Right," Occidental Observer, May 18, 2016, www.theoccidentalobserverl.net/2016/05/18/guillaume-faye-seven-mistakes-that-explain-the-failure-of-the-european-new-right; Michael Walker, "Alain de Benoist's *Against Liberalism*," Counter-Currents Radio, https://counter-currents.com/2019/11/alain-de-benoists-against-liberalism; John Law, "Natural Rights vs. Human Rights: A Critique of Alain de Benoist," Counter-Currents Publishing, August 13, 2015, https://counter-currents.com/2015/08/natural-rights-vs-human-rights; Roger Devlin, "Human Rights between Ideology & Politics: Alain de Benoist's *Beyond Human Rights*," Counter-Currents Publishing, April 11, 2012, https://counter-currents.com/2012/04/alain-de-benoists-beyond-human-rights/print; and Greg Johnson, "Remembering Guillaume Faye: November 7, 1949–March 7, 2019," Counter-Currents Publishing, November 7, 2019, https://counter-currents.com/2019/11/remembering-guillaume-faye-2. This last article provides links to twenty-seven articles by and twenty-five articles about Faye published by Counter-Currents Publishing.

17. A full copy of the Daily Stormer's style guide is available at Ashley Feinberg, "This Is the Daily Stormer's Playbook," *Huffington Post*, December 13, 2017, www.huffpost.com/entry/daily-stormer-nazi-style-guide_n_5a2ece19e4b0ce3b344492f2. The complete document is also available at https://assets.documentcloud.org/documents/4325810/Writers.pdf. Excerpts from the guide are also available at Vox Day, "The Andrew Anglin Style Guide," Vox Popoli, September 6, 2017, https://voxday.blogspot.com/2017/09/the-andrew-anglin-style-guide.html. The quotes cited here are from pages 10, 11, and 14.

18. Regarding the Drudge Report's promotion of false stories of Clinton family scandals, see: Brian Stelter, "Drudge Report Misleads Readers with Hillary Clinton Photo," CNN Money, August 8, 2016, https://money.cnn.com/2016/08/08/media/drudge-report-hillary-clinton-fall/; BBC News, "Hillary Health Myth: From Twitter Theories to a Trump Speech," August 19, 2016, www.bbc.com/news/election-us-2016-37090082; and Tara Golshan, "Drudge Report Is Spreading a Conspiracy about Bill Clinton It Debunked in 1999," Vox, October 3, 2016, www.vox.com/policy-and-politics/2016/10/3/13147842/bill-clinton-son-danney-williams. Regarding the Drudge Report's promo-

tion of the false Obama birth certificate story, see: Drudge Report, "BOOK TO REVEAL OBAMA'S 'TRUE' IDENTITY," April 20, 2011, www.drudge report.com/flash7.htm; and Brian Stelter, "In Trying to Debunk a Theory, the News Media Extended Its Life," *New York Times*, April 27, 2011, www.nytimes .com/2011/04/28/business/media/28birth.html. For a list of fact-checks failed by the Drudge Report previous to its improved journalistic standards, see: Media Bias/Fact Check, "Drudge Report," April 24, 2021, https://mediabiasfact check.com/drudge-report/.

Regarding Breitbart's climate change denial, see: James Delingpole, "Climate Change: The Hoax that Costs Us $4 Billion a Day," Breitbart, August 8, 2015, www.breitbart.com/politics/2015/08/08/climate-change-the-hoax-that -costs-us-4-billion-a-day/; and John Nolte, "Scientists Prove Man-Made Global Warming Is a Hoax, Breitbart, April 9, 2019, www.breitbart.com/politics/2019 /04/09/nolte-scientists-prove-man-made-global-warming-is-a-hoax/. For Breitbart's promotion of false claims of election fraud, see: Tom Fitton, "Hope for a Failed Election," Breitbart, December 23, 2020, www.breitbart.com/poli tics/2020/12/23/fitton-hope-for-a-failed-election/; Joel B. Pollak, "The Real 'Big Lie' Is that the 2020 Election Was Free and Fair," Breitbart, June 7, 2021, www.breitbart.com/2020-election/2021/06/07/pollak-the-real-big-lie-is-that -the-2020-election-was-free-and-fair; and Tiffany Hsu, "Conservative News Sites Fuel Voter Fraud Misinformation," *New York Times*, published October 25, 2020, updated November 6, 2020, www.nytimes.com/2020/10/25/business /media/voter-fraud-misinformation.html?smtyp=cur&smid=tw-nytimes. For Breitbart's characterization of promoters of mask use during the COVID-19 pandemic as "mask fascists," see: John Nolte: "The Era of the Mask Fascists Has Begun," Breitbart, May 26, 2020, www.breitbart.com/politics/2020 /05/26/nolte-the-era-of-the-mask-fascists-has-begun/; and John Nolte: "66% of Democrats Are Anti-Science Mask Nazis," Breitbart, August 2, 2021, www .breitbart.com/politics/2021/08/02/nolte-66-democrats-are-anti-science-mask -nazis/. For a list of fact-checks failed by Breitbart, see: Media Bias/Fact Check, Breitbart, April 3, 2021, https://mediabiasfactcheck.com/breitbart/.

19. Links to some forty articles by and about Carl Schmitt published by Counter-Currents Publishing are provided by Greg Johnson, "Remembering Carl Schmitt (July 11, 1888–April 7, 1985), Counter-Currents Publishing, July 11, 2020, https://counter-currents.com/2020/07/remembering-carl-schmitt-9.

20. Rodolphe Lussac, "Why Are We Political Soldiers?" Counter-Currents Publishing, July 15, 2010, https://counter-currents.com/2010/07/why-are-we-polit ical-soldiers.

21. David Horowitz Freedom Center, www.davidHorowitzfreedomcenter .org/.

22. David Horowitz, *The Art of Political War: How Republicans Can Fight to Win* (Los Angeles: The Committee for a Non-Liberal Majority, 1999), pp. 15–16.

23. Joseph Klein, "Borderline Treason: How Democrats Continue to Betray

Their Country," FrontPage Magazine, January 8, 2020, https://cms.frontpage mag.com/fpm/2020/01/borderline-treason-joseph-klein.

24. Quoted in J. E. S. Hayward, "Finer's Comparative History of Government," *Government and Opposition* 32, no. 1 (Winter 1997), p. 131.

25. S. E. Finer, "Perspectives in the World History of Government—A Prolegomenon," *Government and Opposition* 18, no. 1 (Winter 1983), pp. 21–22.

26. Francis Fukuyama, *Political Order and Political Decay* (New York: Farrar, Straus and Giroux, 2014), p. 37.

27. "A Letter on Justice and Open Debate," *Harper's Magazine*, July 7, 2020, https://harpers.org/a-letter-on-justice-and-open-debate.

Chapter 3

1. A list of the URLs of websites included in this analysis is available from the author at thomas.main@baruch.cuny.edu. Unless otherwise noted, characterizations of websites and their content mostly refer to the time period January 2019 to November 2019.

2. The source sites that provided lists of Left Illiberal sites included Sprout Distro, "an anarchist zine distro [distributor] and publisher based in the occupied territory currently known as the United States"; Contra Info, a "worldwide counter-information website"; Anarres Press, "an all-volunteer anarchist small press in Seattle . . . We print seditious materials"; Semo Distro, "an anarchist distribution project"; Untorelli Press, "an anarchist publishing project . . . As *untorelli* (plague-carriers), we seek to propagate our textual diseases and contribute to the plague of anarchy"; the Torch Network, "a network of militant antifascists . . . We are dedicated to confronting fascism and other elements of oppression. We believe in direct action"; *Three Way Fight*, "a blog that promotes revolutionary anti-fascist analysis, strategy and activism. . . . We believe that 'defending democracy' is an illusion as long as 'democracy' is based on a socio-economic order that exploits and oppresses human beings"; What's Left?; Rocky Mountain Antifa; Denver Anarchist Black Cross; and the Ruin of Capital.

3. For example, Joe Biden, the *New York Times*, and the entire Democratic Party are all part of DTN's charts. Under the classification of "Groups>>Radical," DTN includes several sites that could be classified as Far Left. However, I had to make judgment calls in using this source, which admittedly was a drawback. Nonetheless I decided to use the leads provided by DTN because information on the Far Left is hard to come by. In recent years, the Far Right has been tracked by organizations like the Southern Poverty Law Center, received much journalist coverage, and been analyzed by many academics. Far-Left groups receive much less attention, and therefore, identifying their web outlets is more difficult than tracking down Far-Right outlets. I wanted to be certain that I had left no stone unturned in my search for the web presence of the Far Left, and therefore I decided to make use of data from DTN despite the drawbacks.

4. Overcoming Bias, About, www.overcomingbias.com/about.

5. NextBigFuture, About, www.nextbigfuture.com/about.

6. Steve Keen's Debt Deflation Page, www.debtdeflation.com/. Overlawyered: Chronicling the High Cost of Our Legal System, About, www.over lawyered.com/about/.

7. The Knights Party: The Premier Voice of America's White Resistance, http://kkk.bz/. Reconquista Europa: Reclaiming Our Heritage, https://alt-right .com/who-we-are/.

8. RationalWiki, https://rationalwiki.org/wiki/RationalWiki.

9. According to its mission statement, an "important purpose of Metapedia is to become a web resource for pro-European activists. Metapedia makes it easy for our cadres to expand their knowledge on various important subjects, and also functions as a searchable reference. Furthermore Metapedia gives us the opportunity to present a more balanced and fair image of the pro-European struggle for the general public as well as for academics, who until now have been dependent on strongly biased and hostile 'researchers' like Searchlight, Anti-Defamation League, Southern Poverty Law Center, Simon Wiesenthal Centre, and such" (https://en.metapedia.org/wiki/Metapedia:Mission_statement).

10. InfoGalactic was founded by Theodore Beale, better known by his pen name, Vox Day, and for his role in the Gamergate controversy, which was a formative episode for the Alt-Right. According to its website, "InfoGalactic is intended to have less alleged politically progressive, left-wing, or 'politically correct' bias than Wikipedia, and to allow articles or statements that would not be allowed on Wikipedia because of problems with Wikipedia's policies on reliable sources, or due to alleged biases held by Wikipedia editors" (https://infoga lactic.com/info/Main_Page).

11. RationalWiki has write-ups on the *New York Times* columnist Ross Douthat, former Fox News and NBC host Megyn Kelly, and long-time neoconservative writer William Kristol. Say what one will of these figures, none of them is illiberal in any sense. In its *Intelligence Report* for 2017, the SPLC devotes considerable space to Donald Trump. His election is relevant to the rise of illiberalism and will be discussed elsewhere in this book. But the mention of Trump in an SPLC document does not, in our judgment, represent confirmation that he is accurately described as illiberal without qualification.

12. Over a public affairs career of 40 years, Main has read, contributed to, and edited many political publications. He holds advanced degrees in public administration and politics, and is a professor of public affairs. Most importantly, Main is the author of a comprehensive book on the Alt-Right and has interviewed, read the works of, and visited the sites edited by many of the leaders of that movement. It was on the basis of these qualifications that Main undertook to distinguish Hard-Core Right Illiberal sites from Soft-Core Right Illiberal sites.

13. One of the earliest uses of the term "alternative right" was in the title of the published version of a speech Gottfried delivered to the H. L. Mencken

Club in 2008. The text of the speech appeared as "The Decline and Rise of the Alternative Right" in *Taki's Magazine*. Richard Spencer, a prominent figure of the early Alt-Right, was editor of the magazine and gave the printed version of Gottfried's speech its title. Gottfried claims he and Spencer "co-created" the name "alternative right." See Jacob Siegel, "The Alt-Right's Jewish Godfather," Tablet, November 29, 2016 (www.tabletmag.com/jewish-news-and-poli tics/218712/spencer-gottfried-alt-right).

14. Rod Dreher, "The End of Liberal Democracy?" American Conservative, September 26, 2016, www.theamericanconservative.com/dreher/the-end -of-liberal-democracy/.

15. Editors, "Decius Out of the Darkness: A Q&A with Michael Anton," American Greatness, February 13, 2017, amgreatness.com/2017/02/12/decius -darkness-qa-michael-anton/.

16. Workers World Party: Who We Are, https://workersworld-party.org/ about/.

17. It's Going Down, About, https://itsgoingdown.org/about.

18. There were four sites categorized by MBFC as Left but not mentioned by the Illiberal Left sources we consulted. These were socialistworker.org, an outlet of the International Socialist Organization ("We stand in the Marxist tradition, founded by Karl Marx and Frederick Engels, and continued by V. I. Lenin, Rosa Luxemburg and Leon Trotsky"); themilitant.com, which is associated with the Socialist Workers Party ("The SWP and the *Militant* are part of the continuity of revolutionary Marxism—from Marx and Engels, V. I. Lenin and Leon Trotsky, and the lessons of revolutionary struggle through to the Cuban Revolution"); c4ss.org, the platform of the Center for a Stateless Society ("A Left Market Anarchist Think Tank and Media Center"); and wsws. org, or the World Socialist Web Site ("published by the International Committee of the Fourth International, the leadership of the world socialist movement, the Fourth International founded by Leon Trotsky in 1938"). All these sites explicitly express a Left Illiberal ideology. But, strictly speaking, they do not represent an overlap between the Illiberal Left and the ordinary left, because they are mentioned by MBFC but not by my Illiberal Left sources. These sites have a combined audience of about 603,000 visits and 255,000 unique visitors. Adding these audiences to that of the four overlapping Ambiguous Left sites still does not raise the audience to even a tenth of one percent of the audience for the traditional Left sites. So the main point of this discussion remains: the overlap between the traditional Left and the Illiberal Left is vanishingly small, very much smaller than the overlap between the traditional Right and the Illiberal Right.

19. Michael Walzer, "Which Socialism?" Dissent, Summer 2010, www.dis sentmagazine.org/article/which-socialism.

20. Richard D. Wolff, "Socialists Need to Fight for Economic Change—Not Just Another Version of Capitalism," PopularResistance.org, August 18, 2018,

https://popularresistance.org/socialists-need-to-fight-for-economic-change
-not-just-another-version-of-capitalism/.

21. Richard D. Wolff, "Capitalism, Democracy, and Elections," MRonline, June 21, 2013, https://mronline.org/2013/06/21/wolff210613-html/. Emphasis in original.

22. Ben Gliniecki, "What Will Socialism Look Like?" In Defense of Marxism, April 14, 2015, www.marxist.com/what-will-socialism-look-like.htm.

23. RationalWiki, "Fourteen Words," rationalwiki.org/wiki/Fourteen_Words; Anti-Defamation League, "14," www.adl.org/education/references/hate-symbols/14.

24. Anti-Defamation League, "88," www.adl.org/education/references/hate-symbols/88.

25. National Socialist Movement, "25 Point Plan," www.nsm88.org/25points/25points.html.

26. Ibid.

27. Barbara Perry, "'Button-Down Terror': The Metamorphosis of the Hate Movement," *Sociological Focus* 3, no. 2 (May 2000), p. 121; Carol M. Swain, *The New White Nationalism in America: Its Challenge to Integration* (Cambridge University Press, 2002), pp. 6, 31.

28. Mario Calabresi, "We Will Stop Barack Obama We Are the New Ku Klux Klan," La Repubblica, October 29, 2008, www.repubblica.it/2008/10/sezioni/esteri/verso-elezioni-usa-5/nuovo-kkk/nuovo-kkk.html?refresh_ce.

29. "Intro Material for People New to Stormfront," posted February 2006, www.stormfront.org/forum/t538924/. Emphasis in original.

30. DJ Noble Protagonist, "National Socialism—The Fundamentals (Part 1)," Renegade Tribune, www.renegadetribune.com/national-socialism-the-fundamentals-part-1/. Emphasis in original.

31. See chapter 2, "How Big Is the Alt-Right?" in Thomas J. Main, *The Rise of the Alt-Right* (Washington, D.C.: Brookings Institution Press, 2018).

32. Ibid., p. 24.

33. Ibid., chapter 2.

34. See "Alt-Right," RationalWiki, rationalwiki.org/wiki/Alt-right; "List of alt-right political cartoonists," RationalWiki, rationalwiki.org/wiki/List_of_alt-right_political_cartoonists.

35. "Theodore Beale," RationalWiki, rationalwiki.org/wiki/Theodore_Beale.

36. Vox Day, "Fantaisie, utopie, égalité," Vox Popoli, April 9, 2018, http://voxday.blogspot.com/2018/04/fantaisie-utopie-egalite.html. Emphasis in original.

37. Ibid. Emphasis in original.

38. Main discusses the Daily Stormer in *The Rise of the Alt-Right*, pp. 5–6, 11, 14, 23, 27–29, 98, and 162.

39. Ashley Feinberg, "This Is The Daily Stormer's Playbook," *HuffPost*, December 13, 2017, www.huffpost.com/entry/daily-stormer-nazi-style-guide_n_5a2ece19e4b0ce3b344492f2.

40. Daily Stormer, Style Guide, https://assets.documentcloud.org/docu ments/4325810/Writers.pdf.

41. Andrew Anglin, "Emperor Trump Defends the Rights of the People of Crimea!" Daily Stormer, August 1, 2016, https://web.archive.org/web/2017 0721120541/http://www.dailystormer.com/emperor-trump-defends-the-rights -of-the-people-of-crimea/.

42. Andrew Anglin, "Glorious Leader Calls for Complete Ban on All Moslems," Daily Stormer, December 7, 2015, https://dailystormer.su/glorious -leader-calls-for-complete-ban-on-all-moslems/.

43. Max Roscoe, "6 Ways Liberal Democracy Destroys the Goodness of Humanity," Return of Kings, April 8, 2016, www.returnofkings.com/84753/6 -ways-liberal-democracy-destroys-the-goodness-of-humanity.

44. Roosh Valizadeh, "How to Save Western Civilization," rooshv.com, March, 6, 2017, www.rooshv.com/how-to-save-western-civilization. Emphasis in original.

45. Matt Forney, "Why Feminists Want Men to Rape Them," mattforney. com, February 22, 2016, mattforney.com/feminists-want-men-rape/. Emphasis in original.

46. InfoGalactic, "Chateau Heartiste," infogalactic.com/info/Chateau_Hear tiste.

47. Chateau Heartiste, "Witnessing the Death of a Religion," April 11, 2019, heartiste.org/2019/04/11/witnessing-the-death-of-a-religion/.

48. Urban Dictionary, meaning of "SWPL," www.urbandictionary.com/ define.php?term=SWPL.

49. Also see Chateau Heartiste, "A Very Special Kind of Double Standard," March 7, 2019, heartiste.org/2019/03/07/a-very-special-kind-of-double-standard/, which claims that, "[Special people] in America overwhelmingly support population replacement levels of immigration and refugee resettlement. . . . In Israel, they are hyper nationalist. In America, they are pluralist, with the goal of ensuring [special people] are just one of many other minority populations." Brackets in original. Other posts at this site that use the code terms "special people" or "specials" when denigrating Jews include "PA on Environmentalism," April 23, 2019, heartiste.org/2019/04/23/pa-on-environmentalism/; "Comment of the Week: Lessons from Jesus on How to Disrupt the Establishment," April 18, 2019, heartiste.org/2019/04/18/comment-of-the-week-lessons-from-jesus-on -how-to-disrupt-the-establishment/; and "All the Humor Is on the Dissident Right," April 12, 2019, heartiste.org/2019/04/12/all-the-humor-is-on-the-dissi dent-right/.

50. Chateau Heartiste, "The Earnest Futility of 'Proposition Nation' Magical Thinking," August 31, 2016, https://heartiste.org/2016/08/31/the-earnest -futility-of-proposition-nation-magical-thinking/. Emphasis in original.

51. Boyd Cathey, "The Egalitarian Myth and Secession," *Abbeville Institute* (blog), June 2, 2020, https://abbevilleinstitute.org/blog/the-egalitarian-myth -and-secession/.

52. Ibid.

53. The following sentences are based on the analysis found in Daniel A. Farber, *Lincoln's Constitution* (University of Chicago Press, 2003), pp. 78–79 and pp. 110–11.

54. Abraham Lincoln, "First Inaugural Address," March 4, 1861, found at Lincoln Home National Historical Site Illinois, www.nps.gov/liho/learn/historyculture/secanarchy.htm#:~:text=First%20Inaugural%20Address%20March%204,sovereign%20of%20a%20free%20people.

55. RationalWiki, "Neoreactionary movement," https://rationalwiki.org/wiki/Neoreactionary_movement.

56. Brett Stevens, "End of the Nation-State Signals the End of Liberal Democracy," Amerika, November 11, 2019, www.amerika.org/politics/end-of-the-nation-state-signals-the-end-of-liberal-democracy/.

57. *Federalist* No. 9, www.congress.gov/resources/display/content/The+Federalist+Papers#TheFederalistPapers-9.

58. Ann Barnhardt, "The Big Pulchra Vera Essay Part 1," Barnhardt, February 28, 2013, www.barnhardt.biz/2013/02/28/the-big-pulchra-vera-essay-part-1/.

59. Ibid. Emphasis in original.

60. James Delingpole, "Delingpole: Liberalism Is a Mental Disorder Which Feeds Islamic Terror," Breitbart News, July 26, 2018, www.breitbart.com/politics/2018/07/26/we-need-to-confront-the-liberals-whose-excuse-feed-islamic-terror/.

61. Dr. Sebastian Gorka, "Exclusive Excerpt—Sebastian Gorka's 'The War for America's Soul': The Plotters and Their Plan to Destroy America," Breitbart News, October 28, 2019, www.breitbart.com/politics/2019/10/28/exclusive-excerpt-sebastian-gorkas-the-war-for-americas-soul-the-plotters-and-their-plan-to-destroy-america/.

62. James Delingpole, "Delingpole: Tony Blair Is a Traitor. Where's Capital Punishment When You Need It?" Breitbart News, March 11, 2019, www.breitbart.com/europe/2019/03/11/tony-blair-has-betrayed-britain-to-the-european-union/. Emphasis in original.

63. Michelle Moons, "Palin on Paid Anti-Trump Protesters: 'Not Even President Yet and Our Guy's Already Creating Jobs,'" Breitbart News, July 1, 2016, www.breitbart.com/politics/2016/07/01/palin-paid-trump-protesters-not-even-president-yet-guys-already-creating-jobs/; Snopes, "Breitbart Duped by Fake News (Again)," August 3, 2016, www.snopes.com/news/2016/08/07/breitbart-duped-by-fake-news-again/.

64. Thomas D. Williams, "Planned Parenthood Teams Up with Satanists to Promote Abortion in Missouri," Breitbart News, September 13, 2017, www.breitbart.com/politics/2017/09/13/planned-parenthood-teams-up-with-satanists-to-promote-abortion-in-missouri/; Dan MacGuill, "Did Planned Parenthood 'Team Up' with Satanists to Promote Abortion Rights in Missouri?" Snopes, September 14, 2017, www.snopes.com/fact-check/planned-parenthood-satanists/; Joseph Bernstein, "Here's How Breitbart and Milo Smuggled White

Nationalism into the Mainstream," BuzzFeed News, October 5, 2017, www
.buzzfeednews.com/article/josephbernstein/heres-how-breitbart-and-milo
-smuggled-white-nationalism#.ejewGBW00.

65. Aaron Sharockman, "Breitbart Gets the Wrong Loretta Lynch in Whitewater Claim," Politifact, November 10, 2014, www.politifact.com/factchecks/
2014/nov/10/breitbart/breitbart-gets-wrong-loretta-lynch-whitewater-clai/.

66. M. Huitsing, "Breitbart," Media Bias/Fact Check, July 14, 2018, updated
February 4, 2020, mediabiasfactcheck.com/breitbart/.

67. Michelle Malkin, "Triggering the Google Social Credit System," Creators Syndicate, August 21, 2019, www.unz.com/mmalkin/triggering-the
-google-social-credit-system/?highlight=treason; Michelle Malkin, "DUH:
HUD Housing Should Put Americans First," Creators Syndicate, May 22, 2019,
www.unz.com/mmalkin/duh-hud-housing-should-put-americans-first/?high
light=DUH; and Michelle Malkin, "The Terror-Tipping NYTimes," Creators
Syndicate, June 28, 2006, www.unz.com/mmalkin/the-terrorist-tipping-times
/?highlight=treason.

68. For an example of Fuentes's anti-Semitism, see Nicholas J. Fuentes, "The Cookie Question," YouTube, January 11, 2019, www.youtube.com/
watch?v=WgN4ipYosPs. According to YouTube, "This video has been removed
for violating YouTube's policy on hate speech."

69. Pat Buchanan, "Democracy—A Flickering Star?" Patrick J. Buchanan
website, August 8, 2008, buchanan.org/blog/pjb-democracy-a-flickering-star-
1045.

70. Pat Buchanan, "Why the Authoritarian Right Is Rising," April 20, 2018,
buchanan.org/blog/why-the-authoritarian-right-is-rising-129153.

71. Pat Buchanan, "Is Liberal Democracy an Endangered Species?" January
5, 2017, buchanan.org/blog/liberal-democracy-endangered-species-126366.

72. Buchanan uses the spurious Jefferson quote in "After the Revolution,"
March 11, 2011, buchanan.org/blog/after-the-revolution-4619; and "How
Middle America Is to Be Dispossessed," March 12, 2019, buchanan.org/blog/
how-middle-america-is-to-be-dispossessed-136645. He uses the alleged Madison quote in "After the Revolution" and "Another God That Failed," January 8,
2010, buchanan.org/blog/another-god-that-failed-3435.

73. The Jefferson Monticello, "Democracy is nothing more than mob rule
. . . (Spurious Quotation)," Thomas Jefferson Encyclopedia, www.monticello.org
/site/research-and-collections/democracy-nothing-more-mob-rulespurious
-quotation.

74. Regarding the quote attributed to James Madison, in a personal communication of July 1, 2021, Hilarie M. Hicks, senior research historian of Madison's home Montpelier, stated: "As far as I can tell, the quote is spurious." In
a note of July 9, 2021, Jurretta Jordan Heckscher, reference specialist for early
American history at the Library of Congress, wrote to me that: "The most
complete searchable source of Madison's writings is the Founders Online proj-

ect at the National Archives. . . . I can tell you that an admittedly cursory survey of this invaluable resource fails to yield any statement resembling the one that you quote, which sounds suspiciously un-Madisonian in any case."

75. John Adams, "From John Adams to John Taylor, 17 December 1814," Founders Online, https://founders.archives.gov/?q=%20Author%3A%22Adams %2C%20John%22%20Democracy%20suicide&s=1111311111&r=1.

76. Ibid.

77. John Adams, "VII. An Essay on Man's Lust for Power, with the Author's Comment in 1807," Founders Online, https://founders.archives.gov/documents /Adams/06-01-02-0045-0008.

78. Founders Online, Adams Papers, IX. "Letters from a Distinguished American," No. 5, Paris, February 1, 1782, founders.archives.gov/?q=%E2%80%9CLet ters%20from%20a%20Distinguished%20American%2C%E2%80%9D%20 No.%205%20&s=1111311111&sa=&r=8&sr=.

79. Buchanan, "How Middle America Is to Be Dispossessed." Also see, Pat Buchanan, "Web Exclusive! Nation or Notion?" Patrick J. Buchanan website, October 4, 2006, buchanan.org/blog/web-exclusive-pjb-nation-or-notion -120.

80. James Madison, *Federalist* No. 10, *The Federalist Papers*, https://guides.loc .gov/federalist-papers/text-1-10#s-lg-box-wrapper-25493273. Emphasis added.

81. James Madison, *Federalist* No. 14, *The Federalist Papers*, https://guides.loc .gov/federalist-papers/text-11-20#s-lg-box-wrapper-25493285.

82. Quoted in *American Government: Institutions and Policies*, James Q. Wilson et al., enhanced 16th edition (Boston: Cengage, 2021), p. 5.

83. Pat Buchanan, "After the Revolution."

84. Media Bias/Fact Check defined "conspiracy-pseudoscience and questionable sources" as follows: "Sources in the Conspiracy-Pseudoscience category *may* publish unverifiable information that is *not always* supported by evidence. These sources *may* be untrustworthy for credible/verifiable information, therefore fact-checking and further investigation is recommended on a per article basis when obtaining information from these sources. A questionable source exhibits *one or more* of the following: extreme bias, consistent promotion of propaganda/conspiracies, poor or no sourcing to credible information, a complete lack of transparency and/or is fake news. Fake News is the *deliberate attempt* to publish hoaxes and/or disinformation for the purpose of profit or influence. . . . Sources listed in the Questionable Category *may* be very untrustworthy and should be fact-checked on a per article basis. Please note sources on this list *are not* considered *fake news* unless specifically written in the reasoning section for that source." Emphasis in original. "Questionable Sources," Media Bias/Fact Check, https://mediabiasfactcheck.com/fake-news/.

85. Chrysanthos Dellarocas, Zsolt Katona, and William Rand, "Media, Aggregators, and the Link Economy: Strategic Hyperlink Formation in Content Networks," *Management Science* 59, no. 10 (October 2013), p. 2361.

86. D. Van Zandt, "Drudge Report," Media Bias/Fact Check, September 25, 2020, https://mediabiasfactcheck.com/drudge-report/.

87. D. Van Zandt, "Drudge Report," Media Bias/Fact Check, October 7, 2019.

88. According to the agency, Ivandjiiski neither admitted nor denied wrongdoing.

89. Tracy Alloway and Luke Kawa, "Unmasking the Men Behind Zero Hedge Wall Street's Renegade Blog," Bloomberg.com, April 29, 2016, www .bloomberg.com/news/articles/2016-04-29/unmasking-the-men-behind-zero -hedge-wall-street-s-renegade-blog. The Bloomberg.com article was based on an interview with Colin Lokey after he left the blog. Zero Hedge responded to the Bloomberg article with an article by Tyler Durden, "The Full Story Behind Bloomberg's Attempt To 'Unmask' Zero Hedge," www.zerohedge.com/news /2016-04-29/full-story-behind-bloombergs-attempt-unmask-zero-hedge. According to the article, "In short: **in its desire to obtain ad-revenue generating clicks, Bloomberg provided a platform to a deranged person who held a major grudge**." Emphasis in original.

90. See Media Bias/Fact Check, "Zero Hedge," mediabiasfactcheck.com/ zero-hedge/.

91. Tyler Durden (Authored by Charles Hugh-Smith via OfTwoMinds blog), "Our Hopelessly Dysfunctional Democracy," Zero Hedge, March 22, 2017, www.zerohedge.com/news/2017-03-22/our-hopelessly-dysfunctional-demo cracy.

92. Ibid. Emphasis in original.

93. Tyler Durden (Submitted by James Miller of the Ludwig von Mises Institute of Canada), "Guest Post: What Democracy?" August 5, 2012, www .zerohedge.com/news/guest-post-what-democracy.

94. Gary Galles, "Ben Franklin on Liberty," Mises Institute, February 3, 2003, mises.org/library/ben-franklin-liberty.

95. "Megyn Kelly Reports on Alex Jones and 'Infowars,' " *Sunday Night with Megan Kelly*, June 18, 2017, www.nbcnews.com/megyn-kelly/video/megyn-kelly -reports-on-alex-jones-and-infowars-970743875859.

96. Eli Rosenberg, "Alex Jones Apologizes for Promoting 'Pizzagate' Hoax," *New York Times*, March 25, 2017, www.nytimes.com/2017/03/25/business/alex -jones-pizzagate-apology-comet-ping-pong.html. Guardian Staff, "Alex Jones Retracts False Stories about Chobani in Defamation Settlement," *The Guardian*, May 17, 2017, www.theguardian.com/us-news/2017/may/17/alex-jones-re tracts-false-stories-chobani-defamation-suit.

97. D. Van Zandt, "Infowars-Alex Jones," Media Bias/Fact Check, August 11, 2019, mediabiasfactcheck.com/infowars-alex-jones/.

98. RationalWiki, "Alex Jones," rationalwiki.org/wiki/Alex Jones#Infowars.

99. Internet Archive, "Globalist Elite—Guidance by Machine Elves Contacted Through DMT," https://archive.org/details/GlobalistElite-GuidanceBy MachineElvesContactedThorughDmt.

100. Andrew Napolitano, "What If Democracy Is Bunk?" Infowars, February 24, 2012, www.infowars.com/what-if-democracy-is-bunk/; Paul Craig Roberts, "Is Western Democracy Real or a Facade?" Infowars.com, February 14, 2012, www.infowars.com/is-western-democracy-real-or-a-facade/; Gary Galles, Mises.org, "Why Democracy Doesn't Give Us What We Want," Infowars, January 30, 2020, www.infowars.com/why-democracy-doesnt-give-us -what-we-want/.

101. Discover the Networks, www.discoverthenetworks.org/about. The site shows that there is or has been some overlap between some Illiberal Left movements and mainstream liberalism. Thus it notes that "the radical organizers of the mass anti-war demonstrations pretended that their only interest was to 'Bring the Troops Home,' when in fact their agendas embraced a radical menu that was anti-capitalist and welcomed a Communist victory." This is true of a few tiny radical organizations, but of course the vast majority of people who opposed the Vietnam War were not communists and objected to the war on grounds consistent with liberal democracy. But overlaps of this sort do not establish any real tie between old-left communism and present-day liberalism.

102. David Horowitz Freedom Center, www.davidHorowitzfreedomcenter .org/.

103. David Horowitz, *The Art of Political War: How Republicans Can Fight to Win* (Los Angeles: The Committee for a Non-Liberal Majority, 1999) p. 15–16.

104. Sol Stern, "The Captive Mind of Trump True Believer David Horowitz," Daily Beast, February 25, 2017, updated July 13, 2017, www.thedailybeast .com/the-captive-mind-of-trump-true-believer-david-Horowitz?ref=scroll.

105. Carl von Clausewitz, *On War* (New York: Pelican Books, 1968), pp. 119–120. Clausewitz is often quoted as having written "war is politics conducted by other means." See "Politics Is War and Conservatives Need to Learn How to Fight," Maverick Philosopher, December 4, 2012, maverickphilosopher.type pad.com/maverick_philosopher/2012/12/politics-is-war-and-conservatives -need-to-learn-how-to-fight.html. Strictly speaking, the quote is inaccurate but not really misleading, for after defining war as a "mere continuation of policy by other means," Clausewitz goes on to state that all forms of war "may all be regarded as political acts." He regards policy as "the intelligence of the personified State," and war is one of "the constellations in the political sky whose movements it has to compute." This makes all wars a subdivision of politics.

106. Don Feder, "The Left Owns The Riots," FrontPageMag, June 4, 2020, https://cms.frontpagemag.com/fpm/2020/06/democrats-have-spent-decades -playing-fire-now-don-feder.

107. Daniel Greenfield, "Obama's Genocidal Treason," FrontPageMag, September 24, 2015, https://archives.frontpagemag.com/fpm/obamas-genocidal -treason-daniel-greenfield/.

108. Daniel Greenfield, "The Civil War Is Here," FrontPageMag, March 27, 2017, https://archives.frontpagemag.com/fpm/civil-war-here-daniel-green field/.

109. United States Constitution, Article 3, Section 3, www.archives.gov/founding-docs/constitution-transcript#toc-section-3--2.

110. David Horowitz, "Acts of Treason," FrontPageMag, May 19, 2020, https://cms.frontpagemag.com/fpm/2020/05/acts-treason-david-Horowitz.

111. James Madison, *Federalist* No. 43, https://guides.loc.gov/federalist-papers/text-41-50#s-lg-box-wrapper-25493407.

112. Media Bias/Fact Check, "American Thinker," April 12, 2021, https://mediabiasfactcheck.com/american-thinker/.

113. Pamela Geller, "Report: Obama said 'I Am a Muslim,'" American Thinker, June 16, 2010, www.americanthinker.com/articles/2010/06/report_obama_said_i_am_a_musli.html. The alleged report is based on thirdhand information and has not been corroborated. See David P. Goldman, "Barack Obama Is Not a Muslim," *First Things* (blog), November 5, 2010, www.firstthings.com/blogs/firstthoughts/2010/11/barack-obama-is-not-a-muslim; Lee Carpenter, "Prominent Anti-Islam Conspiracy Theorist to Speak at Jersey Event," Medium, April 24, 2018, https://medium.com/nine-by-five-media/prominent-anti-islam-conspiracy-theorist-to-speak-at-jersey-event-92d8a68aee44.

114. F. W. Burleigh, "Obama and the Muslim Gang Sign," American Thinker, February 18, 2015, www.americanthinker.com/articles/2015/02/obama_and_the_muslim_gang_sign.html#ixzz6I2CXf7le. The fact-checking site Snopes rated the claim "false." See David Mikkelson, "Obama Flashes Muslim 'Shahada' Gang Sign: Rumor: President Obama Secretly Signaled African Leaders Using a Muslim Hand Signal Known as the Shahada," Snopes, August 20, 2015, www.snopes.com/fact-check/shahada-been-there/.

115. Daniel John, "Was Seth Rich Killed over the Steele Dossier?" American Thinker, January 12, 2018, www.americanthinker.com/articles/2018/01/was_seth_rich_killed_over_the_steele_dossier.html.

116. Mathew Ingram, "Getting to the Bottom of the Seth Rich Conspiracy Theory," *Columbia Journalism Review*, July 10, 2019, www.cjr.org/the_media_today/seth-rich-conspiracy-theory.php. Bethania Palma, "Did DNC Staffer Seth Rich Send 'Thousands of E-Mails' to WikiLeaks Before He Was Murdered? A man claiming to be a private investigator is making uncorroborated claims about the deceased staffer," Snopes, May 16, 2017, www.snopes.com/fact-check/seth-rich-dnc-wikileaks-murder. Sarah Mervosh, "Seth Rich Was Not Source of Leaked D.N.C. Emails, Mueller Report Confirms," *New York Times*, April 20, 2019, www.nytimes.com/2019/04/20/us/mueller-report-seth-rich-assange.html.

117. See Bethania Palma, "The Seth Rich Conspiracy Theory," Snopes, May 25, 2017, www.snopes.com/news/2017/05/25/seth-rich-conspiracy-theory/; and Sarah Mervosh, "Seth Rich Was Not Source of Leaked D.N.C. Emails, Mueller Report Confirms."

118. Allison Nichols, "The Hoax of 'Climate Change,'" American Thinker,

December 11, 2018, www.americanthinker.com/articles/2018/12/the_hoax_of_
climate_change.html.

119. Nikki Forrester, editor; "Sea Levels Rose Faster in the Past Century
than in Previous Time Periods," Climate Feedback, March 12, 2020, https:/
/climatefeedback.org/claimreview/sea-levels-rose-faster-in-the-past-century
-than-in-previous-time-periods/.

120. Todd Keister, "The Dangers of Democracy," American Thinker, June
21, 2013, americanthinker.com/articles/2013/06/the_dangers_of_democracy.
html. Other articles that disparage democracy include Bruce Walker, "Democracy Is Not Freedom," American Thinker, June 19, 2019, www.americanthinker
.com/blog/2019/06/democracy_is_not_freedom.html; and Chris Talgo and
Emma Kaden, "Is Democracy Doomed?" American Thinker, October 29, 2018,
www.americanthinker.com/articles/2018/10/is_democracy_doomed.html.

121. Philip Ahlrich, "Towards a Conservative Democracy," American
Thinker, June 26, 2017, https://tmp.americanthinker.com/articles/2017/06/to
wards_a_conservative_democracy.html. Another article that confuses liberal
democracy with progressive democracy is Peter Skurkiss, "What Is a Liberal
Democracy?" American Thinker, June 16, 2018, www.americanthinker.com/
articles/2018/06/what_is_a_liberal_democracy.html.

122. Ahlrich, "Towards a Conservative Democracy."

123. For a video of Gugino being shoved to the ground by police, see Mirna
Alsharif and Alec Snyder, "75-year-old protester pushed by Buffalo police files
lawsuit against city, mayor and officers," CNN, February 22, 2021, www.cnn
.com/2021/02/22/us/buffalo-protester-lawsuit/index.html.

124. "Buffalo Officials Duped By Professional Antifa Provocateur—Arrest
and Charge Two Police Officers—Righteous Police Team Stand Together
and Walk Out . . . ," The Last Refuge, June 6, 2020, theconservativetreehouse
.com/2020/06/06/buffalo-officials-duped-by-professional-antifa-provocateur
-arrest-and-charge-two-police-officers-righteous-police-team-stand-together
-and-walk-out/.

125. Media Bias/Fact Check, "The Last Refuge (Conservative Treehouse),"
mediabiasfactcheck.com/the-last-refuge/.

126. "Hoax and Chains—President Obama Again Calls the United States
a 'Constitutional Democracy,' " The Last Refuge, May 6, 2014, https://thecon
servativetreehouse.com/2014/05/06/hoax-and-chains-president-obama-again
-calls-the-united-states-a-constitutional-democracy/.

127. Glenn Kessler, "Trump Tweets Outrageous Conspiracy Theory about
Injured Buffalo Man," *Washington Post*, June 9, 2020, www.washingtonpost
.com/politics/2020/06/09/trump-tweets-outrageous-conspiracy-theory-about
-injured-buffalo-man/. Also see Kevin Poulsen, "Trump's New Favorite Chan-
nel Employs Kremlin-Paid Journalist," Daily Beast, July 22, 2019, www.the
dailybeast.com/oan-trumps-new-favorite-channel-employs-kremlin-paid
-journalist?ref=scroll.

128. See Jack Goodman, "Martin Gugino: Donald Trump's Police Scanner Tweet Fact-Checked," BBC News, June 9, 2020, www.bbc.com/news/52984295; and Kessler, "Trump Tweets Outrageous Conspiracy Theory About Injured Buffalo Man."

129. Hannah Gais and Michael Edison Hayden, "Extremists Are Cashing in on a Youth-Targeted Gaming Website," Southern Poverty Law Center, November 17, 2020, www.splcenter.org/hatewatch/2020/11/17/extremists-are -cashing-youth-targeted-gaming-website.

130. DLive, Announcements, "Building a Safe and Welcoming Community," January 9, 2021, https://community.dlive.tv/2021/01/09/building-a-safe -and-welcoming-community/.

131. For an account of Michelle Malkin's support of Nick Fuentes, see Amanda Carpenter, "Michelle Malkin: Mother of Groypers," The Bulwark, March 9, 2020, https://thebulwark.com/michelle-malkin-mother-of-groypers/.

132. Hannah Gais, "Meet the White Nationalist Organizer Who Spewed Hate Against Lawmakers," Southern Poverty Law Center, January 19, 2021. For a video clip of Fuentes making the statement attributed to him, see https:// twitter.com/MeganSquire0/status/1346478478523125767.

133. Left Coast Right Watch (@LCRWNews), Twitter post, January 11, 2021, https://twitter.com/LCRWnews/status/1348549176343216132?s=20.

134. Mallory Simon and Sara Sidner, "Decoding the Extremist Symbols and Groups at the Capitol Hill Insurrection," CNN, January 11, 2021, www .cnn.com/2021/01/09/us/capitol-hill-insurrection-extremist-flags-soh/index .html. Washington Post Staff, "Identifying far-right symbols that appeared at the U.S. Capitol riot," *Washington Post*, January 15, 2021, www.washingtonpost .com/nation/interactive/2021/far-right-symbols-capitol-riot/. ProPublica has collected videos of the Capitol riot uploaded to the social media service Parler. Among the videos that show America First flags displayed by participants are: "1:35 pm-Near Capitol" at 0:01–0:30; "1:42 pm-Near Capitol" at 0:10–0:20; "1:49 pm-Near Capitol" at 0:10–1:27; "2:10 pm-Near Capitol" at 0:40–1:25. See Lena V. Groeger, Jeff Kao, Al Shaw, Moiz Syed, and Maya Eliahou, "What Parler Saw During the Attack on the Capitol," ProPublica, January 17, 2021, https://projects.propublica.org/parler-capitol-videos/.

135. Doc Lindenbrook, "Nick's—The Patriot's Attitude," January 7, 2021, YouTube, www.youtube.com/watch?v=-hZZTkD98Qc.

136. Washington Post Staff, "Identifying far-right symbols that appeared at the U.S. Capitol riot."

137. Ibid.

138. Ibid.

139. For articles on QAnon, the Three Precenters, and the Oath Keepers see: "QAnon," RationalWiki, https://rationalwiki.org/wiki/QAnon. Hate Watch Staff, "What You Need to Know about QAnon," Southern Poverty Law Center, October 27, 2020, www.splcenter.org/hatewatch/2020/10/27/what-you

-need-know-about-qanon. "QAnon," Anti-Defamation League, www.adl.org /qanon. "Oath Keepers," Anti-Defamation League, www.adl.org/resources/ backgrounders/oath-keepers. "Oath Keepers," Southern Poverty Law Center," www.splcenter.org/fighting-hate/extremist-files/group/oath-keepers. Rachel Tabachnick, "Profile on the Right: Oath Keepers," Political Research Associates, April 23, 2015, www.politicalresearch.org/2015/04/23/profile-on-the -right-oathkeepers. Spencer Sunshine, Profile on the Right: Three Percenters, Political Research Associates, January 5, 2016, www.politicalresearch.org /2016/01/05/profiles-on-the-right-three-percenters. "Three Percenters," Anti-Defamation League, www.adl.org/resources/backgrounders/three-percenters . For articles on the role these groups played at the Capitol on January 6, 2021, see, Devlin Barrett and Spencer S. Hsu, "FBI probes possible connections between extremist groups at heart of Capitol violence," *Washington Post*, January 18, 2021, www.washingtonpost.com/national-security/oath-keeper -three-percenter-arrests/2021/01/17/27e726f2-5847-11eb-a08b-f1381ef3d207 _story.html. Adam Goldman, Katie Benner, and Alan Feuer, "Investigators Eye Right-Wing Militias at Capitol Riot," *New York Times*, published January 18, 2021, updated January 24, 2021, www.nytimes.com/2021/01/18/us/politics/ capitol-riot-militias.html

140. An accurate description of the video of the Capitol riot that Democrats presented at Trump's second impeachment trial notes that "The video then cuts back to the rioters, clashing violently with police on their way toward the building . . . They swarmed through windows and the halls, many of them chanting 'treason.'" See, Claire Lampen, "This Chilling Video of the Capitol Riot Speaks for Itself," The Cut, February 9, 2021, www.thecut.com/2021/ 02/watch-democrats-capitol-riot-montage-from-trump-impeachment.html; Rioters can be heard chanting "traitor" on the prosecution's video at 3:31, 8:04–8:13, 8:14–8:20, and 10:41–10:44. See Glenn Thrush, "Graphic Video at Impeachment Trial Shows Riot and Trump's Comments," *New York Times*, February 10, 2021, www.nytimes.com/2021/02/10/us/politics/impeachment -graphic-video.html.

141. "Decoding the extremist symbols and groups at the Capitol Hill insurrection," CNN.

142. Aleszu Bajak, Jessica Guynn, and Mitchell Thorson, "When Trump started his speech before the Capitol riot, talk on Parler turned to civil war," *USA Today*, February 1, 2021, www.usatoday.com/in-depth/news/2021/02/01/civil -war-during-trumps-pre-riot-speech-parler-talk-grew-darker/4297165001/.

143. UVA Center for Politics, *Sabato's Crystal Ball*, "New Poll: Some Americans Express Troubling Racial Attitudes Even as Majority Oppose White Supremacists," September 14, 2017 (centerforpolitics.org/crystalball/articles/new -poll-some-americans-express-troubling-racial-attitudes-even-as-majority -oppose-white-supremacists/). Also see, Reuters/Ipsos/UVA Center for Politics Race Poll, September 11, 2017 (www.centerforpolitics.org/crystalball/

wp-content/uploads/2017/09/2017-Reuters-UVA-Ipsos-Race-Poll-9-11-2017
.pdf).

144. *A Portrait of Jewish Americans*, chapter 1, "Population Estimates, Pew
Research Center," October 1, 2013, p. 1 (www.pewforum.org/2013/10/01/chap
ter-1-population-estimates/). This estimate "refers only to people whose religion is Jewish (Jews by religion). . . . If one includes secular or cultural Jews . . .
then the estimate grows to 2.2 percent of American adults, or about 5.3 million." *Fast Facts Study Guide* (State Populations): The US50 (www.theus50.com
/fastfacts/population.php). "New York Cities by Population," New York Demographics by Cubit (www.newyork-demographics.com/cities_by_population).

Chapter 4

1. *Federalist* No. 10, www.congress.gov/resources/display/content/The+Fed
eralist+Papers#TheFederalistPapers-10.

2. *Federalist* No. 51, www.congress.gov/resources/display/content/The+Fed
eralist+Papers#TheFederalistPapers-51.

3. Ibid.

4. *Federalist* No. 10.

5. Ibid.

6. William Voegeli, "Republics, Extended and Multicultural," *Claremont
Review of Books* XX, no. 2 (Spring 2020), p. 26.

7. Quoted in Mayra Rivera and Stephen D. Moore, "A Tentative Topog-
raphy of Postcolonial Theology," chapter 1 in *Planetary Loves: Spivak, Postcolo-
niality, and Theology*, Moore and Rivera (eds.) (New York: Fordham University
Press), p. 11.

8. *Oxford Learners Dictionaries*, definition of "identity politics," www.oxford
learnersdictionaries.com/us/definition/english/identity-politics.

9. Masha Gessen, "The Queer Opposition to Pete Buttigieg, Explained," *The
New Yorker*, www.newyorker.com/news/our-columnists/the-queer-opposition
-to-pete-buttigieg-explained.

10. Hunter Wallace [Brad Griffin], "What Is the Alt-Right?," Occidental
Dissent, August 25, 2016, www.occidentaldissent.com/2016/08/25/what-is-the
-alt-right/. Emphasis in original.

11. Guillaume Faye, *Why We Fight: Manifesto of the European Resistance*
(London: Arktos Media, 2011), p. 36.

12. Ibid., p. 237. Emphasis in original.

13. Ibid., p. 113.

14. Ibid., p. 128.

15. Ibid., pp. 185–86. Emphasis in original.

16. Ibid., p. 359.

17. Ibid., p. 139. Emphasis in original.

18. Ibid., pp. 126–27. Emphasis in original.

19. Ibid., pp. 43–45. Emphasis in original.

20. Ibid., p. 365.

21. Ibid.

22. *The Landmark Thucydides: A Comprehensive Guide to the Peloponnesian War*, edited by Robert B. Strassler (New York: Simon & Schuster, 1996), pp. 352.

23. "Ethnopluralism," Revolution Europea, September 8, 2016, https://revolutioneuropa.com/2016/09/08/ethnopluralism/.

24. Benoist, *Beyond Human Rights: Defending Freedoms* (London: Arktos Media, 2011), pp. 22, 36. Emphasis in original.

25. Ibid., pp. 22–23.

26. Ibid., pp. 81–82. Emphasis added.

27. Ibid., pp. 89–90.

28. Ibid., p. 56.

29. Don Howard, "Two Left Turns Make a Right: On the Curious Political Career of North American Philosophy of Science at Midcentury," in *Logical Empiricism in North America*, edited by Gary L. Hardcastle and others (University of Minnesota Press, 2003), p. 25.

30. Bertrand Russell, *The History of Western Philosophy* (New York: Simon & Schuster, 1945), pp. 827–28.

31. Bertrand Russell, *The Scientific Outlook* (New York: W. W. Norton, 1931), p. 260.

32. Russell believed that "Huxley had stolen almost every idea for his novel from him." Alan Ryan, *Bertrand Russell: A Political Life* (New York: Hill and Wang, 1988), p. 136. The similarities between *The Scientific Outlook* and *Brave New World* are discussed in detail in Peter Firchow, "Science and Conscience in Huxley's 'Brave New World,'" *Contemporary Literature* 16, no. 3 (Summer 1975), pp. 301–16.

33. Russell, *The Scientific Outlook*, p. 242.

34. Ibid., pp. 265, 260.

35. Ibid., p. 265.

36. Thomas S. Kuhn, *The Structure of Scientific Revolutions*, 4th ed. (University of Chicago Press, 1962), pp. 166–67.

37. Ibid., p. 170.

38. Ibid., p. 169.

39. Ibid., p. 167.

40. Ibid., pp. 163–64.

41. Ibid., p. 166.

42. Sandra Harding, "After the Neutrality Ideal: Science, Politics, and 'Strong Objectivity,'" *Social Research* 59, no. 3 (Fall 1992, Science and Politics), p. 576.

43. Sandra Harding, "'Strong Objectivity': A Response to the New Objectivity Question," *Synthese* 104, no. 3 (September 1995, Feminism and Science), p. 331.

44. Harding, "After the Neutrality Ideal," pp. 579–80.

45. Ibid., pp. 580–81. Emphasis in original.

46. Ibid., pp. 582–83.

47. Ibid., p. 581.

48. C. S. Peirce, "The Essentials of Pragmatism," in *Philosophical Writings of Peirce*, edited by Justus Buchler (New York: Dover Publications, 1955), p. 256.

49. Sandra Harding, "Standpoint Theories: Productively Controversial," *Hypatia* 24, no. 4 (Fall 2009), p. 195.

50. Ibid., pp. 192–200.

51. Sandra Harding, "Feminist Epistemology In and After the Enlightenment," chapter 7 in *Whose Science? Whose Knowledge? Thinking from Women's Lives* (Cornell University Press, 1991), p. 174.

52. Nancy C. M. Hartsock, "Comment on Hekman's 'Truth and Method: Feminist Standpoint Theory Revisited': Truth or Justice?" *Signs* 22, no. 2 (Winter 1997), pp. 368.

53. Harding, "'Strong Objectivity,'" p. 341. Emphasis in original.

54. Very briefly, Lukacs argues that in a capitalist society, everything is turned into a commodity, including the workers. Therefore when the workers realize they are commodities, they understand the totality of society. But this argument overlooks the fact that even in a completely capitalist society, there are still some things that are not commodities: public goods. So the knowledge of the proletariat is not knowledge of the totality, because it excludes knowledge of public goods. But since public goods are the domain of the state in capitalist societies, the standpoint of the proletariat leaves out understanding of the state in principle and therefore never considers the reformist position that political action through the state can address the distress of the workers.

55. Harding, "After the Neutrality Ideal," pp. 583–84.

56. Alison Wylie, "Feminist Philosophy of Science: Standpoint Matters," *Proceedings and Addresses of the American Philosophical Association* 86, no. 2 (November 2012), pp. 47–76.

57. Daniel Hicks, "Is Longino's Conception of Objectivity Feminist?" *Hypatia* 26, no. 2 (Spring 2011), p. 337.

58. Ibid., p. 339.

59. Harding, "What Is Feminist Epistemology?" chapter 5 in *Whose Science? Whose Knowledge?* (Cornell University Press, 1991), p. 116.

60. Sandra Harding, "Comment on Walby's 'Against Epistemological Chasms: The Science Question in Feminism Revisited': Can Democratic Values and Interests Ever Play a Rationally Justifiable Role in the Evaluation of Scientific Work?" *Signs* 26, no. 2 (Winter 2001), p. 518.

61. Harding, "After the Neutrality Ideal ," p. 571.

62. André Breton, *Manifesto of Surrealism*, 1924, www.tcf.ua.edu/Classes/Jbutler/T340/SurManifesto/ManifestoOfSurrealism.htm.

63. Robin Adèle Greeley, "Dali's Fascism; Lacan's Paranoia," *Art History* 24, no. 4 (September 2001), p. 466.

64. Ibid.

65. Mark Dyal, "'We Are the Real Subalterns,'" Counter-Currents Publishing, March 7, 2013, www.counter-currents.com/2013/03/we-are-the-real-subalterns/print/. The word "subaltern" in the first sentence of this quote links to the Wikipedia entry "Subaltern (postcolonialism)," which explains that, "The identity of the subaltern native is conceptually derived from the cultural-hegemony work of Antonio Gramsci, an Italian Marxist intellectual" (https://en.wikipedia.org/wiki/Subaltern_(postcolonialism). So, apparently the editors of Counter-Currents Publishing are aware of the Gramscian nature of this contribution.

66. Roman Bernard, "Got Metapolitics?" Radix Journal, December 14, 2015, https://radixjournal.com/2015/12/got-metapolitics/.

67. "A Gentle Introduction to White Nationalism, Part II," Radix Journal, May 14, 2015, https://radixjournal.com/2015/05/2015-5-13-a-gentle-introduction-to-white-nationalism-part-ii/.

68. James Lawrence, "Contra Cosmopolitanism," Affirmative Right, May 7, 2017, https://affirmativeright.blogspot.com/2017/05/contra-cosmopolitanism.html.

69. Hateful Heretic, "Cuckservatism: The Alt-Right," The Right Stuff, July 29, 2015, https://archive.is/zUoYg#selection-61.0-64.0.

70. James Lawrence, "Marginstreaming," Affirmative Right, June 2, 2016, https://affirmativeright.blogspot.com/2016/06/marginstreaming.html. Emphasis in original.

71. Guillaume Faye, *Archeofuturism: European Visions of the Post Catastrophic Age* (London: Arktos Media, 2010), pp. 15–16. Emphasis in original.

72. Gregory Hood, *Waking Up from the American Dream* (San Francisco: Counter-Currents Publishing, 2016), pp. 6–7. Emphasis in original.

73. Herbert Marcuse, *An Essay on Liberation* (Boston: Beacon Press, 1969), p. 84.

74. Seyla Benhabib, *Situating the Self: Gender, Community, and Postmodernism in Contemporary Ethics* (New York: Routledge, 1992), p. 14.

75. Ibid., p. 16.

76. Georg Lukacs, *Lenin: A Study on the Unity of His Thought*, translated by Nicholas Jacobs (MIT Press, 1971), pp. 25–26. Emphasis in original.

77. Ibid. Emphasis in original.

78. George Hawley, *Making Sense of the Alt-Right* (Columbia University Press, 2017), p. 48.

79. Andrew Anglin, "A Normie's Guide to the Alt-Right," Daily Stormer, August 31, 2016, www.dailystormer.com/a-normies-guide-to-the-alt-right/.

80. Vox Day, *SJWs Always Lie: Taking Down the Thought Police* (Kouvola, Finland: Castalia House), pp. 279–80.

81. Ibid., pp. 186–89. Emphasis in original.

82. John Dewey, *Reconstruction in Philosophy* (New York: Henry Holt and Company, 1920), p. 98.

83. One wonders if Day has given any serious thought to his rhetorical principle of "total indifference to the consequences," for earlier he said that rhetoric is effective when its consequences are tears, shock, and gasps from the audience. Perhaps Day means one should be indifferent to the consequences of his or her rhetoric for oneself. In that case, not only loss of a job, but also self-destruction, infantilism, or madness should be a matter of indifference. So once again, the total indifference principle involves a descent into meaninglessness.

84. Day, *SJWs Always Lie*, pp. 181–82. Emphasis in original.

85. Ann Coulter, *How to Talk to a Liberal (If You Must)* (New York: Crown Forum, 2004), p. 10.

86. David Horowitz, *The Art of Political War: How Republicans Can Fight to Win* (Los Angeles: The Committee for a Non-Liberal Majority, 1999), p. 15; David Horowitz, *Take No Prisoners: The Battle Plan for Defeating the Left* (Washington, DC: Regnery Publishing, 2014), p. 123. Horowitz's other four principles of political warfare are, "3) In political war the aggressor usually prevails, 4) Position is defined by fear and hope, 5) The weapons of political war are symbols that evoke these emotions, 6) Victory lies on the side of the people."

87. Horowitz discusses the position of the underdog as "the key to American politics" in *Take No Prisoners*, pp. 12–14, 121, 129, 134–35, 138, and 157–61.

88. Fyodor Dostoyevsky, *The Possessed (or, the Devils)*, translated by Constance Garnett (London: Global Grey Ebooks, 2014), pp. 254–256.

89. Ibid., p. 256.

90. Ibid., p. 257. Ellipses in original.

91. Ibid., p. 256.

92. Deborah J. Schildkraut, chapter 3, "Does Becoming American Create a Better American? How Identity Attachments and Perceptions of Discrimination Affect Trust and Obligation," in *Fear, Anxiety, and National Identity*, edited by Nancy Foner and Patrick Simon (New York: Russell Sage Foundation, 2015), pp. 83–114, ProQuest Ebook Central edition; Deborah J. Schildkraut, "Boundaries of American Identity: Evolving Understandings of 'Us,'" *Annual Review of Political Science*, 2014 (17:441–60); Deborah J. Schildkraut, "Defining American Identity in the Twenty-First Century: How Much 'There' Is There?" *Journal of Politics* 69, no. 3 (August 2007), pp. 597–615; Deborah J. Schildkraut, chapter 3, "Theories of American Identity," from *Press "ONE" for English: Language Policy, Public Opinion, and American Identity* (Princeton University Press, 2005), pp. 38–66.

93. Schildkraut, "Boundaries of American Identity," p. 443.

94. Ibid., p. 441.

95. Schildkraut, "Defining American Identity in the Twenty-First Century," p. 601. According to Schildkraut, "The remaining respondents either identified as mixed race, Native American, or answered the race question in a way that could not be incorporated into this breakdown (e.g., 'human'). These respondents have been dropped from all analyses."

96. Schildkraut, "Does Becoming American Create a Better American?" p. 81.

97. Schildkraut, "Boundaries of American Identity," p. 448.

98. Ibid., p. 447. Emphasis in original.

99. Schildkraut, "Defining American Identity in the Twenty-First Century," p. 599. Emphasis in original.

100. Greg Johnson, "Fukuyama on Identity Politics," Counter-Currents Publishing, January 11, 2019, www.counter-currents.com/2019/01/fukuyama -on-identity-politics/.

101. Ibid.

102. Ibid.

103. Schildkraut, "Defining American Identity in the Twenty-First Century," pp. 599–600.

104. John Sides, *Race, Religion, and Immigration in 2016: How the Debate over American Identity Shaped the Election and What It Means for a Trump Presidency* (Democracy Fund Voter Study Group, June 2017), pp. 16–17.

105. Michael J. Sandel, "The Procedural Republic and the Unencumbered Self," *Political Theory* 12, no. 1 (February 1984), pp. 81–96.

106. However, Alt-Rightists are incorrect when they argue that white racial consciousness was formally incorporated into the principles of the American founding documents.

107. Kai Hammerich and Richard D. Lewis, *Fish Can't See Water: How National Culture Can Make or Break Your Corporate Strategy* (Chichester, UK: Wiley, 2013).

Chapter 5

1. Johannes Lindvall, "The Real but Limited Influence of Expert Ideas," *World Politics* 61, no. 4 (October 2009), pp. 703–30.

2. Another qualification is that expert knowledge is not necessarily about cause-and-effect relationships. Cartographers, surveyors, sherpas, and trail guides are experts in the lay of the land, which is not a matter of cause and effect. The same could be said about critics of all types, investigators, lawyers, judges, accountants, and many other professionals who are undoubtedly experts but whose knowledge is not usually about causes and effects. And finally, expert knowledge is not necessarily about policy in the sense of laws, regulations, standards, practices, plans, and other authoritative rules. The expertise this book is concerned with is any special knowledge relevant to public affairs and politics.

3. Mark H. Moore, "What Sort of Ideas Become Public Ideas?" in *The Power of Public Ideas*, edited by Robert B. Reich (Harvard University Press, 1988), p. 79.

4. F. A. Hayek, "The Intellectuals and Socialism," *University of Chicago Law Review* 16, no. 3 (1949), article 7, http://chicagounbound.uchicago.edu/uclrev/vol16/iss3/7.

5. Plato, *The Republic*, Book VI, 509c–511e. Plato gives a similar account of the process of learning in his *Seventh Letter*, 342d–344d.

6. Plato, *Seventh Letter*, 344a–344b.

7. Hayek, "The Intellectuals and Socialism."

8. Karl Mannheim, *Ideology and Utopia: An Introduction to the Sociology of Knowledge* (New York: Harcourt Brace Jovanovich, 1936), pp. 155, 154. Emphasis in original.

9. Irving Howe, "This Age of Conformity," in Nina Howe, ed., *A Voice Still Heard: Selected Essays of Irving Howe* (Yale University Press, 2014).

10. Russell Jacoby, *The Last Intellectuals: American Culture in the Age of Academe* (New York: Basic Books, 1987), p. 30.

11. Ibid., p. 31.

12. Richard Hofstadter, *Anti-Intellectualism in American Life* (New York: Vintage Books, 1962), p. 393.

13. Patrick Baert and Josh Booth, "Tensions within the Public Intellectual: Political Interventions from Dreyfus to the New Social Media," *International Journal of Politics, Culture, and Society* 25, no. 4, Public Intellectuals (December 2012), p. 124. Peter Dahlgren, "Public Intellectuals, Online Media, and Public Spheres: Current Realignments," *International Journal of Politics, Culture, and Society* 25, no. 4, Public Intellectuals (December 2012), pp. 95–110.

14. Baert and Booth, "Tensions within the Public Intellectual."

15. Robert H. Bork, *Slouching Towards Gomorrah: Modern Liberalism and American Decline* (New York: HarperCollins, 1996), p. 63.

16. Allan Bloom, *The Closing of the American Mind: How Higher Education Has Failed Democracy and Impoverished the Souls of Today's Students* (New York: Simon & Schuster, 1987), p. 215.

17. Richard M. Weaver, *Ideas Have Consequences* (University of Chicago Press, 1948), p. 44.

18. Ayn Rand, "Apollo and Dionysus," Ford Hall Forum lecture (1969).

19. Robert Curry, "The War on Common Sense," American Greatness, September 14, 2019.

20. The need for a new sociological account of intellectuals is strikingly summarized in Gil Eyal and Larissa Buchholz, "From the Sociology of Intellectuals to the Sociology of Interventions," *Annual Review of Sociology* 36 (2010), pp. 117–37. My analysis builds on this discussion of the literature on "postmodern intellectuals as 'interpreters.'" Eyal and Buchholz use the phrase "epistemic community" to mean "a network of professionals with recognized expertise and competence in a particular domain and an authoritative claim to policy-relevant knowledge within that domain or issue area" (p. 128). I use the term much more broadly, to refer to any group of people who share a particular epistemic standpoint.

21. See Michael Walzer, *Interpretation and Social Criticism* (Harvard University Press, 1987) and Michael Walzer, *The Company of Critics: Social Criticism and Political Commitment in the Twentieth Century* (London: Peter Halban, 1989).

22. Walzer, *Interpretation and Social Criticism*, p. 35.

23. Bruce A. Williams and Michael X. Delli Carpini, *After Broadcast News: Media Regimes, Democracy, and the New Information Environment* (Cambridge University Press, 2011), p. 303.

24. Ibid., 117.

25. Oscar Wilde, "The Decay of Lying: An Observation," 1889, file:///C:/Users/tmain/Downloads/the_decay_of_lying.pdf.

26. Ihab Hassan, "The Critic as Innovator: A Paracritical Strip in X Frames," *Chicago Review* 28, no. 3 (Winter 1977), pp. 10–11.

27. For a brief but convincing refutation of these arguments, see Karl R. Popper, *Objective Knowledge: An Evolutionary Approach*, rev. ed. (Oxford University Press, 1979), pp. 42–43.

28. Özlem Sensoy and Robin DiAngelo, *Is Everyone Really Equal? An Introduction to Key Concepts in Social Justice Education*, 2nd ed. (New York: Teachers College Press, 2017), p. 16. Emphasis in original.

29. Karl Popper, *The Open Society and Its Enemies: Volume II, Hegel and Marx*, 5th ed. (Princeton University Press, 1966), p. 217.

30. Chris Cillizza, "This Poll Number Proves How Powerful Trump's Misinformation Machine Really Is," CNN, October 2, 2019, www.cnn.com/2019/10/02/politics/donald-trump-ukraine-transcript/index.html?fbclid=IwAR2Un cyhFeklBfNFWnkF1rsREFTDpjhk4Cwd_MyQ7D8brVs1g588YT2FEac.

31. Ibid.

32. Williams and Delli Carpini, *After Broadcast News*, p. 38.

33. Samuel J. Abrams, "The Contented Professors: How Conservative Faculty See Themselves within the Academy" (2016), www.researchgate.net/publication/312229229_The_Contented_Professors_How_Conservative_Faculty_See_Themselves_within_the_Academy/citation/download.

34. Jon A. Shields and Joshua M. Dunn Sr., "Forget What the Right Says: Academia Isn't So Bad for Conservative Professors," *Washington Post*, March 11, 2016.

35. Richard Posner, *Public Intellectuals: A Study of Decline* (Harvard University Press, 2001), pp. 388–89.

36. Jose Ortega y Gasset, *The Revolt of the Masses* (New York: Norton, 1932), p. 63.

37. Ibid., p. 70.

38. Andrew Rich, *Think Tanks, Public Policy, and the Politics of Expertise* (Cambridge University Press, 2004), p. 35.

39. *Public Papers of the Presidents of the United States: Lyndon B. Johnson, 1966, Book II* (Washington, DC: Government Printing Office, 1967), pp. 1096–97. Quoted in Rich, *Think Tanks*, p. 1.

40. Fred Block, "Think Tanks, Free Market Academics, and the Triumph of the Right," *Theory and Society* 42, no. 6 (November 2013), p. 650.

41. Rich, *Think Tanks*, p. 204.

42. John L. Campbell and Ove K. Pedersen, *The National Origins of Policy Ideas: Knowledge Regimes in the United States, France, Germany, and Denmark* (Princeton University Press, 2014), p. 329.

43. Ibid., p. 330.

44. Ibid., pp. 336–43. By "high-intellect learning," the authors mean trying "to understand the causal structure of the events that have been associated with past successes and then derive actions based on those explanations." This approach is opposed to " 'low-intellect learning' where organizations look to the prior successful experiences of their own or other organizations and try to replicate them through mimicry." The assumption is "that high-intellect learning is often more successful than low-intellect learning because the world is too complex and past experiences are too limited to achieve success by replication. Furthermore, the lessons of experience are often ambiguous and subject to many interpretations, which can be greatly distorted by one's long-standing, taken-for-granted ideologies and worldviews."

45. Mark Lilla, *The Once and Future Liberal: After Identity Politics* (New York: Harper, 2017), pp. 102, 132.

46. Bob Guccione Jr., "Signs of the Times," interview with Frank Zappa, *Spin*, July 1991, www.afka.net/Articles/1991-07_Spin.htm.

47. Michael X. Delli Carpini and Scott Keeter, *What Americans Know About Politics and Why It Matters* (Yale University Press, 1996), p. 116.

48. Pew Research Center, "Public Knowledge of Current Affairs Little Changed by News and Information Revolutions: What Americans Know: 1989–2007," April 15, 2007, pp. 1, 3, www.pewresearch.org/politics/2007/04/15/public-knowledge-of-current-affairs-little-changed-by-news-and-information-revolutions/.

49. Personal correspondence with Scott Keeter, Senior Survey Advisor, Pew Research Center, October 2, 2019.

50. Pew Research Center, "Public Knowledge of Current Affairs," p. 4.

51. Delli Carpini and Keeter, *What Americans Know About Politics and Why It Matters*, pp. 105–06. Emphasis in original.

52. Jennifer L. Hochschild and Katherine Levine Einstein, *Do Facts Matter? Information and Misinformation in American Politics* (University of Oklahoma Press, 2015), p. 148.

53. Ibid., p. 164.

54. Ibid., p. 165.

55. Alan I. Abramowitz, "The Engaged Public," in *The Disappearing Center: Engaged Citizens, Polarization, and American Democracy* (Yale University Press, 2010), p. 33.

56. George Pillsbury, *America Goes to the Polls 2018: A Report on Voter Turnout and Election Policy in the 50 States* (Cambridge, MA: Nonprofit VOTE, March 2019).

57. Emily Stewart, "2018's Record-Setting Voter Turnout, in One Chart,"

Vox, November 19, 2018, www.vox.com/policy-and-politics/2018/11/19/181031
10/2018-midterm-elections-turnout.

58. Center for Information and Research on Civic Learning and Engagement (CIRCLE), "New National Youth Turnout Estimate: 28% of Young
People Voted in 2018," May 30, 2019, https://civicyouth.org/new-national
-youth-turnout-estimate-28-of-young-people-voted-in-2018/.

59. Bianca DiJulio, Cailey Muñana, and Mollyann Brodie, "The Kaiser
Family Foundation/Washington Post Survey on Political Rallygoing and Activism," Henry J. Kaiser Family Foundation, April 6, 2018, pp. 2, 11–12.

60. Kevin Schaul, Kate Rabinowitz, and Ted Mellnik, "2020 Turnout Is the
Highest in Over a Century," *Washington Post*, November 5, 2020, www.washing
tonpost.com/graphics/2020/elections/voter-turnout/.

61. Adam Seth Levine, "The Myth of Civic Engagement During Trump's
Presidency," *Behavioral Scientist*, November 6, 2017, https://behavioralscientist
.org/myth-civic-engagement-trumps-presidency/.

62. Stanley B. Greenberg, *R.I.P. G.O.P.: How the New America Is Dooming the
Republicans* (New York: Thomas Dunne Books, 2019).

63. Greenberg, *R.I.P. G.O.P.*, p. 258.

64. Steve Phillips, *Brown Is the New White*, Kindle Edition (New York: The
New Press, 2016), pp. xiii, xv.

65. John B. Judis, "Redoing the Electoral Math," *The New Republic*, September 2017.

66. Maureen A. Craig, Julian M. Rucker, and Jennifer A. Richeson, "Racial
and Political Dynamics of an Approaching 'Majority-Minority' United States,"
ANNALS, *AAPSS*, 677 (May 2018), p. 208.

67. Ibid, p. 212.

68. Ibid.

69. Phillips, *Brown Is the New White*, p. 181.

70. Ibid., p. 47.

71. Ibid. Phillips is here quoting from a *Washington Post* article about changes
made by the College Board to the content of the Advanced Placement History
test. Phillips claims the "College Board caved to conservative criticism" and
endorsed a "neutered version of history."

72. Deborah J. Schildkraut, "Defining American Identity in the Twenty-
First Century: How Much 'There' Is There?" *Journal of Politics* 69, no. 3 (August
2007), pp. 597–615.

73. Deborah J. Schildkraut, "Theories of American Identity," chapter 3 in
Press "ONE" for English: Language Policy, Public Opinion, and American Identity
(Princeton University Press, 2005), p. 53.

74. Ibid.

75. Ibram X. Kendi, *How to Be an Antiracist* (New York: One World 2019),
p. 230.

76. Ibid.

77. Ibram X. Kendi, *Stamped from the Beginning: The Definitive History of Racist Ideas in America* (New York: Nation Books, 2016), p. 510.

78. Kendi, *How to Be an Antiracist*, p. 231.

79. Works documenting the importance of ideas in policymaking include: Steven Kelman, *Making Public Policy: A Hopeful View of American Government* (New York: Basic Books, 1987); Robert B. Reich, editor, *The Power of Public Ideas* (Harvard University Press, 1988); Marc K. Landy and Martin A. Levin, editors, *The New Politics of Public Policy* (Baltimore: Johns Hopkins University Press, 1995); and Martin A. Levin, Mark K. Landy, and Martin Shapiro, editors, *Seeking the Center: Politics and Policymaking at the New Century* (Washington, DC: Georgetown University Press, 2001).

80. *How to Be an Antiracist*, p. 232.

81. Kendi, *Stamped from the Beginning*, p. 508.

82. The best introduction to the literature questioning the primacy of self-interest in politics remains Jane J. Mansbridge, editor, *Beyond Self-Interest* (University of Chicago Press, 1990).

83. Vladimir E. Medenica, "How the Few Persuade the Many: Overcoming Marginality in the Fight for Public Opinion," Ph.D. dissertation, Princeton University, 2017, p. iii.

84. Ibid., p. 79.

85. Ibid., pp. iv, 100.

86. Ibid., p. 98.

87. Ibid., pp. 100–01.

88. Ibid., p. 101.

89. Ibid., p. iii.

90. Ibid., pp. 42–43.

91. Ibid., pp. 59–66.

92. Ibid., p. 108.

93. Alan I. Abramowitz, *The Disappearing Center: Engaged Citizens, Polarization, and American Democracy* (Yale University Press, 2010), p. 168.

Chapter 6

1. Whitney Phillips and Ryan M. Milner, *The Ambivalent Internet: Mischief, Oddity, and Antagonism Online* (Cambridge, U.K.: Polity Press), pp. 51–52.

2. David Kirkpatrick, "Pronouncements on Irony Draw a Line in the Sand," *New York Times*, September 24, 2001; Roger Rosenblatt, "The Age of Irony Comes to an End," *Time*, September 24, 2001; Michiko Kakutani, "The Age of Irony Isn't Over After All," *New York Times*, October 9, 2001; David Beers, "Irony Is Dead! Long Live Irony!" www.salon.com/mwt/feature/2001/09/25/irony_lives/?sid=1048586; see also Matthew Stratton, *The Politics of Irony in American Modernism* (Fordham University Press, 2014), p. 1.

3. Alan Gibbs, *Contemporary American Trauma Narratives* (Edinburgh University Press, 2014), p. 117.

4. Alan Wilde quoted by Neil Brooks in "On Becoming an Ex-Man: Postmodern Irony and the Extinguishing of Certainties in the Autobiography of an Ex-Colored Man," *College Literature* 22, no. 3 (October 1995, Race and Politics: The Experience of African-American Literature), p. 23.

5. John N. Duvall, "Homeland Security and the State of (American) Exception(alism): Jess Walter's 'The Zero' and the Ethical Possibilities of Postmodern Irony," *Studies in the Novel* 45, no. 2 (Summer 2013), p. 279.

6. Matthew Stratton, *The Politics of Irony in American Modernism* (Fordham University Press, 2014), p. 2. Emphasis in original.

7. Wayne C. Booth, "The Empire of Irony," *Georgia Review* 37, no. 4 (Winter 1983), p. 727.

8. Nick Fuentes, "Irony is so important for giving . . . plausible deniability for our views," January 25, 2020, www.youtube.com/watch?v=jrBbZq7GddI.

9. Greg Johnson, "Identity vs. Irony," Counter-Currents Publishing, August 23, 2017, www.counter-currents.com/2017/08/identity-vs-irony/print/.

10. Nick Fuentes, "Ironic Detachment," November 7, 2019, www.youtube .com/watch?v=eOzVXDZllX8.

11. Wayne C. Booth, *A Rhetoric of Irony* (University of Chicago Press, 1974), p. 59.

12. Of course, the Liar Paradox is ancient, having been mentioned by Aristotle and Cicero. In this age of YouTube, a more recent iteration is easily available in the form of a clip from a *Star Trek* episode. Captain Kirk and his confederate, Harry, short-circuit the android Norman as follows:

> Kirk: "Everything Harry tells you is a lie."
> Harry: "Now listen to this carefully Norman: I am lying."
> Norman: "You say you are lying. But if everything you say is a lie, then you are telling the truth. But you cannot tell the truth because everything you say is a lie. But you lie. You tell the truth. But you cannot for you lie. Illogical! Illogical!" [Smoke pours out of Harry's ears as he blows a fuse]

Alt-Right adolescents who mouth the Liar Paradox do not short-circuit, at least not in the short run.

13. Phillips and Milner, *The Ambivalent Internet*, pp. 51–52.

14. See Paul Mager, "The Theoretical Impact of Poe's Law on Political Discourse," November 27, 2016, ssrn.com/abstract=2876299 or dx.doi.org/10.2139 /ssrn.2876299; and Anand Manikutty, "Manikutty's Poevian Hypothesis: A Hypothesis on the Frequency of Poe's Law in Action," December 7, 2017, ssrn. com/abstract=3084197 or dx.doi.org/10.2139/ssrn.3084197. Manikutty's paper reads as if it is itself an example of Poe's Law.

15. Phillips and Milner, *The Ambivalent Internet*, p. 203.

16. Ibid., p. 199.

17. Booth, *A Rhetoric of Irony*, p. 59.

18. Booth, "The Empire of Irony," p. 728.

19. C. S. Peirce, *The Collected Papers of Charles Sanders Peirce*, CP 1.344 Cross-Ref, pp. 153, 344, https://colorysemiotica.files.wordpress.com/2014/08/peirce-collectedpapers.pdf.

20. C. S. Peirce, "The Essentials of Pragmatism," in *Philosophical Writings of Peirce*, edited by Justus Buchler (New York: Dover Publications, 1955), p. 256. Emphasis in original.

21. Wayne C. Booth, *Modern Dogma and the Rhetoric of Assent* (University of Chicago Press, 1974), p. 111. Emphasis in original.

22. Ibid., p. 110. Emphasis in original.

23. Ibid., p. 106.

24. Ibid., p. 108.

25. C. S. Peirce, "The Fixation of Belief," in *Philosophical Writings of Peirce*, edited by Justus Buchler (New York: Dover Publications, 1955), pp. 12–13.

26. Booth, *Modern Dogma and the Rhetoric of Assent*, p. 108.

27. Peirce, "The Fixation of Belief," p. 14.

28. Stephen Macedo, *Liberal Virtues: Citizenship, Virtue, and Community in Liberal Constitutionalism* (Oxford University Press, 1991), p. 272.

29. Robert B. Talisse, "Towards a Peircean Politics of Inquiry," *Transactions of the Charles S. Peirce Society* 40, no. 1 (Winter 2004), p. 30. Emphasis in original.

30. Ibid.

31. Ibid., pp. 30–31. Emphasis in original.

32. The term "democracy friendly" is from Albert O. Hirschman, *The Rhetoric of Reaction* (Harvard University Press, 1991), p. 168.

33. Chrysanthos Dellarocas, Zsolt Katona, and William Rand, "Media, Aggregators, and the Link Economy: Strategic Hyperlink Formation in Content Networks," *Management Science* 59, no. 10 (October 2013), p. 2361.

34. Michael Burke, "Cracks in the Armor? The Future of the Communications Decency Act and Potential Challenges to the Protections of Section 230 to Gossip Web Sites," *Boston University Journal of Science & Technology Law* 17, no. 2 (Summer 2011), p. 11.

35. Tom Goldstein, "Drudge Manifesto: The Internet's Star Reporter vs. Politics, Big Business, and the Future of Journalism," *Columbia Journalism Review* 39, no. 5 (January 2001), https://go.gale.com/ps/i.do?&id=GALE|A70495771&v=2.1&u=cuny_baruch&it=r&p=AONE&sw=w.

36. Matt Drudge, "Anyone with a Modem Can Report on the World," address before the National Press Club, June 2, 1998, www.bigeye.com/drudge.htm

37. See, John V. Pavlik, *Journalism and New Media* (New York: Columbia University Press 2001), p. 92, www.jstor.org/stable/10.7312/pavl11482.10; and Andrew Glass, "Drudge says Newsweek sitting on Lewinsky story, Jan. 17, 1998," Politico, January 17, 2013, www.politico.com/story/2013/01/this-day-in-politics-086305.

38. Jack Goldsmith and Andrew Keane Woods, "Internet Speech Will Never Go Back to Normal," *The Atlantic*, April 25, 2020, www.theatlantic.com/ideas/archive/2020/04/what-covid-revealed-about-internet/610549/.

39. Ibid.

40. Ibid.

41. Ibid.

42. Peter Baker and Maggie Astor, "Trump Slams MSNBC Host with a Smear," *New York Times*, May 27, 2020.

43. D. Van Zandt, "True Pundit," Media Bias/Fact Check, mediabiasfactcheck.com/true-pundit/. Also see Craig Silverman, "Revealed: Notorious Pro-Trump Misinformation Site True Pundit Is Run by an Ex-Journalist with a Grudge Against the FBI," BuzzFeed News, August 27, 2018, www.buzzfeednews.com/article/craigsilverman/revealed-notorious-pro-trump-misinformation-site-true.

44. Kara Swisher, "Timothy Klausutis's Full Letter to Jack Dorsey, and Twitter's Response," *New York Times*, May 28, 2020.

45. Peter H. Schuck, "Trump May Have Crossed a Legal Line," *New York Times*, May 29, 2020.

46. Ibid.

47. Kate Conger and Davey Alba, "Twitter Refutes Inaccuracies in Trump's Tweets About Mail-In Voting," *New York Times*, May 28, 2020.

48. Kate Conger and Mike Isaac, "Defying Trump, Twitter Doubles Down on Labeling Tweets," *New York Times*, May 29, 2020.

49. Ibid.

50. Rebecca Klar, "Dorsey Defends Decision to Fact-Check Trump Tweet: 'More Transparency From Us Is Critical,'" *The Hill*, May 27, 2020, thehill.com/policy/technology/499866-dorsey-defends-decision-to-fact-check-trump-tweet-more-transparency-from-us.

51. Kevin Roose, "Silencing Trump, Tech Giants Show Where Power Now Lies," *New York Times*, January 10, 2021, p. 1.

52. Elizabeth Dwoskin and Craig Timberg, "Misinformation Dropped Dramatically the Week after Twitter Banned Trump and Some Allies," *Washington Post*, January 16, 2021, www.washingtonpost.com/technology/2021/01/16/misinformation-trump-twitter/.

Chapter 7

1. Robert A. Dahl, *How Democratic Is the American Constitution?* (Yale University Press, 2001), p. 156.

2. For discussions of RAND's system analysis of fire company placement in New York City, see Joe Flood, "Quantifying the Unquantifiable," in *The Fires: How a Computer Formula, Big Ideas, and the Best of Intentions Burned Down New York City—and Determined the Future of Cities* (New York: Riverhead Books, 2010), pp. 197–209.

3. David Brady, Jason Beckfield, and Wei Zhao, "The Consequences of Economic Globalization for Affluent Democracies," *Annual Review of Sociology* 33 (2007), p. 316.

4. Dani Rodrik, "Populism and the Economics of Globalization," *Journal of International Business Policy* 1 (2018), p. 23.

5. Josh Bivens, "Adding Insult to Injury: How Bad Policy Decisions Have Amplified Globalization's Costs for American Workers," Economic Policy Institute, July 11, 2017, pp. 5–6.

6. Rodrik, "Populism and the Economics of Globalization," pp. 17–18.

7. Pippa Norris and Ronald Inglehart, *Cultural Backlash: Trump, Brexit, and Authoritarian Populism* (Cambridge University Press, 2019), p. 454.

8. Ibid., pp. 458–59.

9. Ibid., p. 463.

10. Ganesh Sitaraman, "Economic Inequality and Constitutional Democracy," chapter 30 in *Constitutional Democracy in Crisis?* edited by Mark A. Garber, Sanford Levinson, and Mark Tushnet (Oxford University Press, 2019), pp. 534–35.

11. R. Kent Weaver and Bret A. Rockman, "Assessing the Effects of Institutions," in *Do Institutions Matter? Government Capabilities in the United States and Abroad*, edited by R. Kent Weaver and Bert A. Rockman (Brookings Institution Press, 1993), p. 28.

12. William G. Howell and Terry M. Moe, *Relic: How Our Constitution Undermines Effective Government—and Why We Need a More Powerful Presidency* (New York: Basic Books, 2016), p. 68.

13. See Tom Nichols, *The Death of Expertise: The Campaign against Established Knowledge and Why It Matters* (Oxford University Press, 2017).

14. Alan I. Abramowitz, *The Disappearing Center: Engaged Citizens, Polarization, and American Democracy* (Yale University Press, 2010), p. 170.

15. "Towards a More Responsible Two-Party System: A Report of the Committee on Political Parties of the American Political Science Association," part 2, supplement to *American Political Science Review* 44, no. 3 (September 1950).

16. Abramowitz, *The Disappearing Center*, pp. 159–60.

17. Greenberg, *R.I.P. G.O.P.*, p. 258.

18. Ibid., p. 279.

19. Woodrow Wilson, "Introductory" in *Congressional Government: A Study in American Government* (Boston: Houghton Mifflin, 1885), www.gutenberg .org/files/35861/35861-h/35861-h.htm.

20. Ibid., "The Executive."

21. Ibid.

22. Kenneth M. Roberts, "Populism, Democracy, and Resistance," in *The Resistance: The Dawn of the Anti-Trump Opposition Movement*, edited by David S. Meyer and Sidney Tarrow (Oxford University Press, 2018), p. 56.

23. Ibid., p. 72.

24. For a discussion of the downsides of a polarized political environment, see Morris P. Fiorina with Samuel J. Abrams, *Disconnect: The Breakdown of Representation in American Politics* (University of Oklahoma Press, 2009), pp. 150–59.

25. Jacob S. Hacker and Paul Pierson, "After the 'Master Theory': Downs, Schattschneider, and the Rebirth of Policy-Focused Analysis," *Perspectives on Politics* 12, no. 3 (September 2014), p. 652.

26. Soren Jordan, Clayton McLaughlin Webb, and B. Dan Wood, "The President, Polarization, and the Party Platforms, 1944–2012," *The Forum* 12, no. 1 (May 2014), p. 179, https://doi.org/10.1515/for-2014-0024.

27. Donald J. Trump, "Let Me Ask America a Question," *Wall Street Journal*, April 14, 2016, www.wsj.com/articles/let-me-ask-america-a-question-1460 675882.

28. William H. Riker, *Liberalism Against Populism: A Confrontation Between the Theory of Democracy and the Theory of Social Choice* (San Francisco: W. H. Freeman, 1982), pp. 238–39.

29. Ibid., pp. 242–44. Emphasis in original.

30. Robert A. Dahl, *How Democratic Is the American Constitution?* (Yale University Press, 2001), pp. 154–56.

31. Akhil Reed Amar, "Conclusions and Further Questions," chapter 14 in *Is the American Constitution Obsolete?* edited by Thomas J. Main (Durham, NC: Carolina Academic Press, 2013), p. 238.

32. See Robert Curry, "Protecting the Electoral College from the Progressive Assault," American Greatness, November 21, 2016, https://amgreatness.com /2016/11/21/protecting-the-electoral-college-from-the-progressive-assault/; Michael M. Uhlmann, "As the Electoral College Goes, So Goes the Constitution," *The American Mind*, October 9, 2019, https://americanmind.org/essays/ as-the-electoral-college-goes-so-goes-the-constitution/; George F. Will, "The Electoral College Is an Excellent System," *Washington Post*, December 16, 2016, www.washingtonpost.com/opinions/the-electoral-college-is-an-excellent-sys tem/2016/12/16/30480790-c2ef-11e6-9a51-cd56ea1c2bb7_story.html.

33. Bruce E. Cain and Roger G. Noll, "Constitutional Change: Malleable Constitutions: Reflections on State Constitutional Reform," *Texas Law Review*, 87 (June 2009), p. 1519.

34. Ibid.

35. "State constitutional conventions," Ballotpedia, ballotpedia.org/State_ constitutional_conventions.

36. Robert F. Williams, "Evolving State Constitutional Processes of Adoption, Revision, and Amendment: The Path Ahead," *Arkansas Law Review* 69, no. 2 (2016), pp. 572–73.

37. Jesse McKinley, "Fear vs. Hope: Battle Lines Drawn over a Constitutional Convention," *New York Times*, October 26, 2017.

38. Editorial, "Constitutional Convention: Thanks, but No Thanks," *New York Times*, October 31, 2017.

39. The Principle of Unripe Time and other arguments against change were apparently presented in an essay by the early-twentieth-century English classicist F. M. Conford, entitled "Guide to the Young Academic Politician." The essay is discussed in Albert O. Hirschman, *The Rhetoric of Reaction* (Harvard University Press, 1991), pp. 81–83.

40. Joshua Braver, "New York Isn't Ready for a Constitutional Convention," *Dissent*, November 6, 2017, www.dissentmagazine.org/blog/new-york-isnt-ready -constitutional-convention.

41. Gerald Benjamin, "The Mandatory Constitutional Convention Question Referendum: The New York Experience in National Context," *Albany Law Review* 65, no. 4 (Summer 2002), p. 1049.

42. Much of the information in this and the following paragraphs on constitutional commissions comes from Robert F. Williams, "Are State Constitutional Conventions Things of the Past? The Increasing Role of the Constitutional Commission in State Constitutional Change," *Hofstra Law & Policy Symposium* 1, article 4 (1996), pp. 1–26.

43. Ibid., p. 15.

44. Ibid., p. 16.

45. "Florida Constitution Revision Commission," Ballotpedia, https:// ballotpedia.org/Florida_Constitution_Revision_Commission#2017-2018; "Florida 2018 Ballot Measures," Ballotpedia, https://ballotpedia.org/Florida _2018_ballot_measures; "Florida 1998 Ballot Measures," Ballotpedia, https:// ballotpedia.org/Florida_1998_ballot_measures.

46. Ibram X. Kendi, "Pass an Anti-Racist Constitutional Amendment," Politico, n.d., www.politico.com/interactives/2019/how-to-fix-politics-in-america /inequality/pass-an-anti-racist-constitutional-amendment/.

47. William G. Howell and Terry M. Moe, *Relic: How Our Constitution Undermines Effective Government and Why We Need a More Powerful Presidency* (New York: Basic Books, 2016), p. 145.

48. Ibid., p. 105.

49. Ibid. Emphasis in original.

50. Tom Ginsburg and Aziz Z. Huq, *How to Save a Constitutional Democracy* (University of Chicago Press, 2018), p. 211.

51. Peter H. Schuck, *Why Government Fails So Often and How It Can Do Better* (Princeton University Press, 2014), pp. 30, 380. Emphasis in original.

52. Ibid., pp. 211–12.

53. Ibid., p. 212.

54. Daniel Bell and Irving Kristol, "What Is the Public Interest?" *The Public Interest* no. 1 (Fall 1965), pp. 3–5.

55. Editor's prospectus for *The Public Interest.*

56. Bell and Kristol, "What Is the Public Interest?"

57. John Gordon, "Notes on Liberal Democracy and Its Alternative," Counter-Currents Publishing, January 31, 2013, https://counter-currents.com/2013/ 01/notes-on-liberal-democracy-and-its-alternative.

58. Ginsburg and Huq, *How to Save a Constitutional Democracy*, p. 212.

59. Juan J. Linz, "The Perils of Presidentialism," *Journal of Democracy* 1, no. 1 (Winter 1990), p. 53.

60. Ibid., pp. 63–64.

61. Dana D. Nelson, "Going Corporate with the Unitary Executive," in *Bad for Democracy: How the Presidency Undermines the Power of the People* (University of Minnesota Press, 2008), pp. 155–57. As the title of his book suggests, Nelson is unhelpfully critical of the whole institution of the presidency. But his characterization of the "unitary executive" theory as it applies to relations between the president and Congress is apt.

62. Thomas J. Main, ed., *Is the American Constitution Obsolete?* (Durham, NC: Carolina Academic Press, 2013).

63. Jeremy Rabkin, "We Should Preserve, Protect, and Defend the Constitution—Not Trash It," chapter 3 in *Is the American Constitution Obsolete?* edited by Thomas J. Main, pp. 25–39.

64. Ibid., pp. 26–28.

65. Schuck, *Why Government Fails So Often*, pp. 1, 4. Emphasis in original.

66. Rabkin, p. 27.

Chapter 8

1. Peter H. Schuck, *Why Government Fails So Often and How It Can Do Better* (Princeton University Press, 2014), pp. 411–12.

2. See Marc K. Landy and Martin A. Levin, eds., *The New Politics of Public Policy* (Johns Hopkins University Press, 1995), and Martin A. Levin, Marc K. Landy, and Martin Shapiro, eds., *Seeking the Center: Politics and Policymaking in the New Century* (Georgetown University Press, 2001). Among the legislative breakthroughs discussed in these works are the Clean Air Act of 1970, the Education for All Handicapped Children Act of 1975, the Tax Reform Act of 1986, and the Personal Responsibility and Work Opportunity Reconciliation Act of 1996.

3. Peter H. Schuck, "The Politics of Rapid Legal Change: Immigration Policy in the 1980s," in *The New Politics of Public Policy*, edited by Marc K. Landy and Martin A. Levin (Johns Hopkins University Press, 1995), pp. 49–51. Emphasis in original.

4. Ibid. Emphasis in original.

5. Ibid., pp. 78, 83. In 2001, Schuck updated his analysis of immigration policy in his contribution to *Seeking the Center: Politics and Policymaking in the New Century*. There he reiterated the importance of ideas in immigration policy: "I was not wrong about the role of ideas in 1990 but some of the ideas affecting immigration policy have changed since then, certain interests have become more salient and powerful, and the policy-relevant ideas about immigration have acquired a new resonance in light of these changes in the political context." See Peter H. Schuck, "Immigration Reform Redux," in *Seeking*

the Center: Politics and Policymaking in the New Century (Georgetown University Press, 2001).

6. Ashley Feinberg, "This Is the Daily Stormer's Playbook," *HuffPost*, December 13, 2017, www.huffpost.com/entry/daily-stormer-nazi-style-guide_n_5a2ece19e4b0ce3b344492f2. The style book itself can be found at https://assets.documentcloud.org/documents/4325810/Writers.pdf.

7. Matt Forney, "Why Feminists Want Men to Rape Them," mattforney.com, February 22, 2016, mattforney.com/feminists-want-men-rape/. Emphasis in original.

8. Roosh Valizadeh, "How to Save Western Civilization," rooshv.com, March 6, 2017, www.rooshv.com/how-to-save-western-civilization.

9. Eli Rosenberg, "Alex Jones Apologizes for Promoting 'Pizzagate' Hoax," *New York Times*, March 25, 2017, www.nytimes.com/2017/03/25/business/alex-jones-pizzagate-apology-comet-ping-pong.html.

10. Greg Johnson, "Answering Sargon of Akkad," Counter-Currents Publishing, July 24, 2019, https://counter-currents.com/2019/07/answering-sargon-of-akkad/print/.

11. Alain de Benoist, "Critique of Liberal Ideology," Counter-Currents Publishing, May 28, 2012, www.counter-currents.com/2012/05/critique-of-liberal-ideology/print/.

Index

Tables are indicated by "*t*" following the page number.

www.ingramcontent.com/pod-product-compliance
Lightning Source LLC
Chambersburg PA
CBHW021116270326
41929CB00009B/903